★ ★ ★ ★ ★ ★ ★ ★ ★ ★

JOHN TYLER
the *Accidental* President

JOHN

THE UNIVERSITY OF NORTH CAROLINA PRESS ★ CHAPEL HILL

TYLER

the
Accidental President

Edward P. Crapol

© 2006
The University of North Carolina Press
All rights reserved
*This book was published with the assistance of
the William R. Kenan Jr. Fund of the University
of North Carolina Press.*
Designed and typeset in Bodoni Book and
Torino by Eric M. Brooks
Manufactured in the United States of America
The paper in this book meets the guidelines
for permanence and durability of the Committee
on Production Guidelines for Book Longevity of
the Council on Library Resources.

Library of Congress Cataloging-in-Publication Data
Crapol, Edward P.
John Tyler, the accidental president / by Edward P. Crapol.
    p. cm.
Includes bibliographical references and index.
ISBN-13: 978-0-8078-3041-3 (cloth: alk. paper)
ISBN-10: 0-8078-3041-0 (cloth: alk. paper)
1. Tyler, John, 1790–1862. 2. Presidents—United States—
Biography. 3. United States—Politics and government—
1841–1845. I. Title.
E397.C73   2006
973.5′092—dc22   2005037963

10 09 08 07 06   5 4 3 2

★ *For my grandchildren*

★ CONTENTS
★
★
★
★ Introduction 1

MAP & ILLUSTRATIONS

★ ★ ★ ★ ★ ★ ★ ★ ★ ★

JOHN TYLER
the *Accidental* President

★ ★ ★ ★ ★ ★ ★ ★ ★ ★

Introduction

The facts of my public life are matters of record,
and can neither be expunged nor altered. The impartial
future will see the motive in the act, and the just
historian will look to the good or evil only which will
have been developed, and find in the one or the other
cause of censure or of praise. To this ordeal I submit
myself without fear.

★ *John Tyler, 1847*

That a fair history of my administration should be
written by a competent person is a matter very near
to my heart.

★ *John Tyler, 1857*

ohn Tyler is not one of the famous or better-known American presidents. If known at all, it usually is because of the catchy political slogan, "Tippecanoe and Tyler too," which was the rallying cry in the 1840 campaign of presidential candidate William Henry Harrison and his vice-presidential running mate, John Tyler. Perhaps when questioned, a number of Americans also might know that Tyler was the first vice president to succeed to the presidency upon the death of the incumbent president. Maybe even some would also remember from their school days that his opponents mocked Tyler as "His Accidency," because of the manner in which he became the nation's tenth president.

His obscurity has not been for want of historical accounts of his life and career. A decade after his death, one of Tyler's good friends and political allies authored a highly laudatory biography of his long public life intended to salvage the tenth president's historical reputation. In the late nineteenth century one of his sons published a three-volume work also designed to burnish John Tyler's image in America's historical memory. More recently, Tyler has been the subject of several biographies as well as more specialized works that deal with his presidency, his commitment to republicanism, and his dedication to states' rights. Competent and just historians intent on presenting a fair history of Tyler's life and administration wrote each of these earlier works.

This book too is intended to be a just and fair accounting of John Tyler's life and presidency. I appreciate and am guided by Tyler's clear-eyed "let the chips fall where they may" attitude and his willingness to accept censure or praise from future historians. I believe this book meets his criteria and offers a tough analysis of good and evil that seeks to explain and understand his mindset and actions. John Tyler's story is, like few others in the national experience, one of American failure and tragedy, and the degradation of constitutional and republican principles. It is above all a tragic tale of one man's blind faith in the belief that endless territorial and commercial expansion could preserve the institution of slavery and maintain the Union as a slaveholding republic. As such, it is an exploration of what one of Tyler's contemporaries called the "disease" of empire "deep down in the human heart."

Lastly, because it is focused on the reasons why he believed in the quest for national destiny and greatness, I hope this book provides a different and fresh historical interpretation of the life of John Tyler that helps readers better understand his important place in American history. Unlike any previous Tyler biography or specialized study on some aspect of his public career, this book presents a full account of his pursuit of national destiny as a means to sustain the Union. It also provides an original analysis of the tenth president's ambivalent views on slavery, his racial outlook, his belief in white supremacy, and his faith in an American exceptionalism.

Other biographers and historians have argued that John Tyler was a hapless and inept chief executive whose presidency was seriously flawed. Although acknowledging that Tyler was not a great president, I believe he was a stronger and more effective president than generally remembered. The book also breaks new ground by emphasizing that not only was John Tyler a tragic figure, he also was a personification of the great American tragedy that led to bloody civil war and the loss of over 600,000 American lives. The inability of Tyler and many other Americans of his generation to reconcile their republican principles with their slaveholding institutions represented both a personal and a national tragedy. No other biographer has identified John Tyler's personal tragedy as being akin to America's tragedy. For that reason I think the book provides a key insight into his life and public career that helps explain why John Tyler is almost totally absent from American memory.

It all began very well. John Tyler was born to wealth and privilege in one of Virginia's first families. He was raised on a slave plantation as a member of the political elite and social aristocracy of his state and nation. His father was a member of the Revolutionary generation and a friend to leading founding fathers, including Thomas Jefferson. Educated at William and Mary in Bishop James Madison's school of empire and national destiny, John Tyler had been groomed to assume as his birthright a career dedicated to public service and political leadership. He practiced law and was elected to the Virginia House of Delegates at age twenty-one. He would serve in the U.S. House of Representatives and as a U.S. Senator. As governor of Virginia in 1826 he presented an eloquent eulogy upon Thomas Jefferson's death. Elected vice president in 1840, he assumed the republic's highest office when Harrison died the following year. Near the end of his political career, as a member of the Virginia State Convention, he voted for the Old Dominion's secession from the Union. At the time of his death in 1862, John Tyler was a representative-elect to the Confederate Congress.

Contrary to the singularly stern and austere visage that comes across from his official portraits, Tyler in life was a warm, affectionate, and gracious man with a keen sense of humor. Tall and slender with an angular face featuring a distinctive aquiline nose, he relished parties and champagne, dancing the Virginia Reel and playing the fiddle, and had a robust love of life. He fathered fifteen children, the most of any president, and had babies on his knee and toddlers underfoot until he was in his late sixties and early seventies. A master of the self-deprecating quip, Tyler frequently poked fun at himself and made light of his supposed follies and foibles. For instance, he is said to have named his James River estate Sherwood Forest because he, like the legendary Robin Hood, was ostracized by many of his countrymen for being a political renegade and outlaw.

At a time in the nation's history when public speaking was a highly valued political skill, Tyler was known as an accomplished orator with a mellifluous voice. On the one extended political excursion of his presidency to major eastern seaboard cities, he drew huge crowds and displayed that he could be a charismatic campaigner and popular public figure. Tyler was a prolific writer of letters and political tracts, and many of his contemporaries believed his prose to be inspiring. At least one of his political colleagues thought John Tyler's words touched the soul. Others, however, found his writing verbose and convoluted, and it is true that he never penned any ringing or memorable lines that live on like those of Thomas Jefferson or Abraham Lincoln.

John Tyler loved books and had an extensive library—some 1,200 volumes at the time of his death. Shakespeare was his first love and he frequently quoted the Bard in his correspondence and public addresses. Tyler read widely, was well versed in the classics and ancient history, and was familiar with the works of Joseph Addison, Richard Steele, Samuel Johnson, and Lord Byron. For his bookplate John Tyler chose the motto "Luxuria et egestas commodis cedunt," which may be translated as "Wealth and poverty are inferior to what is comfortable." The motto would seem to be a statement of the quest for the Epicurean ideal, the golden or happy mean, and reflected Tyler's disposition to follow a path of moderation in all things. As a political leader who helped shape public policy, Tyler avidly read newspapers and journals to keep current on the issues of the day. His intellectual curiosity led as well to an interest in geography and discovery, and the advancement of science and technology.

Not well traveled beyond the eastern and midwestern reaches of the United States, John Tyler nonetheless was a vicarious sojourner who had a cosmopolitan sense of the world and international affairs. A stay-at-home president, Tyler enjoyed hobnobbing with a wide array of foreign dignitaries at White House receptions and dinners. With the guidance of Daniel Webster, he held his own in policy disputes with European statesmen, and on one occasion his unorthodox diplomacy bewildered Queen Victoria and her prime minister. He entertained the famous English writer Charles Dickens, who complimented the president on his good manners and regal bearing.

Tyler also met and accommodated a Hawaiian prince who sought American recognition of the sovereignty and independence of his islands. He traded stories with dashing naval explorers who brought back exotic artifacts and treasures from the far reaches of the Pacific that became a prize collection for the Smithsonian Institution. Caleb Cushing, Tyler's intrepid envoy to China, returned with America's first treaty with the Celestial Empire and a gift of two exquisite Chinese vases that remain in the possession of the Tyler family to the present day.

But for all his worldliness, the Virginian, like most other white Americans of his time, looked upon other societies through a lens of racial, cultural, and religious superiority. It was axiomatic for Tyler that lesser races of the world needed the help of advanced Western, Christian peoples to guide them on the path of spiritual redemption and cultural regeneration. A believer in American exceptionalism, Tyler thought it was America's mission to bring the blessing of liberty to the oppressed and wretched of the earth. In his imagination, Tyler said, "I have seen her overturning the strong places of despotism, and restoring to man his long-lost rights." Confident that his nation's global mission was divinely ordained, the accidental president identified himself as an "instrument of Providence."

Early on in his public life John Tyler did confront the great contradiction between his lofty beliefs in liberty and freedom and the reality of the United States as a slaveholding society. During the 1819–20 Missouri crisis Tyler recognized that the issue of the future of slavery in the republic was a looming political thunderhead that jeopardized national unity and threatened to undercut his hopes for America's national destiny. In debate on the Missouri controversy in the House of Representatives, Tyler conceded that slavery had "been represented on all hands as the dark cloud" hovering over the Union. "It would be well," he recommended, "to disperse this cloud." Tyler's solution was a further expansion of slavery and the admission of Missouri as a slave state. He saw territorial expansion as a way to thin out and diffuse the slave population. With fewer blacks in some of the older slave states, it might become politically feasible to begin a process of gradual emancipation in Virginia and other states of the upper South.

Tyler's logic of diffusion was a tacit admission that the South's peculiar institution was a fatal anomaly in a republic dedicated to liberty and justice. And although he knew slavery was an evil, Tyler was unable to take the next crucial step. He did not enter the fray to abolish slavery. Quite the opposite: he strongly defended slavery for the remainder of his public life. For all that he had in his favor as a member of the nation's political elite, John Tyler nonetheless felt trapped by the slave system he had inherited from the founding fathers. That system of human bondage dominated the politics of Virginia and the South.

In his remarks during the Missouri crisis, Tyler acknowledged the trap he was in when he confessed that it would be "an act of political suicide" for him to become an advocate of universal emancipation. Seeing no way out, Tyler adhered to accepted southern political rules by defending slavery and promoting its expansion. As his mentor and idol Thomas Jefferson lamented: "We have the wolf by the ear, and we can neither hold him, nor safely let him go." That was Tyler's and America's tragedy. Unable in the end to conceive of an American Union without slavery, Tyler followed the path of disunion and civil war.

The purpose of this book is to explain that tragedy and provide a full understanding of the man and his life. I believe John Tyler is generally misunderstood as a national leader and underrated as a president. He may have been a champion of the old South, a defender of states' rights, and a spokesman for a strict interpretation of the Constitution. But in the White House Tyler was not always faithful to those precepts. In the course of his presidency Tyler occasionally trampled on states' rights and exercised executive prerogatives that did violence to a strict constructionist view of the Constitution.

Operating on the assumption that the Constitution "never designed that the executive should be a mere cipher," Tyler grasped the possibilities of the executive system. Without hesitation, he exploited the institutional malleability of that executive system to enhance the power of the presidency. Never the weeping willow of a creature his enemies loved to mock and deride, President Tyler was a decisive and energetic leader who established several important executive precedents that helped shape the direction of America's nineteenth-century imperial destiny. But with the exception of the one establishing the presidential succession principle, historians and presidential scholars rarely if ever acknowledge his landmark achievements. Perhaps this historical neglect stems from the stigma of being the nation's only traitor president, a distinction he gained from his support for secession and the Confederacy. That unique precedent is another facet of the tragedy of John Tyler that this book explores.

★ ★ ★ ★ ★ ★ ★ ★ ★ ★

Forewarned,
Forearmed

1

We will vote for Tyler therefore, without a why
or wherefore.
★ *Whig campaign verse, 1840*

The Constitution never designed that the executive
should be a mere cipher.
★ *John Tyler, July 2, 1842*

In presenting the foregoing views I can not withhold
the expression of the opinion that there exists nothing
in the extension of our Empire over our acknowledged
possessions to excite the alarm of the patriot for the
safety of our institutions.
★ *John Tyler, June 1, 1841*

fter just under a month in office, President William Henry Harrison died of pneumonia at 12:30 A.M. on April 4, 1841. Popular legend has it that Vice President John Tyler was momentarily stunned when Fletcher Webster, a State Department official and son of the secretary of state, pounded on the door of his Williamsburg, Virginia, home at sunrise on April 5 to awaken him with the news of President Harrison's death. Another tale about that momentous day, delightful for its rustic simplicity and republican innocence, had the fifty-one-year-old aristocratic Virginian playing marbles with his sons in front of his home when the young Webster arrived from Washington.

Tyler initially may have been startled by the dispatch from Harrison's cabinet announcing the president's death, but surely the marbles tale is apocryphal. It surfaced decades later in the early twentieth century, long after the principal parties involved had died, in a breezy and unreliable collection of personal reminiscences about former presidents.[1] Whatever the case, and however shocked Tyler may have been at receiving the news, he was not totally unprepared. He had been alerted days beforehand of Harrison's grave illness and probably anticipated receiving word at any moment that the ailing sixty-eight-year-old president had died. James Lyons, a Richmond attorney and Tyler's political ally and frequent correspondent, had apparently written him several days earlier, passing on news appearing in the public presses that Harrison's condition had worsened. He also wrote on April 3, again telling Tyler of the seriousness of Harrison's condition. Although we do not know the date and time this letter arrived at the vice president's Williamsburg home, in all likelihood Tyler received Lyon's message late on Saturday evening, or sometime on Sunday, April 4, the day Harrison died. In his letter, Lyons informed Tyler that the president was at death's door and confided to his friend that "I shall not be surprised to hear by tomorrows mail that Genl Harrison is no more."[2]

Upon learning of the president's life-threatening illness, the courtly Virginian abided by the dictates of his age and did not rush to Washington to hover over Harrison's deathbed in anticipation of succeeding to the nation's highest office. Such behavior would have been unseemly for a man of Tyler's refinement, gentility, and aristocratic sensibilities. But having been alerted to the president's grave condition, Tyler had time to prepare himself—emotionally, psychologically, and intellectually—for the almost certain eventuality of Harrison's death. He also later acknowledged that a premonition from his friend Littleton Waller Tazewell that the elderly Harrison would die in office had led him to contemplate the possible constitutional consequences of the president's death.

After his inauguration as vice president, John Tyler had returned to Williamsburg to consider how to respond if an anticipated presidential succession crisis arose. There was no precedent to instruct him because no previous president had died in office. Also of little guidance was the wording of the Constitution, which was vague and ambiguous on the question of succession. It was unclear whether the vice president became president in his own right, or whether he was to be the acting president until a new chief executive was duly elected.

Although Tyler prided himself on being a strict constructionist, in this instance he opted for a loose interpretation of the language of the Constitution and decided that the vice president in fact became the president outright. By decisive action and adroit political maneuvering during his first weeks in office, Tyler forever made moot any future constitutional objections and established by usage the precedent for the vice president to become president on the death of an incumbent. As one perceptive historian of the United States's first presidential succession crisis has observed, "Tyler's whole course of conduct in the first few days after he arrived in the capital demonstrated plainly that he acted with conscious deliberation to establish himself as a President in his own right and not as a mere caretaker for the departed Harrison."[3]

From the outset, John Tyler used his foreknowledge to full advantage. Shortly after receiving the official cabinet notification of Harrison's death, pointedly addressed to Vice President Tyler, he calmly informed his family at breakfast of the breathtaking turn of events that now placed him in the nation's highest office. Tyler next consulted his Williamsburg neighbor, Nathaniel Beverley Tucker, a law professor at the College of William and Mary. Among other things, Beverley Tucker, as he was known to friends, advised the new president to follow Harrison's example and announce immediately that he intended to serve only one term and would not seek election in his own right in 1844. Only through such a disclaimer, Tucker argued, would Tyler have any success in leading Congress and the American people.

Tyler politely granted the wisdom of Professor Tucker's suggestion but made no commitment about a second term before hastily proceeding to the capital. He and his entourage made the 230-mile trip in twenty-one hours—a remarkable feat in that early age of steam transportation—first by taking a boat on the James River to Richmond and then going by train to Washington.

Once he reached the nation's capital at 4:00 A.M. on April 6, Tyler executed what can only be described as a master stratagem to win unqualified acceptance as president of the United States from friend and foe alike. Crucial to this scheme was Tyler's unwavering certainty that he was now the nation's president, possessing all the powers and privileges of that office, and not "Acting President," as John Quincy Adams and several other members of Congress would have it. Even three years later, when some of his detractors and enemies persisted in addressing letters to him at the White House as "Vice-President-Acting President," Tyler routinely returned the offensive mail unopened.

On the morning of his arrival, Tyler immediately met with the six cabinet members he had inherited from Harrison. When informed by Secretary of State Daniel Webster that under his predecessor the cabinet had made decisions on the basis of majority vote, Tyler rejected that method because he did not believe cabinet members were co-equals of the president. As the chief executive Tyler said he would listen to their counsel, but would "never consent to being dictated to" by his cabinet advisers. He and he alone bore responsibility for his administration, and they were welcome to remain in the cabinet on that understanding of executive prerogative. When and if they found such a procedure untenable, their resignations would be accepted.[4]

Perhaps awed by President Tyler's unexpected decisiveness, the entire cabinet agreed to his stipulations and remained on board to serve their new chief. Upon learning of this decision to retain the entire Harrison cabinet, a handful of the new president's closest allies decried it as a serious early blunder that subsequently would jeopardize Tyler's desire to steer an independent political course. As the new president would quickly learn, being forewarned did not guarantee immunity from the harsh political consequences of hasty miscalculation and human error.

The next step in Tyler's well-orchestrated plan involved taking another oath to certify his claim to the presidential office. Although he believed a second swearing-in ceremony was unnecessary because his previous vice-presidential oath qualified him "to perform the duties and exercise the powers and office" of the president, Tyler took a new oath in the presence of the cabinet on April 6, the day of their initial meeting. As the federal judge who administered the oath explained Tyler's reasoning and action, the new president, "yet as doubts may *arise*, and for greater caution, took and subscribed the foregoing oath before me."

Three days after the symbolic oath-taking, John Tyler issued an inaugural address to further buttress the legitimacy of his presidency. In a somber and forthright manner the new chief executive informed Congress and the American people that for the first time in the nation's brief history, an individual elected as vice president "has had devolved upon him the Presidential office." Referring to himself several times as "Chief Magistrate" or "President," Tyler left no room for doubt that he had assumed the mantle and accompanying powers of the presidency.

To calm any fears about possible foreign threats in this moment of uncertainty, President Tyler promised his fellow citizens that in dealing with other nations, "my policy will be justice on our part to all, submitting to injustice from none." To ensure that the nation's honor "shall sustain no blemish," the newly minted president pledged to improve "the condition of our military defenses." He hailed the army as one of fame and renown, and declared the navy to be "the right arm of the public defense." Betraying his abiding belief in America's destiny and national greatness, Tyler also proudly singled out the navy for already having "spread a light of glory over the American standard in all the waters of the earth."[5]

The inaugural message next addressed an apprehension shared by many Americans since the founding of the republic, the tendency of all human institutions "to concentrate power in the hands of a single man." To avoid the dangers of consolidated executive power, Tyler believed that "a complete separation should take place between the sword and the purse." Tyler's promise of a separation of executive and legislative powers was consistent with his republican faith that the legislative branch "was the direct agent of the people and the mainspring of the constitutional system." In fact, the prevailing Whig orthodoxy espoused by Senator Henry Clay and his supporters called for legislative supremacy and a servile chief executive. Prior to becoming president, Tyler had adhered to this view of government and saw himself as a protector of republican virtue and defender of legislative autonomy.

It was arguable whether Tyler fully agreed with Abel P. Upshur, who later would serve in his cabinet as secretary of the navy and secretary of state, that the "most defective part of the Constitution" was "the loose and unguarded terms in which the powers and duties of the President are pointed out." But in the early 1830s, while serving as a U.S. senator, John Tyler had been alarmed by President Andrew Jackson's abuse of executive power and ultimately resigned his Senate seat rather than vote to rescind a censure of "King" Andrew. Ironically, and despite the disclaimer in the inaugural address and his previous record in the Virginia legislature and

U.S. Congress, Tyler's actions over the next four years demonstrated a preference for enhancing the power of the executive office. In wielding executive power, Tyler later explained to his constituents, he was in reality preserving the separation of powers. As would prove to be the case a number of times during his presidency, John Tyler talked the talk of republicanism, but did not always walk the walk.[6]

On the day that he released his inaugural address, Tyler confided to Senator William C. Rives his innermost feeling about the succession crisis and the emotions he felt upon being placed in the chief executive's chair. Tyler thanked his fellow Virginian and occasional political rival for his kind expressions of support and encouragement in these difficult times. He then confessed that, despite having been forewarned, the "death of our late patriotic president, while it has devolved upon me the high office of President of the United States, has occasioned me the deepest pain and anxiety." "I am," Tyler explained, "under Providence made the instrument of a new test which is for the first time to be applied to our institutions. The experiment is to be made at the moment when the country is agitated by conflicting views of public policy, and when the spirit of faction is most likely to exist. Under these circumstances, the devolvement upon me of this high office is peculiarly embarrassing."

Summarizing his tangled feelings on a note of optimism and hope, Tyler promised Rives, who throughout 1841 proved to be the only member of the Senate who consistently supported the new president, that he would govern upon the principles and teachings of Jefferson and Madison and to rely on "the virtue and intelligence of the people." Tyler's emphasis on following the principles of old republicanism, by which he meant states' rights, a strict construction of the Constitution, restrictions against consolidation of federal power, and corresponding limitations on federal programs such as the national bank and high protective tariffs, became the mantra of his administration for the next four years. Despite his best intentions, President John Tyler was not entirely faithful to the republicanism of the founding fathers.[7]

Tyler rounded out his busy public campaign to establish his legitimacy as president by immediately moving into the White House. He also called for a public day of prayer and fasting to honor the memory of William Henry Harrison, which the new president believed would enable the American people to express their grief and reaffirm the national purpose. To alleviate whatever international concerns existed about this unprecedented transfer of power, the new chief executive next officially met with the ministers of foreign nations at a ceremonial gathering and proclaimed that "the people of the United States regard their own prosperity as intimately connected with that of the entire family of nations."

By June 1, the second day of the special session of Congress originally called by the late president, both the House and the Senate easily passed resolutions acknowledging John Tyler as president of the United States, putting to rest any lingering doubts among the press and the public that he was merely an acting president. This confirmation came after only minimal debate and without division in the House. When one House member questioned whether the Constitution sanctioned Tyler's claim that he was president, he was silenced by Representative Henry Wise of Virginia, who asserted that John Tyler believed "he was by the Constitution, by election, and by the act of God, President of the United States." When similar constitutional objections were raised in the Senate, Robert J. Walker of Mississippi, overcoming his own initial misgivings, argued that Tyler rightly had succeeded to the presidency. The Senate concurred with Walker's assessment by a vote of 38-8.

Tyler's plan had worked to perfection. What was potentially an extremely controversial and bitterly contested transition of power in the nation's highest executive office was deftly handled and smoothly finessed by a states' rights southerner known for his strict constructionist interpretation of the Constitution. If for nothing else, John Tyler's place in history was secure as the author of the precedent that established vice-presidential succession to the presidency.[8]

Why had this transfer of executive power gone so smoothly and uneventfully without any historical precedent or clear constitutional mandate? John Tyler proved to be tenacious and cool under pressure and was able to establish what became known as the "Tyler precedent" because he had ample time to plan his course of action. The early April forewarnings from James Lyons that President Harrison was dying were important in the immediate sense, but Vice President Tyler knew much beforehand that he might succeed to the presidency.

After making a campaign trip to Ohio and Pennsylvania in the fall of 1840, which included major speeches in Columbus and Pittsburgh, the Whig vice-presidential candidate returned to his home state of Virginia and was immediately confronted with the succession issue by the political opposition. A committee of Virginia Democrats from Henrico County who foresaw the possibility that the elderly Harrison might die in office cleverly raised that question publicly in October 1840. Undoubtedly, the main goal of the Democratic questionnaire was not to get Tyler's thoughts on the succession question but to trip up Harrison's running mate on highly contentious issues such as the national bank and the tariff, and thereby aid the reelection campaign of President Martin Van Buren, a Democrat who was Andrew Jackson's protégé.

In a thoughtful reply to his Democratic antagonists, Tyler denied any ambition or desire to hold the highest office in the land, made clear his opposition to a national bank, and expressed his belief in a tariff for revenue only. Tyler concluded by reiterating his adherence to republican principles and candidly announcing, "You see I am a Jeffersonian Republican." His answers initially appeared in the *Richmond Enquirer* and were rapidly reprinted in newspapers throughout the Union. Tyler's political consistency aside, it was clear that people throughout the country were thinking that if elected, Old Tippecanoe could die before completing his term. That fact was not lost on John Tyler. The Henrico query, along with extended conversations with his friends, put Tyler in the frame of mind that he might succeed to the presidency and he had best be ready for that contingency.[9]

The widespread public speculation about the prospects for Harrison's longevity in the White House if he were elected was accompanied by private advice to Tyler about the wisdom of running as the vice-presidential candidate on the Whig ticket. His friend Littleton Waller Tazewell, a fellow William and Mary alumnus who had represented Virginia in the Senate with Tyler during the Jackson administration, and after whom Tyler had named one of his sons, warned him prior to the election in the fall of 1840 of the possible consequences if Harrison died in office. As Tyler remembered the episode in a letter to Tazewell a year later, "I have had frequent occasion to call to mind the last conversation which I had with you in Williamsburg at my house, in which you indulged in certain anticipations, which have received all the fulfillment of actual prophecy. I well remember your prediction of Gen. Harrison's death, and with what emphasis you enquired of me whether I had thought of my own situation upon the happening of that contingency. You declared in advance much of the difficulty by which I have already been surrounded."

Shortly after reminding Tazewell of his prophecy of Harrison's death, President Tyler once again sought his friend's advice and good counsel. In a note studded with literary allusions, the president asked: "Do, my dear sir, turn over your Sibyl leaves and read to me their recorded prophecies. If they augur very badly for me, I may by being forewarned become forearmed. Your early prophecy was of infinite service to me from the moment of my assuming the helm, as without it my ship, already tempest tost, might ere this have been stranded." In this flattering private letter, and again publicly a few years later, Tyler acknowledged that Tazewell's prescient advice had prepared him to resolve quickly a momentary crisis that arose over the constitutionality and legitimacy of vice-presidential succession. Thus forewarned, John Tyler was forearmed and ready to establish the Tyler precedent.[10]

The constitutional legitimacy of Tyler's succession principle was reaffirmed less than a decade later on July 10, 1850, when Millard Fillmore became president on the death of Zachary Taylor. Fillmore's accession to the presidency went unremarked and the transfer of power occurred without opposition. When President Taylor died during the late evening of July 9, cabinet members immediately sent an official notification to the vice president. Fillmore did not hesitate in following the precedent set by John Tyler, replying with alacrity to the cabinet that same evening that "I shall avail myself of the earliest moment to communicate this sad intelligence to Congress, and shall appoint a time and place for taking the oath of office prescribed to the President of the United States. You are requested to be present and witness the ceremony." The following day, Fillmore officially notified Congress of President Taylor's death. He also proposed "this day at 12 o'clock, in the Hall of the House of Representatives, in the presence of both Houses of Congress, to take the oath prescribed by the Constitution, to enable me to enter on the execution of the office which this event has devolved on me."

Thus was the thirteenth president of the United States sworn in before the members of the Senate, House, and cabinet in Statuary Hall. Unlike John Tyler, President Fillmore did not believe it was necessary to present an inaugural address following the swearing-in ceremony. After announcing the funeral plans and calling for a period of national mourning, Fillmore simply plunged into the day-to-day routine of the presidency. In all, this succession tradition was observed seven times after Tyler. Following Fillmore were Andrew Johnson (1865), Chester A. Arthur (1881), Theodore Roosevelt (1901), Calvin Coolidge (1923), Harry Truman (1945), and Lyndon B. Johnson (1963). There were eight successions in all under the Tyler precedent. Four followed assassinations—Lincoln, Garfield, McKinley, and Kennedy were murdered during their presidencies—and two other presidents—Harding and Franklin Roosevelt, like Harrison and Taylor—died in office. In 1967 Tyler's precedent was officially codified with the adoption of the Twenty-fifth Amendment to the Constitution: "In case of the removal of the President from office or of his death or resignation, the Vice-President shall become President."[11]

John Tyler's decisive action placed all future vice presidents a heartbeat from the presidency. Whether or not the framers of the Constitution intended this method of presidential succession and would have approved of Tyler's precedent is arguable. Why then did such a cautious politician and strict constructionist act so uncharacteristically and unconventionally? He employed a loose and more flexible construction of the Constitution, he later explained, not to undermine the Constitution, but to maintain the viability of the system of government erected by the founding fathers.

In justifying his succession precedent and the ensuing power struggle with the congressional Whigs and members of his cabinet, Tyler said he moved swiftly and deliberately in order to demonstrate to the nation and the world that American constitutional procedures for a peaceful transfer of executive power worked. The president further revealed that his controversial actions were designed to preserve executive autonomy and guarantee the separation of the executive and legislative branches. He charged that the Whigs had sought "to merge all executive powers in the legislative branch of the government," which was a challenge to the separation of powers outlined in the Constitution. Surely, he asserted, "The Constitution never designed that the executive should be a mere cipher." In the course of his struggle with Congress, Tyler successfully resisted legislative dominance by implementing an independent executive policy and liberally using the presidential veto. President Tyler had no regrets and was proud of his record in office because "I considered the path of my duty was clearly marked out before me, and I resolved to pursue it."[12]

President Tyler's defiant independent course during his first months in office stunned his Whig allies in Congress and the party faithful throughout the nation. No one was more surprised than Senator Henry Clay of Kentucky, a friend of Tyler's for some twenty years. Clay fully expected the Virginian to endorse the Whig congressional agenda calling for a national bank and a protective tariff. But Clay was mistaken and quickly realized he had underestimated the new president's resolve to be his own man as the nation's chief magistrate. In a tense interview with Tyler on bank legislation at the White House, Senator Clay flatly rejected the president's compromise proposal for a national bank that guaranteed the principle of states' rights. Clay insisted on a national bank with sweeping authority unhampered by states' rights limitations. Irritated at his old friend's arrogance, President Tyler said: "Go you now, then, Mr. Clay, to your end of the avenue, where stands the Capitol, and there perform your duty to the country as you shall think proper. So help me God, I shall do mine at this end of it as I shall think proper."[13]

Thus began a nasty political feud that overturned the Whig political bandwagon and crippled Tyler's presidency. The Virginian's accidental ascendancy to the nation's highest office was a galling turn of fate for Clay and salt in the open wounds of his thwarted ambitions. A man who desperately wanted to be president of the United States, "Harry of the West," as he was affectionately known to legions of his admirers, confidently had anticipated he would be the Whig nominee in 1840. When the party instead chose General Harrison of Ohio as its presidential candidate, a disappointed Clay vented his anger in a drunken rampage that dismayed even his closest allies. Perhaps in a gesture of conciliation to the Kentuckian, Tyler, one of Virginia's delegates for Henry Clay at the Whig convention, was selected as the vice-presidential nominee, ostensibly to placate the South and to give the ticket geographic balance. All knew it was an odd choice and one that would prove calamitous for the Whig Party.

American electoral politics were forever transformed by the Whigs' imaginative presidential campaign that year. The election of 1840 was a sweeping Whig victory as Harrison easily won the presidency and both branches of Congress came under Whig control. Voter turnout was phenomenal. Roughly 80 percent of the eligible male electorate went to the polls, energized by massive parades, outdoor rallies, campaign songs, and a circus-like hoopla never before witnessed by the American public. Gimmickry and humbug became hallmarks of the campaign.

A widely used antic was the rolling of large leather balls festooned with catchy slogans such as "Van, Van, Van—Van's a Used Up Man" across the rural landscape and through villages and towns. The Whigs also changed traditional electioneering practice by bringing along their wives, daughters, and sisters since many of the political activities were family oriented, such as the glee clubs that appeared everywhere along the campaign trail singing patriotic and inspiring tunes. Even one Democratic editor candidly admitted he found the Whig songfests unforgettable and said the melodies "rang in my ears wherever I went, morning, noon, and night" as "men, women, and children did nothing but sing."[14]

Quite fortuitously, the Whig ticket of military hero Harrison, the victor over the Shawnee Indians at the 1811 battle of Tippecanoe in frontier Indiana, and his patrician running mate John Tyler "inspired the most famous alliterative campaign slogan in American history—Tippecanoe and Tyler too." It became an iconic political jingle that remains popular to the present day, even though most contemporary Americans know little to nothing about either Harrison or Tyler. The motto "Tippecanoe and Tyler too" may have been a ringing rallying cry on the campaign trail, but as the New York Whig diarist Philip Hone later observed, "there was rhyme but no reason in it." A loyalist to his party, Hone understood that John Tyler was a renegade Democrat without allegiance to Whig principles.[15]

The Whigs capitalized as well on a Democratic journalist's disparaging characterization of their sixty-seven-year-old candidate as a decrepit frontier soldier eager for a pension so that he might spend his remaining days drinking hard cider in his log cabin. In a bit of flummery that became commonplace in nineteenth-century American political campaigns, the Whigs turned the jibe to their advantage by embarking on a "Log Cabin and Hard Cider" campaign. In this scenario, General Harrison was cast as a common man of humble origins who imbibed the preferred drink of farmers and working folk. Nothing could have been further from the truth. Harrison, like his running mate Tyler, had aristocratic Virginia roots and the general's home on the banks of the Ohio River was a palatial estate, not a rough-hewn cottage.

Unhindered by the truth, the Whigs used the log cabin motif whenever possible. Log cabins were featured on transparencies and banners in parades and at rallies and sprang up in communities nationwide, where the impromptu structures served as local Whig election headquarters. Hard cider became the other prominent symbol of the campaign and it flowed freely at all Whig political gatherings. For good measure, coonskin caps, which highlighted Harrison's supposed frontier origins, were worn by the party faithful and became prized souvenirs. One enterprising distiller introduced pocket whiskey bottles shaped like log cabins. The E. C. Booz Distillery of Philadelphia produced these popular bottles under the brand name "Old Cabin Whiskey." In another tale of the era that may well be apocryphal, legend has it that the nationwide fame of the Booz bottles led to whiskey being identified forever after in the American vernacular as booze.[16]

But despite all the precedent-setting campaign shenanigans and the euphoria of victory at the polls, the chickens came home to roost in the summer of 1841. The man who had received the Whig Party's vice-presidential nomination by default now thwarted Whig legislative initiatives. The man the Whigs had barely given a second thought during the election campaign, dismissed with the ditty "We will vote for Tyler therefore, without a why or wherefore," twice vetoed legislation creating a national bank. Having chosen

Tippecanoe Log Cabin, corner of Main and Eagle Streets, Buffalo. Erected on March 18, by the Whigs of Buffalo, and dedicated to the cause of Harrison and Tyler on March 20, 1840. *Buffalo and Erie County Historical Society.*

to ignore Tyler's earlier hostility to the old Bank of the United States and his campaign speeches expressing opposition to the creation of a new national bank, Senator Clay and the Whig leadership in Congress now cried foul and branded the president a traitor. In the streets of Washington angry citizens burned him in effigy. Whig newspapers across the nation denounced Tyler as an apostate who had abandoned the republican school of Washington, Madison, and Jefferson, all of whom had approved a national bank.

As the titular head of the Whig Party, Clay did everything in his power to curb the usurper in the White House. According to one of his most recent biographers, Clay bore the brunt of responsibility for the feud with Tyler because he tried to force the president and the Whig Party to accept what he alone "had decided the American people had mandated in the election of 1840." It was Clay who "almost single-handedly shattered his own party by his obsessive desire to fashion a third national bank." Although Tyler had not deceived Clay or anyone else about his opposition to a bank, he was not blameless in the fallout with the Whigs. At times during the controversy the president's conduct had been tricky and deceptive. He made equivo-cal statements that were interpreted to mean one thing but turned out to mean quite the opposite. In this way, an earlier biographer of Clay observed, President Tyler made himself "contemptible" as a public figure.[17]

In September 1841, after Tyler's second bank veto, the entire Whig cabinet, except Secretary of State Daniel Webster, resigned in protest. A few days after the cabinet resignations Senator Clay addressed the Whig caucus and likened President Tyler to the nation's most notorious turn-coat—Benedict Arnold. Asking them to hold fast to their principles, Clay told his Senate colleagues: "Our policy has been arrested by an Executive that we brought into power. Arnold escaped to England after his treason was detected" and "Tyler is on his way to the Democratic camp." Clay was confident the Democrats would give Tyler "lodgings in some outhouse, but they will never trust him. He will stand here, like Arnold in England, a monument of his perfidy and disgrace."[18]

In addition to being castigated as a traitor, Tyler also faced assassination threats and was officially drummed out of the Whig Party for allegedly having betrayed the will of the people. Not satisfied with making President Tyler a political outcast, wrathful House Whigs later censured him and un-successfully sought his impeachment. Ironically, at issue in this rancorous dispute were competing but not dissimilar perceptions of republicanism. In the eyes of his antagonists, President Tyler's primary sin was the use of the veto power to overturn the glorious 1840 victory with its promise to reduce executive power and separate the purse from the sword. For his part, Tyler believed his course was the path of true republicanism, and the Whigs, not he, were the betrayers of the republican virtues of the founding fathers.

As a man without a party, John Tyler maintained a brave front after being publicly humiliated by his former Whig allies, although the charge that he had abandoned hallowed republican doctrine undoubtedly stung. His frus-tration was evident in a conversation he had with Beverley Tucker in No-vember 1841. Tucker earlier had advised Tyler to announce that he would not seek reelection in 1844, advice the president had ignored. Now Tyler confided to his friend, "I must have a party." Tucker tersely replied, "Make one!" Tyler shot back: "I have not time. I must have one ready made."

In truth, John Tyler recognized the necessity of creating his own party, and found the time to try, unsuccessfully as it turned out, to build one. Over the next two and a half years, Tyler attempted to marshal public support for his cause by proclaiming he was the true disciple of Jefferson and Madison. He reminded his fellow Americans that a commitment to civic virtue, states' rights, executive restraint, and a strict interpretation of the Constitution had been the bedrock of his beliefs before he entered the White House.[19]

But there was another feature of John Tyler's republicanism, usually downplayed or ignored by biographers and historians of his administration, that was consistent with the thinking and outlook of his Virginian mentors, Thomas Jefferson and James Madison. As the original architects who drafted and implemented the blueprints for an American continental empire, Madison and Jefferson stressed the vital connection between territorial expansion and the viability of republican government. From the onset of his presidency, Tyler extolled the merits of an "extended republic" and in formulating his foreign policy was true to the republican faith that had guided the territorial expansion of the American empire throughout the first half-century of its existence.

What James Madison had wrought at the Constitutional Convention in 1787 was a workable formula for retaining popular government by allowing for an expanding territorial empire. Just after the convention had adjourned, he explained some of the features of the Constitution in a letter to Jefferson, who was serving as the United States's representative in Paris. There had been a fear among the delegates that the newly independent United States might fracture over differing sectional and economic interests. "It appeared," Madison informed his friend, "to be the sincere and unanimous wish of the Convention to cherish and preserve the Union of the States. No proposition was made, no suggestion was thrown out in favor of a partition of the Empire into two or more Confederacies."

Madison went on to dismiss "the concurrent opinions of theoretical writers," an obvious reference to the theory of the French philosopher Montesquieu, that to succeed republics had to be small. Madison believed quite the opposite was true, and maintained that republican government, "in order to effect its purpose must operate not within a small but an extensive sphere." After providing this private explanation of the inner workings of the Constitution to Jefferson, Madison went public with his "extend the sphere" analysis in Federalist no. 10, proposing, among several other safeguards, that republican government would be best secured by expanding and enlarging the territorial empire. As historian Walter LaFeber has noted, Madison's analysis announced that the "relationship between expansion and the viability of republican institutions was now reciprocal."[20]

For his part, Thomas Jefferson confirmed both in thought and deed that he accepted Madison's argument about the necessity of extending the sphere. In March 1801, a few weeks after his inauguration as the nation's third president, Jefferson gave the Vermont politician and preacher Nathaniel Niles his appraisal of the success of the American republican experiment thus far: "It furnishes a new proof of the falsehood of Montesquieu's doctrine, that a republic can be preserved only in a small territory. The reverse is the truth.

Had our territory been even a third only of what it is, we were gone." At the conclusion of his presidency, which was highlighted by his having doubled the territory of the United States with the Louisiana Purchase, Jefferson still wanted more.

He continued to contemplate future territorial expansion through the acquisition or annexation of east and west Florida, Cuba, and perhaps Mexico and Canada to the Union. Bring all those areas under the American flag, Jefferson wrote to Madison upon the latter's inauguration as president, and the United States would become "such an empire for liberty as she has never surveyed since the creation; and I am persuaded that no constitution was ever so well calculated as ours for extensive empire and self-government." Jefferson's self-congratulatory tone and respectful praise for his friend's amazing handiwork, the Constitution of 1787, clarified for posterity his commitment to the Madisonian solution to the age-old dilemma of how to secure a republic while at the same time creating an extensive and powerful empire.[21]

Jefferson's validation in his private correspondence of the necessity of territorial expansion for the survival and health of republican institutions was reaffirmed anew some years later by his protégé, James Monroe. The fourth of Virginia's Revolutionary dynasty of presidents, Monroe publicly made the case for an "extensive republic" in his 1823 annual message to Congress, partially in response to those critics who feared that unrestrained expansion jeopardized the stability of the Union. Marveling at the growth of the nation since the Revolution of '76 from three million to about ten million people, he proudly announced that this "expansion of our population, and accession of new States to our Union, have had the happiest effect on all its highest interests. That it has eminently augmented our resources, and added to our strength and respectability as a Power, is admitted by all. . . . It is manifest that, by enlarging the basis of our system and increasing the number of States, the system itself has been greatly strengthened in both its branches. Consolidation and disunion have thereby been rendered equally impracticable."

Although this 1823 message later gained fame and renown because it contained the announcement of what became known as the Monroe Doctrine, it was a hallmark as well for its restatement of the Madisonian/Jeffersonian faith in territorial expansion and the benefits derived from an ever-expanding republic. In an exercise that had become a routine annual stocktaking, the equivalent of today's State of the Union address, Monroe was unable to resist the opportunity to glory in the unfolding of America's national destiny and uniqueness. He proudly noted, "If we compare the present condition of our Union with its actual state at the close of our Revolution, the history of the world furnishes no example of a progress in improvement in all the important circumstances which constitute the happiness of a nation, which bears any resemblance to it."[22]

A thoughtful reviewer of this aspect of the nation's history would be struck by the constancy in this line of thinking about expansion and empire among American leaders. Less than two decades after Monroe's message, and forty years after Thomas Jefferson's expression of satisfaction with how well the "extend the sphere" principle worked in practice, a post–Revolutionary generation Virginian, John Tyler, once again enunciated the connection between territorial expansion and the viability of republican institutions. In notably similar language to that of his predecessor Monroe, and sharing an admirable consistency of thought with his idols Madison and Jefferson, Tyler wasted little time in making the case for territorial expansion as the cement of Union and generator of national prosperity. After less than two months in office and in his first official message to Congress on June 1, 1841, the tenth president recited the near obligatory statistics of the nation's growth from three million at the time of the Revolution to seventeen million in 1840. This latest increase, Tyler claimed, represented a 30 percent growth in population for the fifth consecutive decade in the nation's history.

In this first of his many homilies on the virtues of extending the sphere, Tyler further contended that the "old States contain territory sufficient in itself to maintain a population of additional millions." And, he continued, "the most populous of the new States may even yet be regarded as but partially settled, while of the new lands on this side of the Rocky Mountains, to say nothing of the immense region which stretches from the base of those mountains to the mouth of the Columbia River, about 770,000,000 acres, ceded and unceded, still remain to be brought into market." Summarizing his appraisal of the nation's phenomenal territorial and population growth, both actual and potential, Tyler reassured members of Congress and the American people "that there exists nothing in the extension of our Empire over our acknowledged possessions to excite the alarm of the patriot for the safety of our institutions. The federative system, leaving to each State the care of its domestic concerns and devolving on the Federal Government those of general import, admits in safety of the greatest expansion." As he began his presidency, John Tyler recognized and understood, as his fellow Virginians Jefferson and Monroe before him clearly had, that expansion was

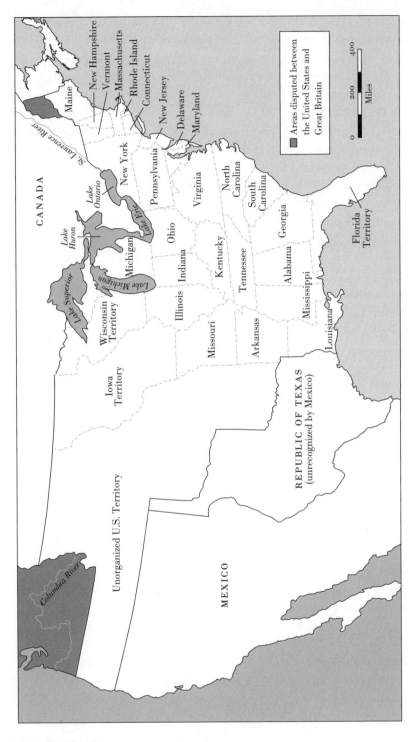

Territorial limits of the United States in 1840, including disputed claims with Great Britain in Maine and Oregon.

the republican key to preserving the delicate balance between national and state power.[23]

President Tyler's nuanced reference to vast "unceded" acres subtly announced his administration's expansionist ambitions. Even a quick glance at a map of the United States's boundaries in 1841 would reveal that Tyler's remark about "unceded" acres was a clear allusion to land the United States did not yet possess, including the Lone Star Republic of Texas east of the Rocky Mountains on the one hand, and the disputed Oregon country along with Mexican territory west of the Rockies on the other. Oddly, this illuminating maiden message to Congress and the American public generally has been overlooked in historical accounts evaluating and discussing the Tyler administration's expansionist diplomacy. A careful reading of the document, however, reveals that two of President Tyler's future foreign policy initiatives were quietly announced in the special session address. First, Tyler signaled his desire to annex Texas. Second, he sought to bring a sizable chunk of the Pacific coast of North America "to market."

As presently became clear, bringing Texas into the Union headed Tyler's acquisitive agenda. Oregon, jointly claimed by the United States and Great Britain, and the Mexican province of California were high on Tyler's list of foreign policy priorities as well, but for the time being diplomatic attempts to acquire those territories would remain on the back burner. He moved quickly to promote Texas annexation. In October 1841, shortly after having filled the cabinet vacancies created by Whig resignations with his own men, Tyler sounded out the lone holdover, Secretary of State Webster, "as to the probability of acquiring Texas by treaty." President Tyler was confident "it could be done," but acknowledged that slavery would cause objections in the North. But if the North could "be reconciled to it, could anything throw so bright a lustre around us? It seems to me that the great interests of the North would be incalculably advanced by such an acquisition."[24]

Daniel Webster was not persuaded by his boss's rationale for adding additional slave states to the Union. Instead, he concentrated on settling a troublesome northeastern boundary dispute and improving relations with Great Britain. Only after Secretary Webster left the cabinet in the spring of 1843 was President Tyler able to set his Texas annexation plans in motion and pursue his goal of creating a continental empire that stretched from the Atlantic to the Pacific Ocean.

In addition to the ambitious expansionist agenda projected in the special session message, President Tyler studded his prose on this occasion with images of the glorious national destiny that lay ahead for the United States.

A believer in the gospel of American exceptionalism, Tyler thought that the American experiment was unique and had universal implications. America with its enlightened republican institutions would serve as an inspiring model and shining example to the world. The immediate national task and civic duty was to "reclaim our almost illimitable wildernesses and introduce into their depths the lights of civilization."

America would be a haven also to those who hungered for liberty. Displaying an appalling moral obtuseness, this man who denied liberty to the more than fifty human beings he held as property urged opening America's shores to Europe's downtrodden and oppressed masses. In language presaging the sentiments expressed in Emma Lazarus's poem "The New Colossus," engraved at the base of the Statue of Liberty, Tyler stated: "We hold out to the people of other countries an invitation to come and settle among us as members of our rapidly growing family, and for the blessings which we offer them we require of them to look upon our country as their country and to unite with us in the great task of preserving our institutions and thereby perpetuating our liberties."[25]

Remarkably, in this initial speech to Congress at the opening of his presidency, John Tyler candidly placed all the signposts for his goal of national destiny in public view for everyone to see. For all the cruel jokes and jibes about "His Accidency" being a fraud and a pretender in the White House, this Virginia aristocrat had a clear and ambitious foreign policy agenda. Just as Tyler had been forearmed to masterfully confront the presidential succession controversy, this disciple of Jefferson and Madison was fully prepared, based on his schooling in their beliefs, to pursue the lofty quest for an extensive republic, preserve republican institutions, and offer the United States as the beacon of liberty to the world. Tragically, even the best-prepared and most visionary leaders sometimes fail to fulfill their dreams.

Despite President Tyler's almost immediate expression of his belief in America's mission of national greatness, rarely has he been credited, either by his contemporaries or later historians, for having such a broad vision of national destiny. Routinely Tyler has been dismissed as a narrow states' rights ideologue who as president pursued continental expansion solely, as in the case of Texas, to preserve the institution of slavery. Indelibly etched in the American public's mind was an image of John Tyler as a stereotypical aristocratic southern slaveowner who, at all costs, defended the region's "peculiar institution." Sometimes John Tyler was a strict constructionist, sometimes not. He had a states' rights agenda, but he also had a nationalist agenda, one which increasingly came to the forefront during his presidency. He would set aside these principles and his strict constructionism, as he had shown in the adroit handling of accession to the presidency, when opportunities for territorial expansion arose and he felt political expediency demanded a more flexible response.

It is frequently forgotten that John Tyler was a key participant in the leadership of an antebellum generation that grappled with the issues of sectionalism and the preservation of the Union. When Tyler's public career is considered in its entirety, it becomes evident that he persistently rose above sectional partisanship and promoted a vision of national destiny designed to sustain, not destroy, the Union of 1789. The rub, of course, came when Tyler insisted that the United States must remain the inviolable slaveholding republic inherited from the founding fathers. An instinct for political survival and a stubborn determination to make his mark on the national scene drove John Tyler to pursue a foreign policy that would achieve these goals and "must look to the whole country and the whole people." As was the case with other occupants of the White House both before and after President Tyler's residency, chief executives who were blocked by political obstacles at home turned to foreign affairs as an ostensibly easy avenue to gain popular support and acclaim.[26]

John Tyler made the most of having been forewarned and forearmed. He met the challenge of being the first vice president to navigate the uncharted waters of presidential succession in the young republic by establishing the Tyler precedent. From this time forward, the vice presidency assumed a new importance. The holder of that formerly disdained office now found himself a heartbeat from the chief executive's chair and, thanks to John Tyler, the presidency, as an institution, became independent of death. The man who had been mocked as "His Accidency" accomplished what he had set out to do. He ignored the objections of those who claimed the framers had not intended the vice president to become president in his own right on the death of an incumbent.

Tyler's carefully planned assumption of the executive office when William Henry Harrison died demonstrated to the nation and the world that the constitutional provisions adopted fifty-two years earlier by the framers worked in practice. The peaceful transition of presidential power achieved by Tyler's precedent lent stability to the American republic by avoiding the possibility of factious and violent disputes about the legitimacy of succession. Tyler's willingness to take a broad interpretation of the Constitution strengthened the system, but it undercut his claim to be a strict constructionist and set the pattern for constitutional flexibility throughout the remainder of his administration.

After having established his right to the office and powers of the chief executive, Tyler turned to a host of other challenges that confronted his accidental presidency. As he explained "to a gathering of his political friends" in Philadelphia celebrating George Washington's birthday in February 1842, his presidency from the outset faced severe trials that included "private and public credit prostrated—industry in all its departments paralyzed—a Treasury deficient in its supplies—and our foreign relations perplexed and embarrassed." He vowed to restore the nation's economic health by launching a foreign policy that fostered territorial and commercial expansion "without a surrender of national honor."

President John Tyler hoped to build upon the legacy of his Jeffersonian mentors; he was a true believer who shared their optimism about America's future as the moral and republican exemplar to the world. Musing some years later on what his unprecedented action meant for posterity, Tyler hoped that because he had followed the path of honor and duty, "future vice-presidents, who might succeed to the presidency, may feel some slight encouragement to pursue an independent course."[27]

★ ★ ★ ★ ★ ★ ★ ★ ★ ★ ★

Visions of National Destiny

2

I see a people but just beginning to move in their political orbit, giving the surest testimony that the love of virtue pervades the breast of every citizen, and that they possess a force which will retain them, throughout their long career, in the path of social felicity, and social greatness; I see, from this principle, this sincere love of virtue, the future glories of my country, already to commence.

★ *Bishop James Madison, 1800*

We direct the destinies of a mighty continent.
Our resources are unlimited; our means unbounded.
If we be true to ourselves, the glory of other nations,
in comparison with ours, shall resemble but a tale
from the days of chivalry.

★ *John Tyler, 1820*

My imagination has led me to look into the distant future, and there to contemplate the greatness of free America. I have beheld her walking on the waves of the mighty deep, carrying along with her tidings of great joy to distant nations. I have seen her overturning the strong places of despotism, and restoring to man his long-lost rights.

★ *John Tyler, 1832*

hroughout the nineteenth century the country's cultural, political, and religious leaders spewed forth an excessive amount of bombast and hyperbole about national greatness and America's global mission. Not even a bloody and bitter Civil War tempered or moderated this patriotic excess. At century's end a host of chauvinistic patriots, or "jingoes" as they were called, reveled in the fact that the United States had gained an overseas empire and had joined the club of imperial nations shouldering the white man's burden. Years before, in the antebellum period, John Tyler was at the forefront of these shining lights among the post-Revolutionary generation who confidently hailed the nation's future glory and international luster.

How did someone like Tyler, an aristocratic Virginian slaveowner and outwardly parochial champion of the Old South and its peculiar institution, come to be one of the early republic's most passionate drumbeaters for national greatness and splendor? How did an individual who barely traveled much beyond the nation's east coast and Midwest, who never journeyed to Texas or California, who never saw the Pacific Ocean or visited its tropical isles, and who never did the Grand Tour of Europe, acquire such grandiose visions of national destiny and become so ardently Pacific-minded? One cannot answer these questions with total certainty, but his upbringing and education in the heady and exhilarating atmosphere of the early republic, amidst Virginia's legendary Revolutionary heroes and founding fathers, undoubtedly nurtured and shaped his sense of mission and faith in the American republican experiment.

Despite being cast as humble republicans of modest origins while running for president and vice president on the Whig ticket in the "Cider and Log Cabin" campaign of 1840, both William Henry Harrison and John Tyler were to the manor born, privileged sons of politically prominent and socially prestigious tidewater Virginia families. Charles City County, located on the north side of the James River, was the native soil of the two future presidents of the United States. Harrison's birthplace was Berkeley plantation, which was less than twenty miles from Greenway plantation, where John Tyler was born on March 29, 1790. Benjamin Harrison, father of William Henry, was a signer of the Declaration of Independence.

Judge John Tyler, the president's father, was Thomas Jefferson's roommate at the College of William and Mary, a passionate revolutionary, a member, along with the elder Harrison and James Madison, of the Virginia House of Delegates, and a noted jurist who three times was elected governor of the commonwealth. The senior Tyler also counted Patrick Henry and James Monroe among his friends and political allies. Throughout the first years of the new republic, during the long and lazy months of summer, he regularly would gather his children, including his second son and namesake John, under a favorite willow tree to amuse them with his fiddle playing and regale them with awe-inspiring tales of the American Revolution. Not unexpectedly, and as was entirely befitting of someone of his high station and privileged childhood, the younger Tyler came to prefer champagne to cider, and neither he nor William Henry Harrison were the self-made men the log-cabin imagery implied.

The Tyler family estate known as Greenway, which actually was the name of the mansion house and included two other adjoining farms designated Mons-Sacer and the Courthouse tenement, was a magnificent plantation composed of 1,200 acres of level, fertile farming land bounded by two flowing creeks. The mansion house was a comfortable, well-finished, genteel residence of six rooms, surrounded by numerous and sundry outbuildings, including a kitchen, laundry, storehouse, dairy, ice house, spinning house, meat house, barn, granaries, and, of course, slave quarters. Wheat, corn, tobacco, and other crops were cultivated and all manner of animals were raised, making the plantation virtually self-sufficient and self-contained. To keep the place humming and well tended, forty slaves did most of the cooking, gardening, domestic and household chores, and all forms of manual labor and farm work. John Tyler grew to young manhood at Greenway plantation, learning to love music, poetry, and literature, and dreaming of serving his state and nation as his father's Revolutionary generation before him had done.[1]

In the latter half of the eighteenth century, and continuing into the first decade of the nineteenth century, the College of William and Mary was the center of learning of choice for many of the sons of Virginia's political elite and its first families. Jefferson and Judge Tyler had been scholars at the college, as had George Washington and James Monroe. Continuing a Tyler family tradition of attendance there that began shortly after the school opened its doors to students in 1693 and extends to the present, John entered William and Mary in 1802 at age twelve and graduated in 1807 at age seventeen. Although tutored broadly in liberal arts and the sciences, the young scholar's favorite academic pursuits became ancient history and the study of Shakespeare. The love of Shakespeare's sonnets and plays remained with Tyler throughout his life. He was fond of quoting or alluding to the Bard in private correspondence, public speeches, and political commentary, and during the romantic courtships of the two women he would wed, Letitia Christian and Julia Gardiner.

Other young men attending William and Mary during and just after Tyler composed a nascent Who's Who of southern public leaders and government officials, many of whom rose to national prominence in pre–Civil War America. Among the most notable were John J. Crittenden, future senator from Kentucky, the military hero General Winfield Scott, and the diplomat Charles S. Todd, who would become the American minister to Russia during Tyler's presidency. Others of note included future Virginia senators Littleton Waller Tazewell, William S. Archer, William C. Rives, Benjamin Watkins Leigh, and the distinguished linguist, historian, author, and State Department translator Robert Greenhow. As William and Mary students in their adolescent and teenage years, these men of promise had been nurtured and groomed in the traditions of classical learning, republican virtue, and public service.[2]

The man most responsible for William and Mary's glory days as "Alma Mater to a nation" during the American Revolution and the first decades of the early republic was the Reverend James Madison, Episcopal Bishop of Virginia, the college's president for thirty-five years, and a second cousin of the founding father of the same name. Bishop Madison was a true believer in America's republican virtue and its regenerative mission in a corrupt world. A believer as well in the necessity of an "extensive republic," the bishop admired his cousin's contributions to the *Federalist Papers* and singled out Federalist no. 10 as especially "valuable."

To see Bishop Madison in action in the classroom and pulpit must have been a spellbinding and memorable experience for generations of his students. The scope and virtuosity of his ideas about what lay ahead for the United States were awe-inspiring—the new nation would be at once a republic of virtue, beacon of liberty, moral exemplar to the world, and a divinely ordained rising empire. Bishop Madison's outstanding contribution to the intellectual capital of the new republic was all the more remarkable because, as a consequence of the American Revolution, the College of William and Mary had lost its major revenue sources, leading one historian to remark that in the post-Revolutionary years "the institution was a financial cripple."[3]

Well known and much admired by legions of his students and the network of his contemporaries serving as leaders of state and nation, Bishop Madison's public and patriotic reputation arguably rested upon his 1795 discourse, *Manifestations of the Beneficence of Divine Providence towards Amer-*

ica, and his well-received and much admired eulogy to George Washington. In his *Manifestations* sermon of thanksgiving and prayer, the republican clergyman exalted America's mission to be one of "holding an eminent rank among the nations of the earth" and linked its destiny to divine guidance when he rhetorically asked his Christian flock, "Is there one throughout this rising empire, who doth not trace, in the eventful history of America, the conspicuous display of the hand of providence?" He envisioned a young and vigorous republic coming to the aid of a decrepit Europe, and intoned that "America, as a tender and affectionate daughter, is ready, from her exuberant breasts, to afford the milk of regeneration to her aged and oppressed relatives."

Such florid imagery of American exceptionalism initially gained the bishop a wide, if localized, audience of admirers. But it was the eulogy of President Washington, delivered in Williamsburg's Bruton Parish Church on February 22, 1800, that accorded him national acclaim and renown. Among hundreds of eulogies that appeared in the outpouring of the nation's grief, Bishop Madison's memorial address struck a responsive chord with his fellow citizens and remained in print until 1844. George Washington had served as William and Mary's chancellor, an honorific post, from 1788 until his death. Although some Jeffersonians thought Washington too closely aligned with Alexander Hamilton and therefore a betrayer of their version of republicanism, Bishop Madison always held the first president in high esteem, even while disagreeing with his Federalist policies. He presented Washington's life as an example for his students and all patriots to emulate and follow. To a reader in the twenty-first century, Madison's language may seem overly verbose and ornate, but it resonated with Americans at the opening of the nineteenth century who were searching for a national identity, hoping like the bishop that a republican people's "sincere love of virtue" foretold "the future glories of my country."[4]

Not surprisingly, the charismatic Reverend James Madison was John Tyler's most beloved and influential teacher during his formative years as a William and Mary student. Whether as spiritual guide or intellectual mentor, Bishop Madison mesmerized his impressionable young protégé with his "eminently eloquent" sermons and speeches and "strikingly impressive" personal manner. Years later, Tyler affectionately remembered that his old professor's republican virtues were "indelibly impressed upon my heart and mind." Bishop Madison, another of his former students reflected, "was also a man of enlarged and patriotic views, and looked beyond mere party and sectional interests to the good of the country at large."

Little wonder that throughout his adult life John Tyler would remain one of his mentor's most unwavering and appreciative disciples. The bishop had served as the precocious boy's "second father" and in his lectures and classes inspired, just as Judge Tyler had done earlier on the lawns of Greenway, the future president of the United States with visions of national greatness and dreams of glory for the American republic. Bishop Madison's fragile and wispy dreams of national destiny and American exceptionalism were of such power and attraction that they beguiled John Tyler until the year before his death, only then dissolving and turning to ashes when the Union dissolved and civil war erupted.[5]

Thomas Jefferson was in the White House throughout young Tyler's student days. Although we do not know for certain, it would be reasonable to assume that Tyler and his classmates closely followed the events of the day, including the nation's exciting and crisis-laden foreign relations. We do know that his father avidly followed current affairs, as did his professors at the college. Under Bishop Madison's tutelage, the controversy swirling around the wisdom and legality of the 1803 purchase of Louisiana from France undoubtedly was being discussed and debated at a republican stronghold such as William and Mary.

On the national scene one voice had been clearly heard on these issues, that of Bishop Madison's former student and friend, Senator John Breckinridge of Kentucky. During the Senate debate on whether or not to approve the purchase, Breckinridge was true to the teachings of the William and Mary school of empire. In response to concerns about the size of the republic, he dismissed the "old and hackneyed doctrine; that a Republic ought not to be too extensive." The opposite was the rule, Breckinridge avowed, because rather than territorial expansion weakening union, "the more extensive its dominion the more safe and more durable it will be."[6]

The Jeffersonians won the day. The Louisiana Purchase agreement received Senate approval, the requisite funding from the House of Representatives, and unqualified popular support. Relishing the victory, John Tyler Sr. wrote Jefferson: "I congratulate you on the great acquisition of Louisiana—obtained, not by the sword, which stabs to the heart the individual and the country for the aggrandizement of a few, but by the peaceable and honorable means of friendly negotiation."

But there was a darker side to this transaction and its constitutional legitimacy, as Jefferson earlier had admitted to Secretary of State Madison: "I infer that the less we say about constitutional difficulties respecting Louisiana the better, and that what is necessary for surmounting them must be

done sub silentio." The Jeffersonian majority had, according to one historian, "few qualms about continued expansion and, on the grounds of necessity, was prepared to accept an expanding concept of presidential power."
Judging from his handling of the Texas annexation issue when he was president in the 1840s, this lesson on the expediency and merit of the extension
of presidential power to promote continental empire was not lost on John
Tyler.[7]

A corollary to Tyler's indoctrination into the national destiny school of
thought was membership in a distinguished corps of anti-British national-
ists. Among Jeffersonian expansionists, the rhetoric celebrating the virtues
and rewards of an extensive republic and future national greatness often
was accompanied by outbursts of anti-British nationalism. Anglophobia
was an integral part of John Tyler's educational heritage. He grew up in a
household that feared and reviled the former mother country. His patriot
father bitterly remembered the hardships inflicted by the British during the
struggle for independence.

Such memories were still fresh in 1810 when the senior Tyler, now governor of Virginia, complained to President James Madison about Britain's
disdain for America's maritime rights and angrily said that "if another impressment shou'd take place I wou'd make prisoners of every british Subject
in the States." Incomprehensible as it may be to most twenty-first century
Americans nurtured on Anglo-American friendship, a slavish fascination
with the antics of British royals, and a pervasive spirit of Anglophilia, the
atmosphere of the post-Revolutionary republic was poisoned by a hatred
for Great Britain. John Tyler was no exception. He and many of his fellow
Virginians grew up detesting and distrusting the British.[8]

Tyler's anti-British nationalism intensified during the War of 1812, a conflict that he and his father believed was young America's second struggle for
independence from England. As a fledgling member of the Virginia House
of Delegates, John Tyler called for a full and unrelenting prosecution of the
war against the British invader. When in the summer of 1813 British troops
captured and plundered the tidewater Virginia city of Hampton, Tyler organized a company of Charles City County militia to protect neighboring
communities and Richmond from British assault. No further British attack
came and his month-long service as "Captain" in the Virginia militia, a military rank that mockingly would be applied to him by his enemies when he
became president, was bloodless.

Upon his graduation from William and Mary, John Tyler had read law
under his father, then a judge of the Virginia General Court. He completed

his legal studies in Richmond under the guidance of Edmund Randolph, who had served as attorney general and secretary of state in George Washington's cabinet. After passing the bar, Tyler began what became a lucrative private practice. As an up-and-coming country lawyer, he was not above playing the anti-British card. In a trial in which the opposing attorney made a big display of citing English authority and precedent, Tyler won the case by shamelessly appealing to the jury's anti-English prejudice. He told them: "Our late war was fought in the face of this English authority, which sought to make slaves of our seamen and destroy the independence of America. Sir, this jury . . . will have none of your English authority! Away with it!"[9]

Later in life when the Anglophobic John Tyler toured Niagara Falls, so the story went, he refused to enter Canada, which offered the better and more breathtaking view of the Horseshoe and American Falls, because he did not wish to set foot on British soil. Tyler's ingrained anti-British nationalism never left him and a visceral Anglophobia unwaveringly prevailed as the flip side of his patriotic calls for the fulfillment of national destiny.[10]

John Tyler learned invaluable lessons about public virtue and personal honor and about the precarious nature of republican government and diplomacy from his father, family friend Thomas Jefferson, Bishop Madison, and his other tutors at William and Mary. They were lessons that remained with him throughout a public career that spanned more than four decades of the nation's early political life. His mentors had infused his learning with visions of national greatness and a belief in the American republic's God-given destiny. Or, as his father was fond of saying, "America stood fairest of any spot on the globe to erect the standard of virtuous liberty." Along with these expressions of American exceptionalism, the senior Tyler and Bishop Madison also heralded the nation's "great code of human rights," a theme about America's mission in the world that has echoed throughout American history to the present day.[11]

In parallel fashion, the younger Tyler was being groomed for greatness himself. From his entry into public life at age twenty-one when he was elected to the Virginia House of Delegates, John Tyler aspired to political glory and fame. He ardently wished to emulate his father's success and desired to achieve a good deal more, perhaps even the highest office available to a citizen of the republic. John Tyler not only was intellectually nurtured and politically primed for the presidency, but he had the talent, drive, and ambition to become the nation's chief executive. He tailored his career with that goal in mind, marrying well to cement his social and economic stature in Virginia's aristocratic society, and carefully positioning himself to avoid political minefields. There is no doubt that John Tyler could be a calculating and devious politician, but to his credit he tried to live up to his principles and remain a man of republican virtue.

The first challenge to Tyler's youthful visions of national destiny came with the Missouri crisis of 1819–20. He initially put many of his republican beliefs to the test when, as a member of the Virginia delegation in the House of Representatives, he denounced the contentious sectional debate that erupted over the question of Missouri's admission as free or slave state as a grave threat to the Union. In a February 1820 speech in the House, he defined sectional feelings and local prejudices that divide a people "as the bane of a republic." As he noted years later about the seriousness of the Missouri crisis: "The alarm bell, as Mr. Jefferson expressed it, had sounded, and the sections stood in array facing each other." Sparked by the hope that the pursuit of national greatness and glory would overcome the dangers of sectionalism, Tyler proudly informed his colleagues that Americans "direct the destinies of a mighty continent. Our resources are unlimited; our means unbounded. If we be true to ourselves, the glory of other nations, in comparison with ours, shall resemble but a tale from the days of chivalry."[12]

From that day forward John Tyler, slaveholding member of Virginia's elite ruling class, doggedly tried to sell his vision of America's mission and destiny to the majority of his fellow white Americans of the South, the North, and the emerging West. Tyler envisaged and championed a comprehensive foreign policy that would provide mutual, if not equal, benefits to all sections of the republic. He was a true disciple of Madison and Jefferson in his belief that territorial and commercial expansion would allay sectional differences, maintain the Union, and create a nation of power and glory unparalleled in history.

Despite his optimism about the healing power of an "extensive republic," the Missouri crisis forced Tyler to confront the divisive issue of slavery and its further expansion. The future of slavery in the republic became a looming political thunderhead that endangered national harmony and obscured his clear vistas of national destiny. Ironically, slavery as the ominous cloud in the otherwise clear and sunny skies that shone upon the Union's prospects made the attraction of an "extensive republic" even more compelling and logical for Tyler because he believed in a theory of "diffusion" as a way to end slavery gradually and peaceably. Development over space would thin out and diffuse the slave population and, with fewer blacks in some of the older slave states of the upper South, it might become politically feasible to abolish slavery in states like Virginia.

According to Tyler's new line of thinking, instead of the healing powers inherent in territorial expansion being diminished, continuing to extend the sphere would not only abate sectionalism and bring national greatness, it also eventually would bring the end of slavery as well. No matter that critics of this reasoning denounced it as a cynical and self-serving doctrine, believers in the logic of diffusion thought their argument was irrefutable. Missouri must enter the union as a slave state so that the African American population might be thinned out from the existing slave states. Consequently, Representative Tyler voted against proposals that restricted slavery in Missouri or any other portion of the remaining territory of the Louisiana Purchase.

During the course of the Missouri debate Tyler candidly explained his rationale for a policy of diffusion. "Slavery has been represented on all hands as the dark cloud," he admitted, and readily concurred with a House colleague from Massachusetts who recommended that "it would be well to disperse this cloud." Tyler approvingly noted that "the gentleman from Massachusetts also conceded that for which we contend—that by diffusing this population extensively you increase the prospects of emancipation. What enabled New York, Pennsylvania, and other States, to adopt the language of universal emancipation? Rely on it," he argued, "nothing but the paucity of the number of their slaves. That which would have been *criminal* in those States not to have done, would be an act of political suicide in Georgia or South Carolina to do." By admitting Missouri as a slave state, Tyler concluded, "You advance the interest and secure the safety of one-half of this extended republic: you ameliorate the condition of the slave, and you add much to the prospects of emancipation, and the total extinction of slavery." Whatever else it may have represented for Tyler and other adherents to the theory in the North and South, the cynical logic of "diffusion" was a tacit admission that the institution of chattel slavery was a potentially explosive and fatal anomaly in a republic dedicated to liberty and justice.[13]

Two months after these extraordinarily revealing remarks about the connections between slavery, expansion, and eventual emancipation, Tyler elaborated further on his vision of national destiny and mission. On this occasion it was a speech before the House in which he opposed a protective tariff and, for the first time, identified Great Britain as the United States's chief rival in the quest for global commercial supremacy. At this point in his political career, Tyler represented and exclusively spoke for the interests of agriculture and commerce; they, he declared, "are twin sisters" and should not be restricted by the folly of high duties and tariff restrictions. "America," he announced, "is now the granary of the world; she supplies the wants of foreign nations as they arise." Free and unfettered trade would assure that the United States ultimately would become a leading world power.

However, Tyler was in no particular hurry to force the issue of America's mission and destiny. In order to surpass Great Britain in this contest, Tyler acknowledged that at some stage of the United States's economic development, manufacturing and industry would become essential ingredients in the drive for national greatness. "When it shall correspond with the interest of this nation to become a manufacturing nation," he prophesied, "such will it become," but "natural causes produce the result," not an artificial protective tariff. With these two speeches in the House of Representatives in 1820, Congressman Tyler established his credentials as a major spokesman for what historian Michael H. Hunt has depicted as a canon of "national greatness." John Tyler also anticipated the expansionist doctrine labeled "manifest destiny" by John L. O'Sullivan, editor of the *Democratic Review*, almost twenty years later.[14]

Tyler's fascination with America's destiny and its role as moral exemplar for the world surfaced again and again in his political speeches and public oratory. He could not say it often enough, as if constant repetition would make it come true. It was the leitmotif of his republican ideology. For example, upon his retirement from the House of Representatives in 1821 because of poor health, Tyler said farewell to his constituents by urging them to look to a future that promised "the march of this favored land in the road of power and glory" and "the high destinies that await us." Despite this temporary setback to his physical well-being, John Tyler completely recovered from his illness and within two years was back on his career path and in the midst of the political fray. After another stint in the Virginia House of Delegates, he followed his father's footsteps to the governor's mansion in Richmond in 1825.

As governor, John Tyler had the sad and solemn duty to deliver the state's official eulogy to Thomas Jefferson, who died on July 4, 1826, the fiftieth anniversary of American independence. Praising Jefferson as the brilliant author of a universal document of human liberty and freedom, Tyler predicted that "when the happy era shall arrive for the emancipation of nations, hastened on as it will be by the example of America, shall they not resort to the Declaration of our Independence as the charter of their rights, and will not its author be hailed as the benefactor of the redeemed?" Thomas Jefferson originally had served as Tyler's inspiration and principal role model. John Tyler was forever grateful to his illustrious mentor and, in the Virginia

John Tyler,
governor of
Virginia.
Special Collections,
Swem Library,
College of William
and Mary.

tradition, this future president became one among many disciples who was prepared and honored to carry forth the Jeffersonian legacy.[15]

Almost immediately after Jefferson's death, James Monroe symbolically passed the torch of republicanism to the next generation. In what amounted to a virtual laying on of hands, the former president praised Governor Tyler for a splendid eulogy that in "warm & glowing terms" conveyed to the American public an appreciation of Jefferson's monumental achievements. As Jefferson's earliest protégé, Monroe confided that having "studied the law under him in my youth, and been long engaged in the same career of public service since, I have known his great integrity, patriotism & important services. It is very gratifying to me to see a just tribute of respect paid to his memory."

Monroe's courtesy and praise undoubtedly gratified John Tyler, who, with a certain measure of pride, justifiably believed he was one of the anointed heirs to the Virginia dynasty of presidents. Further confirmation came the following year when he was elected to the U.S. Senate. Only thirty-seven years old, John Tyler had surpassed his father's political attainments and appeared to be on the fast track to the presidency.[16]

In his quest for national prominence and as presumptive heir to the Jeffersonian legacy, Tyler tried to adhere to a states' rights agenda and a strict constructionist interpretation of the Constitution. Although he prided himself on his consistency and unwavering dedication to these principles, in the 1828 presidential campaign Senator Tyler warily supported Andrew Jackson over incumbent John Quincy Adams as the lesser of two evils. He abhorred Adams's consolidationist policies and was ambivalent as well about Jackson because he feared that as president "Old Hickory" might have similar tendencies to centralize federal authority and abuse executive power. Initially all seemed well when President Jackson vetoed a plan to use federal funds to support road construction.

But some of Jackson's other actions were less comforting to Tyler and his ally Senator Tazewell. The two Virginians were appalled that during a Senate recess Jackson had appointed three commissioners to negotiate a treaty with Turkey without the advice and consent of the Senate. This perceived abuse of the executive prerogative in foreign affairs led them in early 1831 to battle for Senate disapproval of Jackson's actions. After extended debate the Senate adopted a Tyler proviso mildly rebuking the president for his appointment and use of executive agents without its advice and consent. As one scholar has noted about consistency to principle in the use of executive agents, "John Tyler was a sharp critic of the practice during the presidency of Andrew Jackson, but employed a considerable number during his own incumbency."[17]

Tyler's aggressive diplomacy when he became president in the early 1840s, including his liberal use of executive agents, was part of what historian John Belohlavek has labeled as a broad diplomatic continuum in American foreign relations during the antebellum era. Tyler's foreign policy outlook, with its emphasis on expanding commerce and opening foreign markets, mirrored that of his immediate predecessors, and was especially consistent with Andrew Jackson's little-known attempts to foster and promote American commercial dominance in the Pacific Basin. In the 1830s President Jackson dispatched diplomatic missions under the leadership of New Hampshire merchant Edmund Roberts to secure commercial treaties with Japan, the countries of southeast Asia, and those bordering the Indian Ocean. Roberts, who in 1833 made one of the United States's early diplomatic contacts with present-day Vietnam, failed to "open" Japan, but he did succeed in negotiating the nation's first treaty with Siam, now Thailand.

Senator Tyler undoubtedly approved of Jackson's commercial and diplomatic goals in Asia even while questioning Old Hickory's alleged abuse of executive power. As president, Tyler matched Jackson's success in the Pacific Rim by extending diplomatic recognition and protection to the Hawaiian Islands, and by securing the United States's first treaty with China in 1844. This continuity of diplomatic purpose was reflected as well in Martin Van Buren's commissioning of the U.S. Exploring Expedition of 1838–42 that charted the Pacific Ocean and Antarctica, and in Matthew Perry's opening of Japan two decades after Roberts's earlier abortive attempt.[18]

A Pacific-minded Senator Tyler also frequently and eagerly draped himself in the republican mantle of his Virginian mentors by revisiting the themes of Jeffersonian political economy and national greatness. For instance, in an extended debate on the tariff in early 1832 he reaffirmed his commitment to free trade and the necessity of finding foreign markets for the nation's surplus agricultural production. On this occasion, he elaborated on the mutuality of benefits to be attained from unrestricted international commerce and doubted, as advocates of protectionism charged, that a policy of free trade would lead to the United States being recolonized by Great Britain, its fierce economic rival and top commercial competitor. With uncanny prescience, Tyler instead correctly predicted that when in the not too distant future Britain repealed its restrictive Corn Laws, a huge market would be opened for American grains and foodstuffs.

Tyler next went from discussing mundane economic data to more sublime pretensions. Never tiring of rhapsodizing on his visions of American mission and national destiny, Tyler said his imagination led him "to look into the distant future, and there to contemplate the greatness of free America" that extended westward to the Pacific Ocean and the markets of Asia. Notably, what this armchair expansionist and visionary senator from Virginia who had never ventured beyond his east coast environs beheld for his country was Columbia "walking on the waves of the mighty deep, carrying along with her tidings of great joy to distant nations" and "restoring to man his long-lost rights." Undoubtedly, Tyler's critics and detractors sensed something was amiss here. Without hint of irony or hypocrisy, this allegedly principled slaveowner who traded in human beings as property was offering a lofty, if incongruous, vision of "free" America's mission in the world.[19]

However insensible he may have been about the contradiction inherent in a slaveholding republic's mission to spread universal freedom and liberty, a serious matter of principle and loyalty did arise for Tyler during the 1832–33 nullification controversy. In being true to his states' rights beliefs, he found himself in the uncomfortable position of attacking one of his republican icons, James Madison. The nullifiers and secessionists from South Carolina to Virginia were berating Madison for what they purported was his unqualified support for a strong central government at the 1787 convention. During a major speech on the Senate floor, Tyler charged Madison with being an advocate of a centralized plan of government, and the "design of this plan, it is obvious, was to render the States nothing more than the provinces of a great Government, to rear upon the ruins of the old confederacy a consolidated Government, one and indivisible."

Quickly published and circulated throughout Virginia, Tyler's speech unquestionably validated his states' rights credentials, but at James Madison's expense. Apparently the boldness of Senator Tyler's attack on the "father of the Constitution" raised some eyebrows in the Old Dominion. Explaining his recent actions to Virginian constituent John Coalter, Tyler maintained that "in my recent public course, no other motive has governed me but a desire to uphold the Constitution and the laws, and to restrain executive power already grown too great, within the limits which they prescribe."[20]

While many of his southern brethren were bedeviled by the threat to states' rights inherent in the nullification crisis, John Tyler saw a more ominous challenge to the slave South on the horizon. Unlike John C. Calhoun, his friend and sometime political ally, Tyler as a senator from Virginia placed national interests above those of his region and supported the compromise that effectively ended South Carolina's confrontation with the federal government. To Senator Tyler's mind the more serious danger to the existing Union and southern interests in the mid-1830s was the gathering storm of abolitionism. Northern abolitionist societies primarily led and directed by Christian clergymen who espoused a misguided evangelicalism, according to Tyler, had proliferated at an astounding rate in a few short years.

Congress was being inundated with their petitions calling for the national government to support a host of antislavery measures. Pulpit and podium from New England to New York to Pennsylvania and Ohio abounded with abolitionist invective; the federal mails were rife with what southerners believed was incendiary literature savagely denouncing slavery and depicting slaveholders as vicious beasts. Much to Tyler's disgust and outrage, these devilish abolitionists, with their array of divisive and disruptive attention-grabbing maneuvers, seemed possessed in their determination to capture center stage in the national political arena.

A besieged and now defensive Tyler presumably knew all that he needed to know about the evils of slavery, and he had learned it from the lips and pens of fellow Virginians, not northern abolitionists. Just a few years earlier during public debate in the Virginia House of Delegates about the future of slavery, speaker after speaker described what John C. Calhoun had dubbed the South's "peculiar institution" as a national calamity, a cancer, a pestilence of filth and corruption that was "a grinding curse upon the state." Many but not all of this homegrown band of abolitionists were from the western counties of Virginia beyond the Blue Ridge Mountains. Some, such as Henry Berry of Jefferson County, were slaveowners who recognized the need to eradicate this accursed evil and favored legislation that instituted gradual emancipation. Others, such as Samuel M. Garland of Amherst County, used the logic of republican virtue by touting "the principles of our free institutions." Garland echoed Tyler himself by noting that "the genius of liberty which is now walking abroad over the earth" demanded an end to this "odious and abominable" practice of human bondage.

At the conclusion of this debate, Virginia remained a "house divided" as the delegates on the one hand rejected both immediate emancipation and, on the other hand, dismissed all proposals for an open-ended commitment to perpetual slavery. For a slaveowner like Tyler, apparently there was one important distinction between the charges leveled in the Virginia debate and those made by northern abolitionists—a perceived distinction that perhaps explained his more vehement reaction to the latter. Unlike the inflammatory literature and the pesky petition campaigns of their northern brethren that excoriated brutal slave masters, antislavery Virginians concentrated their attacks on the evils of the institution and not the aberrant transgressions of a few isolated individuals.[21]

If Tyler accepted this supposed distinction between northern and southern antislavery forces, he was guilty of oversimplification. Since the time of the sectional controversy over Missouri's entry into the Union, a number of northern abolitionists had concentrated their fire on the evils of the peculiar institution. Their arguments were nearly identical to those made by most antislavery Virginians before and during the intense legislative debate over the future of slavery in the Old Dominion. In fact, one female critic from New England, the author and novelist Lydia Maria Child, drew upon the analysis made by Virginia's unsuccessful opponents of slavery to make a highly influential and logical argument for emancipation.

In her 1833 book, *An Appeal in Favor of That Class of Americans Called Africans*, Child emphasized, "It is the *system*, not the *men*, on which we ought to bestow the full measure of abhorrence." She too framed her critique within the context of republican virtue. Implicitly challenging Senator

Tyler's brand of republicanism, Child offered her own selfless republican remedy to the American people. "If we were willing to forget ourselves," she suggested, "and could, like true republicans, prefer the common good to all other considerations, there would not be a slave in the United States, at the end of half a century." To accomplish the lofty goal of emancipation, Child urged her fellow Americans to pursue political action, including the time-honored practice of petitioning state legislatures and the federal Congress.[22]

Petitioning legislative bodies had been a favorite tactic of antislavery groups since the 1790s. But it remained a decentralized endeavor until late 1834 when the American Anti-Slavery Society, heralded as the first nationwide organization of its kind, offered national leadership and direction in a renewed petitioning campaign. Instrumental to its success was the "Fathers and Rulers" petition form created by abolitionist Theodore Dwight Weld. It was a printed form designed to be circulated and signed exclusively by women that called upon the fathers and rulers in Congress to abolish slavery in the District of Columbia. Weld's standard petition had women pleading for the oppressed slaves "as wives, as mothers, and as daughters," and expressing their apprehension about the nation's future by paraphrasing Thomas Jefferson: "We tremble for our country when we remember God is just, and his justice cannot sleep forever." The "Fathers and Rulers" form quickly became the most frequently used "female petition" as tens of thousands were submitted to Congress prior to 1840.[23]

Even with the new petitioning momentum generated by women volunteers throughout the North, abolitionism spread too slowly to satisfy the ambitious leaders of the national organization. The lack of progress was especially evident in the South, where antislavery forces were making little, if any, headway. At the instigation of Lewis Tappan, a member of the executive committee of the American Anti-Slavery Society, the 1835 annual meeting agreed to finance a monumental pamphlet campaign directed primarily at the slave states. It already had become hazardous for antislavery lecturers to venture into the South, yet the national organization remained optimistic that moral suasion might still bring slaveholders and southerners in general to their Christian senses. It was a foolish hope. The flood of antislavery literature sent to the South touched off an unprecedented, and for abolitionist leaders totally unexpected, negative reaction. Anti-abolitionist violence erupted on a frightening scale, and 1835 became the year of the mob as a furious backlash to antislavery agitation swept the North as well as the South.

In Charleston, South Carolina, mail sacks containing antislavery newspapers, pamphlets, and other abolitionist paraphernalia, including kerchiefs, medals, and emblems, were burned by a mob that then proceeded to hang in effigy both Arthur Tappan and William Lloyd Garrison, editor of the *Liberator*. An informal postal censorship emerged in South Carolina when mail was searched for "incendiary" literature that, if located, was confiscated. These high-handed actions against federal authority within a state met no resistance from the Andrew Jackson administration as Postmaster General Amos Kendall tacitly sanctioned South Carolina's virtual censorship of the U.S. mails.

In his annual message to Congress in December 1835, President Jackson denounced the abolitionist pamphlet campaign, incorrectly and irrationally labeling it as "unconstitutional and wicked." Speaking as southerner and slaveowner, Jackson requested that northern legislatures curtail abolitionist fanaticism by placing restrictions on the mailing of antislavery tracts. His call was seconded by resolutions of the state legislatures of South Carolina, North Carolina, Georgia, Alabama, and Virginia demanding that their northern counterparts pass restrictive legislation to suppress the circulation and mailing of abolitionist publications. Passions ran high as the state of Alabama, in an extraordinary move, demanded that New York State extradite an abolitionist named Robert G. Williams, publisher of the antislavery newspaper the *Emancipator*, for his unspectacular yet allegedly criminal role as a simple cog in the "machinery" of organized antislavery.[24]

Northern reaction to the American Anti-Slavery Society's "postal campaign" was one of equal outrage to that of southerners, but considerably more violent and physically threatening to the personal safety of abolitionists. An anti-abolitionist hysteria stirred by white fears of racial amalgamation swept the cities and towns of the Northeast from Maine to Pennsylvania. Antislavery lecturers were verbally harassed, pelted with eggs and rocks, and frequently threatened with bodily harm. On one particular day in October 1835, mobs dragged William Lloyd Garrison through the streets of Boston with a rope around his neck and attacked Henry B. Stanton, a prominent abolitionist and future husband of Elizabeth Cady Stanton, as he spoke to a gathering in Newport, Rhode Island.

That same day hooligans tormented and terrified a convention of six hundred delegates meeting in Utica, New York, to establish a statewide antislavery organization. American Anti-Slavery leaders in New York City such as Tappan and Elizur Wright were the targets of assassination threats. For a time in the summer and early fall of that year the fury of the anti-abolitionist attacks frightened and tested the mettle of even the most stout-hearted and dedicated among the antislavery ranks.[25]

Beyond the petitioning and postal campaigns, one other facet of the antislavery enterprise evoked the wrath of many Americans. The abolitionists were believed to be in the service of Great Britain and hence an unpatriotic and subversive element in American society. The abolitionists themselves certainly had contributed to this perception, especially the leadership of the American Anti-Slavery Society. The national organization quite consciously had been patterned after the British model of antislavery societies. Garrison and the other founders of the AASS had timed its creation to coincide with the news that Britain had emancipated the slaves in its West Indian colonies, to take full political and psychological advantage of that victory for the enemies of human bondage.

An invitation to come lecture in America extended by Garrison and other leaders to two "foreign emissaries," the British abolitionists Charles Stuart and George Thompson, seemingly confirmed the subversive imagery. Thompson's visit especially enraged public opinion in the Northeast, and when Garrison was dragged through Boston's streets, the mob thought they had Thompson at the end of the rope. Garrison's life was spared when one of the crowd identified him as an American. Several weeks after this incident, Thompson fled the country by rowing himself to a vessel in New York harbor bound for New Brunswick, Canada.[26]

Among those who feared a British conspiracy to undermine the nation's destiny and destroy the American republic was John Tyler. His earlier concerns about an Anglo-American abolitionist cabal jeopardizing the Union seemed to be confirmed. In a speech delivered to some constituents and neighbors at Gloucester Court House in Virginia in the summer of 1835, an alarmed and agitated Senator Tyler warned his local audience and the American people, "I have seen the Union twice in great danger." The first occasion was the Missouri crisis, which as a member of Congress he had witnessed, and "insignificant as the question was in comparison with the present, it produced the most fearful agitations." The second threat to the Union was the current northern antislavery agitation. Abolitionists, aided and abetted by their British allies, were "libelers of the South" who cast slaveholders as "demons in the shape of men," and who had the audacity to interfere with the domestic institutions of Virginia and her sister slave states below the Mason-Dixon line.

The intrusive postal and petition campaigns of the antislavery societies, Tyler further informed his fellow Virginians, incited slave insurrection—the "unexpected evil is now upon us; it has invaded our firesides, and under our roofs is sharpening the dagger for midnight assassination, and exciting cruelty and bloodshed." Giving credence to the charge of British collusion and adding insult to injury, these nefarious schemers, led by Arthur Tappan and "Mr. Somebody Garrison," had imported an outside agitator from England, a "Mr. Foreigner Thompson," to teach southerners "the principles of civil liberty and the rights of humanity." Revealing once again his deep-seated and lifelong antipathy for Great Britain and its smug attempts to refashion American society, Senator Tyler intemperately castigated this British "foreign emissary" who had "dared to venture across the broad Atlantic" to aid the antislavery abomination and "to sow the seeds of discord among us."[27]

But perhaps the most despicable aspect of this attack on southern home and hearth was the abolitionist practice of enlisting and employing women "to accomplish their mischievous purposes." In his capacity as chairman of the Senate's District of Columbia Committee, Tyler had "brought to my knowledge" the full impact of one female petition "praying the abolition of slavery in the District, signed by fifteen hundred women." "Yes," lamented this incredulous southern patriarch, "woman is to be made the instrument of destroying our political paradise, the Union of these States; she is to be made the presiding genius over the councils of insurrection and civil discord; she is to be converted into a fiend, to rejoice over the conflagration of our dwellings and the murder of our people."

Alas, the horrendous specter conjured by Tyler's rhetoric was one in which Eve, succumbing to the temptations of the British serpent, would destroy man's earthly paradise, cloud all visions of a glorious national destiny, and lead the American republic to hell. Despite his frequent optimistic forecasts of national greatness, in the mid-1830s a dismayed John Tyler believed the Union was imperiled. The United States faced apparent disintegration, its political and social fabric seemingly unraveling as the result of this fiendish abolitionist onslaught.[28]

With Senator Tyler's gloomy admonitions about this threat to their political and social system still fresh and vivid in their minds, the Gloucester meeting proceeded to adopt five resolutions to meet and counter the challenge of antislavery fanaticism. The resolutions decried abolitionist and foreign interference in the domestic affairs of the state of Virginia and affirmed that Virginians had the right to demand restrictive legislation from its northern sister states to curb such "incendiary" activities. In addition, the resolutions demanded that Virginia and Maryland be provided veto power over any proposals to eliminate slavery in the District of Columbia.

Finally, the Gloucester meeting called for the appointment of one hundred persons to a Committee of Vigilance and Safety to allow the people of the state "to protect themselves against the machinations of the abolitionists and their emissaries."

Repression of the abolitionists appeared to be the order of the day for many southerners, even from the normally cautious and circumspect Tyler. At an earlier meeting during the summer of 1835 in Williamsburg, one of the birthplaces of the American Revolution, the assembled citizens, after a fiery address by their senator, approved one of the harshest southern resolutions to appear in response to the pamphlet and petition campaign. Tyler and his Williamsburg constituents resolved that "we regard the printing and circulating within our limits, incendiary publications, tending to excite our slaves to insurrection, as treasonable acts of the most alarming character, and that when we detect offenders in the act, we will inflict upon them condign punishment, without resort to any other tribunal."[29]

Fortunately, such high-handed and illegal proscriptions to halt the antislavery crusade were never carried out. But for abolitionists, and even many neutral observers in the North, the Williamsburg resolution was tantamount to lynch law and a clear and menacing signal conveying the degree to which slaveholders and their southern supporters would go to restrict the civil rights of northern whites. Perhaps an even more ominous threat to the constitutional liberties of abolitionists was the fact that several southern state legislatures passed resolutions urging their northern counterparts to enact legislation to curb antislavery publications and tracts.

The emotional intensity displayed by John Tyler in his response to the abolitionists at Gloucester Court House and in Williamsburg reflected his moral anxiety about slavery. To be sure, he was incensed and frustrated by the self-righteous attitude of the abolitionists and their certainty about the viability of their calls for immediate emancipation. Undoubtedly, Tyler also was angry because his argument during the Missouri crisis debate for the diffusion theory as the way to abolish slavery implicitly conceded the moral high ground to the antislavery position. He had been caught short by the likes of "Mr. Somebody Garrison" and he knew it. Overlooked by an agitated Senator Tyler and his enraged allies in their frenzied effort to censor and silence the antislavery forces was the fact that Congress routinely had, admittedly over loud protests from Deep South representatives, received petitions against slavery since George Washington's administration. Petitioning legislatures was a legitimate and accepted constitutional right accorded to a free people.[30]

This precedent did not deter Senator John C. Calhoun of South Carolina. He sought in the 1835–36 session of Congress to muzzle the petitioning enterprise of the American Anti-Slavery Society and the more than 500 other local or regional antislavery societies that had sprung up like mushrooms in the free states over the past four or five years. The campaign to effectively deny the right of petition was initiated by Congressman James H. Hammond, one of Calhoun's South Carolina lieutenants, who proposed that the House of Representatives refuse to receive or accept antislavery petitions. Calhoun sponsored a similar motion in the Senate. For over a month the House and Senate debated these repressive, undemocratic resolutions. The major objective of the South Carolinians and their proslavery allies was to shut off debate on the contentious slavery issue and deny the abolitionists access to a national forum and the widespread media publicity it would generate.

In the end a compromise of sorts was reached that maintained the fiction of the right of petition. Both the House and Senate ultimately adopted the motion of Representative Henry L. Pinckney, another likeminded South Carolina ally of Calhoun, to receive all antislavery petitions but to immediately table them without discussion or debate. This infamous "gag rule," which curtailed for countless northern citizens a basic right guaranteed in the Constitution's Bill of Rights, was in place until 1844. John Quincy Adams of Massachusetts, who would be instrumental in securing an end to this odious practice, defiantly responded when his name was called to vote on the original gag resolution: "I hold this resolution to be a direct violation of the Constitution of the United States, the rules of the House and the rights of my constituents."[31]

Despite his highly emotional reaction to the abolitionist challenge to the South's peculiar institution, Senator Tyler had not supported Calhoun on the gag measure. He predicted that such action would be counterproductive by giving the petitions too much consequence. A gag rule also would give abolitionists the moral and constitutional high ground by mixing up the right of petition with the question of slavery. Tyler believed it would be wiser to let Congress simply say it could not do what the petitioners demanded and not deny them the sacrosanct right of petition. In the end, Senator Tyler did not vote on the gag measure. He had resigned from the Senate on February 29, 1836, because he refused to obey the Virginia legislature's instruction to vote to expunge the censure of President Andrew Jackson.

Although he temporarily lost his constitutional bearings the previous summer during the pamphlet contretemps, Tyler had regained his composure in opposing Calhoun's gag proposal. He understood that restricting the right of petition was not only wrong and bad public policy, but politically unwise because it would make martyrs of the abolitionists and unite northern whites behind their struggle for civil rights. Tyler was prescient. The infamous "gag rule" stimulated rather than stifled petitions and bestowed a measure of credibility to the abolitionist campaign. Arguably, John C. Calhoun's insistence on the gag rule had elicited the northern reaction that the circumspect John Tyler had most feared.[32]

Like John Tyler, other members of his intellectual circle publicly and privately expressed their apprehension over abolitionism's unprecedented assault on the South and slavery. For two of his close confidants, the states' rights stalwarts Beverley Tucker and Abel Parker Upshur, the threat of disunion was their uppermost concern, and paradoxically a possible remedy for the South's dilemma. In their private correspondence the three friends commiserated about the fate of their region. In the midst of the frightening abolitionist challenge, Tucker, a law professor at the College of William and Mary, anonymously published a novel, *The Partisan Leader*, which forecast disunion and the creation of a separate southern confederacy.

Upshur, a respected judge and future secretary of the navy and secretary of state in the Tyler administration, privately may have shared Tucker's disunionist agenda. But instead of publicly urging an end to the Union, Judge Upshur chose to become an open and ardent defender of the South's system of human bondage. Black slavery was essential to white freedom, argued Upshur, because having this "lower condition" of servitude to which not even the poorest whites could descend guaranteed a "republican equality" for all white men. Upshur was among those who believed that the South's peculiar institution was "a great positive good, to be carefully protected and preserved." Historian Sean Wilentz has labeled the argument made by Upshur and other slaveholders that the equality of white men depended on the enslavement of blacks as "Master Race democracy." According to Wilentz, the slaveholding aristocracy blurred the class distinction between themselves "and non-slaveholders by appealing to their basic equality as white citizens regardless of property—creating a Master Race democracy."[33]

Senator Tyler, indirectly and prudently siding with Judge Upshur rather than Professor Tucker on the question of what might be the best future course for Virginia and the South, rejected disunion as an option at this stage as well. However, he had too many qualms about the evils of slavery to follow Upshur's lead in describing that institution as a positive social good and a blessing for all concerned blacks as well as whites. For a politician with aspirations for high national office, the paths of moral justification and political extremism offered by his old and cherished friends struck an ambitious Tyler on the one hand as too negative, and on the other as too defensive.

The Virginia senator, who at this stage of his career took justifiable pride in his strict constructionist beliefs, remained a committed unionist and a firm believer in the nation's destiny. After having sponsored repressive and potentially unconstitutional measures in the heat of his anger and outrage, Tyler rejected that response to the abolitionists' attack on the South. Instead he returned to the formula he had outlined when he was a young congressman during the Missouri crisis. The pursuit of national destiny again became the recommended antidote to sectional discord and fears of disunion.

At a patriotic celebration in Yorktown, Virginia, in October 1837 commemorating the fifty-sixth anniversary of the Revolutionary battle that signaled victory over the British in the war for independence, Tyler returned to an earlier, less conflicted, and less clouded vision of national purpose. "I would exorcise," he told the gathering, "the spirit of sectional feeling, which is too rife in the land. I would point to a common country—a common glory, and a common destiny." In urging the remedy of national greatness to allay the malady of sectional strife, Tyler preferred that the United States should achieve its shining destiny without resort to force of arms. "I would have her victories priceless, but bloodless," he stipulated, "and won only by the force of great example."[34]

However, at no time during these spread-eagle flourishes of Americanism did Tyler betray the slightest awareness that the pursuit of national greatness invariably would lead to a strong centralized government. He seemed oblivious to yet another contradiction in his ideology. Just as slavery mocked Tyler's notion of "free" America's global mission, the chase for national glory ultimately would clash with his traditional Jeffersonian view of limited government and his dedication to restricting executive power and preventing its extension at the expense of Congress and the sovereign states.

Despite his lofty and unifying patriotic rhetoric at Yorktown, Tyler had not entirely curbed his emotions nor wrestled his internal demons to the ground. A scant few months later in January 1838, when he addressed the Virginia Colonization Society in Richmond as its newly selected president, his speech to the assembled leaders of the city and state bristled with the same outrage that had marked his Williamsburg and Gloucester tirades a few years earlier. "Philanthropy, when separated from policy," he observed, "is the most dangerous agent in human affairs. It is in no way distinguishable from fanaticism." This fanaticism sought to destroy the Constitution and acted "in league with foreign missionaries, and gives open countenance to the people of another hemisphere to interfere in our domestic affairs. It is sectional, altogether sectional; in a word, it is the spirit of abolition." In yet another allusion to the biblical Garden of Eden and man's fall from grace at the hands and folly of woman, he reviled these fanatics for enlisting females to "expel us from the paradise of union in which we dwell."

Beyond venting his spleen, however, Tyler made clear his belief that a program of colonization to Africa was the responsible way for the American nation to deal with slavery and the numerous blacks in their midst. He suggested that if the abolitionists, who claimed to be motivated by Christian charity, really sought to help America's blacks, then they should support the work of the Colonization Society, which Tyler contended was "the great African missionary society." Tyler was supplementing his earlier diffusion theory for gradually eliminating slavery with a paternalistic call for the colonization of blacks to Africa as a means of exporting the nation's "Negro" problem. Yet Tyler probably never fully overcame his earlier skepticism about shipping blacks to Liberia as a solution to the slavery problem, for he recognized that colonization was "a dream of philanthropy, visiting men's pillows in their sleep, to cheat them on their waking."[35]

Another of the antislavery movement's objectives that riled John Tyler was its opposition to the annexation of Texas. In March 1836 the Texans had declared their independence from Mexican rule, and established the Lone Star Republic. Many abolitionists detected a conspiracy among southern slaveowners to bring Texas into the Union. Unwilling to jeopardize the election of Martin Van Buren in the 1836 presidential campaign, Andrew Jackson had not sought immediate annexation. His administration's political reluctance to act quickly on annexation, although recognition was granted in early 1837 after Van Buren was safely elected, reflected a fairly widespread northern uneasiness that taking Texas would add a number of slave states and upset the congressional balance between North and South.

For their part, the abolitionists defied the obnoxious gag rule by inundating the House and Senate with memorials against Texas annexation. During the third session of the Twenty-fifth Congress, December 1838–March 1839, abolitionist petitions with a total of 500,000 signatures were presented on eight separate topics, including opposition to the annexation of Texas, and for the first time, the call for the recognition of the black republic of Haiti. Actually the inauguration of petitions for Haitian recognition was a ploy to evade the gag rule, as abolitionists hoped to force a debate on the floor of Congress on the diplomatic and commercial merits of the Haitian case and ultimately the evils of slavery. The stratagem failed, as petitions for Haitian recognition were routinely tabled in the same manner as other antislavery memorials. The abolitionists, however, could claim a minor victory because the fervor for Texas annexation had cooled and President Van Buren had no inclination to resurrect such a politically divisive policy.

Although Haitian petitions were quickly relegated to oblivion on most occasions, in December 1838 two memorials calling for recognition of the black republic did provoke an angry and excessive outburst in the House of Representatives from the normally cool and collected congressman from South Carolina, Hugh S. Legare. A slaveowner from Charleston who later would serve in Tyler's cabinet as attorney general and acting secretary of state, Legare opposed accepting the Haitian petitions because they were "got up by abolitionists for purposes of political effect, and to promote the ends of abolition." Admitting with mild embarrassment that he perhaps spoke "with too much ardor," the southern aristocrat cried "treason" and labeled "the authors of such things traitors—traitors not to their country only, but to the whole human race."

As another fervent believer in the future national greatness of the American republic, Legare feared that the continued political agitation by abolitionists jeopardized the "destinies of such an empire—I speak prospectively as well as of the present—as the sun has never yet shone upon." Expressing visions of republican glory and empire eerily identical to those of his ideological soulmate John Tyler, Legare confessed, "I have been nursed from my youth in an idolatrous love of that most noble of all forms of polity, republican government, and I have dreamed of my country the highest things within the reach of humanity—a career of greatness such as the world has never yet witnessed." Congressman Legare similarly evoked the clouded skies metaphor much favored by Tyler when he said abolitionism "threatens to cloud this glorious prospect" of America's national destiny.[36]

One of the more apparent, if no less surprising, features of the opposing worldviews of slaveholders Hugh Legare and John Tyler and their northern abolitionist adversaries was their common appeal to republicanism as the basis for two distinct but not entirely dissimilar foreign policy agendas for the nation. In his public addresses and political speeches future president Tyler invariably held up the example of the founding fathers, extolling their unselfish adherence to freedom, liberty, and republican principle. It was their legacy of government based on "popular rights" that must be preserved. If those elements of common heritage and common pride—republican virtue, liberty, and freedom—were allowed to flourish, the United

States would become "a blessing to the whole human race." Tyler's and his friend Legare's patriotic Americanism reflected the feelings of many other antebellum southern leaders. Pride in the glory and future of the United States of America was a shared legacy among southerners because, as historian William J. Cooper has noted, their "fathers and grandfathers had helped bring it into being and had nurtured its early growth. Feelings and expressions of patriotism and allegiance to the Union marked southern Americanism."[37]

Ironically, in the late 1830s and early 1840s the northern antislavery enterprise laid claim to a virtually identical republicanism that stressed liberty, freedom, and patriotic virtue. But for the thousands of men and women in the abolitionist ranks, the South's peculiar institution of human bondage betrayed America's fidelity to republican principles. Slavery was a blot on the nation's republican honor and "inconsistent with the genius of republicanism." Only through the elimination of chattel slavery could the American republic be purified. Emancipation would lead to a new direction in the nation's diplomacy that truly might fulfill America's destiny as the beacon of liberty and the wellspring of republican virtue.

But unlike John Tyler and other champions of slavery, the abolitionist forces rarely linked the concept of republican virtue to the republicanism of Jefferson, and on those infrequent occasions the connection made would be with his universal sentiment that all men were created equal. Jumping into the fray over what constituted legitimate republicanism, the British abolitionist George Thompson, the same man John Tyler had derided as "Mr. Foreigner Thompson," announced to the world that the men and women committed to the abolition of slavery were "the only true republicans of America."[38]

Based on a belief in human freedom and a demand for the immediate emancipation of all the slaves in the republic, an abolitionist vision of a future American foreign policy was enunciated. Initially expressed in the 1840 presidential campaign by Liberty Party candidate James G. Birney and Joshua Leavitt, editor of the *Emancipator*, among others, this vision was characterized by the concept of a "free diplomacy" untainted and unencumbered by the contradiction of black slavery, and dedicated to "diffusing the blessings of commerce, peace, civilization, and liberty over the globe."

The Liberty Party platform also rejected proposals for Texas annexation, opposed the expansion of slavery and any future acquisition of slave territory, and called for the immediate recognition of the black republic of Haiti. In his letter accepting the nomination, James Birney praised the

Haitians because they had "achieved their Independence as our forefathers did ours—by *rebellion*." But Birney also revealed that he understood that the issue was not simply a question of diplomatic recognition. The Haitians "are black, and to treat a nation of blacks as *free*, would lead the slave of the South into some knowledge of his dignity as a man." A former slaveowner himself, Birney had touched the heart of the matter, and although the Liberty Party did poorly at the polls, its foreign policy agenda persisted as an antislavery counterpoise that clouded and imperiled Tyler's vision for the future of the American republic.[39]

In one of those unforeseen events that dramatically change the course of a nation's history, Vice President John Tyler became the nation's first accidental president in April 1841. A slaveholder intent on annexing Texas was now in the White House. Although labeled "His Accidency" by political pundits, with the unmistakable implication that he was incompetent, Tyler had been groomed and cultivated for the office by the republican mentors of his youth and early manhood, all of whom, not incidentally, were slave-owners. The teachings and inspiration of his father, of Thomas Jefferson, and of Bishop James Madison, as well as his extensive public service at the state and federal level, well prepared him to manage the nation's affairs. It was no accident that Tyler had come to the White House forewarned, fore-armed, and ready to lead the nation.

In the Jeffersonian tradition, President Tyler also was primed to pursue an expansionist agenda and promote the concept of an extensive republic. Not surprisingly, after swiftly establishing his presidential legitimacy, the new chief executive confronted the sectionalist challenge of the antislavery forces by counteracting, replacing, and unabashedly co-opting their program for a free diplomacy with a foreign policy dedicated to national greatness and glory. The most critical phase of this expansionist timetable would be the Tyler administration's crusade for the annexation of the Lone Star Republic of Texas. President Tyler's vision of national destiny, threatened as it was by thunderclouds of discord and disunion, no longer was just a lofty dream. It had become an essential feature in a tragically flawed scheme to finesse abolitionism, ensure the survival of slavery, mute sectionalism, and secure the Union. Necessity may be the mother of invention, but in Tyler's case it was an imagined necessity to preserve the anomaly of a slaveholding republic that became the guiding inventive principle in his administration's formulation and conduct of American foreign policy.

Defending Slavery

3

I feel *now* that the abolitionists & others who would harm us, are failed. That the Constitution & with it the Union will be preserved—and that come Peace or War, our hand is secure & we shall be saved.

★ *S. Jones, of Kings Creek, to John Tyler, April 14, 1841*

Tyler is a political sectarian, of the slave-driving, Virginian, Jeffersonian school, principled against all improvement, with all the interests and passions and vices of slavery rooted in his moral and political constitution—with talents not above mediocrity, and a spirit incapable of expansion to the dimensions of the station upon which he has been cast by the hand of Providence, unseen through the apparent agency of chance.

★ *John Quincy Adams, April 4, 1841*

Wherever black slavery existed there was found at least, equality among the white population. . . . The principle of slavery was a leveling principle. . . . Break down slavery and you would with the same blow destroy the great democratic principle of equality among men.

★ *Henry A. Wise, 1842*

ohn Tyler spent much of his public career defending slavery from its enemies at home and abroad. This was especially apparent during his presidency, when the aristocratic, slaveholding Virginian unwaveringly guided the nation's diplomacy in support of the South's peculiar institution. In adopting a proslavery course in foreign relations, Tyler placed himself within a prevailing national tradition and he became part of a continuum in foreign policy that extended back to George Washington's administration. Slavery was supported diplomatically by all presidents who preceded him, including later critics of this strange "species of property," such as John Quincy Adams and Martin Van Buren. In fact, despite evolving private doubts expressed in his diary, Adams publicly defended the peculiar institution from foreign infringement for twelve years, eight as secretary of state and four as the republic's chief executive.

As one distinguished historian has observed, "In its handling of foreign relations, the federal government actively supported the institution of slavery from the very outset of the nation's existence. In ongoing negotiations with Great Britain, the United States government especially defined itself as an agent for the slaveholding interest. Challenged by England's growing commitment to the antislavery cause, American government officials invariably reacted as proslavery spokesmen." Prior to the election of Abraham Lincoln, it was the unwritten rule that any reservations about or opposition to slavery stopped at the water's edge for America's chief executives and its corps of diplomats. John Tyler's diplomacy was consistent with this antebellum tradition. But in his handling and conduct of the nation's foreign relations Tyler arguably was the most active proslavery president in the period, 1789–1861.[1]

In a broader sense President Tyler's fixation on defending slavery from its enemies at all cost was curious, even tragic, because he had a lifelong ambivalence about the morality of the South's peculiar institution. Unlike many of his southern contemporaries, he never defined slavery as a positive good. As a slaveowner with a conscience, John Tyler mirrored the nation's concerns about the evils of slavery. However, America's moral confusion about slavery was not apparent in its conduct of foreign relations. The republic's unequivocal proslavery diplomacy during the antebellum era obscured the fact that Americans were not of one mind about the morality of slavery. Slavery represented the most obvious contradiction of principle in a republic founded on human liberty and the proposition that all men were created equal.

John Tyler was among those who epitomized the nation's moral uncertainty about slavery. Why? Because in the Virginia of Tyler's youth chattel slavery seemed to be the natural order of things. His earliest and most influential mentors—Bishop James Madison, Thomas Jefferson, and his father, John Tyler Sr.—were prominent slaveowners. Yet these men also were revolutionaries who had secured American freedom and independence, and each privately questioned the morality of slavery. Young Tyler must have sensed his elders' ambivalence. Probably compounding the boy's moral confusion was his father's claim that there was a clear distinction—perhaps a distinction without a difference to the modern eye—between the odious practice of trafficking in human flesh and owning African slaves as chattel property. John Tyler Sr.'s moral aversion to the buying and selling of human beings led him in 1787 to vote against adoption of the Constitution because of the clause that allowed for the continuation of the slave trade for twenty years. It was the elder Tyler's wish "that it should be handed down to posterity that he had opposed this wicked clause." Ever faithful to his father's legacy, the son as well became a lifelong opponent of the African slave trade.[2]

On one occasion during his time in the Senate in the 1830s, John Tyler apparently became physically ill at the sight of slaves being sold on the auction block in the nation's capital. His revulsion at the public display of selling men, women, and children on the streets of the federal city inspired him to seek the abolition of the slave trade in the District of Columbia. Objecting "to the District of Columbia being made a slave mart, a depot for slaves brought from the two neighboring States," Senator Tyler sponsored a new legal code for the District that prohibited the buying and selling of slaves at public auction. Although unsuccessful in his efforts to end the slave trade in Washington, D.C., Tyler's aversion to the practice of trading in human flesh was yet another manifestation of his moral qualms about slavery's corrosive impact on America's civic virtue.

Senator Tyler's concern for the humane treatment of slaves resident in the federal District, including punishment of masters for cruelty, clearly revealed the senator's underlying uneasiness about the evils of the South's peculiar institution. His distaste for the slave depot atmosphere in Washington placed Tyler in agreement with those whom he most despised—northern abolitionists. In their emotional appeals to the country's moral sensibilities, the abolitionists likewise denounced the sight of slave coffles and human auctions in the nation's capital. Throughout the 1830s their voluminous petitions to Congress calling for an end to the slave trade and the institution of slavery in the District embarrassed and enraged Tyler. It was quite acceptable and proper for a Virginia senator to attempt to end the slave trade in the District. But to Tyler's mind the self-righteous abolitionist petition campaign calling for both the abolition of slavery and the elimination of the auction block was an unwelcome and irritating intrusion.[3]

In an influential antislavery tract published at about the same time that Senator Tyler sought an end to the D.C. slave trade, one female abolitionist recounted tales about slavery in Washington that pierced to the heart of the nation's great republican contradiction. In what might well have been an apocryphal account, Lydia Maria Child offered her readers some glimpses of black slavery in the republic's first city: "Whole coffles of them, chained and manacled, are driven through our Capital on their way to auction. Foreigners, particularly those who come here with enthusiastic ideas of American freedom, are amazed and disgusted at the sight. A troop of slaves once passed through Washington on the fourth of July, while drums were beating, and standards flying. One of the captive negroes raised his hand, loaded with irons, and waving it toward the starry flag, sung with a smile of bitter irony, 'Hail Columbia! *Happy* land!'"[4]

Despite Tyler's revulsion at slave auctions and his demonstrated ambivalence toward the South's peculiar institution, he would not follow the abolitionist lead in demanding an end to slavery either in the District or in the nation as a whole. Openly conflicted about the morality of slavery, he nonetheless strongly defended it against abolitionist assaults. Tyler held true to his father's distinction and opposed the slave trade but would not take the next step. Senator Tyler, on this occasion in accordance with his strict constructionist and states' rights principles, saw abolitionist demands for Congress to eliminate slavery in the District of Columbia without consulting Virginia and Maryland as "a gross violation of good faith." Apparently there were ideological limits to Tyler's humanity and he drew the line on this point — no federal legislation to abolish slavery. He remained consistent on that score until the break-up of the Union in 1861.

This was one of the tragic aspects of Tyler's life and career. He could not and would not take the next step to manumission and abolition, as Liberty Party candidate and former Alabama slaveowner James G. Birney had done, even though twenty years earlier during the Missouri crisis, John Tyler had conceded slavery was an evil. Perhaps his reticence is best explained by the fact that he knew it was political suicide to advocate emancipation in a state like Virginia with its large slave population; abolition also would bring personal economic disaster and spell an end to Tyler's national political aspirations.[5]

Although Tyler may have been uneasy about his region's system of human bondage, he was economically dependent on the institution of slavery. He may not have been one of those antebellum southerners who publicly pronounced that slavery was a positive good benefiting American society as a whole, but throughout his life Tyler did enjoy on a day-to-day basis the fruits of labor extracted from human beings held as chattel property. In 1813, at the age of twenty-three, he inherited land and thirteen slaves when his father died. In that same year he obtained a number of additional slaves as the result of his marriage to Letitia Christian. Over his life span of almost seventy-two years, Tyler probably owned a total of several hundred blacks as chattel. These slaves, sometimes numbering as many as seventy men, women, and children of various ages and individual characteristics, prepared and cooked his food, washed his clothes, cleaned his home, waited on his personal needs, and did the routine brute labor on his plantation. Without question, the South's peculiar institution bestowed on him a level of privilege and luxury unknown to the vast number of his fellow white Americans.

And although he had nagging doubts about the morality of slavery, in his lifetime John Tyler never manumitted a single slave, nor did he follow either Washington's or Jefferson's example by providing for the freedom of all or some of his slaves upon his death. The reasons why he did not grant freedom to any of his slaves are lost to history. What was clear, however, was that whether as an aristocratic, privileged, up-and-coming member of the ruling class, or as a mature and successful politician who held the republic's highest office, many of John Tyler's personal hopes and dreams were bound up in the institution of slavery. Tyler believed the South's slave population was "the most important article of southern property." Along with the vast majority of antebellum slaveowners, he made his world out of the slaves he bought, sold, and possessed.[6]

One episode in John Tyler's life as slavemaster, the only one of its nature that has come down to us as part of the historical record, revealed much about the career-enhancing opportunities of the slave mart and the auction block. Her name was Ann Eliza. She was a slave on John Tyler's plantation and, according to one of his biographers, a favorite family house servant. The master put her up for sale in order to raise cash to finance the start of his career in the U.S. Senate. On September 4, 1827, Tyler wrote to ask his brother-in-law, Dr. Henry Curtis, "Do you propose to purchase Ann Eliza or not? By this time I presume you have made up your mind. If not I wish you would sell her for me as soon as you can. My monied affairs are all out of sorts—so much so that I scarcely know how I shall reach Washington. Let not this however influence you since I shall in any event prefer to consummate the sale to you in January—but if you have concluded not to take her, I should prefer as speedy a sale as can be made."

Apparently Dr. Curtis declined the offer to buy Ann Eliza. Over a month later a concerned Tyler again implored his brother-in-law to sell Ann Eliza as quickly as possible because he needed the money from her sale to begin his duties at the nation's capital. "I have to request," Tyler wrote, "that if you cannot meet with a *ready sale* in your neighborhood, which I would prefer, you will hand her over to the Hubbard's for public auction." Just weeks before the congressional session was scheduled to open in December, the future senator sent another letter saying his needs were "very pressing, more so than at any previous period." If Ann Eliza was not yet sold, it was time for the auction block and "the better way would be to put her in the wagon and send her directly to the Hubbard's. Her sale has become indispensably necessary to meet the demands of my trip," a seemingly desperate John Tyler confessed to Dr. Curtis.[7]

We do not know if Ann Eliza was sold at Hubbard's, which presumably was a slave pen in Richmond, or at public auction elsewhere in Virginia during the late autumn of 1827. At present no historical evidence has come to light that would provide the age, or a physical description, including any scars or distinguishing marks, of John Tyler's female slave. Did she have children and a husband? How long had she been John Tyler's chattel property? The public record available to the historian does not provide any of this information, nor does it disclose whether or not Dr. Curtis was able to make the sale. Quite simply we do not know what happened to Ann Eliza. Her story is lost to history. What we do know is that John Tyler found the money to travel to Washington, secure lodging, and assume his position as junior senator from Virginia.

Although the historical data on slaves such as Ann Eliza is sparse, the existing documentary sources, both public and private, tell us a lot about John Tyler, the planter class, and the antebellum South's peculiar institution. Senator Tyler, like many slaveholders, frequently was strapped for ready cash. To meet his immediate needs he readily would sell a human being just as he would a horse, a cow, or other livestock. Apparently Tyler's preference was to sell her to a family member like Dr. Curtis, probably for the ease of the sale and perhaps with a sincere concern for Ann Eliza's future welfare. But in the end he was willing and ready to put her on the wagon and sell her on the auction block at Hubbard's. John Tyler's hopes for his future career advancement and his dreams of national political prominence were tied to the sale of this woman. It was in this manner that the "slave market held dreams of transformative possibilities" for Tyler and thousands of the South's other existing and aspiring slaveowners. As slaveholders they quite literally would make their world out of the human beings they possessed as chattel property. They became, as historian Walter Johnson has shrewdly observed, "men made out of slaves."[8]

The southern aristocracy's privileged and comfortable world made from the labor of black chattel was being seriously and persistently challenged by the time John Tyler first set foot in the White House as president of the United States. The abolitionist onslaught that whirled onto the national scene in the 1830s continued unabated and grew in strength during Tyler's administration. Congressman John Quincy Adams's private denunciation of "Acting President of the Union" Tyler, which he recorded in his diary at the news of William Henry Harrison's death, as "a political sectarian, of the slave-driving, Virginian, Jeffersonian school," was a bitterly partisan characterization. Not surprisingly, such vitriolic rhetoric steadily seeped into the public discourse and became standard fare on both sides of the slavery debate in the 1840s.

The antislavery enterprise quickly mobilized in opposition to this latest and perhaps most cunning slavemaster in the White House. Joshua Leavitt and Theodore Weld were dispatched to the nation's capital to monitor and report back to the faithful on the daily machinations of John Tyler and his proslavery entourage. They became the abolitionist watchdogs who had links to the antislavery caucus in Congress led by Adams and Joshua Giddings of Ohio. Washington circles from breakfast table and drawing room to formal social receptions and the halls and cloakrooms of Congress were all abuzz about the audacious political lobbying and aggressive advocacy journalism of this small company of abolitionists. Leavitt, Weld, and a few of their colleagues even appeared at President Tyler's New Year's Day levees, although they avoided the receiving line and declined to shake hands with the "presidential digits." Weld, whose republicanism ran to the plain and simple, was astounded at the ostentatious exhibition "of pomp and tinsel and fashion" in the presidential palace.[9]

Similar complaints from "plain republicans" about Tyler's aristocratic demeanor and flamboyant planter extravagance surfaced repeatedly in the abolitionist press during his presidency. Abolitionist writers also were scandalized that the American republic's chief executive had his slaves as personal servants in the presidential mansion. On occasion even non-abolitionist northern visitors to the White House who had an audience with the president, such as Dr. Peter Parker, the renowned medical missionary to China, momentarily were taken aback by the incongruity of being greeted at the door of liberty's showcase by Tyler's slave butler and male body servant. Upon his return from his historic four-year exploring expedition to Antarctica and the far-flung island groups and coastal waters of the Pacific Rim, Charles Wilkes, who came to detest President Tyler, also was appalled at the slavemaster atmosphere he encountered during a visit to the executive residence.

Most distressing, at least in the eyes of the moralistic and self-righteous abolitionists Weld and Leavitt, was the glaring contrast between the austerity, simplicity, and integrity of John Quincy Adams's antislavery lifestyle and that of John Tyler's band of southern aristocratic slaveholders then ascendant in Washington. For Weld, Leavitt, and countless other abolitionists, the conspicuous display of wealth and power by slaveowners revealed much about the degradation and corruption of a formerly virtuous and noble American republic.[10]

Charges of John Tyler's sexual exploitation of female slaves appeared almost immediately as well in the antislavery press. As was the case with a number of prominent antebellum slaveowners, President Tyler was accused of fathering slave children. Just as Thomas Jefferson earlier had faced allegations of having mixed-race children by one of his slaves, so too did Tyler. Jefferson's accuser was the scandalmonger and embittered office-seeker James Callender. Tyler's was the abolitionist editor Joshua Leavitt. Of the two, Leavitt was the more honorable and credible critic, although his fierce abolitionism might have led him to distort evidence and even disregard the truth. In December 1841, Leavitt's *Emancipator* ran a lengthy story titled "Tyler-Ising" that claimed President Tyler had slave children and sired at least two mulatto sons by one of his Negro slaves. Leavitt further alleged that Tyler had sold some of his slave children, and made the highly inflammatory and sensational claim that it was "altogether probable he has supported his family by selling the increase of his slave stock."

The tale about the two sons, named John and Charles Tyler, evolved from the recollections of a Baptist minister known to editor Leavitt. The minister was said to have visited Richmond several years earlier and while in the home of his hostess encountered a light-skinned and well-mannered servant. The minister conversed with the servant and inquired if he was a slave. The servant replied yes, he was a slave who had been born on Governor Tyler's plantation and then sold to his mistress, "down at Williamsburgh." "What is your name," asked the minister. "My name is John, sir," he replied; "my mother called me John Tyler, because she said Governor Tyler was my father. You know such things happen sometimes on plantations." By now thoroughly intrigued, the minister asked the slave if his mother had other children by his master. The reply was "Yes, sir, several," and "I reckon they are all sold before now."

The story of Charles Tyler was equally compelling. According to the *Emancipator*'s account, Charles had been John Tyler's highly prized body servant when his master was a senator in Washington. "In the year 1837, or the beginning of 1838, a colored man passed through Poughkeepsie, on his way to Canada, who called his name Charles Tyler, and who seemed to have a good deal of knowledge of things in Washington." Making good his escape to Canada, Charles Tyler gained "the good will of all, until Lord Durham, then governor-general, returned to England, when he took Charles with him, as his waiter, or in some other confidential capacity, and it is supposed he is still in England, perhaps in the service of the Durham family." Leavitt sarcastically suggested that Tyler make a claim against Great Britain for a slave "named Charles, sometimes called Charles Tyler, who had first escaped from his master's services, and was afterwards tortiously harbored by one Lord Durham, a British subject, a servant of the crown, so that the right owner had never been able to recover his said property."[11]

The adventures of Charles Tyler, said to be an escaped slave and the bastard mulatto son of the president of the United States, and who allegedly fled to freedom in Canada and ultimately was taken to Britain as the servant of an English lord, made a gripping tale and was the stuff of antislavery melodrama in antebellum America. But the fate of Charles Tyler remains a historical mystery, and the questions of whether he existed and if his story was true also are unresolved to the present day.

What President John Tyler's personal reaction was to these fantastic charges is unknown as well. One would assume he was furious and aghast at what he considered the abolitionist editor's lack of propriety and decorum. And as a Virginia gentleman, he must have been stung by these attacks on his personal honor and morality. Quite outrageously, the chief magistrate of the American republic was publicly being accused of violating at least three antebellum societal taboos—illicit sex with a slave, miscegenation, and selling his bastard offspring.

The Tyler administration's official newspaper, the *Madisonian*, did print an indignant rebuttal several weeks after Leavitt published the "Tyler-Ising" article. John B. Jones, the newly installed editor of the *Madisonian*, said the *Emancipator* was guilty of "Gross Slander" and angrily denied the abolitionist newspaper's "wretched fabrications." "All the charges made by that paper against the father of the President, or the President himself," Jones concluded, "are false in every particular." In its pages a few days later, the *Madisonian* further clarified the administration's position: "To attempt a refutation of some of the slanderous charges made against President Tyler, we deem not only useless, but degrading. They are such as no honest or candid man would believe, and none but the vilest pander of falsehood would propagate. We cannot descend to the level of the authors or propagators of them."

Editor Leavitt quickly rejoined that he supposed the Tyler administration's denial was "satisfactory," if "a most disingenuous attempt of the official paper to bring in the reputation of the President's father into the case. Now there certainly was not, in the Emancipator, the slightest allusion to the *first* Governor Tyler, respectful or otherwise." The elder Tyler was an "illustrious man" in Leavitt's estimation, well respected for his opposition to the Constitution because it contained the clause that extended the slave trade for twenty years. Leavitt suspected the first Governor Tyler had been dragged into the fray in order "to turn public odium against the two slaves," as slanderers of the dead. As he had no way of communicating with the mulatto slaves, Leavitt concluded there was no way to determine the veracity of the *Madisonian*'s refutation of their claims.

This conclusion was a disingenuous sleight of hand on Leavitt's part, because he, and not the mulatto slaves, whose actual existence was in question, made the charges against President Tyler. Unlike Callender's attack on Thomas Jefferson, Leavitt's accusations were not picked up and circulated in the mainstream opposition press. And unlike the sustained notoriety of the Jefferson tale, the "Tyler-Ising" story has virtually disappeared from the nation's historical memory and is not widely known among the scholarly community or the American general public.[12]

Was it possible that these stories about John and Charles Tyler were indeed true and not fabricated? The standard response among John Tyler biographers and historians of the antebellum era has been to ignore completely Leavitt's charges, or to dismiss his allegations as unworthy of serious scholarly inquiry. But in light of new information that has appeared over the past two decades about the Thomas Jefferson and Sally Hemings relationship, including a recently discovered DNA link between a Hemings descendent and the Jefferson male line, and the resulting scholarly consensus that master and slave were sexual partners, the claims that John Tyler fathered children by his slaves must be taken seriously and examined thoroughly.

In present-day tidewater Virginia there are a number of African Americans who believe they are descendents of John Tyler. Just as there was an oral tradition in the Hemings family about Jefferson fathering children by Hemings, so too was there an oral tradition in the Brown family of Charles City County that President John Tyler fathered children by slave and free women of their family. In an August 1999 newspaper account of a Brown family reunion, Daryl Cumber Dance, a professor of English at the University of Richmond and organizer of the gathering, told a reporter she believed Tyler fathered many children by black women, including her own great-great-grandfather. Within the Brown family, she added: "It's absolutely accepted. It's just the Jefferson story all over again." Professor Dance candidly admitted she had "been unable to find any documentation to support that family legend, other than a land deal involving Tyler and two of the children he allegedly fathered." Current members of the Tyler family, including the president's grandson Harrison Tyler, are skeptical about Dance's claims. No DNA evidence has been sought to substantiate a Tyler-Brown family connection, and so the charges, at least at present, remain unproven.[13]

Far more damaging to President Tyler's credibility as a national leader than these sensational accusations were the persistent abolitionist attacks on the legitimacy of his administration and his political agenda. Editor William Lloyd Garrison of the *Liberator*, perhaps one of the more rabid and fanatical of abolitionists in Tyler's estimation, hammered away at the incongruity of having a notorious slaveholder occupy the top office in a republic supposedly dedicated to liberty and freedom. "A Slaveholder," Garrison believed, was "*ipso facto* disqualified to rule, or to hold office, in a free republic." Editor Leavitt, when not titillating the public with details of the chief executive's sex life in the slave quarter, joined his political allies in the Liberty Party in exposing the evils of the slave power, of which the Tyler administration was the most recent and flagrant incarnation.

The slave power thesis appeared in the 1830s as an integral part of an abolitionist ideology that energized and mobilized the antislavery forces. The main argument of the thesis was that the slaveholding South controlled all the levers of federal power. Adherents to the belief that southern slaveowners ran the country were John Quincy Adams, editors Lydia Maria Child and Horace Greeley, and rising politicians such as Charles Sumner and

Salmon Chase. When the slave power thesis reached its peak of popularity in the 1850s, included among its numerous true believers were prominent Republicans such as Abraham Lincoln. The thesis also attracted its share of the "lunatic fringe," but "oddly enough," according to one recent scholarly analysis, "many southerners also regarded the Slave Power thesis as self-evident truth."[14]

For most abolitionists it also was self-evident that John Tyler's proslavery cabinet appointments confirmed the validity of the slave power thesis. For instance, Abel Parker Upshur, an apologist for slavery and a suspected disunionist, was first named secretary of the navy and then elevated to secretary of state in the wake of Daniel Webster's decision to leave the administration. Another prominent southern slaveowner, Hugh Swinton Legare of South Carolina, served as attorney general and interim secretary of state in the cabinet and was a key adviser to President Tyler.

Then there was the example of John C. Calhoun of South Carolina, the self-anointed leader of the proslavery forces, who was appointed to the nation's top diplomatic post as head of the State Department after Upshur's death in an explosion aboard the navy's prized steamship the *Princeton*. Calhoun was every bit as extreme in his proslavery beliefs as was a Leavitt or a Garrison in their antislavery convictions. But, as one prominent historian has observed, so ingrained and accepted was the proslavery bias of the federal government that "while no president ever appointed an outspoken abolitionist to high office, much less a man of Garrison's views, in 1844 President Tyler nominated Calhoun as secretary of state, and the Senate confirmed the nomination without bothering to hold a hearing and without giving the matter a second thought." One of Tyler's diplomatic appointees, executive agent Duff Green, did elicit congressional scrutiny, but on constitutional grounds involving legislative oversight of financial allocations from the president's secret service or contingency fund, and not because of his proslavery stance.[15]

Antislavery poet and editor John Greenleaf Whittier undoubtedly spoke for many of his northern countrymen when he lamented John Tyler's ascension to the presidency as a "sore evil," but a host of the new president's southern compatriots rejoiced when he entered the White House. As one fellow Virginian exulted, "I feel *now* that the abolitionists & others that would harm us, are failed." In the chief executive's office, Tyler arguably became the most ardent of slavery's defenders at home and abroad the nation had yet seen. However, unlike his emotional and highly charged public reaction while a U.S. senator, the new president only occasionally took public umbrage at the activities of those he dismissed out of hand as fanatics. Tyler preferred to let supporters among the press and his attack dogs in Congress deal with the immediate domestic abolitionist challenge.

Editor John B. Jones, chief scribe of the administration's official mouthpiece, periodically rebutted the most egregious abolitionist attacks. More important, the proslavery forces concocted their own conspiracy thesis to counteract the slave power argument. In the thinking of the Tyler cadre, the abolitionist challenge had both a domestic and an international component. And to meet this growing challenge, Tyler's adherents, and for that matter a considerable number of southerners, defined Great Britain as the main antagonist and a huge part of the problem. Tyler's proslavery forces conjured up an Anglo-American abolitionist conspiracy thesis that identified the British as being behind the plot, not for humanitarian reasons but for economic hegemony and world dominance. The British were the source of abolitionist agitation, and their overall goal was not simply to end slavery but to undermine the United States's economic growth and prosperity.[16]

Even for the most casual political observer, evidence seemed to abound in support of an Anglo-American abolitionist conspiracy thesis. Had not the Liberty Party's presidential candidate, James G. Birney, attended and chaired some sessions at the World's Anti-Slavery Convention in London during the summer of 1840? Was not this convention called and sponsored by the British and Foreign Anti-Slavery Society, some of whose leaders had close ties with leading British politicians? Were not the political abolitionist Henry B. Stanton and Wendell Phillips, the Boston Brahmin and notorious antislavery orator, also in attendance?

And then there was the case of the Ohioan John Curtis. He was a true believer in a highly questionable scheme, originally concocted by Joshua Leavitt, to undermine the slave power by gaining access to the British market for wheat exports from the free states of the American Northwest. It was an incipient version of the King Wheat over King Cotton argument of Civil War fame. Simply put, it was premised on the assumption that repeal of the British Corn Laws would allow King Wheat to slay King Cotton and thereby destroy slavery in the southern United States.

In the summer of 1841 John Curtis sailed for England as a "missionary" of antislavery who, reported several abolitionist newspapers, "goes out to aid the anti–Corn Law League." Upon his arrival in Britain Curtis immediately went on the lecture circuit spreading the abolitionist gospel on the need for repeal of the Corn Laws. For someone like Tyler who had a well-developed hatred of the British dating back to his youth, and who had witnessed the disruptive antics of meddling English abolitionists of the likes of George Thompson in the 1830s, little more evidence was needed. He was convinced of the existence of an Anglo-American antislavery network dedicated to the elimination of slavery worldwide. Most ominously for Tyler and other slave-owners, this British-led antislavery campaign would begin by promoting abolition in the United States and the republic of Texas.[17]

Before John Curtis departed for the British Isles he accidentally encountered Joseph Sturge, an English Quaker who was on an antislavery crusade to America, in Buffalo, New York. Sturge was en route to Niagara Falls, an obligatory stopover for nineteenth-century visitors to the United States. This serendipitous 1841 meeting and symbolic crossing of paths by Curtis and Sturge on the Niagara frontier was a clear indicator, for friend and foe of abolitionism alike, of a blossoming Anglo-American reform partnership. In a letter asking John Greenleaf Whittier to serve as his paid escort and guide during his stay in North America, Sturge explained his mission as one to "promote an entire unity of action and cooperation" between the British and Foreign Anti-Slavery Society and the American Anti-Slavery Society.

Joseph Sturge also carried a message for President Tyler from British abolitionists that he hoped to deliver personally at the White House. He wrote Tyler requesting an interview but received no reply. An affronted Sturge penned an open letter to American abolitionists protesting this presidential discourtesy and rude behavior unbecoming a supposed southern gentleman. He sent copies to Tyler and the members of Congress, but to no avail. Apparently Tyler thought Sturge a dishonorable fellow who needed to mind his own business, and hence deemed him undeserving the common courtesy of a polite response.[18]

In addition to ignoring and snubbing Sturge, President Tyler responded to the challenge represented by abolitionism's private diplomacy, which relied on the all-too-frequent and annoying visits of British antislavery emissaries, by having his friends and allies routinely play the Anglophobia card. On the home front the chief executive directed Representative Henry A. Wise of Virginia, one of the administration's staunchest allies in Congress, to appeal to the nation's latent anti-British feelings by assailing Sturge for meddling in purely American domestic affairs. Wise was further instructed to raise doubts about James Birney's patriotism by labeling him the candidate of the "British Abolitionist—disunionist Party." Congressman Wise also charged that Birney and his cohort Joshua Leavitt were paid foreign agents and that the entire antislavery enterprise, financed and directed by Great Britain, was a subversive scheme aimed at undermining the American Union.

In a speech before the Virginia General Assembly, Thomas Gilmer, another Tyler loyalist, made similar anti-British allegations about the designated 1844 Liberty Party ticket of Birney and his vice-presidential running mate, Thomas Morris of Ohio. The proslavery spokesmen cited what they deemed were clear political and ideological connections between American abolitionists and British reformers as evidence to support these charges. In attempting to discredit abolitionism and cast doubt on its legitimacy as a domestic reform movement, the Tyler forces reflexively played to the American public's residual anti-British nationalism. It was extremely doubtful that the charges were true. But the abolitionists' reliance on the Corn Law panacea and their cultivation of an Anglo-American reform coalition made them vulnerable to such attacks on their patriotism.

On the diplomatic front the president sent forth his own "ambassador of slavery." In the fall of 1841 Tyler dispatched one of his closest advisers, Duff Green, to England as his secret executive agent. Green, a former partisan newspaper editor with a flair for prose that went for the political jugular, was a classic flamboyant nineteenth-century entrepreneur, financial wheeler-dealer, and developer of frontier towns who put the lie to the conventional wisdom that all proslavery southerners were anti-capitalist agrarians. Green, along with many Americans during the depression of the early 1840s, was in financial straits and needed an infusion of capital to keep his enterprises afloat. His cover while abroad was that of a businessman and industrial promoter seeking venture capital from British investors to fund, among other projects, the development of railways and coalmines in Maryland.

A stalwart defender of slavery who despised abolitionism, Green apparently had secret instructions to counteract the influence and undercut the impact of James Birney, Henry B. Stanton, John Curtis, and any other American abolitionists making the rounds in the British Isles. Arriving in London in early December, Green quickly went on the offensive addressing letters to the press and lobbying prominent English aristocrats, leading politicians, and well-heeled financiers. Presumably, he outlined to his hosts the advantages inherent for Britain in a commercial treaty and freer trade with the United States and cautioned against the foolhardiness of a British-inspired global campaign against slavery. Green's analysis probably was heard and considered among the British elite because of his known connections to President Tyler and other leading American politicians such as John C. Calhoun.

At another level, Tyler's ambassador of slavery sought to discredit Anglo-American abolitionism by questioning Britain's motives in pursuing universal emancipation. In a series of essays that usually appeared anonymously in the columns of British newspapers and journals, Green argued that humanitarian concerns or altruistic feelings did not guide Britain's advocacy of antislavery. Its true goal was to enhance Britain's global economic power and commercial dominance. Empire, not philanthropy, inspired Britain's campaign for universal emancipation.

Duff Green's conspiratorial argument was complicated and of questionable validity. Britain had abolished slavery in its empire and, Green charged, wanted to end slavery in Cuba, Brazil, the United States, and the Republic of Texas, in order to eliminate the competition of cheaper slave labor. By exposing Britain's self-interested policies, he hoped to blunt its moralistic attack on slavery, and simultaneously advance the United States's economic interests. What did Duff Green accomplish? The impact of his lobbying efforts remains difficult to assess, although arguably very little was gained through his propaganda campaign and undercover diplomacy. Green's quixotic missions neither produced an Anglo-American commercial agreement nor an end to the British antislavery campaign. Undeterred and unfazed by the amateurish diplomacy of Tyler and Green, Great Britain continued its drive for commercial hegemony and global empire.

The one tangible success for the Tyler administration's proslavery diplomacy during Duff Green's federally funded holiday abroad, and it was only marginally of his doing, was the defeat of the Quintuple Treaty. This 1841 treaty for the suppression of the African slave trade, signed but not formally ratified by Great Britain, France, Prussia, Austria, and Russia, included a provision for a limited right of search on the high seas, but the "said mutual right of search shall not be exercised within the Mediterranean sea." This limitation, and the fact that three of the signatories — Austria, Prussia, and Russia — had never been involved in the African trade, made the treaty an innocuous statement of general principle. But Green insisted that the Quintuple agreement was "one of the measures intended to increase and perpetuate the maritime and commercial supremacy of England" because it would allow the British to extend their objectionable practice of search and visitation.

However, the individual primarily responsible for defeating the treaty was not informal envoy Green, but Lewis Cass, American minister to France. To be sure, Duff Green unofficially collaborated with Minister Cass, even though America's representative in Paris needed little prodding. The Anglophobic Cass, a Democrat from Michigan originally appointed to his post by President Van Buren, hated Britain's intrusive maritime tactics and published a widely circulated pamphlet denouncing British search practices as a violation of America's national honor. Through his friendship with King Louis Philippe and influence with leading politicians, Minister Cass successfully lobbied to block France's ratification of the Quintuple Treaty. Cass's independent diplomacy and indiscreet meddling in French internal affairs were troubling to President Tyler and Secretary Webster, but they did not reprimand their minister and tacitly approved his foray into international intrigue because they were pleased with the results.[19]

Duff Green's transparently proslavery diplomacy in Europe failed to stem abolitionist activities at home or abroad, and unsurprisingly, the Anglo-American antislavery alliance continued to flourish. If anything, Green's overseas machinations strengthened the antislavery enterprise's belief in the veracity of the slave power analysis. Despite the Tyler administration's efforts to conceal his official capacity as a representative of the American government, the subterfuge failed. Everyone in the know on the Washington scene, including those within the abolitionist camp, easily surmised that Duff Green was President Tyler's undercover agent and understood he had been sent to Europe as the administration's ambassador of slavery without official portfolio.

Apparently it was Congressman John Quincy Adams who publicly exposed Duff Green as Tyler's proslavery emissary. In an article that appeared in a prominent newspaper, Adams informed his national audience that "this Duff Green has been for some months a sort of informal negotiator at the court of Great Britain, with the approbation of the president of the United States. He has been charged as being the ambassador of slavery at that court, and I do not understand him to deny it. He has been visiting Queen Victoria and Sir Robert Peel, and trying to convince them of one thing and another, and among them that I could not abolish slavery or dissolve the union." For American abolitionists, Green's defamatory attacks in Britain attempting to discredit former president Adams and to cast him as a conspirator and a demon once again demonstrated the audacity of the slave power. Green's diplomacy also confirmed that America's foreign relations were inextricably bound to a defense of slavery. "Every question that is brought before congress," and not just diplomatic issues said Adams, "is considered in reference to its bearing on slavery."[20]

Perhaps the greatest impact of Duff Green's two trips abroad as America's ambassador of slavery was among the proslavery faithful at home. Through his published writings and frequent correspondence with his superiors back in Washington, Green helped crystallize the thinking of fellow southerners

John Tyler and Abel P. Upshur, both of whom accepted his conspiratorial analysis of Great Britain's drive for world hegemony. John C. Calhoun also was in the company of true believers. Tyler's adherence to this conspiracy thesis originally took shape in the 1830s at the beginning of the antislavery movement's growing militancy. During his presidency, Tyler's anti-British outlook hardened, thanks in part to Green's ready synthesis, and in response to what he believed was clear evidence of an Anglo-American crusade to destroy the South's peculiar institution and instigate disunion. Great Britain, Tyler confided to a member of his family, "steps forward as a pretended philanthropist," but in reality that nation was bent upon breaking up the American Union for its own imperial gain.

Among the Tyler faithful it was received truth that the British were using American abolitionists as their hirelings and dupes in a North American version of the great game of empire. "There can be no doubt, I think," Abel Upshur wrote his friend Calhoun as one Anglophobe confiding his suspicions to another, "that England is determined to abolish slavery throughout the American continent and islands if she can. It is worse than childish to suppose that she mediates this great movement simply from an impulse of philanthropy. We must look for a stronger motive for such an attempt on the part of a great and wise nation. I can find no other motive than a desire to find or to create markets for her surplus manufactures, and to destroy all competition with the laborers of her colonies." The belief that Great Britain meant to bring about the eventual destruction of the United States and "monopolize the commerce of the world" became the conventional wisdom for the Anglophobes of the Tyler administration.[21]

In addition to the use of executive agents to further his proslavery diplomacy, President Tyler moved to strengthen and modernize the American navy. A revitalized navy would protect his envisioned "empire of commerce" and serve as a safeguard against the virus of slave insurrection, which to Tyler's mind loomed as a dreaded possibility in the first year or so of his presidency. He feared war with Great Britain might erupt because of heightened Anglo-American tensions over a number of unresolved issues, most notably the disputed northeastern boundary line between Maine and New Brunswick. The president also believed the forthcoming trial in New York of a British subject, Alexander McLeod, for his part in the 1837 burning of an American vessel in the Niagara River, made another conflict with Britain appear dangerously imminent. War with the world's greatest naval power meant that the United States's vast unprotected coastline was vulnerable to attack from Britain's newly developed shallow draft steam vessels, which had been used so effectively in the 1840 British victory at the Acre fortress in Syria.

For a nervous Tyler administration the exposed and defenseless position of the east coast to a coordinated naval assault raised as well the specter of British-inspired slave revolts in the slaveholding states of the South. There was historical precedent within memory for such fears and apprehensions. Slaveowners of Tyler's generation were well aware that the British had tried this incendiary tactic during the American Revolution when Lord Dunmore, the royal governor of Virginia, issued his 1775 proclamation inviting slaves to gain their freedom by joining his army. Hundreds of black bondsmen flocked to Dunmore's "Ethiopian regiment" and wore uniforms with the slogan "Liberty to Slaves" boldly inscribed across their chests. In the numerous tidewater communities of the antebellum South where blacks outnumbered whites, the prospect of a British-led servile insurrection was a nightmare too horrible to imagine.

In September 1841, when Tyler named Abel P. Upshur to the post of secretary of the navy in his newly reorganized cabinet, many political observers perceived him as a competent provincial judge from the Virginia backwater who owed his nomination to a personal friendship with the president. Predictably, the Whig press, including prominent newspapers in the Old Dominion, denounced Upshur's appointment, angered at what they decried as fresh evidence of Tyler's betrayal of Whig principles since his "accidental" ascendancy to the nation's highest office.

One New York editor, James Watson Webb, went so far as to call for President Tyler's impeachment because he had placed an alleged disunionist at the head of the Navy Department. As evidence of Judge Upshur's disloyalty, Webb claimed the conservative, proslavery Virginian was in fact the seditious author of an anonymously published novel that called for the breakup of the Union and the creation of a southern confederacy. Upshur, who knew that it was his good friend Beverley Tucker who had penned the novel, calmly ignored the rancorous partisan clamor over his appointment. After his relatively easy confirmation by the Senate, he energetically tackled his new duties, hoping to quiet his critics and win much-needed public approval for the beleaguered Tyler administration.[22]

Upshur's stint as head of the Navy Department brought him national prominence and foreshadowed the expansionist foreign policy he later pursued as secretary of state. What established the obscure state judge from Virginia's Eastern Shore as a rising political star to be reckoned with was his first annual report. Submitted a few months after Upshur became navy secretary, the report was a blueprint for naval expansion, modernization, and administrative reform that would alleviate the nation's vulnerability to attack and project American naval power into the Pacific basin. Along with most of his nineteenth-century political contemporaries, Upshur adhered to the traditional belief that one of the navy's primary functions was to protect the nation's commerce and far-flung economic interests.

In order for the navy to fulfill its mission on the world's seas, Secretary Upshur recommended a fleet that would be at least "half the naval force of the strongest maritime power in the world," which of course was an obvious reference to the nation's chief rival and nemesis, Great Britain. Proclaiming that the United States now ranked "in the first class of nations," and recognizing that naval power was imperative to national greatness, Upshur believed Americans must pursue their destiny and announced it was "an absolute necessity to regulate our policy by that of other countries." The new secretary of the navy clearly understood as well that the United States needed naval bases to guard its growing Pacific trade and lucrative whale fisheries. His preferred locations for future bases were at strategic points on the west coasts of North and South America and in the Hawaiian Islands, the "central point" at the crossroads of the Pacific Ocean. Befitting a navy that would serve as the nation's cutting edge of empire, Upshur's far-ranging and visionary report also called for the conversion of the fleet from sail to steam, enlargement of naval ranks to include vice admiral and admiral, a substantial increase in the marine corps, and the creation of a naval academy.[23]

Secretary Upshur shared President Tyler's dread of future slave uprisings and shrewdly justified his recommendations for increased naval strength by playing to the fears of his fellow slaveholders. Talk of war with Britain was rampant and Upshur was not above utilizing the war scare for his own ends. He told the nation that an invading enemy with an antislavery agenda probably would attempt to array "what are supposed to be the hostile elements of our social system against one another." "Steamboats of light draught, and which may be easily transported across the ocean in vessels of a large class," Secretary Upshur warned, "may invade us at almost any point of our extended coast, may penetrate the interior through our shallow rivers, and thus expose half our country to hostile attacks." The destruction and devastation wrought by "these incursions would be terrible everywhere; but in the southern portion of our country they might, and probably would be disastrous in the extreme."

The navy secretary concluded his report by arguing that the threat of foreign invasion, slave insurrection, and race war would become less likely if the nation's weak coastal defenses were strengthened and improved. Upshur's friend, the William and Mary law professor and undercover disunionist Beverley Tucker, praised the report's hard-hitting analysis. "I am pleased that you approve my report," Upshur replied, but he doubted his recommendations would be funded because "Congress I fear, will do little or nothing. They know how delicate and precarious are our relations with England, yet they will not put the country in a posture of defense." His sense of chivalry made the secretary wonder: "How can the *men* of the country, look the *women* of the country in the face, when they are calculating the pence and farthings which it will cost to defend them."[24]

Secretary Upshur's comprehensive naval plans, further outlined in his second report of 1842, were hailed by naval reformers and drew praise and support from the nation's leading newspapers, many of which published the report verbatim. But political objections to the secretary of the navy's proposals arose almost immediately, many critics focusing primarily on the program's overall price tag. Abolitionists, led by *Emancipator* editor Joshua Leavitt, charged that the projected naval buildup, with its provisions for vastly improved coastal defenses, was another hypocritical scheme by defenders of states' rights to employ federal power to protect the South's institution of slavery. They correctly pointed out that Upshur had justified a larger navy to protect America's shores from attack with the argument that a foreign invasion might spark a slave insurrection and instigate political revolution. The abolitionist press, in one of their more outlandish accusations, further disclosed that the report's "real object" was "to furnish convoy for slave traders" and protect the slave trade.

In defense of his recommendations, Upshur waged his own press campaign. In several anonymous editorials published in the *Madisonian*, the secretary once again utilized a war scare in urging public and congressional support for naval expansion and modernization. In an overall sense the navy did prosper and flourish during the Tyler administration, but in the end not even a war scare brought all of Secretary Upshur's desired results, as partisan sectional rivalries sidetracked much of his program.[25]

Upshur's odyssey from state politician and regional jurist to naval reformer and ardent imperialist was strange and mildly puzzling. He had neither been to sea nor traveled beyond America's shores. That is not to suggest he was a confirmed landlubber. Apparently, as a young lawyer starting out in Baltimore, a restless Abel Upshur looked beyond the confines of his legal practice and yearned to travel abroad. As the first step in his projected overseas itinerary, he planned to visit England and tour the European continent. But the death of his father necessitated a cancellation of his scheduled trip. Upshur left Baltimore and returned to "Vaucluse," the family's estate on Virginia's Eastern Shore, to sort out his father's troubled financial affairs. He never fulfilled his youthful dream of crossing the Atlantic and embarking on an uninhibited wanderlust exploring the wonders of Paris, London, and Rome. Instead, after helping restore the family's finances, Upshur became a successful attorney, state legislator, and judge.

Most remarkably, without having seen the wider world and without diplomatic or military experience, Upshur became another of Virginia's deskbound imperialists who guided the Tyler administration's expansionist foreign policy. His Pacific-mindedness and vision for a modernized U.S. Navy came from naval officers and Atlantic seaboard merchants he met through his Norfolk law practice who were engaged in the nation's growing overseas trade. A quick study, Upshur read extensively on international topics and probably was most heavily influenced by the writings of fellow Virginian Matthew Fontaine Maury. In spite of the age difference—Lieutenant Maury was Upshur's junior by more than fifteen years—the younger man became his elder's teacher, and Maury came to believe that their mutual interest in America's naval destiny made them "pretty good friends."[26]

Matthew Fontaine Maury was a seasoned sailor who knew firsthand the adventure and excitement as well as the rigors and hardships of life at sea aboard an American naval vessel in the first half of the nineteenth century. During three naval cruises in the 1820s and early 1830s, he had crossed the Atlantic, sailed the Mediterranean, rounded treacherous Cape Horn, and was a midshipman on the *Vincennes*, the first American man-of-war to circumnavigate the globe. Commanded by Captain William Finch, the *Vincennes* began its voyage across the Pacific in 1829. The American ship visited Tahiti and the Sandwich Islands and then sailed on to China and the Philippines. While visiting the big island of Hawaii, Maury played tourist, visiting the Kilauea volcano and Rainbow Falls.

Maury and his mates of the *Vincennes* crew went on to Oahu, where the captain presented several gifts, including a large map of the United States, to the Hawaiian king, Kamehameha III. The *Vincennes* then became only the second American man-of-war to visit Chinese waters and record the vast commercial opportunities beckoning American entrepreneurs. When the ship arrived back in New York City in June 1830, a band playing the ever-popular anthem "Hail Columbia! Happy Land!" triumphantly welcomed her home. Inspired by his glorious voyages and the refrains of national greatness, and fully aware that a strong navy was essential to America's national destiny, Maury dedicated himself to educating his fellow citizens about what was required to modernize and reform the American navy. As luck would have it, his prize pupil was the future secretary of the navy, Abel P. Upshur.

"Harry Bluff" was one of several pseudonyms Maury adopted to convey his ideas to the public. In a series of articles entitled "Scraps from the Lucky Bag" that appeared in the *Southern Literary Messenger* in 1840–41, sailor "Bluff" urged an extensive overhaul of the navy's administrative procedures and promotion system. Undoubtedly Upshur and Tyler, both of whom were subscribers and contributors to the *Messenger*, a highly respected journal of literary criticism and political commentary published in Richmond, read the articles with enlightenment.

Although Maury, then an active duty naval officer, may have desired anonymity during his brief career as a crusading journalist, it was common knowledge within the naval establishment and among the American populace that he was the author of the "Lucky Bag" exposé. Lieutenant Maury's incisive critique of the U.S. Navy's archaic policies gained him instant national acclaim and recognition as a leading campaigner for naval reform. But "Harry Bluff" wanted more than mere bureaucratic changes. He also called for the conversion of the fleet from sail to steam and highlighted the need for American control of the Columbia River basin and an increased naval presence in the Pacific Ocean to ensure the nation's future commercial dominance in the China market. Apparently, or at least so a fanciful story went, Maury's fame after the publication of the "Harry Bluff" articles was such that he was seriously considered by President Tyler to head the Navy Department, even though Maury was then but a thirty-five-year-old lieutenant without administrative or political experience.[27]

Fortuitously, what did come Maury's way was an appointment that transformed his life and made him an internationally respected marine scientist, hydrographer, and oceanographer. In July 1842, Navy Secretary Upshur rewarded his intellectual mentor and fellow naval expansionist by selecting him for the position of superintendent of the Depot of Charts and Instruments. This appointment launched Maury's career as the scientific investigator of the winds and currents of the oceans and won him fame and distinction as "the Pathfinder of the Seas." President Tyler was pleased with Maury's assignment to this federal research bureau. On several occasions during his presidency, Tyler displayed his engagement in the pursuit of scientific advancement and was especially strong in his support for oceanic studies. When Maury hosted what was the "first National Congress of Scientific men" at the initial meeting of the National Institute for the Promotion of Science in Washington, D.C., in April 1844, President Tyler gave the opening address and presided over the proceedings. Hailed by Maury and his colleagues as a patron of science and supporter of the work of the institute, a flattered Tyler promised to do all in his power to foster the increase and diffusion of scientific knowledge.

Further evidence of the federal government's commitment to scientific endeavors came that year as well with the decision to divide the Navy Depot of Charts and Instruments into two agencies, the Hydrographical Office and the Naval Observatory, both of which Maury was chosen to head. President Tyler was in the forefront of the planning for the Naval Observatory. Displaying all the excitement of a youthful schoolboy embarking upon a new adventure, the president immediately selected the location for the new observatory—an impressive seventeen-acre plot of land that George Washington had earmarked for the site of a future national university and optimistically had named "University Square." Frequently, John Tyler has been cast as a single-minded and ultra-rigid states' righter suspicious of the power of the national government. But when it came to scientific inquiry and applied research he proved as passionate as were his predecessors Washington, Jefferson, and John Quincy Adams in their dedication to federal support for the advancement of knowledge. After all, progress in the quest to understand the physical universe went hand in hand with President Tyler's visions of national greatness.[28]

In his tutelage of Abel P. Upshur, Lieutenant Maury probably was instrumental in shaping the navy secretary's thinking about a good deal more than just the nation's weak coastal defenses and its general unpreparedness for war. Along with most other American naval officers of the time, Maury was suspicious and fearful of Great Britain. He objected to the high-handed visit and search policies of the Royal Navy in its battle against the African slave trade. Maury publicly denounced the Quintuple Treaty, which he charged was designed as convenient cover for Britain's ongoing campaign to ensure its global commercial supremacy.

Closer to home, Maury's concerns about the United States's vulnerability in the face of British naval power undoubtedly fueled and reinforced Upshur's and the South's fears of slave insurrection. The Tyler administration's obsession with the contagion of slave uprisings spreading from the islands of the Caribbean to the American mainland explained its hysterical response and implacable opposition to calls for the recognition of Haiti.

Tyler and other slaveowners were spooked by what the Haitian example foretold for the South and its peculiar institution. If you recognized Haiti, they reasoned, you sanctioned and gave legitimacy to slave revolt and the terror attendant to the violent and bloody overthrow of white rule.

But Haiti symbolized something else that was equally unsettling to many antebellum white Americans irrespective of their sectional or political affiliations. That was the prospect of racial amalgamation. The Haitian example was an alarm bell in the night that awoke Americans to the frightening prospect of racial mixing and the future equality of people of all colors and hues. Opposition to Haitian recognition exposed the unwillingness of the majority of antebellum Americans to contemplate racial equality. That was true for southerners, northerners, midwesterners, and border state leaders alike. To acknowledge the independence of a black republic in the Caribbean was seemingly to acknowledge as well the humanity of black slaves in the American South and the justice of their demands for freedom and liberty. For Tyler, Upshur, Wise, and Calhoun, resistance to the recognition of Haiti was at the heart of their struggle to defend slavery. If one recognized Haiti, then all the barriers to a multiracial society came tumbling down. This band of angst-ridden slaveowners saw it as the dangerous first step of a slippery slope that led to social chaos.

The fear of racial amalgamation evidently haunted even the nation's leading antislavery champion, Congressman John Quincy Adams. Although he was a thorn in the side of the Tyler people and regularly presented petitions for Haitian recognition, one scholar recently has contended that the specter "of future Othellos in American society disturbed John Quincy Adams and caused him to weigh the question of which sin was greater: Negro slavery or increased intermixture of the races." As Upshur and other defenders of the peculiar institution persistently argued, and some antislavery spokesmen hypocritically confirmed, Negro slavery was white society's safeguard, albeit an admittedly porous one given the predatory sexual proclivities of slave masters, against the peril of the increasing intermixture of the races.[29]

"Wherever black slavery existed," according to Tyler's faithful congressional spokesman, Henry Wise, "there was found at least equality among the white population" because "slavery was a leveling principle." If you abolished slavery, Wise feared, "you would with the same blow destroy the great democratic principle of equality among men." Apparently the ever ambivalent John Tyler, who in his early public life defined slavery as a repugnant but necessary evil, gradually came to accept the argument of Wise and other prominent slaveowners that the South's peculiar institution was beneficial to American society as a whole. In the imperfect world bequeathed his generation by the founding fathers, Tyler conceded that black bondage was the only way to preserve white freedom and equality. Although he never publicly articulated this view of slavery as a positive good while in the White House, Tyler privately endorsed this comforting rationalization in his correspondence to family and friends in the years after he left the presidency. John Tyler, like most white Americans of his time, thought black emancipation and racial equality would be detrimental to the status of whites.[30]

As a matter of course the white majority's unrelenting opposition to Haitian recognition elicited some of the more racially charged rhetoric of the antebellum era. Two instances spaced over two decades should suffice to make the point. The first came in response to the possibility of sending American delegates to the Panama Congress. Called by South America's great liberator, Símon Bolívar, in late 1824, this conference of independent American states was conceived as a first step in bringing about hemispheric cooperation and harmony. When President John Quincy Adams sought congressional approval for the United States's participation in the conference, opposition arose because of several concerns, one being that if Haiti participated, attendance by U.S. delegates would imply approval of the Haitian government.

Any possibility of recognizing Haiti, even indirectly, upset one senator, Thomas Hart Benton of Missouri, who pointedly said: "We trade with her, but no diplomatic relations have been established between us. We purchase coffee from her, and pay her for it, but we interchange no consuls or ministers. We receive no mulatto Consuls or black Ambassadors from her." Why does the United States refuse to recognize Haiti, Benton asked? "Because," he answered, "the peace of eleven States to this Union will not permit the fruits of a successful negro insurrection to be exhibited among them. It will not permit black Consuls and Ambassadors to establish themselves in our cities, and to parade through our country, and give their fellow blacks in the United States, proof in hand of the honors which await them, for a like successful effort on their part." It will not, the senator concluded, "permit the fact to be seen, and told, that from the murder of their masters and mistresses, they are to find *friends* among the White people of the United States."[31]

The second example of rhetorical excess came during the Tyler presidency. The abolitionist demand for the recognition of Haitian sovereignty did reach the floor of the Congress on at least one occasion in the 1840s, but then only to be mockingly denounced. Congressman Henry Wise ridiculed the call for recognition in an 1842 speech in the House of Representatives. In the process he again confirmed the racism of the opponents of Haitian recognition. Wise pointed out that if the United States established full diplomatic relations with the black republic, then a Haitian representative would be sent to Washington. Quashipompo, as Wise ludicrously caricatured a possible future Haitian minister, "with his wooly head and his black skin, dressed out in all the negro finery of his diplomatic costume," would expect to attend the president's levees and "be introduced to Southern gentlemen here as their equal, if not a little more, and the next step would be that he must be received at our entertainments, and, as a high foreign functionary, he must of course give entertainments in return."

Receiving Haitian diplomats as social equals, Wise feared, would assuredly lead to racial mixing and amalgamation, which he charged was the barely disguised purpose of the abolitionists' campaign for the recognition of Haitian independence. Wise and his House colleague John Quincy Adams were bitter political adversaries, but the Virginian probably sensed Adams's ambivalence toward the intermixture of the races, an uneasiness that was shared by most white citizens in the early American republic. The racial imagery of Wise's speech played to the prejudices of a national audience and should be understood as having been aimed at all white Americans, not just proslavery southerners.[32]

Even though the United States had been promoting trade with Haiti since the 1790s and had three official commercial agents stationed in the island by the mid-1840s, the American government remained intransigently opposed to granting diplomatic recognition during John Tyler's presidency. While in office, the president and his chief southern advisers, Upshur, Wise, and Calhoun, looked for every avenue and venue to denigrate, degrade, and denounce the Haitian revolution. Such was their obsession with black Haiti that in the eleventh hour of the administration and at the same time they were scrambling to have Congress annex Texas by joint resolution, Tyler and Secretary of State Calhoun moved to undermine and, if possible, destroy the Haitian experiment.

The opportunity came when the eastern half of the island with its predominantly Spanish-speaking inhabitants revolted against Haitian rule and declared its independence. In early 1845 the recently proclaimed Dominican Republic sent a special envoy to Washington to obtain American aid and recognition by exaggerating the whiteness of its population in contrast to the blackness of the residents of the Haitian republic. Tyler and Calhoun jumped at the chance to destabilize the island and terminate black rule in

Haiti. In late February, just a week or two before he was scheduled to leave office, President Tyler dispatched John B. Hogan, a political supporter of the administration from upstate New York, as an executive agent to the Caribbean island. Hogan's mission was to investigate the viability of the new Dominican government and evaluate the possibility of the United States granting diplomatic recognition.[33]

Apparently President Tyler and Secretary Calhoun were prepared to go even further in their campaign to destroy Haiti. There is evidence, fragmentary to be sure, that the American government sent arms and military supplies to the Dominican forces in support of their struggle for independence. Edmund Ruffin, the agricultural expert and southern secessionist who was an admired friend of Tyler, was visiting the nation's capitol in January 1858 when he encountered Virginia senator Robert M. T. Hunter. The two men spoke of the present conditions in Dominica and Haiti. Ruffin recorded the conversation in his diary, noting that "Mr. Hunter told me that when Mr. Calhoun was Secretary of State, & the Dominicans were in great danger from the Haytiens, he used the secret service fund to supply arms to the former, & enabled them to repel their more barbarous invaders." No additional documentary evidence has come to light to substantiate Hunter's claim to Ruffin concerning arms shipments, but it is highly probable that his information was correct given what is known about the Tyler administration's determination to subvert and destroy Haiti.[34]

Further verification of their hostility to the Haitian government came a few months after Calhoun and Tyler left office, when they corresponded about the prospects for the success of the Dominican cause. In October 1845 Tyler wrote Calhoun that "I . . . fully concur with you in the policy of recognizing the independence of the Dominican Republic should Mr. Hogan's report satisfactorily establish the fact of its perfect ability to maintain itself against the Haytien govt. The experiment which blacks have made of governing themselves has resulted in bloodshed, anarchy, and the most fertile island in the world is almost converted into a waste."

When secret agent John Hogan reported to President James K. Polk and Secretary of State James Buchanan that same month, he told them that the Dominicans had successfully organized a government and established a written constitution based on republican principles. Hogan was confident that the Dominican Republic would triumph in its struggle with Haiti, "even to the extent of extending its authority throughout the entire island." Hogan's optimistic prediction proved wrong. In fact, Haiti survived and in 1862 finally received diplomatic recognition from the United States. American recognition of the Dominican Republic did not come until 1866. Both nations coexist on the island to the present day.[35]

In the history of American foreign relations, Haiti may be understood as the nineteenth-century equivalent of a racial contagion comparable to the ideological contagion that Castro's communist Cuba represented in the late twentieth century. Although separated in time by more than a century, the United States's response to these perceived racial and ideological threats to national security was of a remarkably consistent and similar pattern—non-recognition, exaggerated and inflammatory rhetoric about the threat these tiny nations posed, and support for internal subversion by aiding rivals who sought to overthrow these despised regimes. Haiti and Cuba were the pariah nations of their time. Each of these countries was an insignificant small island, but for American leaders they loomed large in their imaginations as racial and ideological challenges that threatened the status quo. In both cases the same irrational fears were evident in the preposterous claims about the nature of the threat to national security posed by a small Caribbean island just miles off the coast of the American mainland.

In its sustained opposition to both the Haitian experiment and the Cuban revolution, the United States was out of step with the international community in each time period. In the last half of the twentieth century a number of nations, including the United States's closest neighbors, Canada and Mexico, granted diplomatic recognition to Cuba. Prior to the American Civil War, Haiti's independence was recognized by France in 1825 and Great Britain in 1833, although the black republic was not granted immediate diplomatic recognition by its neighboring nations of the Western Hemisphere. Despite President Tyler's lofty rhetoric about human liberty and America as the model of freedom for the world, on the issues of the abolition of slavery and the emancipation of blacks, the United States under his leadership fell short of being the beacon of liberty. Clearly, in their campaign for universal emancipation the American abolitionists were far more in tune with enlightened international opinion and the moral sensibilities of the world's leading nation, Great Britain, than they were with the national polity as it found voice in the Tyler administration.[36]

To be fair, in the antebellum era defending slavery from its foreign enemies was the accepted national policy for all presidential administrations regardless of party or sectional affiliation. Protecting the institution of slavery at home and abroad was deemed essential to preserve the Union and prevent the breakup of the United States. In a slaveholding republic haunted by the specter of slave insurrection and the nightmare of a bloody race war, there appeared to be no other choice in the conduct of the nation's diplomacy but to defend the South's peculiar institution from international threats. American foreign relations during John Tyler's presidency epitomized this proslavery bias; his anti-abolitionist and proslavery foreign policy formed a crucial segment in an American diplomatic continuum that prevailed until the election of Abraham Lincoln and the nation's descent into bloody civil war.

Ironically, in vigorously defending slavery from internal and external challenges President Tyler violated his strict constructionist principles and set precedents that expanded executive power. Tyler's cherished and hallowed republican principles were tarnished and undermined in his quest to preserve the South's peculiar institution through the use of federal power and authority, which, it should be noted, was an odd stance for a states' rights Virginian. For example, his willingness to use executive agents financed by the contingency fund, such as the notorious ambassador of slavery Duff Green, to promote a proslavery diplomatic agenda without congressional oversight or approval directly expanded the power of the chief executive.

If Edmund Ruffin's information about military assistance to the Dominicans was correct, President Tyler even went so far as to interfere in a foreign civil war to bring down black rule in Haiti. Once again, Tyler readily dipped into the contingency, or secret service, fund to bypass the Congress's constitutionally mandated fiscal control and guidance of the republic's foreign policy. Despite reservations he had held as a senator during the Jackson administration about presidential prerogatives in foreign policy, President Tyler used executive power to full advantage in behalf of the slaveholding interest.

In carrying the diplomatic banner as the freewheeling and unrestrained agent of a slaveholding republic, President Tyler ignored his own warnings about the danger of concentrating "power in the hands of a single man." When he took office as the first vice president to succeed to the presidency upon the death of the incumbent, Tyler promised to be faithful to his republican principles by respecting the separation of executive and legislative powers. The new chief executive further pledged to maintain a complete separation "between the sword and the purse." As many of his political enemies accurately charged, John Tyler did not live up to that lofty republican standard. His repeated use of the secret service fund to carry on an independent proslavery diplomacy, including the covert backing of internal subversion, jeopardized the fragile constitutional balance that empowered the legislative purse to check the executive sword.

No longer the ardent and vigilant defender of legislative autonomy, John Tyler also sustained precedents set by earlier chief executives that enlarged presidential power and the prerogatives of the office. Tyler apparently relished flexing his presidential muscle, as was the case when he asserted executive privilege in order to withhold information from Congress concerning the administration's diplomatic actions in opposition to the Quintuple Treaty. Remarkably, what previously had been deemed an intolerable usurpation of legislative authority now appeared quite in keeping with republican principle. Tragically for John Tyler and the future of the American republic he so dearly loved, his calculated and at times reckless pursuit of a proslavery diplomatic agenda undermined constitutional restraints on executive power and mocked his pretension to being one of the post-Revolutionary generation's most vigilant guardians of Jeffersonian republicanism.

★ ★ ★ ★ ★ ★ ★ ★ ★ ★ ★

Avoiding War & Preserving Peace

4

The peace of the Country when I reached Washington, on the 6th day of April 1841, was suspended by a thread, but we converted that thread into a chain cable of sufficient strength to render that peace secure, and to enable the Country to weather the storms of faction by which it was in every direction assailed.

★ *John Tyler to Daniel Webster, March 12, 1846*

Blessed are the peacemakers.

★ *John Tyler toast, July 30, 1842*

They do not deem it necessary or expedient to go into a specification of the acts of the agent, who was employed in a secret service, or to inquire into the propriety of employing agents for secret service within the limits of the United States, and paying them out of the contingent fund for foreign intercourse.

★ *Majority Report, Committee to Investigate*
  "Official Misconduct of the Late Secretary of State,"
    June 9, 1846

oung Queen Victoria was understandably perplexed about the American president's unique proposal. In only the fourth year of her glorious and lengthy reign, the relatively inexperienced and impressionable monarch confessed to having never heard of such a thing. Prime Minister Sir Robert Peel shared Her Majesty's bewilderment at President John Tyler's amazing diplomatic gaffe. As he explained in late October 1841 to his twenty-two-year-old sovereign in the formal and deferential third person required when addressing the queen, "Sir Robert Peel humbly assures your Majesty that he fully participates in the surprise which your Majesty so naturally expresses at the extraordinary intimation conveyed to Mr. Fox by the President of the United States." "The measure contemplated by the President," Peel continued, "is a perfectly novel one, a measure of a hostile and unjustifiable character adopted with pacific intentions."

The more experienced and savvy prime minister had put the best face on Tyler's incomprehensible actions by assuring the queen that the brash American president undoubtedly was motivated by "pacific intentions" and earnestly desired "to prevent the interruption of amicable relations with this country." But just in case he was misreading the president's intentions, "Sir Robert Peel assures your Majesty that he has advised such measures of preparation to be taken in respect to the amount of disposable naval force, and the position of it, as without bearing the character of menace, or causing needless disquietude and alarm, may provide for an unfavourable issue of our present differences with the United States." What Peel could not have known, but sagely intuited, was that Tyler was not so much a clumsy and inept diplomat as an alarmed and concerned statesman horrified at the prospect of America once again being at war with the world's most powerful nation.[1]

What had prompted this candid exchange between Queen Victoria and Prime Minister Peel, and what exactly was it that John Tyler had suggested to cause such disbelief and consternation at Buckingham Palace and 10 Downing Street? Peel's intuition about the American president's actions proved correct. Tyler had panicked because, as he later confessed to Secretary of State Daniel Webster, in the first five or six months of his presidency a devastating conflict with Britain appeared imminent and the "peace of the country had been suspended by a thread." The dangerously heightened tensions in Anglo-American relations arose from a lingering dispute over the boundary between the state of Maine and British North America, and from the legacy of violence and discord that had erupted on the Niagara frontier several years earlier when Canadians had destroyed an American vessel, the *Caroline*.

But during the fall of 1841 the contentious issue that threatened to precipitate hostilities at any moment was the possible execution of a British subject, Alexander McLeod, a perpetrator in the burning of the *Caroline* who was charged by the state of New York for the murder of an American named Amos Durfee. It was widely anticipated in both Europe and the United States that the execution of McLeod would lead Britain to recall its minister from Washington, sever diplomatic relations, and declare war on the American republic. To avert such a predictable scenario, John Tyler told British minister Henry S. Fox that if McLeod were to be executed the president intended to refuse Fox his passport and forcibly keep him in the United States under virtual house arrest.

Tyler's threat was quite bold and shocking from a staid and proper nineteenth-century diplomat's point of view. One might expect such a strong-arm routine from a future imperial president—fellow southerner Lyndon Baines Johnson springs to mind—but such gauche behavior was completely out of character for the refined and sophisticated Tyler. In this context it becomes comprehensible why Tyler's high-handed and audacious breach of diplomatic protocol had so puzzled Queen Victoria and Prime Minister Peel.[2]

Minister Fox reported back to London that in the course of making this "extraordinary intimation, privately and personally," the clearly upset and agitated American president had opened the conversation by expressing his sincere desire to avoid war and to preserve peace with Britain. "We have done all that we legally could do," Tyler explained, "to procure McLeod's release and prevent his execution and we have failed." In an even more amazing admission for a self-declared believer in the sanctity of states' rights, Tyler acknowledged that the American Constitution was deficient in providing for federal jurisdiction in such cases. Asking for British patience and understanding in this embarrassing matter, the American president promised Fox that his administration would propose legislation to change the federal law of the United States to guarantee the national government's control of similar situations in the future.

President Tyler aimed to correct an unresolved constitutional issue concerning ultimate authority over foreign relations in a federal system. In a fascinating display of expedient political role reversal, this dispute between the United States and New York State over who had jurisdiction in the McLeod case pitted President John Tyler, the erstwhile champion of states' rights who favored national primacy in this instance, against Governor William H. Seward of New York, a normally ardent nationalist who argued for the primacy of state authority in settling the issue. After McLeod was acquitted and the Anglo-American crisis temporarily defused, the Tyler administration, true to the president's pledge to Minister Fox, backed legislation that would eliminate future federal-state disputes that impinged on the nation's foreign policy. As a result of the administration's efforts, Congress passed and Tyler signed the 1842 Remedial Justice Act, which asserted federal authority in cases such as that of Alexander McLeod.[3]

President Tyler's somewhat irrational and clearly bizarre solution to the McLeod crisis that he proposed during his conversation with Minister Fox was motivated by a mixture of dread and defiance. The normally unflappable Virginian justifiably abhorred the prospect of war with Great Britain because he knew the United States was unprepared for a sustained struggle on the seas with the powerful and technologically advanced British navy. A keen observer of the international scene since his days at William and Mary under the tutelage of Bishop James Madison, John Tyler nervously and helplessly watched from the sidelines as a world colossus was being created. In the late 1830s the British aggressively were expanding their commercial and territorial empire in Central and East Asia, the Mediterranean, and the Western Hemisphere.

Possessing almost complete control of the world's seaways and fighting two imperial wars simultaneously, one in China and the other in Afghanistan, Great Britain's majestic and intimidating global reach was frighteningly apparent to Tyler and other informed American leaders. But it was a brilliant British naval victory in November 1840 over Egyptian forces at the presumably impregnable Syrian fortress of St. Jean d'Acre that awed and inspired military strategists everywhere. The reason for all the excitement among the world's naval professionals and amateur buffs alike was the fact that for the first time in maritime history steam warships had been successfully used in a coordinated sea and land campaign. For fearful and insecure Americans, Acre appeared to foretell the dawn of a new age in warfare.

These fears about Britain's new mode of sea power were publicly aired in a report submitted to the House of Representatives on February 13, 1841, by the Foreign Affairs Committee. Francis W. Pickens, chairman of the committee and author of the report, was a wealthy Anglophobic aristocrat who owned more than 200 slaves and three plantations in his home state of South Carolina, and also had sizable land holdings in Alabama and Mississippi. Pickens's report ostensibly was to focus on what were deemed the twin outrages of the sinking of the *Caroline* and British intransigence in the McLeod affair, but instead became a broad and sweeping indictment of the British Empire's avaricious global designs. As the world's undisputed nineteenth-century hegemon, Britain "moves steadily upon her objects," Pickens charged, "with an ambition that knows no bounds. And wherever she has had a conflict of interest she has rarely yielded to any power."

He also denounced Great Britain as an international menace that "presents to the civilized world the spectacle of the greatest military and commercial power in combination ever known." British naval supremacy had been on display for the entire world to see at the battle of Acre, and Pickens feared that "steam power has recently brought us so near together, that in the event of any future conflict, *war with its effects* will be precipitated upon with much more rapidity than formerly." Uncertain how the nation might defend its coasts from the threat of steam-powered vessels, Representative Pickens recommended quiet and firm diplomacy to ease Anglo-American tensions.[4]

Pickens's inflammatory accusations about Britain's policy of global intimidation created a loud uproar at home and abroad. John Quincy Adams and several other House members wanted the report sent back to the Foreign Affairs Committee for a total revision. After considerable debate on the House floor, Pickens refused to rewrite the report. In Britain the Pickens report was widely denounced in leading newspapers as being provocative and an insult to British honor.

From neighboring Canada, Governor-General Lord Sydenham provided a calmer and more accurate analysis of the political scene in Washington. He wrote his friend Lord John Russell in London, "You must not in the least heed their speeches and declarations in their popular assemblies" because the Americans "are such a set of braggadocios and there is a submission on the part of their public men to pander to this vanity and self-sufficiency, that their language is always in the superlative but their acts are very different." Lord Sydenham anticipated "no cause for alarm of war being rashly entered upon" because, along with other restraining factors, "the South have their cotton interest as well as their slave fears" to consider. In the end, Sydenham in Canada and Pickens in the United States came to the same conclusion — war could be averted and peace preserved through the patient diplomatic efforts of responsible leaders in London and Washington.[5]

Although Vice President–elect John Tyler apparently offered no public comment on Pickens's anti-British allegations, he shared the South Carolinian's Anglophobic outlook. Several years earlier as a member of the Senate, Tyler had made similar charges about the menacing nature of the British Empire. More to the point, barely a week after the report was released President-elect William Henry Harrison and Tyler did their own versions of "twisting the Lion's tail" at a gala celebration of George Washington's birthday in Richmond. Such annual tributes to Washington were commonplace, but the 1841 birthday commemoration hosted an especially distinguished gathering because the Commonwealth of Virginia had decided to belatedly honor with the presentation of magnificently crafted ceremonial swords nine of its native sons who had fought heroically in the War of 1812.

In describing the ceremony the *Southern Literary Messenger* claimed that with "the exception of the welcome given to the good La Fayette, it is probable that the Metropolis of Virginia was never graced with a more imposing assemblage, nor the scene of more interesting ceremonies than occurred on the 22nd February, 1841, the birthday of the Father of his Country." Some five or six thousand people turned out to witness a parade of "the military of the city, in their best and most brilliant array," which "added splendor to the spectacle," and to hear stirring patriotic speeches by Harrison, Tyler, and other dignitaries. Lest there be any doubt about the highly symbolic nature of the presentation of the swords marking the earlier victory over Great Britain, the *Messenger* made clear that a "new generation has sprung up since the last contest with our ancient and powerful foe; and it may not be amiss to recall to the minds of our youth, some of those heroic deeds which held in check, if they did not entirely humble, the lofty pretensions of British pride."[6]

In the wake of Britain's stunning victory at Acre and the arrest of McLeod in Lewiston, New York, both of which came in November 1840 at the time of the American presidential election, U.S. diplomats in Europe were keeping a sharp eye out for any threatening naval maneuvers conducted by their nation's primary rival. On the correct assumption that Daniel Webster was to be appointed secretary of state in the incoming Harrison-Tyler administration, Lewis Cass, the U.S. minister to France, confidentially offered advice to his new chief from Paris in early March 1841. Cass, no friend of Britain's, confided to Webster, "I suppose you are aware of the instructions given by the British Ministry to their Minister at Washington. The subject is no secret here and was freely spoken of to me by *one who knew*. If McLeod is executed, the Minister is to leave the United States. It is the casus belli. But any sentence, short of this, is not to lead to this result."

The American minister in Paris also conveyed alarming news about what appeared to be British war preparations: "Fourteen steam frigates would be ready to be upon the coast of the United States, if necessary, in the month of June, and that the first stroke would be at New York." "Of one thing I am sure," Cass continued. "There is a bad feeling against us in England, and this feeling is daily and manifestly augmenting." Cass also revealed that he fully comprehended the significance of Britain's triumph at Acre: "The next war upon the ocean is to see greater changes, than have occurred in naval operations since the invention of gunpowder. The events upon the Syrian coast have opened all eyes here to surpassing effects of steam. What is to prevent a fleet of steam frigates from being, as it were, its own messenger, and entering at once into the Harbour of New York."[7]

Lewis Cass's shocking revelations about American vulnerability to a future British naval attack probably were presented by Secretary of State Webster for consideration at one of the Harrison administration's initial cabinet meetings. One might assume as well that Webster later discussed the implications of the Cass message at length with Tyler when he became president. If he did, it would help explain why Tyler decided to deny Minister Fox his passports in the event of McLeod's execution.

In concluding his message to Webster, the American minister in Paris had strongly recommended quick action by the federal government to strengthen the country's coastal fortifications and urged "that every exertion be used to create without delay a steam marine." In the early months of his presidency Tyler heeded Minister Cass's warnings and in July introduced legislation in Congress to strengthen the nation's land and sea defenses. Not until the fall of 1841, however, when Abel P. Upshur was appointed secretary of the navy in the reshuffled cabinet did the administration begin to develop a steamship navy.

After several months of intense political and sectional wrangling, Congress passed the fortifications bill on September 4, with a total appropriation of $2,226,401 for seaboard and frontier defenses. The clear danger of war with Great Britain was apparent to all and had spurred members of the House and Senate to action. But even so it was quite a remarkable achievement for the embattled Tyler administration to have succeeded in getting through the hostile Whig-controlled Congress legislation that provided for military expenditures approximately three times larger than the average annual amount appropriated in the previous decade.

In the weeks following the passage of the fortifications bill, both the Peel ministry in London and the Tyler administration in Washington took actions that anticipated a complete breakdown in Anglo-American relations. Each side seriously contemplated war. To suggest that John Tyler's generation of Americans somehow enjoyed an "age of free security" without threat of foreign aggression or war, as one prominent historian nostalgically did in the midst of the angst-ridden Cold War era of the 1960s, was absurd and had no basis in fact. In reality, President Tyler's first year in office proved to be an especially tense and dangerous time in the history of the early American republic.[8]

For their part, British leaders did not panic and took the crisis in stride. After a cabinet meeting at which the possibility of war was discussed, Prime Minister Peel decided that precautionary measures were in order. Britain moved to strengthen its fortifications at Halifax, Nova Scotia, and Bermuda, two of its strongholds in North American waters from which the British navy might launch an attack on the United States. Aware that Britain was preparing for war based upon the earlier intelligence he had received from Minister Cass and more recent warnings from other informants, Secretary Webster dispatched a secret agent to assess the extent of the British military buildup in the West Indies. Webster's spy in the Caribbean was a Bostonian named Albert Fitz who had been recommended by fellow New Englander John Quincy Adams. Fitz's espionage was meticulous and time consuming. His report was not filed until July 1842, just as the crisis in Anglo-American relations was being resolved, but it highlighted how strongly the key island of Bermuda had been fortified and emphasized how seriously the British had taken the possibility of war with the United States.[9]

Albert Fitz's mission also revealed the Tyler administration's fascination with espionage and international intrigue, and its propensity to use secret agents to achieve diplomatic and political goals in a decidedly undemocratic fashion. Secrecy was the rule; undercover agent Fitz would soon be followed by Duff Green, the "ambassador of slavery" in Europe, and provocateur John B. Hogan in the Dominican Republic. Webster also used infiltrators to disrupt the activities of the Patriot Hunters, who were ultra-nationalist Americans seeking war with Great Britain in the hope it would end British rule in Canada. Arguably the most successful covert agent of the Tyler era was Francis O. J. Smith, whose propaganda activities helped convince the leaders and residents of Maine to accept the northeastern boundary settlement contained in the Webster-Ashburton Treaty of 1842. That Albert Fitz understood the game Webster and Tyler were playing was made clear when he concluded his report with the assurance that "I have confidence in asserting, that in no instance, has a suspicion been excited of the purpose of my tour, and that the whole transaction, remains a profound secret." Of course that was exactly what his superiors wanted.[10]

The acquittal of Alexander McLeod on October 12, 1841, momentarily had eased Anglo-American difficulties after the news arrived in London several weeks later. The slow pace of transatlantic communications in an age of sail, before regular steamship service was inaugurated and when the use of an Atlantic cable still lay in the future, had made Tyler's injudicious talk of detaining Minister Fox irrelevant by the time it was considered by the British government. The bemused correspondence between Queen Victoria and Prime Minister Peel about President Tyler's unconventional and impudent proposal actually occurred after the McLeod issue had been favorably resolved in North America.

Luckily for the American president, he did not suffer any serious consequences for his diplomatic misstep. But Tyler's good fortune should not obscure the fact that his actions were taken very seriously in Britain and probably indelibly shaped the Peel government's perception of the unknown and untested Virginian for the remainder of his presidential term. Tyler's proposal to Fox was gutsy and audacious, and for the astute Prime Minister Peel it also was the awkward response of a man apparently dedicated to preserving the peace between the two English-speaking nations. On another occasion several months later, Peel again had the measure of the man when he commented to Foreign Secretary Lord Aberdeen that President Tyler's remarks about the crisis with England in his first annual message were "ambiguous, concealing peaceful desires and intentions under blustering words." Despite his courtly manner and genteel demeanor, a posture that some of his critics mistook for softness and a lack of resolve, John Tyler was becoming an assertive statesman willing to take risks to achieve his diplomatic goals.[11]

The relaxation in tensions between Britain and America following McLeod's acquittal proved to be short-lived. Just a few weeks later a slave revolt aboard the *Creole*, a brig plying the interstate slave trade between the east coast port of Hampton Roads, Virginia, and the Gulf port of New Orleans, reignited the crisis. The *Creole* was carrying a cargo of tobacco and 135 slaves, and in addition to Captain Robert Ensor and his crew, a few whites traveled as passengers, including a man named John Hewell, who owned 39 of the slaves on board.

Just over a week into the voyage, on the evening of November 7, nineteen of the slaves mutinied and took control of the ship after killing Mr. Hewell and severely injuring the captain and three of his crew. Their leader, Madison Washington, no doubt a Virginia-born slave appropriately named for two founding fathers dedicated to American freedom and individual liberty, acted in the spirit of his namesakes and directed the ship to Nassau in the Bahamian Islands, a British colony in which slavery had been abolished by the Emancipation Act of 1833. Evidently the exhilarating news that American slaves, no matter the mode of their arrival, were to be granted their freedom once setting foot on British soil spread like a contagion throughout the South's slave quarters and inspired dreams of liberation among all those held as human chattel.

After some sporadic diplomatic and legal wrangling between American consul John Bacon and British colonial officials, the *Creole* slaves, ultimately even including Madison Washington and his band of mutineers, were set free by the Bahamian authorities. "Thus ended," in the opinion of one prominent historian, an often ignored episode in the chronicles of slave resistance and black revolt that was in fact "the most successful slave rebellion in American history, achieved with British collaboration."

The abolitionist faithful on both sides of the Atlantic, however, were more prescient than later historians and quickly grasped the full import of Madison Washington's actions in their battle to destroy the South's peculiar institution. British and American antislavery societies immediately mobilized a memorial campaign to convince Lord Aberdeen not to bow to the Tyler administration's diplomatic pressure to reverse the earlier decision by British colonial officials in the Bahamas to free the *Creole* slaves. Black abolitionists in America especially rejoiced at Washington's courageous blow for freedom, and at the 1843 National Negro Convention in Buffalo, New York, the young antislavery zealot Henry Highland Garnett praised the liberator of the *Creole* as "that bright star of freedom" who "took his station in the constellation of true heroism."[12]

News of the *Creole* mutiny and the liberation of its slave cargo in Nassau, the capital city of the Bahamian island of New Providence, slowly filtered back to the United States mainland. Not surprisingly, the British decision to free the *Creole* slaves aroused strong feelings of protest throughout the slaveholding South and incited bitter exchanges between the proslavery and antislavery forces in Congress. Word of this latest British assault on the legitimacy of the peculiar institution came too late for President Tyler to address in his first annual message of early December. But later that month Secretary of State Webster informed Minister Edward Everett, who only recently had assumed his posting to the Court of St. James, of this fresh irritant and complication in the nation's continuing crisis with Britain. Webster correctly predicted to Everett that the freeing of the *Creole* slaves in the Bahamas "is likely to give us new & great trouble."

Meanwhile in London, Foreign Minister Lord Aberdeen, after discussing the matter with Prime Minister Peel, solemnly informed Queen Victoria that "several questions of great difficulty" with the United States "might, at any moment, lead to consequences of the most disastrous nature." To avoid the calamity of a third war with the American republic, Aberdeen proposed the appointment of a special mission to Washington to "bring all these differences promptly to an adjustment." Lord Aberdeen suggested to the queen that Alexander Baring, Lord Ashburton, would be the appropriate envoy to undertake the all-important task of preserving peace with the United States, and sought her consent to his appointment.[13]

A few days after addressing the queen, Lord Aberdeen hastily arranged a meeting with American Minister Everett to tell him of the Ashburton mission. Everett was surprised to learn that in order to resolve the contentious issues dividing the two nations, "her Majesty's Government had determined to take a decisive step toward that end by sending a special Minister to the United States, with full power to make a final settlement of all matters in dispute." Such a mission of course undercut any role Everett might play in the negotiations and relegated him to the position of being a mere bystander to these momentous events. If he was chagrined, Everett initially gave no hint of his annoyance and rebounded nicely. He assured Lord Aberdeen "that the President had nothing more at heart than an honorable adjustment of the matters in discussion between the two countries."

Edward Everett also informed the British leader that he "anticipated the happiest results from this overture." Lord Aberdeen quickly corrected the American minister, who obviously had betrayed his desire to remain in the diplomatic loop and participate in the action. The foreign secretary emphatically clarified "that it was more than an *overture*;—that Lord Ashburton would go with full powers to make a definitive arrangement on every point in discussion between the two countries." After his interview with Lord Aberdeen, and on the day the Ashburton mission formally was announced in the London *Times*, Everett conveyed this propitious and exciting intelligence to his chief in Washington.[14]

Tyler and Webster welcomed the news about the Ashburton mission with a sigh of relief. The secretary was especially pleased to learn that his old friend and occasional business associate would be England's "messenger of peace," as Ashburton had characterized himself in a letter to Webster announcing his plans to arrive in America by late February or early March.

From the British perspective, as Everett reported to Webster, "Lord Aberdeen mentioned particularly, that his known friendly relations with you were among the chief inducements to select Lord Ashburton." That, and the fact that Aberdeen had little faith in the ability and overall competence of Minister Fox to carry out such delicate negotiations, made the well-connected Alexander Baring an ideal choice.

Lord Ashburton was a wealthy banker and head of the House of Baring, Britain's premier financial institution. He owned large land holdings in the United States and had married an American woman, Ann Louisa Bingham, daughter of former Senator William Bingham of Pennsylvania. For a number of years Daniel Webster had served as legal counsel and representative of the House of Baring in the United States. He and his wife, Caroline, had stayed with the Ashburtons at their English estate, the Grange, during their tour of the British Isles in 1839, a trip that was partially funded by Baring Brothers. The Webster-Ashburton connection was a cozy social and monetary relationship between members of the American and British ruling classes, but it reeked of corruption and insider favoritism. Such obvious cronyism and blatant conflict of interest at the highest levels of government offended and enraged the critics of the Tyler administration on all points of the political spectrum.[15]

Even before the British envoy's much anticipated arrival in the United States in early April 1842 at Annapolis, Maryland, after a stormy and prolonged Atlantic passage, the *Creole* controversy had stormed up and darkened the horizon of Anglo-American relations. It was just as Secretary Webster had predicted. The American public and Congress were in an uproar. Webster instructed Minister Everett: "You will make the substance known to Lord Aberdeen, by relating it to him, or in any other way. He will at once see what excitement these occurrences occur in the South, and I doubt not will take proper steps to prevent recurrence. The Colonial authorities should be directed not to interfere in such cases, to set slaves at liberty, nor to withhold assistance from any vessel, brought in by mutiny, or driven in by stress of weather." And although Lord Ashburton "deeply regretted the occurrence," he too "thought it would be a source of greater difficulty than any other" because he suspected "Great Britain would never make compensation for the liberated slaves."

Ashburton's premonition was confirmed even before his departure from England. Not only were the innocent slaves released in Nassau in the Bahamas to remain free without compensation to the American owners, but in an even more egregious affront to the Tyler administration, the Crown law officers were unanimous in their decision "against the power to deliver up the 19 slaves guilty of murder in the Creole." Lord Ashburton well knew, as did his American counterpart Daniel Webster, that this legal judgment denying the extradition of Madison Washington and the other mutineers meant trouble for the cause of peace.[16]

To his dismay and annoyance, President John Tyler faced an impossible predicament. He was under intense pressure from his fellow slaveholders to defend the national honor against this latest British outrage and to restore the *Creole* slaves to their rightful owners. Calls for redress and compensation from Great Britain were heard throughout the South. Widespread condemnation and denunciation of these all-too-frequent, high-handed British maritime abuses appeared in the editorial columns of influential newspapers in New Orleans, Charleston, Baltimore, Nashville, Mobile, and Washington, D.C. In Congress, Senator Henry Clay of Kentucky expressed concern that the nation's coastal trade was in jeopardy and at the mercy of British caprice. Senator Thomas Hart Benton of Missouri accused British authorities of condoning lawlessness and mutiny.

Demanding immediate redress, John C. Calhoun of South Carolina, the Senate's leading defender of the peculiar institution and the property rights of slaveowners, called on the Tyler administration to defend the nation's honor and dignity. Calhoun introduced a sharply worded Senate resolution requesting that the executive branch transmit the "correspondence relative to the actions of the authorities of Nassau, New Providence, in the imprisonment of slaves charged with mutiny and murder, the refusal to surrender them to the United States consul for trial in the United States, and the liberation of the slaves, all of said slaves being a part of the cargo of the United States brig, *Creole*." But President Tyler, with a sense of embarrassment and helplessness, rightly suspected from the onset of the crisis that whatever diplomatic or legal blandishments the U.S. government might make, the Peel ministry adamantly would refuse to return the *Creole* mutineers and slaves.[17]

Despite the administration's best efforts to defuse the issue by releasing the entire *Creole* correspondence and publishing Webster's strong protest to the British government, the public outcry did not subside, and if anything, intensified. The *Madisonian*, official mouthpiece of the administration, lamely defended Tyler's handling of the *Creole* affair and demanded that Britain recognize that the institution of slavery was sanctioned by the nation's Constitution and laws, and must be respected as such by all other nations in the international community. Not at all satisfied with the federal government's ineffective diplomacy, the legislatures of Louisiana, Mississippi, and Tyler's home state, Virginia, passed resolutions denouncing this blatant British transgression of American sovereignty and national honor and demanding immediate compensation.

The call from the state capital by the Virginia General Assembly for his administration to gain prompt diplomatic atonement from Britain surely rankled and irritated President Tyler. It had only been a year earlier at Richmond's glorious celebration of Washington's birthday, with its patriotic speeches and anti-British agenda, that he and the since-departed Harrison had been the toast of the town. Now, by implication, Tyler stood accused of toadying to England. And then there was the Mississippi resolution, which was perhaps even more galling to someone who fancied himself a loyal defender of slavery. The Mississippi legislators charged that without monetary restitution and the return of the *Creole* slaves to their rightful owners, "the slaveholdings States would have most just cause to apprehend that the American flag is powerless to protect American property: that the Federal Government is not sufficiently energetic in the maintenance and preservation of their peculiar rights, and that these rights, therefore, are in imminent danger."[18]

The perceived ineptitude of the Tyler-Webster duo in dealing with the *Creole* case and other grievances against England made them figures of fun and ridicule for some of their countrymen. Abolitionist editor Joshua Leavitt, who just weeks earlier had claimed that the president had fathered children with his female slaves, was among those who seriously questioned the Tyler administration's competence in conducting the nation's foreign affairs. Upon learning of the forthcoming Ashburton special mission, Leavitt predicted to his friend Joseph Sturge that the Peel ministry's peace initiative would fail. A leader in the British and Foreign Anti-Slavery Society, Sturge had embarked the previous year on an antislavery pilgrimage to the United States and had sought an interview with slaveowner Tyler, but was ignored by the American president. In the midst of the *Creole* crisis, Leavitt wrote Sturge that "Lord Ashburton will accomplish nothing with the poor imbecile at the head of our Government & the poor debauchee his prime Minister."

Another severe critic of Webster and Tyler, albeit from the other end of the political spectrum, was James Henry Hammond of South Carolina. A wealthy slaveowner, disunionist, and early advocate of southern independence, Hammond in a diary entry privately vented his anger at the British seizure of the American ship and their refusal to "give up the mutineers of the Creole." He feared the United States was "on the eve of a conflict with England," a war from which we "should suffer much." Then, sounding the same refrain as abolitionist Leavitt, Hammond gave his critique of the administration's diplomacy: "With such a stupid imbecile as Tyler at the head of Affairs and such an unprincipled and cowardly Sec. of State as Webster we should fare badly for a time. They are bent on peace. Webster is in the pay of the great English bankers, the Barings, the head of which House, Lord Ashburton is now on his way as a Special Ambassador to this Country." Although this was a secret expression of his disillusionment with Tyler and Webster, Hammond probably openly shared his opinions with his neighbors and slaveholder friends in South Carolina and the other slave states.[19]

Remarkably, two politically active Americans with radically different ideologies expressed the same opinion of Tyler and privately labeled the tenth president an imbecile. Although not privy to either Leavitt's or Hammond's insulting appraisals of his mental capacity, Tyler knew of the widespread dissatisfaction with his administration's handling of the *Creole* matter. This public perception of his failure to defend the national honor was frustrating and annoying to a politician who proudly proclaimed his patriotism and faithful commitment to the accomplishment of America's national destiny. The *Creole* also posed a moral dilemma for John Tyler. From the beginning of his public career, Tyler had been on record as opposing the international slave trade, as his father had been before him. As a U.S. senator he had tried and failed to eliminate the slave trade in the District of Columbia, after having been literally sickened by the gut-wrenching sight of slave coffles trudging through the streets and witnessing the spectacle of men, women, and children being sold on the auction block in the nation's capital.

It must have been unsettling for President Tyler to reconcile his principled opposition to the international slave trade and his revulsion to the buying and selling of human beings in the District of Columbia with the political necessity of having to defend the coastal slave trade as an extension of the nation's internal slave trade. Contending that there was a moral difference between these equally despicable and inhumane practices was an exercise in sophistry. Surely, Tyler recognized that fact and understood the moral inconsistency of such an argument. Grappling on a daily basis with the ambiguities and frustrations presented by the *Creole* quandary in his negotiations with the British envoy made him contentious and difficult to work with. Throughout the course of his mission to America, Lord Ashburton frequently found President Tyler out of sorts and registered numerous complaints about the president's ill humor in his reports back home to Foreign Minister Aberdeen.

Upon his arrival in the United States Lord Ashburton was appalled by the chaotic and unruly status of politics in the American republic. He found the executive branch and the Congress locked in a bitter power struggle over the direction of public policy. The English envoy's initial impression of President Tyler also was unfavorable. Ashburton feared for the success of his mission because he believed Tyler was a "weak & conceited" person and a vacillating, indecisive, and powerless leader. The British freeing of the *Creole* slaves and mutineers was a major sticking point in the negotiations. "The President as a Virginian," Ashburton explained to his superiors in London, "has a strong opinion about [the] Creole case, and is not a little disposed to be obstinate on the subject."

On another occasion after several more weeks of diplomatic haggling, Ashburton said Tyler remained highly agitated and "he is very sore and testy about the Creole." However, Ashburton did not let President Tyler's short-tempered disposition or the partisan political bickering then prevailing in Washington blind him to the reality of American power. He candidly advised Lord Aberdeen: "I would further discharge my duty by cautioning you not to mistake or undervalue the *power* of this country. You will be told that it is a mass of ungovernable & unmanageable anarchy, and so it is in many respects." But, Ashburton continued, "With all these disadvantages I believe that the energies & power of the country would be found to be immense in the case of war and that the jarring elements would unite for that purpose." Nonetheless, the English aristocrat could not resist ending his message with a condescending and disdainful jab at the American republic. He told Aberdeen that to "humour the wild Beast" might be Britain's best and safest course.[20]

Lord Ashburton's healthy respect for the United States as a dangerous potential foe kept him at the negotiating table throughout the oppressively hot and humid summer of 1842. He longed to escape the debilitating heat of Washington and return home to England's more salubrious climate. Occasionally, however, the tedium of hammering out the terms of an agreement was relieved by amiable dinners with Secretary and Mrs. Webster, glittering official functions at the White House, and numerous lavish social receptions in his honor to present him to the citizens of the city. For all his grumping about being in the provinces among parochial folk, the Englishman relished the hearty fresh food served by Americans and clearly preferred such simple fare to the rich sauces and heavy casseroles of French cuisine.

Much to his delight, Lord Ashburton attended a magnificent June wedding reception at the White House for James Monroe's granddaughter and discovered that the Americans could entertain with the best of them. The president's daughter-in-law, Mrs. Robert Tyler, graciously hosted the reception, filling in for the gravely ill First Lady. Over one hundred people were in attendance, including members of the Monroe family, the Websters, Dolley Madison, several prominent politicians, and representatives of the diplomatic corps. Ashburton also found that amidst all the political chaos and partisan bickering of the Washington scene some civility and decency in social relations still existed.

John Quincy Adams, one of Tyler's fiercest critics in Congress, was a guest, and much to the taciturn former president's surprise, he and his family thoroughly enjoyed the party. President Tyler "led the bride to the supper-table" and asked Adams to do the honor of escorting the hostess. The next day Adams recorded his impressions of an enchanting evening: "There was dancing in the now gorgeously furnished East Room, and an elegant supper. The courtesies of the President and Mrs. R. Tyler to their guests were all that the most accomplished European court could have displayed"—effusive praise indeed from the world-traveled John Quincy Adams, an American statesman who in his earlier diplomatic career had witnessed the best the European courts of Paris, London, St. Petersburg, and Berlin had to offer.[21]

President Tyler reveled in playing the affable and courteous host at these extravagant White House entertainments. His generous hospitality was well known to his countrymen and his ability to put his guests at ease duly impressed visiting dignitaries, including literary notables such as Charles Dickens and Washington Irving. Undoubtedly, for Tyler the gaiety of fun-filled parties provided relief from a tedious regimen and took the edge off what otherwise was a demanding and pressure-laden job. As Dickens observed on meeting and conversing with President Tyler, the leader of the American republic "looked somewhat worn and anxious, and well he might, being at war with everybody."

On at least one occasion Tyler privately confirmed what Dickens had sensed—being president was a high-stress occupation. In a letter to his Williamsburg friend, attorney Robert McCandlish, he provided a fascinating glimpse into the everyday routine and busy schedule of a nineteenth-century president of the United States: "My course of life is to rise with the sun, and to work from that time until three o'clock. The order of despatching business pretty much is, first, all diplomatic matters; second, all matters connected with the action of Congress; third, matters of general concern falling under the executive control; then the reception of visitors, and despatch of private petitions. I dine at three-and-a-half o'clock, and in the evening my employments are miscellaneous—directions to Secretaries and endorsement of numerous papers." Tyler admitted he took "some short time for exercise," but "after candle-light again receive visitors, apart from all business, until ten at night, when I retire to bed." "Such is the life led by an American President," Tyler concluded, and he asked his friend, "What say you?—would you exchange the peace and quiet of your homestead for such an office?" There is no record of McCandlish's response, if there was one, to Tyler's hypothetical query.[22]

In the summer of 1842 John Tyler's harried life and political woes were exacerbated by a fellow Virginian, Congressman John Minor Botts. A former backer of Tyler, Botts was an ardent supporter of Henry Clay's legislative program who became outraged by the "acting" president's vetoes of the bank and tariff bills and his flagrant betrayal of Whig principles. In retaliation for Tyler's treachery, Botts took unprecedented action. He called for the president's impeachment on the charge of "high crimes and misdemeanors." The House of Representatives ultimately rejected Bott's resolution, but John Tyler had to live with the ignominy of being the first American president in history to be confronted with impeachment proceedings in Congress.

Understandably, Tyler was stung and hurt by these charges. The proud Virginian tried to disguise his pain by claiming he was too busy with his presidential duties to bother with these frivolous charges and cavalierly dismissed the talk of impeachment as the work of "madcaps." Tyler said that when "the attacks of the malignants come to my knowledge, I only hear them to despise them." But he anguished at being assailed as a "traitor" by former allies, friends, and neighbors. An exasperated Tyler asked Robert McCandlish, "Did you ever expect to see your old friend under trial for 'high crimes and misdemeanors'?" Tyler supplied his own answer to the question. Yes, he defiantly admitted, the "high crimes of sustaining the Constitution of the country I have committed, and to this I plead guilty."[23]

The tariff issue was one of the main sources of tension between the Whigs and President Tyler. His vetoes of Whig tariff legislation had been one of the reasons why Botts labeled the president a traitor and called for his impeachment. Ironically, despite his lifelong adherence to the concept of free trade and minimal duties on imports, Tyler ultimately compromised his principles by signing the highly protective tariff of 1842. Historians have been at a loss to explain Tyler's capitulation to protectionism on this occasion, although most agree he probably did so to meet the desperate revenue needs of the federal government. Some scholars also have linked Tyler's support for a protective tariff to political ambition and his attempt to garner support among northern manufacturers for a reelection bid in 1844. One of his principal biographers suggested that Tyler was weary of the constant pounding he was receiving from the Whigs and that by agreeing to the protectionist legislation he sought to ward off impeachment.[24]

There is evidence for another explanation. Apparently, President Tyler had come to believe that adopting a protective tariff was an essential first step to revive a depression-ridden American economy and restore national prosperity. Acceptance of a tariff that aided industry symbolized his transition from being solely a champion of agriculture and commerce to becoming an advocate for the promotion of domestic manufacturing as well. This shift in Tyler's thinking began before he became president. In the late 1830s he presided over a commercial convention in Norfolk, Virginia, that recommended the appropriation of state funds for internal improvements, specifically railroads and canals, and the encouragement of manufacturing. Perhaps this newly acquired commitment to governmental aid to industry reflected an evolution in Tyler's thinking about what was necessary for the United States to achieve national greatness and become a world power.[25]

Among the other indictments Representative Botts leveled against President Tyler was the charge that the executive branch had withheld information from the Congress and that the chief executive unconstitutionally had denied congressional requests for memoranda, correspondence, and pertinent documents. Technically, Botts's charge was correct because Tyler on occasion had invoked executive privilege to refuse congressional demands for information. But in the past when presidents, beginning with George Washington, had denied a congressional request for information, no member of Congress had viewed such an assertion of executive privilege as an impeachable offense.

Just prior to Lord Ashburton's arrival in the United States, for instance, President Tyler rejected a request by the House of Representatives to turn over all correspondence on the status of the negotiations with Great Britain relating to the Maine boundary dispute. In explaining his refusal of the House request, the president said that "in my judgment no communication could be made by me at this time on the subject of its resolution without detriment or danger to the public interests." Tyler's position was justifiable and in accord with precedent. Earlier chief executives, including Jefferson and Madison, had invoked the same privilege in what they deemed the national interest.[26]

In another exercise of executive power involving the use of executive agents, however, Tyler's actions were more problematic and bordered on the unconstitutional. This undercover escapade, involving the use of secret agents in Maine, began in the spring of 1841 shortly after Tyler became president. In a May meeting at Secretary of State Daniel Webster's home, Francis O. J. Smith, a seasoned Maine politician, lawyer, newspaper publisher, and venture capitalist, presented his friend with a scheme to convince the citizens and leading politicians of his home state to accept a compromise solution to the northeastern boundary dispute with Great Britain. Believing that the people of Maine were intransigent on the issue, Smith earlier had floated this same idea for a federally funded propaganda campaign in Maine to President Martin Van Buren, who judiciously had ignored what appeared to be a highly irregular and legally dubious proposal.

Secretary Webster had no such qualms and immediately accepted Smith's propaganda project. President Tyler authorized the deal in June. Webster then appointed, with the president's approval, Francis Smith as a secret agent in the employ of the State Department, to be paid $12,000 from the chief executive's secret service or contingent fund. Smith's mission was "to prepare public sentiment in Maine for a compromise of the matter through a conventional line." The boundary compromise was to include an exchange of territory between the United States and Britain, and a monetary indemnity for Maine. The tricky part of this caper, Smith explained to his co-conspirators, was to get the citizens of Maine to believe that the compromise solution had "its origin with themselves." This, Smith conceded, was "the most delicate part of the enterprise."[27]

With the Tyler administration's blessing and endorsement, Francis O. J. Smith enthusiastically undertook his well-conceived and now handsomely funded propaganda campaign. He quickly went about hiring assistants and enlisting editors to get the message out to the people of Maine about the benefits of making concessions and readily negotiating a settlement of the boundary dispute. In addition to lobbying prominent civic and business leaders, legislators, and other governmental officials, Smith and his operatives sought "to adjust the tone and direction of the party presses" and major urban newspapers. Under the *nom de plume* Agricola, Smith wrote a series of articles entitled "Northeastern Boundary—Why Not Settle It?" that originally appeared in Portland's *Christian Mirror* and then was reprinted widely in journals and newspapers throughout the state and nation.

After Smith's cadre of secret agents had softened up the Maine populace with a ten-month propaganda and lobbying blitz, Secretary of State Webster put the next phase of the plan into operation. In an attempt to convince the legislatures and governors of Maine and Massachusetts (also party to the original dispute as a claimant to the territory before Maine entered the Union) of the wisdom of accepting a compromise line, Secretary Webster enlisted the help and expertise of the renowned scholar and Harvard historian Jared Sparks. While doing research at the French Foreign Service archives in Paris, Professor Sparks had located a "red line" map of the northeast boundary that completely supported the British claims to the disputed territory. Presumably the map Sparks found was the one used by Benjamin Franklin in 1782 during the peace negotiations, although its authenticity was in question. In what now became a campaign of disinformation and subtle blackmail, Webster sent Professor Sparks with his "red line" map on a mission to Augusta, Maine, to persuade state legislators of the wisdom of compromise before this map fell into the hands of the British.[28]

Apparently the British "messenger of peace" also was party to the Sparks intrigue. Almost immediately after his landing in the United States, Lord Ashburton got in on the espionage and propaganda campaign that his friend Webster had been orchestrating in Maine and Massachusetts. Although the details and extent of Ashburton's involvement in the subterfuge are debated by historians to this day, he did pay or perhaps bribed an unidentified informant a princely sum of almost £3,000, or nearly $14,500, to promote a compromise solution to the northeast boundary dispute. Some scholars have speculated that the American informant was none other than the always cash-strapped Daniel Webster. Other historians vehemently deny Webster was on the take.

Without implicating his friend Webster, Ashburton did later explain in a letter to Foreign Secretary Lord Aberdeen how a portion of his undercover funding was spent: "The money I wrote about went to compensate Sparkes [sic] & to send him, on my first arrival, to the Governors of Maine & Massachusetts." "My informant thinks," Ashburton further confided to Aberdeen, "that without this stimulant Maine would never have yielded" to the boundary settlement he and Webster reached in August 1842.

For Sparks's disinformation efforts in frightening Maine legislators with his spurious map, the Harvard professor received more modest compensation from the parsimonious Tyler administration. When apprised of the mission's expenses, the president worried about overpaying Sparks for his services. "I can only say that I should regard $250 to Mr. Sparks for the map fully enough," Tyler informed the disbursing agent, remarking that "I do not doubt that it will satisfy him." At the very least, President Tyler's frugality with the public's money was far more consistent with his dearly held republican and states' rights principles than was his brazen meddling in Maine politics.[29]

Given that peace with Great Britain was preserved by the Webster-Ashburton agreement, the money expended from the president's contingency fund for Francis Smith's extended propaganda campaign and Jared Sparks's map escapade appeared well spent. The secretary of state certainly thought so. Several months after the treaty with Britain was ratified, Webster told his collaborator Sparks that the "grand stroke" in the successful negotiations with Ashburton "was to get the *previous* consent of Maine & Massachusetts," which in good measure had been attained through the covert work of the administration's executive agents.

But the entire secret operation abounded with ironies. For instance, had Representative John Minor Botts known exactly what the Tyler administration was up to in the state of Maine during the year before he called for impeachment, he undoubtedly would have been able to make a stronger case for the charge that the president was guilty of "gross usurpation of power." Why? Because President Tyler employed executive agents within the United States to violate a state's sovereignty and paid them through a secret service fund that was specifically designated for the executive branch's conduct of the nation's diplomacy.

Neither John Tyler nor Daniel Webster would have had the audacity to proclaim publicly that Congress intended the president's contingency fund to be used covertly for the manipulation of domestic public opinion. But with their approval, supervision, and guidance, that was what occurred. Congressional intent was ignored and the citizens of the American republic became the propaganda targets of their own government. If believers in republican principle had known of the Tyler administration's secret actions, which were not subject to congressional oversight, they would have had direct evidence to substantiate a charge that President Tyler was guilty of the gross misuse of executive power. A decade earlier when the shoe was on the other foot, John Tyler, as a senator dedicated to states' rights, would have howled if Andrew Jackson had deigned to use such tactics to subvert the political process in the sovereign state of Virginia. Not surprisingly, two could play this game. Unbeknownst to President Tyler and a host of other Anglophobes who regularly decried Britain's alleged tampering and control of the nation's destiny, Lord Ashburton was in fact using "British gold" to undermine and corrupt the workings of the American republic.[30]

Perhaps Secretary Webster was guilty of a selective lapse of memory when he later pridefully boasted to Professor Sparks about his "master stroke" in bringing the leaders of Maine and Massachusetts to "previous consent." His faulty recollection minimized the touch-and-go nature of the negotiations during those hot summer days in 1842. Webster had made this clear to Minister Everett in late June when he wrote that our "movement for the last ten days, if any has been made, has been rather backward." "The boundary business," Webster conceded, "is by no means in a highly promising state." To the secretary of state's dismay, it appeared that an impasse in the negotiations had been reached. Lord Ashburton became so discouraged with the continued obstinacy of the Maine commissioners that he threatened to break off the talks and return to England.

At this juncture an admittedly "testy" President Tyler displayed noteworthy equanimity and came to the rescue. The president used his renowned southern charm to persuade the British diplomat to remain at the negotiating table until an agreement had been reached. He flattered the weary and exasperated Ashburton by asking, "If you cannot settle" these "unhappy controversies that now threaten the peace" of the two nations, "what man in England can?" After enduring a further stream of Tyler's honeyed words, Lord Ashburton finally capitulated and proclaimed: "Well! well! Mr. President, we must try again."

Try again they did and after several more weeks of tough bargaining and the administration's successful appeals to Maine's delegates to demonstrate their patriotism by acting in the national interest, the negotiators finally agreed to a compromise settlement of the northeastern boundary. The compromise line gave the United States more than half of the disputed northeast territory, but in return the British received a fifty-mile buffer between the American border and the St. Lawrence River, which satisfied their need for a military road to defend Quebec and the maritime provinces. In addition, the treaty included a settlement of the boundary line from Lake Superior to the Lake of the Woods that was highly favorable to the United States because it included territory rich in iron ore deposits. Without question, the resulting Webster-Ashburton Treaty was a major diplomatic accomplishment and a highlight of the Tyler presidency.[31]

Before the treaty could be finalized, however, the other knotty issues that bedeviled Anglo-American relations had to be resolved. Webster and Ashburton still confronted the question of the suppression of the African slave trade and the right of search, the *Caroline* incident, the lingering *Creole* dispute and extradition of escaped slaves, the issue of impressment, and the Oregon boundary controversy. Ashburton had no instructions on Oregon, so the two diplomats wisely decided to put that issue aside.

The contentious impressment question was resolved informally through an exchange of notes between Webster and Ashburton that temporarily satisfied both sides and preserved each country's national honor. Although he did not disavow Britain's right of impressment, Ashburton, relaying the expressed opinions of Foreign Secretary Aberdeen, assured his American counterpart that England no longer would exercise the right and that impressment of former British subjects would be curtailed. To allay the long-standing anger of his countrymen at this odious British maritime practice, Webster wrote a note on impressment for home consumption that expressed America's outrage and detailed the nation's grievances.[32]

The long-standing *Caroline* issue was defused when the American government accepted Lord Ashburton's unofficial expression of regret for the incident. President Tyler had helped the British diplomat compose the precise wording of the apology, prompting Ashburton to clarify to the Foreign Office in London that the letter was primarily intended for American domestic consumption. "My letter is more wordy than it need be but for the audience for which it was intended," Ashburton uneasily wrote Lord Aberdeen. "I hope you will not think it too apologetic."[33]

On another level, the *Caroline* incident has become enshrined in international law because of Secretary of State Webster's thoughtful and compelling rejection of Great Britain's justification for the burning and sinking of the *Caroline* as an act of self-defense. In a letter sent to British minister Henry Fox in late April 1841, a few weeks after Tyler became president, Webster argued that in order to make its case for self-defense, Britain had to "show a necessity of self-defense, instant, overwhelming, leaving no choice of means, and no moment for deliberation." Webster was duly proud of having completely demolished the British justification for the attack, and when he gave the letter to President Tyler for his perusal said, "Lord Palmerston, sir, may put that in his pipe and smoke it."[34]

Daniel Webster's nineteenth-century criteria for self-defense was adopted by the post–World War II Nuremberg Tribunal trying Nazi war crimes and has been used by the Israeli government to justify its 1976 raid on the Entebbe airport in Uganda. Apparently, the George W. Bush administration also relied on the Webster doctrine in formulating its 2002 policy statement sanctioning preemptive war. At a meeting with newspaper reporters, National Security Adviser Condoleezza Rice said that preemption against Iraq would be justified as "anticipatory self-defense," which "is not a new concept." "You know," she explained, "Daniel Webster actually wrote a very famous defense of anticipatory self-defense." In fact, Webster never used the term "anticipatory self-defense" and in his note to Minister Fox the secretary of state certainly was not making a case for the legitimacy of preemptive war.[35]

Another important feature of the Webster-Ashburton Treaty was Article VIII. It was drafted with the hands-on assistance of President Tyler, and successfully dealt with the thorny right-of-search issue as it applied to the campaign to end the African slave trade. This article called for the creation of joint British and American cruising squadrons along the west coast of Africa, each of which was "to carry in all not less than eighty guns, to enforce, separately and respectively, the laws, rights and obligations of each of the two countries, for the suppression of the Slave Trade." Each squadron would operate independently, but they could act in concert when required. At the insistence of Tyler, who betrayed a lingering distrust of Britain's traditional "right of search" pretensions, the two governments also agreed to exchange copies of their orders to the naval officers commanding the joint-cruising squadrons.

Some years later in a letter to one of his sons, former president Tyler claimed credit for the joint-cruising scheme, which he said "was adopted not only in strict coincidence with my own views, but upon my own suggestion." His pride in the provisions of Article VIII was understandable, given the fact that it finessed the British on the right of visit and search issues and was consistent with his long-held desire to end the African slave trade. The joint-cruising provision proved broadly popular with the American public and a pleasant surprise to the president's abolitionist critics, many of whom openly praised the Tyler administration for its humanitarian commitment to ridding the Atlantic world of this odious commerce in human flesh. That this pledge to halt the international slave trade was sponsored by a notorious slaveholder from Virginia clearly caught some abolitionist leaders off guard, especially the editor of the *Emancipator*, Joshua Leavitt, who was mystified by John Tyler's endorsement of Article VIII.[36]

Much more problematic was the *Creole* controversy, which had so infuriated President Tyler. Ultimately, if reluctantly, he and Webster acquiesced to the British decision not to return the ship's black mutineers and cargo of slaves. But in appended notes to the treaty they did achieve a victory of sorts by getting an important commitment from Lord Ashburton. The British envoy informed Webster that instructions would be given to "the Governors of Her Majesty's Colonies on the southern borders of the United States" to execute their local laws carefully and to be mindful "that there shall be no officious interference with American vessels driven by accident or violence into those ports." Equally important from the American perspective, the question of extradition was addressed directly in the Webster-Ashburton Treaty. Article X of the treaty stipulated that the United States and Britain agreed to the mutual extradition of persons charged with several crimes, including murder, arson, robbery, forgery, and piracy. Although mutiny was not on the list of extraditable offenses, an omission that mildly irked President Tyler, the hope was that the extradition provision would prevent future problems like those arising from the *Creole* case.

It was not until eight years after John Tyler left the White House that a final settlement of the *Creole* controversy was reached. Private citizen Tyler, now enjoying retirement from public life at Sherwood Forest, his plantation in Charles City County, Virginia, was gratified by the decision handed down in 1853 by an Anglo-American claims commission that awarded $110,330 to southern slaveowners who lost their slave property in the *Creole* mutiny. John Tyler may have believed that the long-delayed monetary award vindicated national honor, but as was the rule in the history of antebellum American slavery, the diplomatic sanctity of the South's peculiar institution meant that property rights once again had triumphed over human rights.[37]

In his euphoria at reaching a boundary settlement agreeable to Maine and Massachusetts and supremely confident that his overall diplomatic handiwork readily would be ratified by the Senate, Secretary of State Webster hosted a dinner in late July to honor his co-negotiator, Lord Ashburton. The guests at the celebratory party included the president and members of the cabinet, the Maine and Massachusetts commissioners, several senators, and a handful of other dignitaries. Webster opened the festivities with a warm toast to Queen Victoria, and Ashburton replied with a republican sentiment pleasing to his American hosts: "The President! Perpetuity to the institutions of the United States." President Tyler fittingly and with undisguised relief gave credit where credit was due with the gracious toast: "The Commissioners! Blessed are the peacemakers."

Several days after this gala and somewhat premature celebration, Lord Ashburton and Secretary Webster signed the final draft of the treaty. President Tyler submitted the treaty to the Senate on August 11, 1842. In a ploy to broadcast the administration's confidence that ratification was certain even before the Senate had voted on the treaty, President Tyler followed Webster's lead by publicly expressing his appreciation to Lord Ashburton for his contribution to the preservation of Anglo-American peace and friendship at an elaborate state dinner at the White House.[38]

However, opposition to the terms of the Webster-Ashburton Treaty in the initial Senate debate suggested it might not receive the two-thirds majority required for ratification. Senator Thomas Hart Benton, a Democrat from Missouri, attacked the agreement as a dishonorable betrayal of the national interest and charged Secretary Webster with duplicity in his use of the Sparks red-line map. In response to Benton's criticism, Whig senator William Rives of Virginia, chairman of the Foreign Relations Committee and nominal ally of the Tyler administration, strongly endorsed the treaty. Senator Rives deftly skewered his colleague Benton in floor debate by exposing the inconsistency of his argument about the use of the Sparks map.

The tide turned completely and ratification seemed assured when another prominent Democrat, John C. Calhoun, defended the treaty from its critics. Calhoun, who less than two years later would become Tyler's secretary of state, said the agreement would preserve peace with England and serve the national interest by permitting the nation to recover from a lingering and damaging economic depression. Senator Calhoun's endorsement of the Anglo-American pact proved decisive and on August 20 the Senate overwhelmingly approved the treaty by vote of 39-9. The margin of victory surprised even the ever-confident Webster and thoroughly delighted President Tyler. In a letter to his son-in-law, Thomas G. Clemson, Calhoun gave his personal assessment of the importance of the agreement: "We ratified the treaty yesterday, which will give us time and leisure to settle our domestick troubles, without any from abroad, a thing most desirable."[39]

In the fall of 1842 most Americans seemed to welcome the treaty for the same reasons John C. Calhoun had favored ratification—because it guaranteed peace and promised commercial prosperity. Surprisingly, praise for the treaty, if not for the Tyler administration, even came from antislavery publications in all quarters of the country. In Boston, the hotbed of abolitionism, *Emancipator* editor Leavitt, already puzzled by the treaty's frontal attack on the international slave trade, grudgingly conceded that the "imbecile" president and the "debauchee" secretary of state had scored a diplomatic triumph. Leavitt ate further crow by reprinting several accounts from the British press that generally admitted that America "had got the best of the bargain." In New York City's *National Anti-Slavery Standard*, David Lee Child, husband of the paper's editor Lydia Maria Child, exclaimed: "This treaty appears to me one of the most just, reasonable, and sensible, that two great nations have ever entered into." *The Philanthropist*, Gamaliel Bailey's antislavery newspaper in Cincinnati, printed the entire text of the agreement and the editor announced he was happy to "hail the treaty with delight."

But amidst all the hoopla and favorable commentary on the treaty's virtues came an unwelcome and embarrassing snub of President Tyler from New York City's uppercrust. At a dinner in the Astor House honoring Lord Ashburton before his departure for England, toasts were offered to Queen Victoria and President John Tyler. When one of the guests announced to "The Queen," great cheering and applause broke out among the audience. A similar toast to "The President" was greeted with "dead silence." Although no admirer of Tyler, Philip Hone, a Whig partisan and a prominent New Yorker who witnessed this discourteous affront, was appalled at the lack of respect for the office of the presidency.[40]

Shortly, however, cracks appeared in the façade of Anglo-American unity. Almost immediately after ratification of the treaty, abolitionists looked at Article X more closely and wondered if this provision might not be used to extradite escaped slaves residing in Canada. This was a major concern because it was estimated that 12,000 ex-slaves lived in Canada, presumably including Charles Tyler, the alleged son of President Tyler who was rumored to have fled to this British haven a few years earlier. To clarify the scope and intention of Article X, leaders of the American and Foreign Anti-Slavery Society requested an interview with Lord Ashburton.

In a meeting with the British diplomat in early September 1842, the American abolitionists asked if Article X would be used to allow slaveholders to recapture fugitive slaves. Lord Ashburton assured the gentlemen that caution had been taken to exclude fugitive slaves. Ashburton further said he had deliberately omitted mutineers and deserters from the list of extraditable crimes for fear that they could be used by slaveholders to regain runaway chattel. In any event, only the governor of Canada and not "inferior magistrates" had the authority to surrender individual refugees. Finally, Lord Ashburton proclaimed that if Article X proved injurious, Great Britain would terminate it, as the provision could remain in force only as long as both parties agreed. For his candor and dedication to safeguarding the fugitive slaves in the British colonies adjacent to or near the United States, Lewis Tappan dubbed him "*honest* Lord Ashburton."[41]

Sharing the same concerns as their American counterparts, British abolitionists also were nervous about the implications of Article X. They too sought reassurances from Lord Ashburton. Upon his return to England,

Ashburton was asked the same question from his countrymen that he had faced from abolitionists in America. Did Article X apply to escaped slaves in Canada? He gave the same answer he had given on the other side of the Atlantic—no, it did not. Ashburton also repeated the claim that in drawing up the extraditable crimes covered by the provision, the protection and safety of runaway slaves had been "anxiously in my mind throughout my negotiation." He further promised that Article X would not be used to undermine the principle that British soil was a haven for those seeking freedom.

Members of the British and Foreign Anti-Slavery Society found Ashburton's pledges all well and good. But they wanted further guarantees and thus went to Foreign Secretary Aberdeen to make sure he interpreted Article X in the same way. The Earl of Aberdeen was more cautious and circumspect than his subordinate. He told the abolitionists that protecting the welfare and security of fugitive slaves in Canada was of great interest to the Foreign Office. Although Aberdeen also pledged to prevent "the abuse of the extradition article," he made it clear that the treaty's provisions would be honored and, consequently, escaped slaves would not be exempt from Article X. Aberdeen's reply, while less satisfactory than Ashburton's had been, was acceptable to leading British abolitionists. However, this interpretative qualification of the extradition provision by two of Britain's top diplomats disturbed American slaveholders and their representatives in Congress, several of whom unsuccessfully urged the Tyler administration to abrogate Article X unilaterally.[42]

If the British appeared to be fudging on the extradition clause as it applied to fugitive slaves in Canada, President Tyler reciprocated by offering a unique reading of Article VIII, the joint-cruising provision. In his second annual message of December 1842, the president broadly interpreted the joint-cruising convention to mean that the British had relinquished their claims to the right of visit and search and "that all pretense is removed for interference with our commerce for any purpose whatever by a foreign government." The Peel ministry was aghast at Tyler's take on Article VIII. Foreign Secretary Aberdeen quickly sent a dispatch to Minister Fox, which was to be conveyed to Secretary of State Webster, that flatly rejected Tyler's interpretation and denied that Britain had given up its right of visitation.

In response to attacks by his domestic political opponents concerning President Tyler's assertion about the scope of Article VIII, Prime Minister Robert Peel felt compelled to clarify the issue. In a speech before the House of Commons he was adamantly blunt: "In signing that treaty we consider that we have abandoned no right of visitation." In private correspondence both Ashburton and Aberdeen denounced Tyler as well. "The speech," Ashburton confided to the foreign minister, "imprudently insinuated that the cruising article as founded on some abandonment, at least implied, of our right" of visit. A few weeks later, Lord Aberdeen wrote a friend that you "must know by this time why I expressed myself greatly dissatisfied with the message of the President. The manner in which he treated the subject of the Right of Search was really scandalous." Although years later John Tyler would claim he had forced the British to concede on the issue of visit and search, in early 1843 the possibility of a renewed Anglo-American crisis led him to act more prudently. He publicly admitted in a communication to the House of Representatives "we did not demand of Great Britain any formal renunciation of her pretension."[43]

The Oregon question, which had been removed from the negotiating table by Webster and Ashburton, reemerged as a source of tension in Anglo-American relations after the ratification of the treaty. All went smoothly at first. Soon after Ashburton's return to England, Foreign Secretary Aberdeen decided to take advantage of the good feelings generated by the successful negotiations and suggested to President Tyler that they seek a broad settlement on the Oregon boundary issue as well. After receiving Aberdeen's proposal from British minister Fox, President Tyler initially was receptive and seemed eager to send an envoy to London to begin negotiations. But then things took a disastrous turn. To the amazement and chagrin of Lord Aberdeen, the American president in his 1842 annual message was "most uncandid" about Oregon, just as he had been imprudent and slippery in his language about the visit and search issue. Tyler appeared to be presenting the British government with a fait accompli by claiming that the entire Oregon country was the territory of the United States, and only "a portion of which Great Britain lays claim." The president also told Congress that "I shall not delay to urge on Great Britain the importance of its early settlement."

Why had Tyler's statements so provoked and angered the British leader? Because the president claimed all of Oregon as an American possession, which totally negated the existing Anglo-American joint occupation agreement and overlooked the fact that Britain had as much claim to this territory as did the United States. President Tyler also ignored the fact that Britain had taken the diplomatic initiative. Aberdeen was annoyed at Tyler's lack of good faith and complained to his friend Lord Croker: "When he talked of pressing us to enter into negociation [sic], he had in his pocket a most friendly overture from us, which he had already answered favourably." Tyler's blatant pandering to his domestic political audience need not have agitated the good English lord. He and Ashburton well knew such behavior was standard operating procedure in the American political arena. John Tyler was no more or less slippery than were most other antebellum politicians.[44]

It was highly questionable whether or not President Tyler actually wished to negotiate an Oregon settlement during his time in office. Instead of seeking a compromise solution as he had done with the northeastern boundary controversy, Tyler stalled for time on Oregon and kept the British dangling by tossing out a bold, if impractical, initiative to resolve the Pacific Northwest dispute. This tripartite scheme involving Mexico, Great Britain, and the United States was the brainchild of Secretary of State Daniel Webster. Anticipating Great Britain's support for the plan, Webster and Tyler proposed to drop two million dollars in American claims against Mexico. In return, Mexico would cede all of California north of the thirty-second parallel, which included the harbors of San Francisco and Monterey, to the United States. If Britain urged Mexico to accept this proposal, then presumably the Tyler administration would agree to an Oregon boundary at the Columbia River.

As might be expected, the convoluted tripartite project went nowhere. Mexico had no interest in ceding two of its most splendid California harbors to the United States on the terms offered by Webster, and although Lord Ashburton favored the deal, Peel and Aberdeen declined to strong-arm the Mexicans into accepting the American proposal. A canny President Tyler shrewdly had anticipated this result.

Still, Tyler remained intent on preserving peace with England. To avert a break in negotiations, he made another overture to the British in an attempt to find a solution to the Oregon question that would be highly advantageous to the United States. The revised proposal was to include a commercial treaty with Great Britain and Mexican cession of the coveted California harbors. This time round the president fell back upon his favorite diplomatic device—the use of an executive agent. Duff Green, Tyler's "ambassador of slavery," once again was sent back to London in the guise of a private citizen, although he was, as he had been on his earlier assignment, in the pay of the U.S. government.

In an extraordinary letter to Edward Everett, the American minister in London, Tyler informed him of Green's new mission and outlined what was an outlandish modification of Webster's earlier tripartite proposal. President Tyler still sought to link an Oregon settlement to his expansionist designs in California and Texas, and believed that a commercial treaty with Britain that led to a mutual reduction of tariff duties was essential to his plan's success. "General Green," the president explained to Minister Everett, "acting under limited countenance and known only as a private citizen, might be of great service in bringing facts to our knowledge" that held out the promise of improved commercial relations and sustained peace with England.

In outlining his new variation of the tripartite scam President Tyler may have demonstrated a keen grasp of global politics and an overriding ambition to have the United States replace Britain as "the carrier of the world," but the updated plan proved as impractical as the original version. Secret agent Duff Green accomplished little other than to be obnoxiously self-important in his dealings with British officials and the accredited American minister to the Court of St. James. An aggrieved Edward Everett became a lifelong skeptic about the legitimacy and usefulness of executive agents. Almost twenty years later, when Secretary of State William H. Seward attempted to enlist Everett as a secret agent of the Union during the Civil War, he declined the offer. In explaining his decision to Charles Francis Adams, then the American minister to Great Britain, Everett stated that executive agents "carry no weight with foreign Governments—are justly distasteful to the accredited Minister," and bitterly admitted "such, at least was my own feeling when Mr. Tyler sent General Duff Green to London while I was Minister."[45]

There is evidence to support the argument that President Tyler was playing for time and never seriously sought a solution to the Oregon boundary dispute during his term in office. Instead, he hoped that a policy of delay would lead in a few years to a complete American occupation of the territory to the 49th parallel. For instance, within months after entering the White House he and Webster secretly authorized a deal with a private entrepreneur, Alfred Benson, to ship American settlers at government expense to the Oregon country. Benson's firm was contracted by the Navy Department in 1841 "to establish a line of transport ships to the Oregon Territory, conveying fifty passengers by each trip without charge, upon the condition that they should have the benefit of transporting all the government supplies to the Pacific, at the rate of $3 per barrel freight."

President Tyler sanctioned this clandestine and unprecedented arrangement with the Benson shipping company because it would help secure an American foothold in Oregon without unduly alerting the British government to his administration's ambitions in the Pacific Northwest. Whether or not this government-financed project for sending hundreds of American pioneers to the Oregon country succeeded is unknown. But indisputably this scheme was another example of Tyler's willingness to use executive power in foreign relations without legislative sanction or approval.[46]

More compelling evidence of Tyler's delaying tactics on the Oregon question came in his correspondence with John C. Calhoun just six months after they had left office. In a long letter to his former secretary of state that read like a post-mortem on his administration's diplomatic achievements as well as some of its foreign policy shortcomings, Tyler thanked Calhoun for "the important aid you afforded me" in securing the annexation of Texas. However, Tyler continued, "I left the gov't with but one wish remaining unfulfilled, and that related to the Oregon Question. I wished you to terminate that negociation [sic]. I entered upon it with reluctance believing that under the convention of joint occupation we stood on the most favorable footing. Our population was already finding its way to the shores of the Pacific, and a few years would see an American Settlement on the Columbia sufficiently strong to defend itself and to protect the rights of the U. States to the territory."

This candid admission to Calhoun confirmed that during his tenure in the executive office President Tyler warily pursued negotiations with Britain and disclosed that the elaborate tripartite structure was designed to fail. His revelation to Calhoun about the policy of delay being advantageous to an American takeover in Oregon suggested as well that John Tyler was a believer in what another ardent expansionist later described as the American multiplication table. The chief proponent of the multiplication table analogy was Representative Andrew Kennedy, a Democrat from Indiana, who shared Tyler's Jeffersonian faith in westward expansion as national destiny. "Go to the West," he advised his congressional colleagues, "and see a young man with his mate of eighteen; after the lapse of thirty years, visit him again, and instead of two, you will find twenty-two. That is what I call the American multiplication table." "Westward the course of empire" was the American expansionists' motto. A belief in demographics as destiny became the keystone of their unquestioned expansionist creed.[47]

In negotiating with the Americans to resolve the Oregon dispute, Aberdeen and Ashburton rightly suspected that Tyler and Webster were not always acting in good faith. But this came as no surprise to either man, because both understood from experience how politics worked in the American republic. To appease and placate the electorate, President Tyler would talk tough to Congress and the American people, but then proved much more restrained and conciliatory in the give and take of the negotiating table. Even so, the American style of negotiation occasionally drove the savvy British diplomats to distraction. They privately grumbled that this Virginia gentleman who prided himself on his republican virtue behaved dishonorably and accused him of being most uncandid, a polite way of saying President Tyler was a liar.

Members of Congress such as Democrat Thomas Hart Benton of Missouri were even more despised for their "swagger" and bullying rhetoric. "The truth is," Ashburton complained to a friend after returning from his diplomatic mission to the United States, "that our cousin Jonathan [the United States] is an offensive, arrogant fellow in his manner" and by "nearly all our people he is therefore hated, and a treaty of conciliation with such a fellow, however considered by prudence or policy to be necessary, can in no case be very popular with the multitude." Such condemnation of American republican conduct was common in mid-nineteenth century England, and disgust with American bluster and bombast was especially prevalent among its aristocracy. For Lords Ashburton and Aberdeen, President Tyler's duplicitous negotiating style epitomized the American way of diplomacy. Of course, the disdain was reciprocated because Americans, especially the Anglophobic Tyler, felt the same way about the British and deeply resented Britain's arrogant and condescending treatment of the American republic.[48]

Some Americans on the political fringe, most notably abolitionist spokesmen fixated on the evil machinations of the Slave Power, were uneasy about Tyler's diplomacy and shared British perceptions and concerns about its reliance on deceit and duplicity. At the time, especially during the Webster-Ashburton negotiations, the overwhelming majority of the American public did not know the extent to which the Tyler administration employed secret executive agents in the conduct of its foreign policy. The information about Webster's sponsorship of surreptitious activities in Maine did not come to light until a few years later and it was not until the twentieth century that the Tyler administration's widespread use of secret agents abroad was uncovered by historians and biographers.

To be sure, John Quincy Adams smelled a rat when he labeled Duff Green the "ambassador of slavery" and publicly voiced his suspicions about the general's overseas activities being financed secretly by the chief executive and the State Department. By and large, however, President Tyler and his secretaries of state—Webster, Upshur, and Calhoun—conducted their undercover activities with impunity and without congressional oversight or public scrutiny. In fact, the Tyler administration, under Webster's enthusiastic guidance, was probably the first to sponsor a systematic propaganda campaign to manipulate public opinion, and to do it with funds from the public treasury. Although not quite the direct antecedent of the disinformation tactics so commonly associated with late-twentieth-century Cold War diplomacy, the Webster-Tyler operation in Maine was designed to hoodwink Congress and the American people by keeping them in the dark.

But a policy of official secrecy did not mean everyone in the mainstream was bamboozled or totally unaware of what was happening. Doubts about the legitimacy of this "new mode" of conducting foreign policy were raised and troubling questions about the propriety of using public funds to influence domestic politics ultimately did surface. Daniel Webster was the initial target. In the spring of 1846 Charles J. Ingersoll, chairman of the House Committee on Foreign Affairs, charged the former secretary of state with three counts of official misconduct. An expansionist Democrat from Pennsylvania who enthusiastically had supported Tyler's annexation of Texas, Ingersoll was an old and bitter political foe of Daniel Webster. The charges Ingersoll leveled against his longtime enemy were (1) the unlawful use of secret service funds, (2) "misapplying part of that fund to corrupt party presses," and (3) being a defaulter on public funds upon leaving the State Department.

After a rancorous partisan debate over Ingersoll's resolution, the House of Representatives appointed a committee to investigate the charges. In the course of its inquiry the committee interviewed former president John Tyler, who testified that Secretary Webster had acted with his full approval and consequently was not guilty of using secret service funds unlawfully. Upon his ascendancy to the presidency, Tyler told the committee, he "found the foreign relations of the country in a very delicate condition" which "in his opinion" justified the "employment of confidential agents." A majority of the committee accepted Tyler's explanation and dismissed the first charge.

On the second count of using "public money to corrupt the party presses," members of the committee flinched but again absolved Webster of wrongdoing, and by implication his chief executive John Tyler, by a vote of 4-1. The majority deemed it expedient for reasons of state and in deference to executive prerogative not "to inquire into the propriety of employing agents for secret service within the limits of the United States, and paying them out of the contingent fund for foreign intercourse." However, with this disclaimer, the majority members had raised, and it is difficult to believe they did so inadvertently, the crucial issue of the constitutionality and legality of the Tyler administration's indoctrination enterprise in Maine.

In a dissenting report the minority member of the committee, Democrat Jacob Brinkerhof of Ohio, also wondered whether the Tyler administration's activities were constitutional. Although unwilling to pass judgment and seek impeachment of the former secretary of state, Brinkerhof questioned whether "this direct effort of the general government, through the agency of one of its high functionaries and the employment of pecuniary means for the purpose of influencing the legislative action of a State government, constitutes an impeachable offense in that functionary."

Brinkerhof's nagging doubts about the constitutionality and propriety of a federally subsidized "systematic electioneering" campaign to manipulate the internal politics of a sovereign state of the Union clearly troubled other members of the committee as well. However, in their final report the majority members of the committee expediently exonerated Daniel Webster on all counts of official misconduct, including the charge that he was a public defaulter. But by raising the paramount issues of constitutionality and implied abuse of executive power, the entire committee had insinuated that the Tyler administration was guilty of an ethical lapse and a legal impropriety.[49]

Representative Ingersoll's personal political vendetta against Daniel Webster had failed, although the investigating committee's disclosures about the former secretary of state's cavalier handling of public funds brought into question his honesty and truthfulness and further dishonored the New Englander's already tarnished reputation. In his attempt to destroy his political enemy, Ingersoll also quite inadvertently had opened a can of worms on the use of executive power in conducting the nation's diplomacy. Before bringing his formal charges of Webster's misconduct to the House of Representatives, Ingersoll had gained approval of a resolution requesting that President James K. Polk furnish the House with all documents related to former president Tyler's use of the secret service fund, particularly those concerning the treaty with Great Britain settling the northeastern boundary dispute.

Not unexpectedly, Polk refused to comply with the request. In his reply to the House explaining his decision, President Polk discussed the history of the 1810 law that had authorized an annual appropriation "for the contingent expenses of intercourse between the United States and foreign governments." Polk believed his predecessor's use of the secret service fund was legal and within the bounds of the enabling legislation. Tyler operated under the law as well when he "exercised the power of placing these expenditures under the seal of confidence." "To break the seal of confidence," Polk believed, "would be subversive of the very purpose for which the law was enacted." Polk feared that if he gave the requested information it would set "a precedent that would render such disclosures hereafter inevitable."

President Polk did not touch upon the legality of Tyler's use of these funds to manipulate public opinion at home in a sovereign state, but he did seek the moral high ground by noting that his administration had not spent one dollar in secret and had no intention to do so in the future. While acknowledging that Tyler as the chief executive had a perfect right to use the contingency fund as he saw fit, Polk implied there was a certain impropriety about the previous administration's unprecedented reliance on secrecy in the conduct of the nation's foreign relations.[50]

Undaunted by Polk's rejection of his request for information, Ingersoll blithely and improperly proceeded on his own fishing expedition to locate incriminating evidence about Webster's activities in the files of the State Department. With the help of a bureaucrat at State who obviously had little sympathy for the Tyler administration's covert activities, Ingersoll discovered Francis O. J. Smith's celebratory letter to Secretary of State Daniel Webster of August 12, 1842. A delighted Ingersoll immediately went public with the damning information in a speech on the House floor in April 1846. "It begins by congratulating Mr. Webster," Ingersoll told his colleagues, "on his settlement of the Maine boundary question by *a new mode of approaching the subject*, after forty years of diplomacy, without which *new mode* another forty years of diplomacy would have come to nothing."

Despite his glee at having identified this "new mode" of diplomacy and having uncovered more than just another instance of political corruption and malfeasance in public office, Ingersoll did not seek to broaden the scope of the inquiry beyond his personal desire for revenge and the settling of scores with Daniel Webster. Ingersoll and his colleagues in the House of Representatives made no attempt to launch a full-scale investigation of John Tyler's apparent abuse of executive power. Nor was there a searching evaluation of the danger this "new mode" of diplomacy might present to a healthy and viable balance of power between the executive and legislative branches in the conduct of the nation's foreign relations. Apparently no one in Congress had the stomach for such an inquiry. Better to keep the focus narrow and avoid having to deal with larger constitutional issues.[51]

Congressman Ingersoll's lack of curiosity about Tyler's improper use of executive power was easily explained. He was an avid territorial expansionist who had no objection to the aggressive diplomacy of the former president and heartily supported John Tyler's extralegal use of a congressional joint resolution to annex Texas. In addition, Ingersoll was a highly partisan Democrat who viciously attacked his Whig adversaries, including not only Daniel Webster but the venerable John Quincy Adams as well. In fact, at one point a wounded Adams, reflecting on the ups and downs of his political career, confided to his diary that Charles J. Ingersoll was a base human being and a malignant and lying enemy. As might be expected, Daniel Webster fully shared Adams's low opinion of Ingersoll.

All his enemies might agree that Mr. Ingersoll played dirty and was unscrupulous in his political attacks on Webster. However, Ingersoll did have legitimate policy disagreements with the former secretary of state, chief among them Webster's general distaste for territorial expansion and his stubborn opposition to the annexation of Texas. To Ingersoll's mind, the New Englander had been a nettlesome drag on President Tyler's expansionist agenda and had overstayed his usefulness in the cabinet. Tyler had been correct and acted none too soon in forcing Webster to resign as secretary of state.

The Texas annexation issue had been a nagging point of disagreement in the Webster-Tyler relationship, but it had never undermined their ability to work together on the formulation and conduct of the nation's diplomacy. President Tyler valued Webster's wise counsel and was thankful the secretary of state had chosen to remain in his cabinet after the mass resignation of the other Whig members originally appointed by Harrison. Webster had played a crucial role in the negotiations with Lord Ashburton that led to the treaty with England, which President Tyler much appreciated and readily commended.

Secretary Webster admired Tyler as well and thought their diplomatic agenda had been productive and beneficial. On the completion of the treaty negotiations he warmly thanked President Tyler: "Your steady support and confidence, your anxious and intelligent attention to what was in progress, and your exceedingly obliging and pleasant intercourse, both with the British minister and the commissioners of the States, have given every possible facility to my agency in this transaction." After his resignation from the State Department in May 1843, however, Webster expressed his misgivings about Tyler's obsession with Texas annexation and his hell-bent determination to be elected to a second term in his own right.[52]

Tyler seemingly was unaware of Webster's disapproval of his political ambitions and for years afterward their private relationship remained cordial, even friendly. For both Tyler and Webster securing peace with England had been the happiest result of their successful diplomatic collaboration. Webster never looked back nor doubted the efficacy of the Maine disinformation campaign. Tyler also was untroubled by the larger implications of the questionable tactics they employed during their brief political partnership. He justified his extensive use of executive agents and the secret service fund with the rationale that "concealment was necessary for the public good." As president and later in retirement, Tyler clearly was in denial about how his administration's federally funded propaganda activities in Maine had undermined states' rights. His argument in defense of secrecy illustrated a willingness to accept the ancient dictum that the ends justify the means. Any inconsistency on the question of states' rights and the abuse of executive power was conveniently overlooked.

A policy of official secrecy for the "public good" meant the American people knew little or nothing about the Tyler administration's questionable use of executive agents. The administration's surreptitious activity in New England was carried out with the familiar justification that these actions, no matter how improper, served the national interest. President Tyler would have been outraged if another occupant of the White House, especially a northerner with antislavery leanings, used the justification of national interest or the rationale of the greater good to interfere covertly in Virginia or any of the other slave states in an effort to undermine the South's peculiar institution. Consistency, it would appear, was not John Tyler's hallmark when it came to practicing what he preached about the sanctity of states' rights.

There is a trace of hubris and a hint of tragedy in Tyler's course of action. As the chief executive of the republic, he followed a path of political expediency in the conduct of foreign affairs that sacrificed his long-proclaimed commitment to states' rights at the altar of personal ambition. John Tyler believed a vigorous and successful foreign policy was the best way to assure his future political success. He focused on the diplomatic arena because it allowed him a freedom of action that garnered tangible results and the promise of public acclaim. He could use the contingency funds with impunity, without congressional interference, and with few questions asked. The lure of this avenue of unchecked power in pursuit of the nation's destiny was irresistible. It offered President Tyler an escape from the political dead end of being a mere executive figurehead and a pliant servant of Congress, a fate to which his archrival Henry Clay had hoped to consign him. But in this quest for personal vindication and political glory John Tyler betrayed and abused his most deeply held principles.

★ ★ ★ ★ ★ ★ ★ ★ ★ ★

Pacific Visions

5

The Americans [are] destined by nature to be a great
maritime people. . . . They will become, like the English,
the commercial agents of a great portion of the world.
  ★ *Alexis de Tocqueville, 1835*

A commerce, such as ours, *demands* the protection
of an adequate naval force. Our people, scattered all over
the world, have a right to require the occasional presence
of our flag, to give assurance to all nations that their
country has both the will and the power to protect them.
  ★ *Abel P. Upshur, 1842*

If the attempt now making by ourselves, as well as by
other Christian powers, to open the markets of China to
a more general commerce, be successful, there can be no
doubt but that a great part of that commerce will find its
way over the Isthmus. In that event it will be impossible
to overrate the importance of the Hawaiian group as a
stage in the long voyage between Asia and America.
  ★ *Hugh Legare, June 13, 1843*

n the first half of the nineteenth century, and particularly in the 1830s and 1840s, there existed a small but significant band of private citizens and public officials who persistently lobbied for American commercial and territorial expansion in the Pacific Rim. This disparate and unorganized brotherhood of merchants, missionaries, naval officers, whalers, commercial ship captains, and entrepreneurs composed what might be labeled an influential American Pacific community. Charter members of this unofficial and informal fellowship were the advance corps of "a great maritime people" that the French observer of young America, Alexis de Tocqueville, predicted would come to dominate the commerce of the world.

In pursuing the United States's maritime destiny, self-appointed agents of the American Pacific community sought political and diplomatic support from the federal government in Washington. Many of their number were well connected to politicians in Congress and the executive branch, especially with such leading figures as New Englanders John Quincy Adams, Daniel Webster, and Caleb Cushing, and the Virginians John Tyler and Abel P. Upshur. These national leaders proved receptive to the expansionist message and understood, as Navy Secretary Upshur declared, that Americans were "scattered all over the world" and wanted assurance "that their country has both the will and the power to protect them."[1]

It was fairly commonplace for missionaries and merchants working in Hawaii, the South Sea Islands, or China to crisscross the Pacific Ocean on three-to-six-month excursions to and from the American mainland. During their periodic returns to the United States to visit relatives and friends or to attend to their family and business affairs, these eager and tireless promoters of America's Pacific destiny stopped off in Washington, New York City, Philadelphia, and Boston to spread their expansionist gospel. They were not only doing the day-to-day toil of forging an empire in the Pacific, but they also were educating and influencing the thinking of countless American citizens and instilling an enduring Pacific-mindedness in the nation's leaders.

Chief among those welcoming the imperial message from this cadre of maritime frontiersmen about the marvelous possibilities for American destiny in the Pacific Ocean and East Asia was President John Tyler, himself an enthusiastic if deskbound expansionist. Tyler had been a Pacific-minded visionary for at least a decade before his election as vice president on the 1840 Whig ticket of "Tippecanoe and Tyler too." After ascending to the presidency upon the death of William Henry Harrison in April 1841, Tyler found himself constantly being bombarded by the persuasive blandishments of the American Pacific community. Their letters and petitions simply reinforced the new president's Pacific visions and confirmed his desire to project American influence to the Hawaiian Islands and gain access to the markets of China and Japan. The parade of individuals lobbying to have his administration bolster the official American diplomatic presence throughout the Pacific Rim began only months after he entered the White House and continued until the waning days of his presidency.

One champion of American political and economic ambitions in China, Dr. Peter Parker, met with Secretary of State–designate Daniel Webster as early as January 1841, nearly five weeks before the Harrison-Tyler team took office. A Yale graduate, Parker was a prominent Christian missionary and famed surgeon known for his highly successful medical practice at the Canton Ophthalmic Hospital in China. At the time of the outbreak of the Opium War between Great Britain and China in 1839, Parker suspended his work at the Canton Hospital and returned to the United States to regain his health after "excessive labors."

During his recuperative period in New Haven, Connecticut, Dr. Parker exchanged views with various members of the Yale University faculty about conditions in China, "and of the favorable opportunity for the American government to proffer friendly offices to the contending parties, and to establish treaty relations with China." The New Haven intellectuals were so impressed with Parker's prescription for an American role as peacemaker that they encouraged him to go to Washington to present his views to the national leadership.[2]

Energized by this endorsement of his plan, Peter Parker proceeded to Washington "to call the attention of the men in power to the relations of America to China." He initially had an audience with the lame-duck incumbent, President Martin Van Buren and Secretary of State John Forsyth, who politely suggested that perhaps it would be more appropriate for him to meet with the incoming head of the State Department, Daniel Webster. As directed, the novice lobbyist went to Webster, who carefully listened to Parker's proposal for U.S. mediation of the Anglo-Sino conflict. After briefly reflecting on his visitor's recommendations, Webster in a "grave voice" said: "What you have now stated to me orally will you be so good, sir, as to give me in writing for the benefit of whom it may concern."

A flattered Dr. Parker eagerly complied. Several days later he submitted a six-point report to Webster, which outlined the steps the United States should take to mediate an end to the Opium War and establish formal diplomatic relations with the Chinese empire. Although Parker's impromptu report was not entirely original and echoed the main themes of petitions that had been submitted to Congress a year or two earlier by American Canton merchants, it nonetheless offered a fascinating glimpse of a knowledgeable American's perceptions of China and the Chinese at mid-century. Parker's proposals to Webster also were important because they helped shape the future direction of the Tyler administration's China policy.[3]

In presenting his prescription for promoting American interests in the Celestial Empire, Parker accepted a key assumption about China that came to be widely shared by American policymakers and the general public for more than a century, arguably until 1949 when the creation of the People's Republic of China undermined that supposition. For most nineteenth-century Americans, including old China hands, merchants, and missionaries, it was an article of faith that the Chinese people held America in special favor. Dr. Parker aptly expressed this belief with his observation that the "American nation probably stands higher in the confidence of the Chinese than any other nation."

One reason why the Chinese held America and Americans in high esteem, Parker claimed, was because in the early 1840s few American merchants doing business in Canton were engaged in the opium trade. He also believed that the Chinese were impressed because a handful of these Yankee merchants had taken the moral high ground by publicly speaking out about the evils of opium use and denouncing the drug traffic. On both counts Dr. Parker was misinformed. Contrary to his assertion, most American merchants did not speak out against opium use. In fact, many American firms were heavily involved in the opium trade and in the first half of the nineteenth century drug trafficking provided sizable fortunes for a number of prominent China merchants, including Warren Delano, grandfather of Franklin Delano Roosevelt.

But Dr. Parker's third reason for why China ostensibly looked favorably upon the United States was perhaps the most compelling for his countrymen. Among the Chinese, "America is known not to be a colonizing nation," and precisely because the United States was not seen as an avaricious imperial power, he maintained, China would welcome an American envoy with the authority to establish formal diplomatic relations between the two nations. The medical missionary had someone in mind to be that emissary. Parker suggested that a retired, elderly president be sent as an ambassador to China, believing that the emperor of China would accept such an eminent statesman most heartily. The former president who perfectly fit that description was the venerable John Quincy Adams, at the time a member of the House of Representatives from Massachusetts.[4]

As secretary of state under President Tyler, Daniel Webster chose not to implement all of Parker's recommendations. Other foreign policy crises, most notably the threat of war with Great Britain over the McLeod case and the northeastern boundary dispute, took precedence and precluded taking action in China to bring a peaceful and equitable settlement of the Opium War. Neither was John Quincy Adams given a diplomatic posting to China. But Dr. Parker's report was not thrown in the wastebasket. A scant two years later in 1843, Caleb Cushing was sent by the Tyler administration to negotiate America's first treaty with China. Parker, who served as a translator and consultant for the Cushing mission, later noted with some pride that the American envoy brought with him a "copy of that paper; and essentially the program therein initiated has since been carried out by our government." Perhaps one reason why Parker's original plan for the opening of formal Sino-American relations had not been relegated to history's dustbin was because the good doctor proved to be a persistent and indefatigable lobbyist.[5]

Nine months after his initial interview with Daniel Webster and having just returned from a trip to Europe where he sought support for his missionary enterprise and hospital at Canton, Parker was back in Washington once again pressing his case for American action in China. This time he began his lobbying efforts by having a private audience with President John Tyler at the executive mansion. It quickly became apparent to Parker that President Tyler had read and contemplated his report on China that earlier had been submitted to Secretary Webster. Parker found the Virginia aristocrat "exceedingly affable" and recorded that President Tyler "made kind inquiries respecting my residence in China, visit to England and France, the probable result of the English and Chinese war." Somewhat apologetically, the president confessed to his visitor that in "regard to China nothing had been done."

As an explanation for his administration's inaction, Tyler lamely claimed to be constrained by a respect for legislative prerogative and noted that he "was present in the Senate when the act was passed by which no President can originate a new mission, but can only recommend, etc." Another apprehension his administration had about sending a mission to China, Tyler confided to Parker, was "that they had feared to disgrace the country by having an ambassador rejected, and thought of having a 'floating embassy.'" But as Dr. Parker later revealed in a conversation with John Quincy Adams, President Tyler assured him "that he had his eye fixed upon China, and would avail himself of any favorable opportunity to commence a negotiation with the Celestial Empire."[6]

Although heartened by Tyler's forthright commitment to taking action in China, Dr. Parker apparently was puzzled by President Tyler's reference to "a floating embassy" as a possible form of diplomatic representation in China. In his journal entry for September 16, 1841, recorded after his meeting with the president, Parker placed an emphatic question mark after this phrase. Parker's confusion was justified. President Tyler's suggestion was an odd and peculiar method for how the United States might establish a diplomatic presence in China. One can only speculate about what Tyler meant by "a floating embassy." Did he mean that a U.S. diplomat, without formal recognition from the Chinese government, would reside on a ship floating offshore and move about as necessary to handle the routine diplomacy and business of Americans in China? If so, the president's proposal to Parker was a novel concept, but not uncharacteristic of Tyler's sometimes unique approach to the nation's foreign relations. The "floating embassy" scheme was akin to another of his offbeat diplomatic proposals, made in the same month of September 1841, which was to refuse British minister Henry S. Fox his passports to leave the country and keep him under virtual house arrest in order to avoid war with Great Britain.

In President Tyler's defense, it might be argued that he clearly was attempting to be innovative in broaching the "floating embassy" idea and was unwilling to be restricted by the formalized and unyielding demands of diplomatic protocol. The Pacific-minded Tyler was a well-read and highly informed observer of international relations and obviously was intent on having the United States do something to protect its interests in China. What appeared to be a bizarre suggestion for a "floating embassy" might in fact have been based on his reading of Edmund Roberts's posthumous 1837 memoir of his voyage to Asia, including diplomatic missions to Cochin China (Vietnam), Siam (Thailand), and Muscat (Oman). Roberts's account of his contentious encounter with Chinese officials at Canton probably made Tyler aware of China's arrogant and dismissive treatment of foreigners. Perhaps President Tyler should be credited for having conjured up an imaginative diplomatic initiative that conceivably might have succeeded in cracking open the door without causing an embarrassing rejection by the Chinese government.[7]

Immediately after his heartening chat with President Tyler in the White House, Dr. Parker proceeded to the home of Daniel Webster for an informal visit with the secretary of state. Parker and Webster were fellow New

Englanders and personal friends, and both assumed they had ties of kin by fact of Parker's recent marriage to Harriet Webster. Actually the new Mrs. Parker was not related to the secretary of state, but they both good-naturedly went along with the notion that they were cousins. Even though he had close ties to Webster and was comfortable while gently prodding him to take action in China, it was clear that Dr. Parker was in awe of "the great man." Unlike President Tyler, Parker found Webster to be an engaging, cosmopolitan, well-traveled, and worldly wise intellectual of national stature. Indeed, Webster's unrivalled qualities of mind and intellect led many of Parker's contemporaries to refer to him as the "god-like Daniel."

After an "exceedingly agreeable" hour spent with Webster that September evening, Parker confided in his journal: "I can scarcely refrain from a comparison between the two statesmen. The President, a pleasant and intelligent, ordinary man, evidently conscious of his inadequacy to the high office he holds; the Secretary, perfectly at ease, sensible of his mighty intellect and power to grapple with any subject." Parker's private appraisal of the two men may have reflected a northeasterner's snobbery and bias about inferior southerners in general and slaveholding planters in particular, but he pinpointed one of President Tyler's main political handicaps as a national leader. Despite his administration's solid diplomatic accomplishments, Tyler received little credit for his achievements and forever paled in comparison to the acknowledged political giants of the era such as Daniel Webster, John C. Calhoun, and Henry Clay. One of John Tyler's tragic flaws as politician and president was his inability to convince either northerners or southerners, as South Carolinian James Henry Hammond noted, that he was a man of substance or "capacity."[8]

★ THE TYLER DOCTRINE
★
★ Dr. Peter Parker was only the first of many in the American Pacific community who trekked to the nation's capital during John Tyler's presidency to lobby for a stronger American presence along the Pacific Rim and in East Asia. Although many of them may have shared Parker's enthusiasm for opening relations with China, most of the proselytizing agents of Pacific empire that followed in his footsteps were primarily concerned about the future of the Hawaiian Islands. True, Hawaii was an important stopover and way station for American ships engaged in the China trade, but that was a decidedly secondary factor to their main objectives, which were to prevent European ascendancy in the islands and to preserve the independence and

sovereignty of the Hawaiian monarchy. Just as Parker's cajoling efforts ultimately bore fruit for American diplomacy by helping to persuade the Tyler administration to send a formal mission to China, so too did the insistent lobbying campaigns of numerous like-minded expansionists, most of whom were fellow missionaries, pay off in the long run by assuring an American predominance in Hawaii for the remainder of the nineteenth century.

How Hawaii became American territory and eventually the fiftieth state in the Union is a fascinating and gripping tale, but a story unknown to most contemporary Americans. On one level, it was a heroic saga of missionary fervor and personal courage familiar to an earlier generation of Americans who read James Michener's epic 1959 novel, *Hawaii*, or who saw the Hollywood movie adaptation starring Julie Andrews and Max Von Sydow. But Michener's fictionalized romantic tale ignored or minimized the crucial role played during the nineteenth century by the energetic individuals who were the heart and soul of the American Pacific community. These unheralded private citizens alerted the U.S. government to the need for a formal diplomatic guarantee of Hawaiian independence and sovereignty. Popular fiction obscured historical reality at another level as well. No mention was made of early visionary stateside leaders such as Daniel Webster and John Tyler, who promoted and encouraged policies that contributed to the rapid Americanization of the islands.

Tyler and Webster understood that in the late 1830s and early 1840s the United States had become a major player on a par with Great Britain and France in the international scramble for power and dominance in the Pacific Ocean. American ascendancy in the Pacific at this early stage in the republic's history was quite extraordinary given the fact that the nation did not have a navy to match that of its European competitors, possessed no territory, either insular or continental, on the Pacific Ocean, nor did it have control or access to harbors on the west coast of North America. At best, the United States had disputed and unresolved claims to the Oregon country, which were contested by its chief rival, Great Britain. But, despite all the odds favoring a French or a British triumph in Hawaii, with considerable luck and some formal government assistance provided by the Tyler administration, the eclectic membership of the American Pacific community prevailed in the central Pacific. This loosely knit contingent of missionaries and merchants demonstrated the potency of economic and religious influences and the importance of nonstate actors in antebellum American foreign relations.

France's forceful attempt to protect Catholic converts and priests from discrimination and persecution presented an immediate and pressing challenge to American influence in the Sandwich Islands. The French were outraged when King Kamehameha III, at the urgings of his American Protestant missionary advisers, enacted "An Ordinance Rejecting the Catholic Religion," which outlawed the teachings of the Roman Catholic faith and forbade Catholic priests from setting foot in the Hawaiian kingdom. In a classic display of gunboat diplomacy, the French government responded by dispatching one of its frigates to the islands to teach the impertinent Hawaiian monarch and his intolerant pack of anti-Catholic mentors a lesson.

In July 1839, after a brief blockade of Honolulu harbor and the threat of bombardment of the city, the French naval officer Captain Cyrille Laplace extracted a treaty from the royal government that legitimized the Catholic faith and extended religious equality to all Catholics residing in the islands. Laplace's high-handed diplomacy also forced the Hawaiian chiefs to grant special tariff concessions for imported French products, including brandies and wines, and created a $20,000 guaranty fund to assure future good behavior by the Hawaiians. All this was anathema to the intolerant and bluenose American mission, which feared that the French were intent upon taking possession of the island kingdom.[9]

Within days after the arrival of the French frigate, the missionary community in Honolulu drew up a memorial to be sent to the U.S. Congress protesting Laplace's discriminatory actions and calling for the American government to seek redress. After being presented to the House of Representatives by a congressman who also happened to be a member of the American Board of Commissioners for Foreign Missions, the memorial was forwarded to the State Department. It went unnoticed by the department and was confined to a wastebasket by the Van Buren administration.

The Board of Commissioners, which governed and financed the American mission in Hawaii, was undeterred, however, and some months later opened its lobbying efforts again with what it correctly understood to be a more Pacific-minded Tyler administration. They sent a copy of the memorial to President Tyler in the hope that he might be openly sympathetic to their missionary enterprise and in the belief that the president and Secretary Webster were quite intent upon promoting an American commercial and economic beachhead in the central Pacific. As a follow-up maneuver, the commissioners dispatched one of their most eminent brethren, the Reverend Hiram Bingham, to Washington to meet privately with Tyler and Webster. Reverend Bingham was among the band of original missionaries who sailed for Hawaii in 1819 and, until his return to the mainland some twenty years later because of poor health, was the leader of the American mission in the islands.

Prior to his interviews with the president and secretary of state in the summer of 1841, Bingham sent a private letter to Webster explaining why he believed Hawaiian sovereignty was in jeopardy. Pitching his appeal for the administration's assistance on political and commercial and not spiritual grounds, Bingham warned the secretary of growing European imperial ambitions in the Pacific. The French threat was the most immediate and the retired missionary made the case that "the great importance of the entire independency of the Sandwich Islands to the commercial interests of our country, & the decided ascendancy of American influence there at this moment . . . seem to call for action in this case." Happily for the Reverend Bingham, he found both President Tyler and Secretary Webster responsive to his call for America's diplomatic backing of Hawaii's independence and concerned about further European imperial aggrandizement in the Pacific.

After his most cordial and friendly meetings with Tyler and Webster, lobbyist Bingham wrote a fellow member of the Board of Commissioners that the secretary of state had assured him that American missionaries would be afforded more protection than other U.S. citizens living and working abroad. Apparently, Webster also promised Bingham he would lodge a protest with France over Captain Laplace's coercive actions in Honolulu. In the end Secretary Webster did not honor what Bingham believed was a pledge to take diplomatic measures objecting to France's behavior in the islands. However, the other promise was kept. Although it took some time, well over a year in fact, Daniel Webster ultimately was true to his word about ensuring the safety of America's missionaries serving abroad.[10]

Fearing that the American Board of Commissioners' private lobbying campaign in the United States for the preservation of Hawaiian independence would not succeed, King Kamehameha III initiated his own diplomacy. At the suggestion of his closest and most trusted Western political adviser, William Richards, an American missionary who left his spiritual calling to become a royal mentor, Kamehameha dispatched several official emissaries abroad to gain formal diplomatic recognition of his kingdom's sovereignty. These fledgling and untested diplomats, all more or less affiliated as members of the broader American Pacific community, specifically were instructed to secure complete and unequivocal acknowledgment of the Hawaiian kingdom's status as an independent nation and a full member of the international community. Confident that his own nation would seize the opportunity to prevent possible future European annexation of the islands,

Richards convinced the king to initially target the United States because it was believed to be the one power that might be most receptive to Hawaii's claim to national legitimacy.

Steadfastness became the hallmark of this endeavor as Kamehameha sent waves of his agents to soften up the Tyler administration and convince an apparently reluctant Secretary of State Webster to act in Hawaii's behalf. The first to be sent out was Thomas Jefferson Farnham, an itinerant lawyer from Illinois who only recently had arrived in Honolulu. As an American citizen turned state actor in the employ of the Hawaiian Crown, Farnham was sent abroad with instructions to gain American, British, and French recognition of Hawaii's independence and sovereignty. Farnham proved an unreliable and desultory diplomat and lobbyist. He never made it to either England or France to present the Hawaiian government's case for international recognition.

After a journey of fruitless dilly-dallying, Farnham finally reached Washington in November 1841, several months in the wake of the Reverend Hiram Bingham. Apparently, the sum of Farnham's diplomatic accomplishment was a single letter sent to Daniel Webster requesting formal acknowledgment of his status as the Hawaiian king's envoy. Farnham received no response from the State Department and unlike his forerunner Bingham, he was not granted interviews with President Tyler or Secretary Webster. Farnham's mission to the United States ended in total failure.[11]

Undeterred, the Hawaiian monarch sent yet another special agent. The next delegate of King Kamehameha's amateur diplomatic corps to arrive at the Tyler administration's doorstep was Peter Brinsmade. Originally having studied and trained for the ministry, Brinsmade, instead of answering a spiritual calling as missionary to the heathen, followed a more lucrative worldly path seeking fame and fortune as a businessman and entrepreneur. He was a partner in Ladd & Company, the firm that had the distinction of operating the first sugar plantation in the Hawaiian Islands. Brinsmade also served as the American consul in Honolulu during the years 1839–46. His diplomatic career as the servant of two governments was not unusual and a fairly common practice among members of the influential and growing American community in Hawaii during the first half of the nineteenth century.

Peter Brinsmade, in the opinion of Manley Hopkins, an English gentleman and sojourner in Hawaii during the 1840s, was "one of those rapid, all-sided men which the social hot-bed of the United States produces so quickly and in such numbers." Unlike nineteenth-century Britons who knew and accepted their place in society and who rarely challenged the existing social order, these American "all-sided men" could move from being a surgeon to a merchant, to an editor, and failing in these occupations, to a preacher, or a "candidate for the presidentship." Hopkins was an astute observer. The social and economic mobility of these men on the make, or "all-sided men," was the reason why they were such energetic and effective representatives of the American Pacific community.[12]

In March 1842 Brinsmade arrived in Washington carrying an official message from Kamehameha III to President John Tyler. In his letter to the American president, which undoubtedly had been written under the direction of William Richards, the Hawaiian monarch requested that the United States join Great Britain and France in a mutually agreed upon convention guaranteeing the independence of the Hawaiian Islands. After several weeks of lobbying the administration and Congress on Hawaii's behalf, the amateur and inexperienced diplomat failed in his effort to meet with President Tyler to present the king's letter. Secretary Webster also was uncooperative and apparently never granted Mr. Brinsmade the courtesy of a personal interview.

As a last resort, the frustrated amateur envoy forwarded Kamehameha's message to the State Department and attached a lengthy personal letter to Webster in which he outlined the reasons why the Hawaiian kingdom deserved recognition of its sovereignty. Brinsmade stressed that Hawaii was the "Malta of the North Pacific," and was of crucial geopolitical and strategic importance to the United States. Speaking as a successful American entrepreneur and investor, Brinsmade informed Secretary Webster, who had close ties with the New England merchant and whaling community, that the "importance of the independence and neutrality contemplated in the proposals of the King to our commercial interests touching at these Islands, is incalculable."

In hopes of cinching his case for why the Tyler administration should extend recognition, Brinsmade repeatedly played the British card. He warned that Hawaii must be "protected from the ambition that grasps at the maritime supremacy of the world" and direly predicted that "should the policy of a British Colonial establishment be brought upon the Country American enterprise there would of course wither and die." Secretary Webster did not reply to Brinsmade's correspondence, just as he had ignored the Hawaiian emissary's requests for a meeting, perhaps because he was preoccupied with the treaty negotiations with Lord Ashburton seeking to maintain peace with England. Undoubtedly another more telling reason for Webster's inaction at this juncture was his and Tyler's traditional distrust of entangling agreements with European powers. Both men preferred, if feasible, a unilateral and independent diplomatic course of action for the United States. On this score Brinsmade and William Richards, author of the king's proposal, misjudged the preferences of the Tyler administration and inadvertently revealed they were somewhat out of touch with the political realities in their native land.[13]

Unbeknownst to the king and his advisers, their campaign for recognition of Hawaiian sovereignty also received unsolicited support from Henry A. Peirce, a self-appointed lobbyist and freelance member of the American Pacific community. Peirce unexpectedly popped up in the nation's capital at about the same time that Peter Brinsmade was attempting to see President Tyler and Secretary Webster. A Bostonian who had made a sizable fortune as a merchant and planter in Hawaii and as a shipper in the Pacific trade, Peirce immediately began working the same political corridors of power in Washington that Brinsmade had been frequenting. These two ambitious American entrepreneurs and vocal Pacific expansionists, one with official diplomatic portfolio, the other a private citizen without formal credentials, quite literally must have been bumping into each other at every turn as they lobbied for an independent and diplomatically secure Hawaii.

Perhaps because of his unofficial capacity and less demanding diplomatic agenda and the fact that he was not a man on the make but a wealthy merchant who owned a handsome mansion on Boston's Harvard Row, Peirce, unlike the frustrated Brinsmade, easily secured an audience with Secretary of State Webster. At his meeting with Webster, Peirce gave the secretary a detailed and comprehensive overview of the threats to American interests in Hawaii, and made the case for why the United States should acquire harbors along California's Pacific coast. "In the fitness of things," Peirce pointedly observed, "we must have California." Without hesitation, Secretary Webster answered: "Well, sir, if we must, we probably will."

The commercially minded Webster, who constantly was being deluged by the fervent entreaties of the likes of Peirce and other seafaring entrepreneurs of the Pacific, already had recognized the need for California and its splendid harbors. As Tyler's secretary of state, Webster never wavered from the belief that these "windows on the Pacific" were imminently more valuable to America's destiny than was the slave republic of Texas. For his part, President Tyler was an unabashedly more aggressive territorial expansionist, wanting both a slave Texas and a free California added to the constellation of American states.[14]

Realizing that his government had been poorly served by the incompetent and inept emissaries previously dispatched to Washington, King Kamehameha III decided it was time to send abroad a first-class delegation composed of Timoteo Haalilio and William Richards. Although neither individual was a professionally trained or experienced diplomat, both were men of the highest intelligence and trustworthiness who had the unequivocal backing and confidence of the king. The importance placed on this diplomatic mission by King Kamehameha was apparent in his choice of Haalilio, whose integrity and lofty reputation among native Hawaiians gave enormous respectability and political clout to the monarchy's latest international endeavor. The strikingly handsome and dignified young Hawaiian prince had been the king's much beloved youthful companion and at the time of his diplomatic appointment was Kamehameha's official secretary and trusted confidant.

The other half of Kamehameha's frontline team was William Richards, the American missionary who was the primary architect of the Hawaiian monarchy's campaign for legitimacy and international acceptance. A member of the Hawaiian mission since the early 1820s, Richards made his mark as a preacher, educator, and translator of the Hawaiian language into written form. In recognition of his linguistic talents and impressive service to the Crown, the Reverend Richards was chosen in 1838 to be the principal counselor to the king and his chiefs. It was a fortuitous choice. Self-taught in the science of government and the art of diplomacy, Richards set to work immediately in an effort to modernize the Hawaiian monarchy by relying on the principles of American republicanism as his inspiration and guide.

One of Richards's first tasks, undertaken with the full approval of Kamehameha III, was to write a draft of a proposed "treaty of peace, mutual friendship and trade" between the king of the Hawaiian Islands and the United States of America. The draft treaty, which was designed to protect Hawaiian independence as well as to enhance the United States's influence in the kingdom, was submitted to the Martin Van Buren administration for its consideration. In an accompanying letter urging adoption of the treaty, Richards stressed the advantages that would accrue for an already burgeoning American commerce and investment in the Hawaiian Islands. An indifferent State Department took no action on the Hawaiian proposal and Richards's draft treaty was ignored and forgotten. Richards enjoyed more success in his effort to restructure the Hawaiian monarchy. He played a key role in the creation and adoption of a Hawaiian constitution and a bill of rights, and in the crafting of a code of laws governing the island kingdom.

Testimony to William Richards's effectiveness in refashioning the Hawaiian monarchy and, not incidentally, promoting the United States's influence in the archipelago came from admiring American and somewhat more skeptical British visitors to Hawaii. Lieutenant Charles Wilkes, the head of the United States Exploring Expedition that spent some time in the islands during its extended voyage of discovery in the Pacific Ocean, met the Reverend Richards in 1840. Wilkes was highly impressed by the New England missionary in his role as government official. In speaking of Richards some years later, Wilkes observed that the Hawaiian people were indeed fortunate "in obtaining the services of one who has made such exertions in their behalf, and who is so well qualified for the responsible situation he holds." Other members of the American Pacific community long resident in the islands, especially merchants and venture capitalists, were a bit savvier about the long-range impact of their fellow countryman's accomplishments. They instinctively understood that by serving Hawaiian interests Richards also improved their commercial and entrepreneurial opportunities.[15]

Richards's spiritual and temporal career epitomized a nineteenth-century phenomenon that accompanied the United States's drive for territorial and commercial expansion in the Pacific Rim. It became a fairly common occurrence for a private American citizen in service to a foreign government to also do serious duty as an agent of American empire. Richards and other missionaries in the Sandwich Islands who followed his example were engaged in a very delicate balancing act not only between the religious and the secular, but also in their divided political loyalties to two different nations, one a republic, the other a monarchy.

Apparently the line separating the worldly from the religious was conveniently blurred as American missionaries readily served both secular and spiritual masters. They never shed their American identity or their love for American republican institutions, which prejudiced and biased their political advice to the king. But as the British traveler Manley Hopkins observed after his stay in the islands, the missionaries "never went so far as to attempt to introduce a republic in the Hawaiian Islands." Of course, this judicious restraint and seemingly benevolent disinterest were precisely the qualities that had given the American missionary community, and by extension American commercial and economic interests, the upper hand in the Hawaiian Islands by the early 1840s.[16]

Another British visitor to Honolulu, Sir George Simpson, the head of the Hudson's Bay Company in British North America, quickly recognized this American predominance. He reported back to his superiors in England that the Hawaiian monarchy was "too much under the influence of the Calvinist Missionary Society in the United States." The most active missionary promoting American interests was William Richards, a "narrow minded, illiterate, American installed as Prime Minister, or principal councellor of the King. This man never absents himself from him and being the tool of the Missionary Society, which may be considered in a certain degree, a political Engine in the hands of the Government of the United States, the Sandwich Islands may be said to be greatly under the influence of that government." Ultimately, Simpson gained more respect for Reverend Richards and successfully urged King Kamehameha to appoint him to the diplomatic mission seeking recognition of Hawaiian independence. "I found him as shrewd and intelligent as he was pious and humble," Simpson later admiringly remarked about the American missionary turned public servant.[17]

In the summer of 1842 Timoteo Haalilio and William Richards embarked upon what became more than a two-year pilgrimage to the capitals of the western world, including Washington, London, Brussels, and Paris. Their mission was to seek recognition of Hawaiian sovereignty and independence from the three competing expansionist maritime powers vying for predominance in the islands — the United States, Great Britain, and France. After sailing the Pacific to Mexico's west coast, they went overland to Vera Cruz, took a ship to New Orleans, and finally arrived in Washington in early December.

It was an auspicious time for the Hawaiian delegation to appear in the capital city of the American republic. The recently signed Webster-Ashburton Treaty, which Richards and Haalilio had learned of while crossing Mexico, had cleared the diplomatic decks with Great Britain and future Anglo-American peace now seemed assured. No longer was the Tyler administration preoccupied with threats to America's national security from a menacing British Empire. It was reasonable for Haalilio and Richards to assume that in such a relaxed diplomatic climate the United States might be induced to do something for Hawaii.

The Hawaiian delegation was fortunate as well to arrive in the nation's capital just as Congress began its winter session and the glittering Washington social season officially opened. That particular December what Europeans tended to deride as nothing more than a provincial outpost on the banks of the Potomac River took on an unusually confident tone and cosmopolitan atmosphere. Its inhabitants were awash in a tide of Pacific-mindedness inspired by their pride in the return the previous summer of the United

States Exploring Expedition after a four-year cruise under the command of Lieutenant Charles Wilkes.

The last of the grand sailing voyages of discovery charting the earth's vast oceans that began almost four centuries earlier, the Wilkes expedition embodied the nation's commitment to the belief that westward was the course of discovery and empire. By ambitiously sending a flotilla of six small ships "to extend the empire of commerce and science," the young republic was continuing the glorious exploratory tradition of the great European navigators extending back to Vasco da Gama, Christopher Columbus, Ferdinand Magellan, and concluding with the eighteenth-century voyages of Captain James Cook. Not without justification Americans in the 1840s viewed the Wilkes voyage of discovery as the maritime equivalent of a previous generation's famed continental expedition that had gone out under Lewis and Clark to explore and chart the unknown reaches of Jefferson's landed empire of liberty.

Washington's political and social elites were excited about the return of the Wilkes mission because the heroics of these magnificent voyagers confirmed their belief in America's destiny and national greatness. The exploits of Wilkes and his crew in gathering specimens of the world's flora and fauna were breathtaking achievements that elevated the United States to a level of scientific distinction rivaling that of Great Britain and France, the other maritime powers actively engaged in uncovering the secrets of the boundless Pacific Ocean. These Scientifics, a label bestowed upon civilian crew members, of the Great Exploring Expedition brought fame and glory to the United States through their ethnographic research in the islands of Polynesia and Melanesia, their mapping of eight hundred miles of the western coast of North America, and their surveying and charting of vast sections of the western Pacific. The Wilkes expedition also recorded the first verified discovery of Antarctica. The map work and the nautical charts compiled under Charles Wilkes's direction were comparable in accuracy and quality to those created by the legendary Captain Cook, and many of the Exploring Expedition's charts and maps were still in use by the U.S. Navy in the early stages of World War II.[18]

Almost immediately a representative sample of the enormous collection of natural history specimens and cultural objects of human manufacture brought back by the Exploring Expedition went on display at the National Gallery of the Patent Office. In late June 1842, a few weeks after the return of the voyagers, Charles Wilkes presented a summary of the expedition's

discoveries in a lecture at the Patent Office that sparked widespread public interest in the exhibition. In attendance that evening were a number of
prominent men of science and several national dignitaries, including Secretary of the Navy Abel P. Upshur. In his brief remarks to the distinguished
audience, the navy secretary praised Lieutenant Wilkes's nautical achievements and said his report on the Oregon Territory "was by itself ample compensation for the entire cost of the expedition."

During the following months a tour of this novel exhibit at the nation's
first federally funded museum became a most desired outing for many of
Washington's residents and visitors. An afternoon spent marveling at this
treasure trove of exotica was all the rage and the fashionable thing to do
for Washingtonians who sought stimulating intellectual entertainment. The
objects and artifacts that antebellum Americans rushed to see at the Patent
Office ultimately became the core collection of the Smithsonian Institution.
And to this day Americans coming to the Mall in Washington to see the
exhibits at the Smithsonian's Museum of Natural History experience that
same sense of wonder and amazement when viewing the fascinating specimens of flora and fauna from the South Seas and Antarctica that originally
were collected by Wilkes and his scientific corps.

The public may have been enthralled by the glamour and excitement
of his naval odyssey, but initially Wilkes believed the official reception accorded him by the Tyler administration upon his return was cold and unen-
thusiastic. Despite Upshur's gracious acknowledgment of the expedition's
great accomplishments after hearing the informative Patent Office lecture,
Wilkes was unhappy. He felt aggrieved by what he perceived to be a deliber-
ate attempt by President Tyler and Secretary Upshur to suppress his full
forty-four-page report in order to minimize the importance of the voyage's
findings. The report, Wilkes believed, would not be allowed to see the light
of day because of petty partisan politics. At its inception, President Martin
Van Buren, a Democrat, had sponsored the Exploring Expedition. An embittered Wilkes charged that Tyler's Whig administration did not want to
give any credit to a venture that originated under Democratic leadership.

Wilkes was mistaken about Tyler and politically out of touch for having
been too long at sea. The naval officer had not witnessed the bitter struggle
between Tyler and the Whig Congress over the national bank and other domestic issues that led to the president's ouster from the Whig Party. Tyler
was no longer a Whig, if in fact he had ever been one. The explanation for
Navy Secretary Upshur's unwillingness to release Wilkes's complete report,
which was anti-British in tone and called for American occupation of Or-

egon to 54°40′, had little to do with settling partisan political scores and everything to do with the nation's diplomacy. Publishing the report with its explosive recommendations for aggressive American actions in the Pacific Northwest threatened to scuttle the Webster-Ashburton negotiations, which were at a delicate juncture during the summer of 1842, and thereby effectively torpedo the diplomatic effort to maintain peace with Great Britain. A vainglorious and self-absorbed Charles Wilkes failed to understand that completing and signing the Webster-Ashburton Treaty took precedence over his need for personal recognition and acclaim.[19]

The bitter accusations that Wilkes privately leveled at the Tyler administration did not lead to prolonged public wrangling over the merit and usefulness of his exploratory mission, nor did his personal chagrin dampen the celebratory aura of Pacific-mindedness that greeted Haalilio and Richards upon their arrival in Washington, D.C. For their daring exploits charting the unknown reaches of the Pacific Ocean, several of Wilkes's junior officers were greeted as returning heroes and were lionized by the young ladies of the Washington social set. Chief among the widely traveled sailors being adoringly feted was Richard R. Waldron, a twenty-three-year-old midshipman from New Hampshire who had performed admirably throughout the voyage, especially navigating through the icebergs during the explorations of the Antarctica coast. Waldron had met Haalilio and Richards when the expedition visited the Sandwich Islands in 1840 and he readily renewed his acquaintance with the Hawaiian diplomats, amiably serving as one of their guides to the city's most entertaining and notable salons.

High on the list of drawing rooms to visit was that in Mrs. Peyton's boardinghouse where the David Gardiner family of New York was staying. Young Waldron was courting one of the Gardiner daughters, the beautiful and flirtatious Julia. In addition to taking Julia Gardiner to the Patent Office exhibition, where she was appalled by the sight of a grotesque preserved and bloated head of a Fiji cannibal, Waldron introduced the "Belle of Long Island" and the future Mrs. John Tyler to Prince Haalilio and Mr. Richards. Julia was enchanted by Haalilio and playfully dubbed him "Timothy Hallelujah." She was less taken with the dour and prudish Reverend Richards, as she made clear in describing the two men in a letter to her older brother Alexander: "His complexion is about as dark as a negro, but with Indian hair though at a distance being short and thick it seems the *true wool*. He was in an undress military uniform and his manners were modest and graceful—quite the man of the world in comparison with his Interpreter."[20]

Julia Gardiner may have seen the missionary turned diplomat as a tire-

Timoteo Haalilio, ca. 1843. *Hawaiian Mission Children's Society, Honolulu, Hawaii.*

some bore, but Richards had enjoyed himself that evening at what he pronounced was a "splendid party." He also commented on his companion's popularity with the guests, noting that the "young ladies desired Mr. Haalilio's autograph, wished he had come in his native costume." Apparently Haalilio was flattered by all the attention he was receiving. Desiring to please his newfound admirers, he decided to wear a native shirt made by his wife to the next party, telling Richards "perhaps I had better present this to the ladies." Quite unexpectedly, the dashingly handsome "black" Prince Haalilio became an exotic oddity in the capital of a slaveholding republic where people of color normally were obedient servants and frequently human chattel as well. Much in demand at the salons of the rich and famous, Haalilio was accorded celebrity status and became the trophy guest at Washington's gala soirees and dinner parties during the 1842 winter social season.[21]

In contrast to the warm welcome they received on the social circuit, the official reception extended to Haalilio and Richards by Secretary of State Webster was much more reserved and within the strict confines of diplomatic decorum. Webster proved extremely cautious and cagey in his initial meetings with the Hawaiian representatives, most likely because he feared being trapped into accepting an entangling alliance with Britain and France that would limit American options in the central Pacific. Reverend Richards especially came to feel they were getting the runaround, or the "go by" as he phrased it, from Webster.

After their first interview with the secretary of state, Richards's apprehensions about American indifference to the cause of Hawaiian independence were "considerably awakened by the coldness" of Webster's evasive attitude and noncommittal responses. Secretary Webster feigned a loss of memory about Peter Brinsmade's earlier mission and denied any knowledge of the letter from King Kamehameha to President Tyler calling for joint recognition by the United States, Great Britain, and France. Most troubling because it appeared to be a direct rebuff was the American secretary's suggestion that Haalilio and Richards immediately go to London to first seek British recognition of Hawaiian independence.[22]

There certainly was no lack of support for Hawaiian independence amongst the many influential members of the American Pacific community who were present in Washington that December for the third session of the Twenty-seventh Congress. Within days after their arrival Richards and Haalilio had tested the waters and in numerous private meetings found broad support for Hawaii's cause from whaling, commercial, naval, and missionary spokesmen. They quickly discussed the outlines of their lobbying strategy with several of New England's staunchest advocates of American expansion in the Pacific Rim, including Caleb Cushing and John Quincy Adams.

They also received encouragement and support from knowledgeable and experienced naval officers, most notably Charles Wilkes and Richard Waldron, who had traversed the immense reaches of the Pacific Ocean and understood the strategic importance of the Hawaiian Islands. Representative Thomas Williams of Connecticut, a leading advocate for the whaling industry, emerged as one of the main sponsors and go-betweens for Richards and Haalilio in the halls of Congress. In all, these insider contacts paved the way for Haalilio and Richards to meet on seven occasions with the reluctant and evasive Secretary Webster. Eventually the Hawaiian delegates also succeeded in having an audience with President Tyler and other members of his cabinet.

After initially experiencing the jarring but not totally unexpected cold shoulder from the secretary of state, Richards and Haalilio turned to the venerable John Quincy Adams for advice and help. They found Adams

Timoteo Haalilio and William Richards, from the daguerreotype taken in Europe, probably Paris, ca. 1843. *Hawaiian Mission Children's Society, Honolulu, Hawaii.*

more sympathetic to their cause and were pleased to learn that the New Englander had "a deep interest in the welfare of the Islands." In recounting his first impressions of the Hawaiian emissaries to his diary, Adams expressed the same fascination with Haalilio's complexion and hair as had Julia Gardiner, although he had less difficulty with the pronunciation of his name. A "native of those islands, a Secretary of the King—a strong, stout-built man, nearly black as an Ethiopian, but with a European face, and wool for hair . . . Haa-lee-lee-o has a commission as Ambassador from the King of the Sandwich Islands to this country, to Great Britain, and to France, and is to assume the character first here or in Europe at his discretion." Richards and Haalilio proceeded to have a lengthy discussion with the former president, after which Adams advised them not to leave for England but to persist in pressuring Secretary Webster and President Tyler to grant recognition.[23]

Whatever may have been his own reservations about black equality and nagging concerns about racial amalgamation, Adams believed the Tyler administration was balking at granting recognition of Hawaii's independence because of racial prejudice. "I did not see the wisdom of leaving to Great Britain the option of assuming the islands under her protection," he confided to his diary, "but I see the motive for Webster's advice, which is that they are black." John Quincy Adams, who the previous February had wit-

nessed a vicious racist tirade against the recognition of the black republic of Haiti in the House of Representatives by Henry Wise, a close ally of
President Tyler, suspected the same anti-black sentiment was motivating
the administration in the Hawaiian case. To some extent, Adams may have
been correct. Operating within a racial framework that defined Africans
and other dark-hued people as inferior and incapable of self-government,
recognition of Hawaii's independence initially may have been problematic
for Tyler and Webster because Haalilio "was nearly black as an Ethiopian"
and hence all his countrymen were presumed to be black as well.[24]

It is unknown whether Reverend Richards and Prince Haalilio shared
Adams's belief that the Tyler administration's diplomatic aloofness was due
to racial prejudice. Even if they did sense or suspect an ugly racism was the
reason behind their cool reception, the two men were too polite and wisely
circumspect to raise the issue publicly. For his part, Richards never once
accused Secretary Webster or President Tyler of racial animus in his private
day-to-day journal, which was a copious and detailed account of their mission to the western capitals of the world.

Apparently the many meetings and consultations Haalilio and Richards
had with more than two dozen "persons of influence" such as Senators John C.
Calhoun and Thomas Hart Benton, and Congressmen Cushing and Williams, convinced them that what the Tyler administration most feared was
losing its freedom of action by being tied to a European consortium guaranteeing Hawaiian independence. A preference for a policy of freedom of
action, not blatant racism, would seem to have been the explanation for
the more than two-week runaround they received from Secretary Webster.
Richards, sensing the administration's insecurity about its policy in the Pacific and undoubtedly taking a cue from John Quincy Adams, thought it
might be time to play the British card.

After the next meeting with Secretary Webster, Richards recorded that
they had a "pleasant visit and free talk with *him*." At the end of their open
and candid discussion, the secretary asked Richards to write him officially
about the purpose of their diplomatic mission. Richards dutifully complied
and within a few days hand-delivered the official letter to the State Department requesting the United States to recognize the sovereignty and independence of the Hawaiian Islands. To buttress his case for formal recognition, Richards enumerated the reasons why the islands were important to
the United States and the other maritime powers dominant in the Pacific.
"Their position is such, that they constitute the great centre of the whale
industry for most of the world," and the Hawaiian Islands were essential

to success in the China trade because they "are on the principal line of communication between the Western Continent of America and the Eastern Continent of Asia." In addition, Richards pointed out that American citizens had extensive property interests in the islands that would continue to be protected and safeguarded if the United States granted diplomatic recognition to the Hawaiian monarchy.[25]

Still Webster stalled. More than a week after sending the requested letter, Richards and Haalilio had not received a reply. On Friday, December 23, they called on Webster again only to discover that "he evidently had not read our letter." Without apology, the secretary of state "promised that it should be ready by the middle of next week." Richards was further disappointed that Webster "said nothing about introducing us to the president as he had formerly promised to do—no paper ready to view—evidently giving us the go by." "When I spoke of seeing the President," Richards noted in his journal, Webster coyly responded, "Oh you have not seen him yet, call on your friend Mr. Williams—he will introduce you."

Richards did call on Mr. Williams, but after they talked it over, he "declined going with him to President after Mr. Webster's promise." Instead, Richards finally decided to play the British card and told Williams of "my plan of putting Islands under British protection, if we do not get independence." The next day Richards also passed on the word about seeking a British protectorate to the well-connected Richard Waldron, who was scheduled to dine with Daniel Webster at the secretary's home that evening. Mr. Richards also "informed Lt. Wilkes of my design."[26]

Playing the British card and getting the alarming news out to "persons of influence" did the trick. On December 27 Haalilio and Richards again met with Webster. According to Reverend Richards, this time the secretary politely "inquired if we should like to call on the Pres. I answered 'yes.'" Richards's fascinating journal entry for the momentous day when he and Haalilio had their long-awaited meeting with President Tyler continued: "It was the day for the Cabinet meeting. We waited in the anteroom until the cabinet had assembled and were invited in. All pleasant.—free and full. In reply to some of the President's close questions I hinted my plan in case independence was not acknowledged. He understood it and was quite engaged. Inquired where I was from and as I was leary said that Yankees are shrewd negotiators—and so forth."

President Tyler knew the game being played and admired the Yankee missionary's audacity. The pious evangelist from New England, recently turned canny diplomat, had aroused Tyler and Webster's fears of British imperial expansion in Hawaii. William Richards's diplomatic ploy of raising the specter of British imperialism convinced the Tyler administration to abandon its foot-dragging policy of evasion and delay.[27]

It was a remarkable turnaround. To forestall a possible British protectorate in the islands, the slaveholding John Tyler had willingly granted an audience to a "black" ambassador, Timoteo Haalilio, in order to assure America's continued cultural and commercial dominance in Hawaii. If securing the nation's political and strategic agenda in the Pacific Ocean demanded the unusual and exceptional, the ever Pacific-minded President Tyler was happy to oblige. To put the importance of his Pacific priorities in further perspective, one must realize that President Tyler never would have extended the same courtesy to a black diplomat from Haiti. But then the republic of Haiti was a former slave colony in the Caribbean within threateningly close proximity to the United States's southern coast and not a vitally strategic archipelago at the crossroads of the Pacific Ocean. His flexible and astute Hawaiian policy did in fact give credence to Tyler's oft-repeated claim that his diplomacy was broadly national in scope and aimed at fulfilling America's national destiny.

Although President Tyler may have followed Webster's early policy of stall and delay in dealing with the issue of Hawaiian independence, his face-to-face encounter with Prince Haalilio and Reverend Richards changed all that. Once the Americans understood the Hawaiians were playing hardball, negotiations moved more swiftly if still somewhat enigmatically. Just two days after meeting with the president and his cabinet, Haalilio and Richards finally received Webster's written reply to their formal request for diplomatic recognition. In his letter to the Hawaiian representatives the secretary of state appeared to grant U.S. acceptance of Hawaiian sovereignty but his clear emphasis was on another point—that their "government should not be interfered with by foreign powers."

In diplomatic language that obscured rather than clarified, Secretary Webster did not unequivocally acknowledge Hawaiian independence. Instead, he explained that American commercial predominance in Hawaii "induces the President to be quite willing to declare as the sense of the government of the United States that the government of the Sandwich Islands ought to be respected; that no power ought either to take possession of the Islands as a conquest or for the purpose of colonization, and that no power ought to seek for any undue control over the existing Government, or any exclusive privileges or preferences in the matters of commerce."[28]

Reverend Richards was troubled by Secretary Webster's equivocal statement. He asked him if there would be a formal treaty between the United States and the Hawaiian monarchy granting diplomatic recognition. No, replied Webster, because a treaty between nations "was a solemn thing—it was not best to do too much at once." An obviously disheartened Richards confided to his journal: "Have received Mr. Webster's reply. . . . Not quite what I want but others think it is well." The "others" referred to by Richards undoubtedly were his more sanguine political mentors, the "men of influence" such as Congressmen John Quincy Adams, Thomas Williams, and Caleb Cushing. They, along with naval officers Waldron and Wilkes, were patrons of Hawaiian independence because it forestalled Britain's imperial designs and sustained American commercial and political predominance in the Central Pacific.[29]

Apparently the optimism of the men of influence was justified. In his official diplomatic correspondence to Edward Everett, the American minister to Great Britain, Secretary Daniel Webster made clear that the United States had recognized the independence of the islands. On the same day that he presented his written reply to Haalilio and Richards, Webster wrote his minister in London: "We take the lead in declaring for the Independence of the Islands. We think, also, of recommending to Congress to make provision for a Commission to China." Several months later Webster informed Everett that the Tyler administration "has for its sole object the preservation of the independence of those Islands, and the maintenance by their Government of an entire impartiality in their intercourse with foreign states." Webster also told Everett to assure the British government that the United States had no intention to take control or possession of the Hawaiian Islands.[30]

On December 30, 1842, the day following the secretary of state's last meeting with Haalilio and Richards, President Tyler sent a special message to Congress making public his Hawaiian policy, which became known as the Tyler Doctrine. The president also announced, as Webster had noted in his instructions to Everett, the administration's intention to send an official diplomatic mission to China. In his message, Tyler repeated the familiar arguments earlier expressed by Webster about the importance of the islands to the American whaling industry and to the nation's commerce. Tyler emphasized that five-sixths of all vessels annually visiting Honolulu sailed under the American flag, "and could not but create dissatisfaction on the part of the United States at any attempt by another power, should such attempt be threatened or feared, to take possession of the islands, colonize them, and subvert the native Government."

President Tyler believed the Hawaiian Islands were entitled to American protection because there was "proof that their inhabitants are making progress in civilization, and more and more competent to maintain regular and orderly civil government." "Just emerging from a state of barbarism," he explained, "the Government of the islands is as yet feeble, but its dispositions appear to be just and pacific, and it seems anxious to improve the condition of its people by the introduction of knowledge, of religious and moral institutions, means of education, and the arts of civilized life." An advocate of American exceptionalism, Tyler thought that as an advanced Western, Christian society it was the United States's obligation to guide the Hawaiians on the path to spiritual redemption and cultural regeneration. On behalf of the American people, slaveholder John Tyler readily took up what the British poet Rudyard Kipling decades later characterized as the "white man's burden."

With this message President Tyler extended the 1823 Monroe Doctrine to the central Pacific and claimed an American sphere of influence over a distant archipelago some 2,500 miles from the western shores of North America. If nothing else, the Tyler Doctrine was a breathtaking display of imperial hubris and an unmistakable expression of nineteenth-century American diplomatic brazenness. Despite Secretary Webster's later assurances to the contrary to the British government, the Tyler administration had signaled to the world the United States's intention to establish a de facto protectorate in the Hawaiian Islands.[31]

Tyler's bold China initiative was prompted by the British victory in the Opium War earlier that year. Hostilities between England and China, the president told Congress, "have been terminated by a treaty, according to the terms of which four important ports hitherto shut against foreign commerce are to be open to British merchants." It was imperative that the United States secure the same port privileges for American merchants and businessmen engaged in the China trade. President Tyler recommended "to Congress to make appropriation for the compensation of a commissioner to reside in China to exercise a watchful care over the concerns of American citizens." When appropriate the commissioner should negotiate a treaty with the Chinese government that would grant American citizens access to the four ports previously opened to British traders and merchants. Knowing Congress's penchant for skimping on funds for such ventures, Tyler urged that in order to enlist the services of "a citizen of much intelligence and weight of character," a "compensation should be made corresponding to the magnitude and importance of the mission."[32]

Undoubtedly Webster and Tyler should be given joint credit for setting two path-breaking precedents in the nation's antebellum Pacific diplomacy that led at century's end to the annexation of Hawaii and the creation of the Open Door Policy in China. But another of Tyler's confidants—Caleb Cushing—deserved recognition as well for his role in formulating this policy. Cushing was one of Tyler's most trusted and loyal northern political allies. He had the president's full confidence and his policy advice regarding Hawaii and China probably influenced Tyler as much, if not more so, than that of Secretary Webster. Unlike the secretary of state, Cushing was unequivocal in his call for a strong stance in the Pacific and he was one of the "men of influence" helping Richards and Haalilio negotiate Washington's corridors of power. As legislator, lobbyist, and presidential confidant, Cushing's intellectual and political commitment to promoting American interests in the Pacific Rim was unwaveringly supportive of his friend in the White House.

On the day that Secretary Webster grudgingly brought Haalilio and Richards round to meet with Tyler and the cabinet, Cushing was on the scene. Before the Hawaiian emissaries were ushered into the room, Cushing had presented the president with a succinct geopolitical analysis of events transpiring in the Pacific and Asia. Cushing appealed to Tyler's Anglophobia by raising the specter of a British imperialism on the prowl. It was another version of the British card, but this time played by a fellow Anglophobe. With its recent triumph of arms Britain not only had forced China to admit British vessels to additional ports, but, more alarmingly, "to cede to England in perpetual sovereignty a commercial depot and fortified port on the coast of China." That reference, of course, was to Hong Kong, which while not held by Britain in perpetuity, was only restored to China at the close of the twentieth century after more than 150 years of British rule.

Although it did not appear to Cushing that Britain intended to exclude other nations from China, he urged Tyler to send a special commissioner to China "with instructions to make commercial arrangements in behalf of the United States." The moment was propitious because Cushing had "information from Canton that the Chinese are predisposed to deal kindly with us." Dr. Peter Parker, who earlier had told Secretary Webster and President Tyler that the Chinese held the United States in special favor, probably was Cushing's informant in Canton. Whether or not this news about the receptivity of the Chinese government to an American overture was reliable, Cushing believed it was accurate. He was supremely confident that a mission to China would be successful and added that after completing his diplomatic task of opening relations with China, the American agent should proceed "for the same purpose to Japan."[33]

Great Britain may not have contemplated closing the China trade to its commercial rivals. But Cushing feared the British were in a position "to seize on the Sandwich Islands to have a complete belt of fortresses envisioning the Globe, to the imminent future peril, not only of our territorial possessions, but of all our vast Commerce on the Pacific." To counteract such menacing British imperial designs along the Pacific Rim, Cushing informed President Tyler of Haalilio and Richards's keen desire to enter "into friendly political relations in preference to any of the European Govts." With this diplomatic opportunity at hand, Cushing proposed "that the United States make at once a public recognition of the independent sovereignty of the Sandwich Islands" and follow up by sending a paid consular agent to Hawaii as a "formal manifestation" of recognition. "By taking this step," Cushing argued, "we block the game of England with respect to the Sandwich Islands and assure to ourselves the friendship of a people who by their peculiar geographical position are of the greatest possible consequence to the commerce of the Pacific." With his crucial assistance in the House of Representatives, the Tyler administration was able to implement all of Caleb Cushing's recommendations for an activist diplomacy throughout the Pacific Rim.[34]

Not surprisingly, the Tyler Doctrine was highly popular among the ranks of the American Pacific community. Merchants, entrepreneurs, and spokesmen for the whaling industry were pleased with the president's decisiveness in extending America's protective shield over the Hawaiian Islands. Another group that had strongly lobbied for recognition, the American Board of Commissioners for Foreign Missions, hailed President Tyler's statement in favor of Hawaiian independence and reprinted large sections of his December message to Congress in its official journal, the *Missionary Herald*. The Board of Commissioners had begun their lobbying efforts on behalf of Hawaiian sovereignty by sending Hiram Bingham to Washington in June 1841. Although it had taken Webster and Tyler seventeen months to take favorable action, that troubling and annoying delay made the victory no less sweet.

In addition to its hearty approval of the administration's Hawaiian policy, the missionary community had another good reason to be pleased with the diplomacy of Secretary of State Daniel Webster and President John Tyler. On two recent occasions, Secretary Webster had been directed by President Tyler, "who is profoundly interested in the matter," to issue explicit instructions to the nation's representatives in Denmark and Syria in the Ottoman Empire to protect the interests of American missionaries serving in those countries. This was the first time in the history of the American republic that the federal government had extended official protection to missionaries living and working in foreign lands.

It was not lost upon Webster and Tyler that American missionaries, as Sir George Simpson of the Hudson's Bay Company had enviously observed, were agents of empire who opened the way for the nation's commercial and cultural expansion not only in the Pacific but across the globe. No part of the world escaped the Tyler administration's interest and scrutiny. The remarkable thing was that Tyler and Webster virtually did everything the missionary societies asked. They proclaimed the Tyler Doctrine, granted recognition of Hawaiian independence, and provided a shield of protection for missionaries, which was a precedent-setting endeavor and a significant diplomatic first for the Tyler administration.[35]

John Tyler also received accolades for his Pacific-minded policy from some of his most bitter foes and political adversaries. Rather unexpectedly, the abolitionist editor Joshua Leavitt, who had just run a series of articles on the president's alleged sexual activities in the slave quarters, expressed approval of the Tyler Doctrine. The administration's Hawaiian initiative, according to Leavitt, was "liberal and philanthropic." John Quincy Adams, for all his undisguised distaste for the slaveholder "Acting President" in the White House and distrust of the libertine secretary of state, pronounced Tyler's message, which he believed was "Webster's composition," an "elaborate and able argument for the recognition of the Sandwich Islands Government and the mission to China." Adams worked with the administration to gain congressional funding for its proposals and wrote an influential report for the House Foreign Affairs Committee urging formal recognition of the Hawaiian Islands. A mutual interest in commercial expansion and a shared wariness about the British Empire expediently if temporarily brought Adams and Tyler together in support of American interests throughout the Pacific Rim.[36]

Despite the widespread approval and praise for the Tyler Doctrine at home, on the international scene Great Britain, the United States's chief imperial rival in the Pacific, almost immediately challenged the new policy. Two uncoordinated British maneuvers in early 1843, one a trenchant response by the Peel ministry in London and the second a case of unauthorized gunboat diplomacy in Hawaii, seriously threatened to undercut the American attempt to extend the principles of the Monroe Doctrine to the Central Pacific. These two events occurred almost simultaneously, but because of the slow communications in the mid-nineteenth century, unlike today when television networks instantaneously broadcast events around the globe, it was not until the late spring of 1843 that both challenges were fully understood in Washington.

Lord Aberdeen mounted the initial objection to President Tyler's Hawaiian policy. In meetings with William Richards and Timoteo Haalilio, recently arrived in England on the second leg of their mission seeking recognition of Hawaiian independence, the British foreign secretary raised serious questions about the true nature of American pretensions in the Pacific. After being shown Webster's letter, which they contended granted recognition, Aberdeen was blunt with the Hawaiian diplomats. He said the letter of the American secretary of state "did not acknowledge the independence of the Islands but virtually denied it, inasmuch as it contained a refusal to enter into treaty." His Lordship was wary of the American game of informal empire. He "implied a suspicion that the Government of the U.S.A. was endeavoring, while it could not hold colonies in form to do so in part by exerting an influence over the Sandwich Islands Government in favor of American interests to the injury of the British."

Foreign Secretary Aberdeen also charged that in its dealings with foreign nations the Hawaiian monarchy was not even-handed and fair. "This suspicion," he told Haalilio and Richards, "is grounded on certain complaints made against the Government of the Sandwich Islands, by the British Consul that the Government is partial to the American." A distrustful Aberdeen brushed off their initial request for recognition. To salvage their mission from imminent disaster, Richards and Haalilio wrote Daniel Webster appealing for a clarification of the American position. They informed the Secretary of State that "His Lordship expressed an opinion that the British Government would not concede the independence of the Islands, and one reason which he mentioned why it would not do it, was the fact that the Americans, (who have much greater interests at the Islands than the British), have not done it." Anticipating Britain's unease about American ambitions, Secretary Webster—in a communication that was sent before he had received the Haalilio-Richards appeal—preemptively had instructed Minister Everett to inform Lord Aberdeen that the United States had no "sinister purpose" in the Hawaiian Islands.[37]

Perhaps the more immediately threatening blow to the Tyler Doctrine came from Lord George Paulet, captain of HMS *Carysfort*. Seeking redress for alleged British grievances against the Hawaiian monarchy, Captain Paulet demanded restitution from the government of Kamehameha III. The British naval officer made clear that if his stipulations were not met promptly, he would order a bombardment of Honolulu. Unable to fulfill Paulet's bill of particulars and under extreme duress, the king ceded the islands to Great Britain on February 25, 1843.

To the dismay of the American business and missionary communities in Hawaii, the Union Jack was hoisted throughout the scattered islands of the archipelago. In writing home informing a relative in the United States of the British takeover, one American missionary in Honolulu, although lamenting that "we are now under the British flag," saw some hope in the fact that "the cession is only *provisional* & may be reversed by treaties now being formed by the embassy in Europe." "But," he added, "of this there is very little hope." Probably most of the other members of the American Pacific community in Hawaii viscerally understood and shared their compatriot's anguish and pessimism about the prospect of permanent British rule.[38]

Paulet's impetuous annexation of the Hawaiian Islands confirmed the worst fears of America's Pacific-minded leaders. It was an unwelcome manifestation of their recurrent nightmare in which an avaricious British Empire gobbled up chains of islands all across the Pacific Rim. From London, American minister Everett had warned Secretary Webster some months after the British occupied New Zealand in 1841 that if unchecked, Great Britain next would take Hawaii, then the Society Islands, "and we shall be driven from all the convenient resorts in the Pacific." A frightening scenario of British imperial expansion in the far reaches of the Pacific Ocean seemed to be unfolding, just as a prescient Representative Cushing had predicted to President Tyler when he warned that Britain was in the process of creating a belt of fortresses encircling the world. These dread forebodings now seemed to becoming reality and no longer could be dismissed as simply the wild and exaggerated fears of a handful of the Tyler administration's most vocal Anglophobes.[39]

President Tyler learned of Paulet's takeover in mid-May from Hugh S. Legare, the interim secretary of state. Legare, an aristocratic slaveholding South Carolinian, had replaced Daniel Webster after the latter's resignation from the cabinet a week earlier. Upon receiving the news, the president replied to Legare that he was "quite concerned at the information you give in relation to the Sandwich Islands," particularly because it was in violation of the recently announced Tyler Doctrine. "I had hoped that a declaration so emphatic would have been respected by G. Britain, and regret now to learn the contrary," Tyler confided to Secretary Legare. "Should we not," the president instructed, in order to protect American interests, "enquire without delay into all the circumstances and address a strong note to the British Govt. upon the subject?" Within a few weeks Secretary Legare complied with Tyler's directive. The interim secretary sent a lengthy dispatch to Minister Everett instructing him to lodge a strong protest with Foreign Secretary Aberdeen opposing this "revolting usurpation" of Hawaiian independence by an overzealous and high-handed British naval officer.[40]

Revealing just how pervasive the belief in future American commercial predominance in the Pacific and Asia was among the nation's leaders, whether they were from above or below the Mason-Dixon Line, Hugh Legare of Charleston pursued the same vision that had guided his New England predecessor Daniel Webster. Legare also proved to be every bit as Pacific-minded as the Virginian John Tyler and Caleb Cushing, a son of Massachusetts. In his message to Everett, Legare explicated his nationalist Pacific vision. He stressed that the United States was a non-interventionist power that had "no wish to plant, or to acquire, colonies abroad." America was an exceptional nation and "there is something so entirely peculiar in the relations between this little commonwealth and ourselves, that we might even feel justified, consistently with our own principles, in interfering by force to prevent its falling into the hands of one of the great Powers of Europe."

"If the attempt now making by ourselves," Secretary Legare continued, "as well as by other Christian Powers, to open the markets of China to a more general commerce, be successful, there can be no doubt but that a great part of that commerce will find its way over the Isthmus. In that event it will be impossible to overrate the importance of the Hawaiian group as a stage in the long voyage between Asia and America." Although Legare was to die just a week after penning this message to Everett, in his brief six-week tenure at the State Department the unheralded South Carolinian had succeeded brilliantly in outlining what was to become America's Pacific destiny.[41]

None of this American rhetorical posturing proved necessary. In early June, before Legare had sent his dispatch to London, Lord Aberdeen wrote the British minister in Washington, Henry Fox, that Great Britain would abide by its earlier promise to recognize Hawaiian independence. Upon receipt of this message three weeks later, Minister Fox immediately conveyed Aberdeen's assurances to the newly appointed American secretary of state, Abel P. Upshur. In early July the welcome news that England intended to restore Hawaiian sovereignty was published in several Washington newspapers. President Tyler found "the disclaimer of the British government as to the Sandwich Islands" to be "highly gratifying."

But Tyler, ever suspicious of British intrigue and duplicity, told Secretary Upshur to reply to Minister Fox's letter circumspectly and cautiously "to guard against any ambiguous or hidden intent." Fortunately for John

Tyler and the United States, Britain's imperial restraint was not illusionary. In Honolulu, British Admiral Richard Thomas restored sovereignty to the Hawaiian monarchy on July 31, 1843. A few months later Great Britain, along with France, officially recognized the independence of the Hawaiian Islands. The Tyler Doctrine was upheld, as the Monroe Doctrine earlier had been, by Britain's forbearance and willingness to acquiesce, at least temporarily, to America's pretensions.[42]

As a postscript to their successful diplomatic mission to London and Paris, William Richards and Timoteo Haalilio once again visited Washington in 1844 on their return trip to Hawaii. A nervous Richards wished to verify that the Tyler administration had indeed recognized Hawaiian independence. The pair made the rounds garnering support from their friends in Congress as well as receiving encouragement from the Democratic Party nominee and future president, James K. Polk. Haalilio and Richards met with Secretary of State John C. Calhoun, who was appointed to the post after the tragic death of Upshur in an explosion aboard the *Princeton*. Secretary Calhoun received a formal written request from the Hawaiian diplomats "making inquiry whether the government of the United States consider their various acts in relation to the Sandwich Islands as a full and perfect recognition of Independence."

After consulting with President Tyler on the matter, Calhoun informed Haalilio and Richards that Webster's December 1842 letter to them along "with the Message of the President to Congress of the 31st of December 1842, and the proceedings therein of the House of Representatives, the appropriation made for the compensation of a Commissioner of the United States who was subsequently appointed to reside in the Sandwich Islands, were regarded by the President as a full recognition on the part of the United States of the Independence of the Hawaiian Government." Their sojourn of over two years now fully complete and eminently successful, Richards and Haalilio briefly indulged themselves in tourism and paid a visit to Niagara Falls before beginning the final leg of their return voyage. Sadly, Prince Haalilio never again saw his beloved homeland. He died at sea on December 3, 1844, on board the ship *Montreal*.[43]

★ AN OPENING TO CHINA
★
★ In his 1842 annual message to Congress, John Tyler had accentuated the need for foreign markets to vent the nation's surplus and overcome the paradox of economic distress arising not from a scarcity of goods but from a glut

of agricultural and industrial commodities. The president believed "the greatest evil" the United States had "to encounter is a surplus of production beyond the home demand, which seeks, and with difficulty finds, a partial market in other regions." Asia abounded in ostensibly lucrative markets for America's surplus production of grains, tobacco, and cotton goods. President Tyler argued in justifying his case to Congress for the appointment of an envoy to China that "the opening of several new and important ports connected with parts of the Empire heretofore seldom visited" by American merchants and businessmen offered vast opportunities for increased trade with the Celestial Kingdom.[44]

President Tyler's call for a mission to China was not met with universal approval in Congress. To be sure, the House of Representatives with Adams and Cushing in the lead readily passed a bill appropriating the necessary funds for the China venture. But the administration's proposal met strong partisan resistance in the Senate, especially from Democrat Thomas Hart Benton of Missouri. Senator Benton, who earlier had inveighed against the Webster-Ashburton Treaty without success, now denounced the administration's plan to send a legation to China as an unnecessary and expensive boondoggle.

This lofty diplomatic enterprise professedly designed to promote America's export trade with the world's most populous nation was, according to Benton, merely an elaborate political scheme concocted to allow Tyler to appoint Edward Everett as commissioner to China. Daniel Webster then would fill the vacancy in London as a graceful way for President Tyler to ease him out of the State Department because of his opposition to Texas annexation. Although Senator Benton's scenario of musical chairs did not play out as he forecast, apparently there was some truth to his claim about Webster seeking to save face by succeeding Everett as the American minister to Great Britain.

Despite Benton's vigorous opposition to the proposal, the Senate finally did approve the $40,000 appropriation for the China mission that President Tyler had requested. An amendment to the bill stipulated that Senate approval of the appointment of a commissioner was required. In anticipation of this requirement, the Tyler administration at the very last minute nominated Edward Everett for the post of commissioner to China and the Senate unanimously endorsed his designation as head of the mission.

Whether or not Everett actually would relinquish the prestigious London posting to accept the challenging assignment to the Celestial Kingdom was uncertain. Nonetheless, while he awaited official word from Everett an anxious Secretary Webster went ahead with preparations for the mission. Almost immediately he issued a State Department circular seeking information from a selected group of China merchants "for the purpose of cultivating friendly relations with that Empire, and of opening and enlarging, as far as practicable, commercial intercourse between the two countries."[45]

As a chief executive who proudly claimed he had "his eye fixed upon China," John Tyler relished the opportunity to provision and outfit the upcoming mission to Asia. Ever since the early days of his presidency and his meeting with the missionary Dr. Peter Parker, Tyler was committed to finding a way to establish treaty relations and opening the door to China. His enthusiasm was apparent when he and Secretary Webster excitedly drew up a "List of Articles for the Legation to China." Tyler went through the list of items and specimens, assiduously making notes to Webster instructing him to make sure certain items would be procured, including two pairs of six-shooting pistols, Kentucky rifles, a telescope, a model of a steamship, and an atlas, "and if possible a *Globe*, that the Celestials may see they are not the 'Central Kingdom.'"

Numerous collections of books and reference works also were on the list, including the *Encyclopedia Americana*. Finally, President Tyler personally requested that a history of the United States and "a History of the Revolution or Marshals [*sic*] life of Washington" be packed as gifts for Chinese officials. This meticulous attention to detail in preparation for the mission was a clear indicator of the importance that Tyler and Webster attached to the China venture. In addition, the list of articles and books they so carefully chose offered a fascinating glimpse of what these men thought were the young American republic's most significant and representative cultural artifacts. President Tyler and Secretary Webster evidently believed they had selected the best examples of Western learning and technology to impress and awe the Celestials.[46]

After some hesitation and equivocation, Everett declined the appointment as commissioner to China. Tyler had no problem making another selection. His friend and loyal political ally Caleb Cushing, a man the president earlier had nominated for secretary of the treasury three times and who had been soundly rejected by the Senate on each occasion, was the logical replacement. A nineteenth-century incarnation of the "Renaissance Man," Cushing graduated Phi Beta Kappa from Harvard at age seventeen, had enormous intellectual and linguistic gifts, and was a renowned scholar and an outstanding botanist. He also had a reputation as an unethical opportunist who switched political allegiances willy-nilly. As fellow New Englander John Quincy Adams succinctly put it: "Cushing has no moral principle."

Untroubled by such charges, President Tyler readily named him to succeed Everett. Since Congress was out of session at the time, Tyler employed his executive prerogative to bypass the requirement for the Senate's approval of another nomination and granted Caleb Cushing a recess appointment as U.S. Commissioner to China.[47]

On May 8, 1843, the day that he resigned and in one of his last acts as Tyler's secretary of state, Daniel Webster dispatched a letter of instructions to Cushing outlining the goals for his mission to China. A number of American merchants and representatives of Canton trading houses had responded to Webster's earlier circular requesting advice for the mission, and the secretary incorporated several of their most useful suggestions in his list of instructions to Cushing. Webster informed the newly appointed commissioner that a "leading object of the Mission" was to guarantee that American merchants would have access to the four ports—Amoy (Xiamen), Ning-po (Ningbo), Fow-chow-fow (Fuzhou), and Shanghai—that recently were opened to British trade as a result of the Opium War. Webster believed it was imperative that American ships have entry because those ports along China's east coast "belong to some of the richest, most productive, and most populous provinces of the Empire, and are likely to become very important marts of commerce."

In his message to Congress calling for the creation of a mission to China, President Tyler had stressed that the United States urgently sought foreign markets to absorb the nation's surplus production. Secretary Webster made the same point in his letter to Commissioner Cushing. He emphasized that the need to augment American exports to consumers in all of China's accessible ports "is a matter of moment to the commercial and manufacturing, as well as the agricultural and mining, interests of the United States." The right man for the task of dealing with this "matter of moment" in Sino-American relations was Caleb Cushing. The son of John Newmarch Cushing, a pioneer sea captain in the Far East trade, and a distant cousin of the influential Canton merchant John Perkins Cushing, the younger Cushing had insider knowledge of the China trade and close ties with the New England mercantile community. He long had been an ardent economic expansionist and welcomed the opportunity to open China's vast market to American enterprise and commerce.[48]

Commissioner Cushing also was instructed by Secretary Webster to convey to Chinese officials and the Chinese people without equivocation that his mission was one of a peaceful and nonthreatening nature. He was to go forth as "a messenger of peace, sent from the greatest Power in America to the greatest Empire in Asia, to offer respect and good will, and to establish the means of friendly intercourse." Finally, Cushing was informed that he would be the bearer of a personal letter of friendship from President John Tyler to the Emperor of China, "signed by the President's own hand, which you cannot deliver except to the Emperor himself, or some high official of the Court in his presence." The president's letter, whose authorship remains a mystery to this day, although it has been attributed to Daniel Webster by some historians, was one of the more bizarre diplomatic communications sent to another sovereign state during the entire history of antebellum American foreign relations.[49]

John Tyler's letter to the exulted leader of the Celestial Empire and the Middle Kingdom was a banal and insipid example of cultural arrogance. It had the singsong cadence of correspondence that American leaders frequently used to address Indian chiefs and other supposedly inferior beings, and was written in the simplified and childlike language that such benighted creatures might be able to understand. The letter's prose was grounded in cultural speech patterns that assumed if you spoke loudly, slowly, and distinctly to non-English speakers, somehow they might divine your meaning.

Tyler began the letter to the Chinese Emperor by introducing himself as the president of the United States. He then methodically proceeded to list all the states of the Union from Maine in the east to Michigan in the west. Despite the simplicity and directness of his roll call of the individual states, President Tyler conveniently neglected to mention that his nation was a slaveholding republic, and he also failed to explain which states were free and which were slave. Perhaps Tyler was acknowledging that the American republic's peculiar institution was not an example of progressive Western thought and practice that would impress the Chinese.

The demeaning and insulting presidential recitation continued: "I hope your health is good. China is a great empire, extending over a great part of the world. The Chinese are numerous. You have millions and millions of subjects. The twenty-six United States are as large as China, though our people are not so numerous. The rising sun looks over the great mountains and great rivers of China. When he sets, he looks upon rivers and mountains equally large in the United States." After offering more of the same absurdities, Tyler urged that these two great nations should be at peace.

The president then got to the heart of the matter and spoke of commercial issues: "The Chinese love to trade with our people, and sell them tea and silk, for which our people pay silver, and sometimes other articles. But if the Chinese and Americans will trade, there should be rules, so that they shall not break your laws nor our laws." Tyler concluded by stating that the bearer of the letter, Commissioner Cushing, was sent to the Celestial Empire "to make a treaty to regulate trade. Let it be just. Let there be no unfair advantage on either side." The fact that Cushing succeeded in his task and survived the ignominy and humiliation of this ludicrous letter spoke volumes about his skills as a diplomat.[50]

Before his departure for the Celestial Empire, Cushing attended a lavish banquet in Boston commemorating the dedication of the Bunker Hill Monument. Among the numerous speakers that evening were President Tyler and his newly appointed commissioner to China. In his remarks, Cushing effectively employed the imagery of the open door to highlight the objectives of the Tyler administration's Asian policy. He went to China, Cushing told the audience, "in behalf of civilization, and that, if possible, the doors of three hundred millions of Asiatic laborers may be opened to America." The following day a special dinner in honor of Commissioner Cushing was held at the Tremont House hosted by a number of merchants involved in the China trade. The celebration lasted well beyond midnight as the elite of Boston's mercantile community offered countless toasts to the success of Cushing's mission.[51]

In early August 1843 Cushing left the United States from Hampton Roads, Virginia, with a flotilla of four ships, including the recently commissioned steam frigate *Missouri*, and three sailing ships, the frigate *Brandywine*, the sloop-of-war *St. Louis*, and the brig *Perry*. Overall it was an impressive American squadron that carried more than two hundred guns. In his close attention to every detail involving the preparation for the legation to China, President Tyler wanted the best display of naval power possible and had sought to have the 120-gun *Pennsylvania*, a menacing and dread ship of the line, serve as flagship of the squadron. But fearing congressional parsimony when it came to funding the mission, Tyler sarcastically wrote Webster that if "they make a small affair of it any little cock-boat will do."

Tyler's fears were unwarranted. Although the *Pennsylvania* did not lead the flotilla, the president surely was pleased that Congress had made no "small affair of it" and that the Cushing mission would be escorted by the mightiest American naval force ever sent to Chinese waters. The appearance of the squadron off the coast of Macao in the South China Sea after a five-month voyage had the desired effect as the arrival of Commissioner

Cushing's legation in February 1844 was met with great anticipation and excitement by the European and American merchant community in China.[52]

There also was an impressive collection of individuals in Cushing's official party. Accompanying him to the Celestial Empire as secretary to the legation was Fletcher Webster, son of Daniel Webster. The others in his entourage included a surgeon and four young gentlemen who volunteered their services as attachés in quest of adventure and basic training in the art of diplomacy. Two members of the American Pacific community resident in China who were serviceably fluent in the language, missionaries Dr. Peter Parker and the Reverend E. C. Bridgman, signed on as interpreters and cultural and political advisers. Cushing particularly valued and respected Dr. Parker's knowledge of China and had brought along a copy of the medical missionary's 1841 report to Daniel Webster for guidance. Cushing's diplomatic achievement owed much to Parker, who because of his familiarity with Chinese customs and negotiating practices proved especially instrumental in helping write the final treaty.

At several stages during the long journey to China, Commissioner Cushing had traveled overland, making stops in Alexandria, Egypt, and other points in the Middle East where he gained first-hand knowledge of the practice of extraterritoriality, which was a legal method for bestowing special privileges upon sojourners to foreign lands. After conversations with the famed Viceroy of Egypt, Muhammad Ali, and a handful of the resident European diplomats, Cushing came to the conclusion that the United States deserved extraterritorial rights in China for its citizens as a matter of principle and in accordance with prevailing norms of international law.

Although the American commissioner believed China was a "highly civilized" society, in comparison to the Christian nations of the West it was a decaying and inferior civilization. "I entered China with the formed *general* conviction," Cushing told his superiors at the State Department, "that the United States ought not to concede to any foreign state, under any circumstances, jurisdiction over the life & liberty of any citizen of the United States, unless that foreign state be of our own family of nations, in a word, a Christian State." For Cushing, securing extraterritorial rights was an absolute necessity. The insistence on these rights became the bedrock of his bargaining position during the protracted negotiations with Chinese officials.[53]

Cushing was made to wait several months before serious negotiations commenced. His Chinese counterpart, the imperial commissioner Qiying, had negotiated the treaty with Great Britain ending the Opium War. Qiying was hesitant and wary after his country's humiliation at the hands of the

British, and in dealing with the American "barbarian" he pursued a policy of delay and foot-dragging. Cushing proved untiring, firm, and resilient, qualities much admired and appreciated by the Chinese. The American's patience and forbearance paid off. On July 3, 1844, he and Qiying signed the Treaty of Wangxia, which granted Americans favorable trading privileges, equal access to Canton as well as the four newly opened ports, and, most important, extended extraterritoriality to Americans residing or doing business in China.

Although Qiying in his official correspondence with the imperial court had referred to Commissioner Cushing as a "crafty" barbarian—the standard language used by nineteenth-century Chinese to describe foreigners—in the end a positive relationship apparently developed between the two commissioners. "It is very seldom," Qiying wrote Cushing, "that persons are found like us two men, the same in heart and united in sentiments."[54]

In the relaxed atmosphere of mutual admiration and respect brought on by their success in forging a treaty acceptable to both sides, the new friends exchanged gifts. Qiying sent Cushing Tartar cheesecakes and a painting of himself that to this day hangs in the Boston Museum of Fine Arts. Cushing reciprocated by presenting the imperial commissioner with a portrait of President Tyler. Upon viewing the Tyler portrait, the gracious Qiying declared the American president to be "a person of lofty stature, dignified, and of no common exterior," a description that would have pleased Tyler.

The "crafty" Cushing also finally gave Qiying a copy of President Tyler's offensive letter to the emperor, which he wisely had held back prior to the signing of the treaty. Whether or not the Tyler letter evoked private guffaws is unknown, but the Chinese official played it straight. In a flourish of diplomatic palaver, Qiying told Cushing that the president's letter was "superlatively beautiful" and after reading it he "could not restrain his spirit from delight and his heart from dilating with joy." For all its effusiveness, the good will expressed by Qiying was genuine, and he later wrote Cushing that they should attempt to remain in touch by corresponding regularly.[55]

Flush with his success in China, Cushing hoped to go on to Japan to open the door to American commerce there as well. Cushing had favored seeking a treaty with Japan from the outset, but that had not been part of his charge when he was appointed to head the legation to China. After arriving in Macao and while waiting for the Chinese to begin serious discussions, he wrote Tyler asking for authorization to travel to Japan once his mission in China was complete. President Tyler thought favorably of the Japan venture, but before word could reach Cushing he already had embarked on the return voyage home.

Both Tyler and Cushing lamented having missed the opportunity to open the door to Japan. A decade or so later when Commodore Matthew Perry did succeed in negotiating a treaty with Japan, Tyler took some satisfaction in earlier having advocated establishing diplomatic relations with that nation. Although disappointed that Perry's treaty fell "far short" of expectations, the former president proudly confided to a friend that his letter to Cushing authorizing negotiations was "the *nest egg* of the Japan movement" and he only regretted "that it has not fully hatched."[56]

When a copy of the Treaty of Wangxia finally reached Washington in early December 1844, it was cause for great celebration at the White House. John Tyler's new bride, Julia Gardiner, whom the president had wed the previous June, jubilantly described the president's reaction in a letter to her mother: "The Chinese treaty is accomplished—Hurrah! The documents came in to-day, and will be sent to the Capitol in a few days. I thought the President would go off in an ecstasy a minute ago with the pleasant news."

President Tyler's near ecstasy was justified. The treaty gave the United States, in addition to the identical trade and residence privileges in Canton and the four ports previously opened to the British, a most-favored-nation provision, and the right to maintain hospitals and churches in the port cities. Equally significant, Cushing secured an extraterritoriality guarantee for American citizens that went further than that granted to the British because it extended to criminal as well as civil matters. However, the treaty did not restrict the opium trade and Cushing apparently made no attempt to prohibit American participation in the drug traffic. Nonetheless, and much to Tyler's delight, the United States unexpectedly pulled to the forefront in the Asian commercial and political sweepstakes. Over the next decade America's European rivals would scramble to catch up by negotiating new treaties that granted them similar concessions.[57]

In the remaining few months of his lame-duck administration, at public occasions and in private meetings John Tyler exulted over Caleb Cushing's precedent-setting accomplishment and was barely able to control his joy over the success of the China mission. This Tyler initiative speedily received the Senate's approval and the treaty was ratified unanimously in early January 1845. Upon his return to the United States Cushing was feted and honored by his countrymen, including most prominently President Tyler. At his last formal dinner at the White House on March 3, 1845, Tyler warmly praised Cushing not only for his monumental achievement in concluding a treaty with China that opened the markets of that vast empire to American trade and enterprise, but also for his loyal, unstinting backing of the administration through thick and thin.

After Tyler left office and retired to Sherwood Forest in Charles City County, Virginia, Cushing reciprocated the president's generous accolades by presenting the Tylers with two elegant China vases. Julia Gardiner Tyler was delighted with the gift and exclaimed that the vases were "magnifico." An appreciative John Tyler wrote Cushing "to express my sincere thanks for the beautiful Chinese vases which had reached in safety before my return. Mrs. Tyler has already assigned them their appropriate position in her drawing-room. They will serve continually to remind me of you, and of the happy selection it was my good fortune to make of the first minister to the Celestial Empire ever appointed by the government, as well as of the prompt and able manner in which he acquitted himself of his important mission." For years the two China vases graced the Tylers' Sherwood Forest home and miraculously were not destroyed in the turmoil of the Civil War. To this day the vases remain prized possessions of John Tyler's descendents.[58]

In the summer and fall of 1845 Caleb Cushing did a victory lap of sorts by going on the lecture circuit from Massachusetts to Virginia, giving speeches on his experiences heading the mission to China. During his travels he stopped off at Sherwood Forest and was the honored guest at a dinner for eighteen hosted by Mrs. Tyler. Cushing's toast that evening praised Tyler's presidency and compared him favorably to another Virginian, George Washington. On July 4, Caleb Cushing was the featured speaker at an Independence Day celebration at Tyler's alma mater, the College of William and Mary in Williamsburg, where he regaled students, faculty, and townsfolk with tales of his journey to the Celestial Empire. In October Cushing was in his hometown of Newburyport, Massachusetts, lecturing at the local Lyceum on the China mission and the potential opportunities for trade with its millions of people.[59]

For all his unabashed optimism and exuberant boosterism about China as a market for America's surplus production, John Tyler was not far off the mark. His expectations about the commercial and economic benefits of the opening to China were more than met in his lifetime. After the formal ratification of the Treaty of Wangxia was completed, trade between the two nations ballooned over the next decade or so. For example, in the years 1845–60 total trade between the United States and China more than doubled, increasing from $9.5 million to approximately $22.5 million. Much to the satisfaction of American farmers and manufacturers, exports to China quadrupled in that scant fifteen-year period. The overall trade balance, however, still favored China as the nation's imports from the Celestial Empire nearly doubled in that same period. Nonetheless, in his retirement years at Sherwood Forest prior to the Civil War, the Pacific-minded former president took justifiable pride in the triumph of his diplomacy. He had succeeded in opening the door to China.[60]

★ PACIFIC PRECEDENTS
★
★ John Tyler's visionary foreign policy in Asia and the Pacific, however traditional it was in some respects and however much it reflected the thinking of his predecessors, nonetheless was a significant breakthrough in the course of nineteenth-century American foreign relations. He extended the Monroe Doctrine to the crossroads of the Pacific Ocean and opened the door to the China market and its 400 million inhabitants. In fairness, President Tyler, Secretary of State Webster, and Commissioner Cushing all should be given collaborative credit for setting these two path-breaking precedents in the nation's antebellum Pacific diplomacy that led at century's end to the annexation of Hawaii and the creation of the Open Door Policy in China.

But recognition also must be accorded the select company of the American Pacific community, most notably Peter Parker, Hiram Bingham, Peter Brinsmade, and William Richards, who lobbied and took up their pens on behalf of U.S. political and commercial expansionism all along the Pacific Rim. These enterprising "all-sided men" helped shape the thinking of a host of antebellum leaders such as Tyler and Webster, and in their day-to-day activities also carried on the slow and steady work of American empire in the Pacific.

The importance of the Tyler Doctrine to the United States's strategic and economic interests in the Pacific was recognized by at least two other presidents in the years before the Civil War. Both Zachary Taylor and Millard Fillmore publicly endorsed and reaffirmed the doctrine in their annual messages to Congress. In his 1849 message President Taylor declared that the United States desired "that the islands may maintain their independence and that other nations should concur with us in this sentiment." Echoing his predecessor in the White House, Taylor stated, "We could in no event be indifferent to their passing under the dominion of any other power."

Fillmore, who became president after Taylor's death by invoking Tyler's succession precedent, also upheld the Tyler Doctrine. In his second annual message, President Fillmore confirmed the nation's commitment to protect Hawaii's independence and reiterated that it was the official view of the American government "that those islands should not pass under the control of any other great maritime state." These public endorsements of the Tyler Doctrine undoubtedly owed much to the fact that Daniel Webster, co-author of the original declaration in 1842, returned as secretary of state during the Fillmore administration.[61]

To be sure, the success of Tyler's Pacific-minded diplomacy relied heavily on Great Britain's use of military force in China and its imperial restraint in Hawaii. Without Britain's triumph in the Opium War and Chinese capitulation to British terms in defeat, it is doubtful that the Cushing mission would have succeeded so easily. In a delicious irony, it was the hated British who gave John Tyler the opportunity to knock on and open China's door. In Hawaii, Foreign Secretary Aberdeen's recognition of the strength and influence of the American Pacific community in those islands motivated Great Britain's restraint. Uncharacteristically, in this case Britain said no to a further expansion of its empire. Just as Sir George Simpson understood that American missionaries such as William Richards were the engine of American empire in the islands, so too did Lord Aberdeen realize that annexation was undesirable because of the American Pacific community's dominant presence in Hawaii. Wisely, the British government did not wish to become involved in the difficult process of counteracting the pervasive influence of America's all-sided men.

President John Tyler and his secretaries of state — Webster, Upshur, and Calhoun — responded to the persistent lobbying efforts of nonstate actors and valued their contribution to the success of antebellum America's overseas expansion. To a man they were quite willing to let private citizens, especially merchants and missionaries, prepare the ground for American empire throughout the Pacific Rim. In turn, the Tyler administration reciprocated by promoting the overseas commercial interests of American businessmen, and it was the first in the history of the republic to extend official governmental protection to missionaries serving in foreign lands. The securing of extraterritorial rights for American sojourners in China was but another expression of the Tyler administration's commitment to aid and protect these informal agents of empire. The precedent-setting accomplishments of John Tyler's Pacific-minded diplomacy clearly hinged on this tacitly acknowledged and mutually beneficial partnership between the nation's public and private spheres.

Texas

6

Texas was lost but for my prompt action.

★ *John Tyler, 1848*

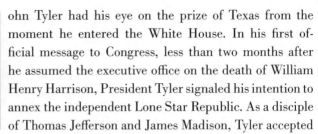ohn Tyler had his eye on the prize of Texas from the moment he entered the White House. In his first official message to Congress, less than two months after he assumed the executive office on the death of William Henry Harrison, President Tyler signaled his intention to annex the independent Lone Star Republic. As a disciple of Thomas Jefferson and James Madison, Tyler accepted their belief in the connection between territorial expansion and the viability of republican institutions. Unfailing in his adherence to the Madisonian doctrine of "extending the sphere," the new president placed Texas at the forefront of his administration's ambitious expansionist agenda.

Americans had long been interested in acquiring Texas. At the time of the Louisiana Purchase in 1803 during Jefferson's presidency, many people thought that all or at least a large part of Texas was included in the bargain. But any pretension that Texas was American territory was disavowed when Florida was acquired in the Adams-Onis Treaty of 1819. That agreement, also known as the Florida treaty, set the United States's boundary with what was then Spanish territory at the Sabine River. Today that is the boundary between the states of Louisiana and Texas. Even though the United States's claim to Texas was legally extinguished in 1819, Americans persisted in their desire to acquire the province, either by purchase if possible or other less official means if necessary. Among those diehard expansionists unwilling to give up hope of getting Texas at a future date was Thomas Jefferson. He assured his friend President James Monroe that, when acquired, Texas would become "the richest State of our Union, without any exception."[1]

The political equation changed after Mexico gained its independence from Spain in the early 1820s and Texas came under its sovereignty. The legitimacy of Mexican ownership of the province went unchallenged by the United States. In fact, Mexican sovereignty was openly acknowledged by the administrations of John Quincy Adams and Andrew Jackson, as both presidents officially tried to purchase all or part of Texas from the Mexicans. The revolution of 1836 altered the situation once again when the Texans, mostly Americans who had emigrated to the province, declared their independence from Mexico. The newly established Republic of Texas adopted a red, white, and blue flag with a single star and joined the international community as a slaveholding republic, a distinction it shared with the United States.

Shortly after independence was declared, Texans held a plebiscite that revealed that the people overwhelmingly supported immediate annexation by the United States. But President Jackson moved cautiously lest he jeopardize

Martin Van Buren's election in 1836 as his successor. After Van Buren was safely elected, Jackson granted formal diplomatic recognition to the Lone Star Republic. A few months later, in August 1837, the Texans officially requested annexation, but Van Buren, fearing an antislavery backlash and domestic turmoil, rebuffed them. The Texans then withdrew their offer in October 1838. Great Britain and France also officially recognized the Texas republic in 1840, even though Mexico refused to grant Texan independence and insisted it still held sovereignty over its rebellious province.

That was more or less where matters stood when John Tyler entered the White House. Aware that the controversy over slavery and its expansion stirred strong political opposition to Texas annexation, and not merely among the radical abolitionist fringe, President Tyler quickly assured members of Congress and his fellow citizens that there was nothing to fear from "the extension of our Empire." On the contrary, he believed it was precisely this continued territorial expansion across the North American continent that would preserve the Union and maintain the precarious balance between national and state power. In this oft-repeated Madisonian formula, empire and liberty became inseparable in order to sustain the incongruity of a slave-holding republic.

Several of the new president's Virginia friends, notably Henry Wise and Abel Upshur, immediately advised him to make Texas annexation the primary objective of his administration. Bringing Texas into the American fold, they argued, would bring glory to his presidency and an indisputable claim to a second term. How, they posited, could Americans not reward a man who succeeded where the venerable Andrew Jackson had failed? John Tyler graciously welcomed these words of encouragement and support, but in truth he needed little coaxing. He already was obsessed with bringing Texas into the Union. Years later when reminiscing about her husband's presidency, his widow, Julia Gardiner Tyler, confirmed his obsession by proudly recalling that "in defiance of every difficulty," John Tyler annexed Texas and "consummated the great object of his ambition."[2]

Tyler's desire for Texas was indeed an intense personal fixation and, as some of his contemporaries grumbled, a tiresome hobby horse. Few in his cabinet or in Congress were spared Tyler's cordial cajoling and gentle arm-twisting in behalf of annexation. Not even his distinguished secretary of state, Daniel Webster, was immune from the gracious and persistent Tyler treatment. In one of his first meetings with the secretary, the president urged Webster to consider the possibility of a treaty of annexation. A few months later, Tyler tried again to convince the skeptical New Englander to support "acquiring Texas by treaty." "Slavery,—I know that is the objection," Tyler conceded, but he thought it could be done by convincing the North "its interests would be incalculably advanced by such an acquisition." Secretary Webster, who years earlier had publicly expressed his opposition to Texas annexation, was not persuaded and politely rejected Tyler's blandishments.[3]

John Tyler anticipated Webster's rebuff. He had no illusions about the magnitude of the task before him and instinctively understood that annexation would not come quickly or easily. To bring Texas into the American union would take careful planning, a large measure of patience, and a boldness of purpose. Consequently, the president respected Webster's anti-annexationist stance and wisely delayed launching an all-out push for Texas. As hungry as he was for national glory and fame, and as ambitious as he was to remain in the White House by securing election in his own right in 1844, Tyler nonetheless bowed to political and diplomatic necessity by temporarily placing the annexation question on the back burner.

More immediate crises threatening national security and domestic harmony took precedence during Tyler's first two years in the executive office. Preserving the peace with England was a high priority for the president and his secretary of state. Equally pressing for both Tyler and Webster was the task of keeping European imperialism at bay in the Pacific Rim. However, when it came to the challenge of defending America's peculiar institution from domestic and foreign foes, slaveholder Tyler was in the forefront of the anti-abolitionist battle with a compliant Webster dutifully in tow. Although they disagreed over the Texas question, the two men fashioned a good working relationship, one of mutual respect and admiration that produced impressive diplomatic successes, such as the Webster-Ashburton Treaty, the Tyler Doctrine for Hawaii, and the mission to China.

Despite being preoccupied by these more urgent diplomatic initiatives, the president kept Texas uppermost on his long-term expansionist agenda. One true indicator of Tyler's undiminished eagerness to bring the Lone Star Republic into the Union fold was his penchant for sending up trial balloons for the annexationist cause in the hope they would uphold and sharpen the American public's focus on Texas. Unfortunately, trial balloons, especially those sent up by Tyler's more exuberant and reckless supporters, tended to explode unexpectedly in the face of an embarrassed administration.

Such was the case in April 1842 when the first of these forays was a spontaneous and unauthorized address by Congressman Henry Wise, perhaps Tyler's most outspoken ally in the House of Representatives. What provoked Wise was an attempt by two antislavery congressmen to eliminate funding for Tyler's newly appointed minister to Mexico, Waddy Thompson, on the charge that his mission was a nefarious scheme to annex Texas. In a rambling speech on the House floor attacking this annoying anti-Texas ploy, Wise took the bait and imprudently confirmed the charge made by his abolitionist adversaries that the Tyler administration was indeed designing to annex Texas.

At first coyly attempting to evade the claim that annexation was the administration's objective, Wise ended up extolling the positive results that would accrue to the entire Union if annexation were achieved. He began by correctly pointing out that in the mid-1820s President John Quincy Adams and Secretary of State Henry Clay had twice tried to purchase Texas, and at a time when slavery still existed in that Mexican province. If two such respected statesmen, one currently a chief opponent of slavery in Congress, could seek to add slave territory to the Union, why was it wrong for the Tyler administration to attempt to do the same? Absolutely nothing was wrong with seeking annexation, he answered, because acquiring Texas was as much in the national interest in 1842 as it had been two decades earlier. Annexation would benefit all sections of the Union by maintaining the United States's global cotton monopoly and boosting its emerging power in the international trading system. This rationale for annexation, preserving America's cotton monopoly, later became President Tyler's frequently recited justification for taking Texas.

Warming to his task and with a straight face, Congressman Wise taunted his abolitionist foes with a challenge—"if they were really sincere in their professed desires to see slavery abolished, their true and only course was to annex Texas to the United States." A number of his colleagues in the chamber could scarcely believe their ears, and Wise's disingenuous argument brought "a laugh in certain portions of the House." Only through annexation, he reiterated, could the abolitionist hope of emancipation succeed because it would bring Texas "within our reach and jurisdiction."

If he was serious, and not just offering a tongue-in-cheek gibe, the puzzling and intriguing aspect of this slaveholder's analysis was his concession of the moral high ground to the antislavery forces by suggesting that emancipation was a worthy and noble goal. Perhaps Representative Wise merely was following the president's lead. Two decades earlier as a member of the House, John Tyler had made the same argument for what became known as the diffusion theory during the debate over the Missouri crisis.[4]

There is no surviving account of Tyler's personal reaction when he learned of Wise's political gaffe, but the president surely was bewildered by his friend's unthinking and premature public disclosure of the administration's Texas strategy. It also remains a mystery as to why the speech was not printed in the *Congressional Globe*, although the journal account of the House proceedings on the day Wise spoke noted that "so much noise and confusion prevailed, that hearing for a full hour was rendered almost impossible." Conceivably, Wise had been inaudible that day because of the commotion his remarks caused on the floor of the House, and the prevailing state of confusion was a plausible explanation for why the speech was not printed and did not appear in Congress's official journal of record.

An equally plausible assumption would be that President Tyler, in an effort at damage control, used his executive influence to suppress the speech and prevent its publication in the *Globe*. If that was the case and Tyler did intervene, his attempt to keep the speech secret failed. Two days after Wise presented his case for Texas annexation on the House floor an account of the speech was published in the widely read and highly respected *National Intelligencer*. His intemperate remarks immediately became ammunition for Tyler's Whig enemies and the entire abolitionist enterprise. As might be expected, Wise's claim that John Quincy Adams sought to acquire Texas when he occupied the White House provoked an immediate backlash from the administration's arch foe. By arousing Adams and placing the administration under the intense scrutiny of the abolitionists, Henry Wise foolishly played into their hands and thus disrupted Tyler's timetable for Texas annexation.[5]

Not wishing to further excite public opinion on the issue, and wanting to avoid another public relations disaster, President Tyler and his associates suspended their Texas annexation campaign for the remainder of 1842. Only after the Webster-Ashburton Treaty had been ratified that summer and the administration's Pacific Rim diplomacy had been successfully launched by year's end did Texas openly become the top priority. President Tyler now took charge of the campaign. To kick off the next public phase of the Texas annexation venture, he chose Representative Thomas W. Gilmer of Virginia, his close friend and a staunch ally of the administration. In January 1843 Gilmer published a letter in the *Baltimore Republican and Argus* making the case for bringing Texas into the Union. Gilmer's letter was quickly reprinted in the *Madisonian*, the official mouthpiece of the Tyler administration, and it received wide circulation and its merits were debated throughout the country.[6]

Striking a decidedly more positive note than Henry Wise had done earlier, Gilmer followed President Tyler's patented script by outlining the national benefits that would result from annexation. He began by making the familiar argument that bringing Texas into the fold would "open a market at home for the manufactures and agricultural products of all the non-slaveholding States" and would bring a "vast acquisition of national wealth, prosperity and harmony" to the entire republic. Gilmer openly acknowledged that "the subject of slavery" was "indeed a subject of extreme delicacy" and might be the basis for strong objections to annexation. Such objections would be misguided because "the annexation of Texas will have the most salutary influence" and "will strengthen the union." Gilmer posited that most citizens of the nonslaveholding states would agree with their counterparts in the South who were content to leave the issue of slavery where the Constitution had placed it — under the jurisdiction of the states.

Without a national consensus on the basic premise that both the present and future condition of slavery should be determined by the individual states, Gilmer feared the Union might dissolve. Parroting the views of President Tyler and a host of other territorial expansionists, Gilmer reiterated the republican dogma that pursuing America's national destiny and creating an extensive republic would be the surest way to preserve the Union. "Nations, like individuals," Gilmer argued, "must live up to their destiny, and we must act the part assigned us by our position on the globe." "Our federative Union," he continued, "in the spirit of its adoption, is capable of indefinite extension. Space and numbers will only add to its strength by multiplying its blessing. In any other spirit it would not have been long preserved, even by the Old Thirteen." Gilmer's analysis was identical to President John Tyler's long-held republican belief that following the Madisonian/Jeffersonian doctrine of continually "extending the sphere" was the only sure way to sustain the Union.[7]

Another standard rationale for Texas annexation invoked by Gilmer was the need to check the threat of a pernicious British imperialism that blocked America's national destiny. Employing the classic logic of imperial competition that dictated taking action to preempt your rival, Representative Gilmer argued that if the United States failed to take Texas, Great Britain would act to bring the Lone Star Republic within its imperial orbit. Mark my words, Gilmer warned his readers, "England, whose possessions and jurisdiction extend over so large a portion of the globe, whose influence is felt every where, will either possess or control Texas, if it does not come under the jurisdiction of the United States." Losing Texas would be calamity enough, but even more frightening to Gilmer and President Tyler was the prospect that Britain would succeed in abolishing slavery in Texas and act on the "disposition to see us dissolve our union on account of it."[8]

Gilmer believed the United States's future path was clearly marked. To disrupt Britain's abolitionist schemes and to avoid the calamity of disunion, Texas must be annexed. He conceded as he had when discussing the delicate issue of slavery that the question of the constitutionality of acquiring foreign territory might cause concern for many Americans. Claiming he was "a strict constructionist of the powers of our federal government," Gilmer nonetheless believed that "the power conferred by the Constitution over our foreign relations, and the repeated acquisition of territory under it," left "this question open as one of expediency." Louisiana and Florida had been acquired on this interpretation of the Constitution, and taking Texas would simply be a case of acting on a precedent that clearly allowed the American republic to acquire foreign territory.[9]

In the months following the successful launching of Thomas Gilmer's trial balloon, President Tyler took another fateful step on the road to annexation. He deftly maneuvered to remove Secretary of State Daniel Webster from his cabinet. The Texas issue persistently had been a point of disagreement in the Webster-Tyler relationship, but it had never bubbled to the surface as a source of friction and tension between the two men, nor had it escalated into a public controversy. The president now believed Webster had outlived his usefulness in the State Department and must go.

Tyler much appreciated Webster's decision to remain in the cabinet after the other holdover Whig members from President William Henry Harrison's brief time in office had resigned en masse in September 1841. He also unfailingly acknowledged Webster's key role in negotiating the treaty with England and preserving the peace. Even after leaving the White House, Tyler was quick to praise in his correspondence and occasional public pronouncements the former secretary of state's diplomatic successes. In the spring of 1843, however, President Tyler needed a secretary of state who favored Texas annexation and unequivocally would pursue that goal.

During his tenure as secretary of state, Webster outwardly reciprocated Tyler's admiration and magnanimity. Predictably for a man known to be untrustworthy, private citizen Webster expressed a less favorable view of President Tyler after his forced resignation from the State Department in May 1843. He was dismayed, Webster confided to a friend, by his former boss's political opportunism and his fixation on annexing Texas. Webster also vented his frustration in a critical editorial ghostwritten for the *National Intelligencer* that appeared only a few days after he left the cabinet.

The anonymous editorial sharply questioned the wisdom of Tyler's abandonment of his Whig supporters and his effort to gain the backing of leading Democrats for his presidential candidacy in the 1844 campaign.[10]

Webster was correct about Tyler's ambition to remain in office by winning the upcoming presidential election. But Tyler did not indulge in wishful thinking as Webster had, and was more realistic than the New Englander about his unpopularity among Whigs. President Tyler regularly was the target of their anger and frustration and Whig partisans branded him a "traitor" to the party that brought him to the White House. Given that he essentially had been drummed out of the Whig Party, it was hardly surprising that John Tyler embarked on an independent course and staked his political future on Texas annexation. For the remainder of his time in the executive office, the despised president "without a party" single-mindedly focused on the Texas issue to secure four more years in the White House in his own right and on his own terms.

In his personal quest to gain broad public affirmation of his presidential record and national voter approval at the polls, John Tyler played political hardball. His polite courtly demeanor and patrician bearing misled many of his contemporaries into thinking he was spineless, "a poor weeping willow of a creature," as Francis Preston Blair, editor of the *Washington Globe*, characterized the Virginia aristocrat at the time Tyler accidentally became president.

It was not unusual for Tyler's critics to underestimate him, despite his record as a politician who stubbornly charted his own course seemingly without fear of the consequences. As president of the United States, John Tyler once again surprised his adversaries and proved to be a tough, iron-willed political infighter. That had been true during his struggle with Congress over a national bank and his rejection of Henry Clay's Whig agenda, and again would be the case in the battle for Texas and his pursuit of a renewed lease on the presidency.[11]

Ironically, the use of political patronage became one of John Tyler's chief weapons in his bid for political glory. Early on in his tenure as president he had opposed removing officeholders for mere political gain as Andrew Jackson had done. Such a blatant and crude application of the "to the victor go the spoils" dictum was contrary to Tyler's republican principles. But political ambition got the better of him and he reversed course. Tyler abandoned his republican scruples and readily used the executive power of political patronage in an effort to build an electoral machine. In May 1843, President Tyler began a purge of federal jobholders and methodically replaced them with men presumed to be loyal administration partisans who would support Texas annexation and his projected presidential campaign wholeheartedly.

Tyler made his newly appointed secretary of the treasury, John C. Spencer, his hatchet man. Spencer, an independent-minded New Yorker who had served ably as head of the War Department, was informed by Tyler that the administration had "numberless enemies in office and they should forthwith be made to quit." "In short," the president continued, "action is what we want, prompt and decisive action." But Tyler cautioned Secretary Spencer, "What I say is that we ought to know whom we appoint." Unquestioning loyalty to the administration and a firm commitment to Texas annexation were the prerequisites Tyler had in mind for all new appointees.

Over the next several months, Tyler directed Spencer to purge more than a hundred federal officeholders, including postmasters, customs collectors, and diplomats. Because these dismissals came so late in the game, the president's attempt to use executive political patronage to build a political party was a dismal failure. However, Tyler's political opportunism once again confirmed that his idealistic brand of virtuous republicanism was unworkable in the rough-and-tumble world of nineteenth-century American politics.[12]

As Daniel Webster—certainly no stranger to the art of political chicanery—earlier had come to appreciate, John Tyler's burning desire to remain in office and secure his place in history was not to be constrained by prior conviction or avowed principle. One of the more illustrative examples of Tyler's shameless expediency was his endeavor to create a political base in New York City through the use of customhouse patronage. Apparently without a second thought, President Tyler anointed Irish immigrant Mike Walsh, a journalist, lithographer, and notorious "practitioner of gang politics," to be his man in Gotham. As leader of the "Spartan Band," Walsh gained notoriety as a tough street fighter and rousing stump speaker who championed the cause of workers and denounced the city's elites as "vultures" and "grub-worms." Nominally a Democrat, Walsh had no compunction about unleashing his Spartan gang members and using violent methods to intimidate the leadership of both the Whig and Democratic Parties.

Tyler probably overlooked Walsh's unsavory strong arm tactics because the gang leader was a proven political organizer and an influential journalist who had no truck with elitist abolitionists, hated the British, and was foursquare for Texas annexation. In one of his public speeches urging annexation, Walsh readily dismissed opponents who argued the United States already had enough territory. He believed for a free people and a free government "the whole continent, or the whole world, would not be sufficient." "I go for the re-annexation of Texas," Walsh continued, and he had no doubt America would prevail if it brought war with Mexico, Great Britain, or the entire international community. Such unbridled and fearless enthusiasm for territorial expansion unmistakably appealed to President Tyler. But it is unknown as to whether the violent antics of Mike Walsh and his gang of toughs actually aided or hindered Tyler's Texas campaign and political aspirations.[13]

Once the political bloodletting of the purges had run its course, federal officeholders, whether newly appointed or holdovers, were subjected to another loyalty test by the administration. In preparation for his presidential run in 1844, John Tyler commissioned journalist Alexander G. Abell to write a flattering campaign biography designed to present to American voters the most compelling case possible for his reelection. To make certain that Abell's *Life of John Tyler* reached a wide national audience, the president appointed his son, John Tyler Jr., to conduct a campaign of blatant political shakedowns of the nation's postmasters and other federal officials who held patronage posts.

The method for coercing postmasters to purchase and freely distribute a number of Alexander Abell's campaign biographies was simple and straightforward. One example will serve to illustrate the process. In this case Alexander Abell wrote Ephraim Spooner, the postmaster of Plymouth, Massachusetts, that as "you will doubtless be pleased to setting the acts of Mr. Tyler's public life properly & truthfully before the people, it is believed that you will cheerfully subscribe for 50 or 60 copies of the work, to be distributed as you shall think best." Abell's letter was accompanied by one from the president's son, making clear what was expected: "As it is considered of importance, in justice to the president, to circulate among the people the work spoken of in Mr. Abell's letter accompanying this, you will confer a favor on the undersigned by taking such measures for that end as Mr. A. suggests." Ephraim Spooner, a political survivor who held on as Plymouth's postmaster until 1854, wisely complied. He purchased sixty copies of Abell's biography. For his part in promoting Tyler's unsuccessful presidential bid, Alexander Abell was compensated in 1845 with a last-minute patronage appointment as consul to Hawaii.[14]

★ A POLITICAL FORAY
★
★ President Tyler's patronage purges and political arm-twisting were accompanied by a barnstorming campaign tour of a number of east coast states in the hope of winning the hearts and political allegiance of countless

disgruntled or indifferent voters. In his first two years in office, Tyler had been a cloistered leader hunkered down in the White House. He rarely had ventured much beyond the confines of Washington or his native Virginia. Aware of his general unpopularity among Americans and anxious to gain much-needed public exposure and to polish his tarnished image, John Tyler traveled north in the late spring of 1843 to Baltimore, Philadelphia, Princeton, and New York City. The presidential party then headed on to New England, with stopovers in Providence and finally Boston, which was to host the featured highlight of the excursion.

The official purpose of the trip was to attend the dedication of the Battle of Bunker Hill Monument on June 17. Former Secretary of State Daniel Webster, who even though he had resigned from the cabinet a month earlier outwardly remained on cordial terms with the president, was scheduled to be the featured speaker at the commemoration. Boston's leading lights invited President Tyler to mark the occasion as the city's honored guest. Tyler eagerly accepted the invitation to stage the only extended political tour of his time in the White House. After the festivities at Boston, the president planned to swing westward and continue on to Springfield, Albany, Buffalo, Cleveland, and Cincinnati.

Tyler's entourage comprised his sons John and Robert, Robert's wife, Priscilla, and several members of the cabinet. The interim secretary of state, Hugh Legare of South Carolina, remained behind because of the press of his new duties and would join the presidential party after its arrival in Boston. From the moment the president left the White House to board a special train to Baltimore, the first stop on the trip, a light-hearted celebratory air of fun and frolic set the tone for the entire journey. Citizens in Washington gave Tyler a rousing send-off as they accompanied his party to the railroad station in carriages and on foot in a joyous procession that included a band of merry musicians.

At its first stop in Baltimore, cheering and enthusiastic crowds warmly greeted President Tyler and his party, to their pleasant surprise. The mayor cordially welcomed the president and proudly proclaimed his city was honored by the visit of the republic's chief magistrate. A visibly moved Tyler basked in this gratifying display of hospitality by the residents of Baltimore. In a brief speech he thanked the mayor and, caught up in the emotion of the moment, remarked that the fair city of Baltimore was like "a swan sitting beautifully upon the water." The presidential party next was feted at a lavish banquet and public gathering in Barnum's City Hotel. Tyler's splendid day in Baltimore ended with a delightful evening theater party. The warmth of the reception given by the citizens of Baltimore buoyed President Tyler's spirits. He hoped it was a true harbinger of what was to come as he ventured north on this fateful political odyssey.[15]

In Philadelphia, President Tyler was enthusiastically welcomed by the city's residents with much the same warmth and cordiality that he had received in Baltimore. The "City of Brotherly Love" officially honored President Tyler as the distinguished guest at a well-attended public reception in Independence Hall. All in all, Tyler's trip was going very well indeed, although there was a discordant note in Philadelphia when Whig members of the City Council boycotted the welcoming ceremony.

The presidential party next journeyed on to Princeton, New Jersey, where they enjoyed "every sort of charming festivity." Their host, naval Captain Robert F. Stockton, was one of the state's most prominent politicians and a close ally of the president. An energetic expansionist who favored the annexation of Texas, Stockton was the driving force behind the navy's conversion to steam and collaborated with Swedish designer John Ericsson to construct a screw-propelled warship, which appropriately was christened the *Princeton*.

Captain Stockton proved to be quite an impresario, showering the leader of the American republic with all the lavish and ceremonious pomp usually accorded European royalty and Asian potentates. Obviously a man of some means, Stockton arranged to have John Tyler greeted, the president's daughter-in-law marveled, "by twenty-six of the most beautiful girls I ever saw, dressed in white, with wreaths of flowers on their heads. They bore with them a long line of flowers, reaching from one end of the group to the other, as thick as my body, all of the choicest kind. This was presented with a very pretty little speech, which Father answered most charmingly." Members of the Tyler entourage then "were all placed in barouches drawn by six horses, and accompanied by forty young collegians—each mounted upon one of Capt. Stockton's splendid race horses. A troop of soldiers followed and a troop preceded us with bands of martial music." After this marvelous welcome to Princeton, the Tyler retinue spent a delightful day and evening as the honored houseguests of Captain Stockton.[16]

The next stop was New York City, where President Tyler and his happy band of sojourners were awed by the magnitude and magnificence of the welcoming ceremonies. They had seen nothing before that equaled what greeted them in the republic's largest city. New Yorkers went wild as they lavishly and enthusiastically spread out the red carpet for the suddenly popular and newly venerated president. The warm and celebratory public reception was quite unprecedented in the city's history and everything the reviled and beleaguered Virginian slaveholder could have hoped for in his wildest imaginings.

Hundreds of pleasure craft with pendants flying and a proud contingent of the Navy's men-of-war with their yards fully manned and their cannons firing salutes in every direction clogged New York's harbor to welcome the president as he crossed over from New Jersey. When the presidential party landed at Castle Garden on the island of Manhattan they were serenaded by bands playing patriotic airs and were officially received by a large honor guard of troops stationed round the Battery. The city's residents "poured forth in mass" and a crowd estimated somewhere between 100,000 and 200,000 New Yorkers thronged the streets to greet President John Tyler as he paraded up Broadway in triumph. "I never saw so magnificent a spectacle in my life," declared native New Yorker Priscilla Cooper Tyler, wife of the president's eldest son, Robert. "All the other cities had done their best," she observed, "but none have the number of inhabitants or the natural advantages of New York. The President had really showers of bouquets and wreaths thrown upon him everywhere. Windows of the houses have been filled with the most beautiful women waving their handkerchiefs and casting flowers in his path."[17]

The famed diarist of mid-nineteenth century America, George Templeton Strong, was at the corner of Broadway and Wall Street on that June morning to see the presidential procession. Then a young man of twenty-three, Strong winced at what he saw that day — "the whole scene was remarkably absurd." That night Strong recorded his reactions to the frenzied excitement generated by the president's arrival: "The Tyler made his triumphal entry today and was received with fuss and parade enough to make him comfortable, it's to be hoped. From eleven o'clock this morning till ten tonight everybody has been in everybody else's way, and everything upside down, and everywhere except Broadway and the other streets along the line of the procession deserted."

Rowdy gangs such as Mike Walsh's Spartan Band were "out in force." "Everybody," Strong believed, "stared at the President much as they would have stared at the Emperor of China and displayed about as much enthusiasm and good will toward him as if he had actually been that potentate." It was a sad scene in a republic. His fellow New Yorkers, Strong lamented, had not come forth to honor a virtuous civic leader; they merely were awed by the trappings and grandeur of the presidential office.[18]

More than one New York newspaper puzzled over this incongruous turn of events and tried to explain why there was such a huge and unforeseen public affection for "His Accidency." The *Morning Express* believed the city of New York had bestowed upon President Tyler "the greatest display ever before made in honor of a public man" and thought many people came out of "curiosity to see this novelty of a President without a party." Quite inexplicably, the newspaper conceded, "a crowd GEN. JACKSON himself could not draw, nor GEN. HARRISON, the most popular of our late Presidents, Mr. Tyler *did* draw."[19]

James Gordon Bennett, editor of the *New York Herald*, placed the event into his personal historical perspective: "One of the most magnificent receptions that ever was given by the people of New York to a public man, was extended yesterday to President John Tyler on his arrival here. We have seen and mingled with the reception of Lafayette—we have seen and mingled with the reception of General Jackson—and in fact we have seen every public reception for the last twenty years—but that extended to President Tyler yesterday far excels any similar event of former days." For Bennett and other politically attuned New Yorkers it was a strange phenomenon to behold. There appeared to be no surge of political support for Tyler's quest for reelection, just crowds of folks, gawking at the president as if he had just dropped to earth from Mars.[20]

It certainly was a baffling and wholly unfathomable spectacle. No one could have predicted that John Tyler, an accidental president reviled as a traitor by the Whigs and the first chief executive to confront the ignominy of impeachment charges, would be accorded such a triumphal passage. As unbelievable as it may seem, the aristocratic, charming, if slightly aloof Tyler actually was welcomed as a popular president, the favorite of the people, and the idol of his countrymen, not only in the nation's premier metropolis, but in the major cities along the northeastern coast. Even the notion that John Tyler may have been accorded the spontaneous if fleeting accolades of his fellow citizens is not the conventional historical image present-day Americans have of their tenth president. If they have any memory of him at all, the American public today dismisses John Tyler as an unimaginative leader and a resounding failure who invariably lands near the bottom of historians' rankings of the most significant and successful presidents.

Clearly flattered and bemused by the unparalleled hubbub and fuss in his honor, President Tyler did not delude himself about its significance for his political fortunes. He understood, he told New York audiences, that their warm greeting was a public expression of devotion to the office itself and not to the man holding the office. This was clearly the case at official functions with civic leaders and partisan politicians in attendance. The tone of the welcome at these events was far less exuberant, more politely restrained, with only "feeble cheers" for the chief magistrate. But such lukewarm receptions did not deter John Tyler from trying to convince his fellow Americans in whatever city he happened to be speaking that their president was a patriotic leader of vision and purpose. On numerous occasions during his journey, Tyler reiterated that he was dedicated to preserving the Union and allowing America to achieve its mission of national greatness.

He told his audiences that the United States had a clear mandate from "Divine Providence" to serve as the model democracy for the entire world to emulate. America was "a land of civil and religious liberty," and this oft-stated belief in American exceptionalism was the bone and marrow of John Tyler's political ideology. For instance, in his response to the mayor of New York's welcoming remarks, the president emphasized this precept in his trademark stilted and detached rhetorical style: "For how can the example of a democratic America be resisted? Do you not perceive that a light is breaking forth every where? That this same free America has already civilized a continent, which when we were boys was almost all in a wildness state, sir?" Soon a superior and ever-expanding civilization would stretch forth from the Atlantic to the Pacific, "overshadowing a continent, and the dews of two oceans resting on its branches." In 1843 such faith in America's continental reach may have seemed a bit premature, but it drew cheers from the crowd and illustrated Tyler's utter conviction that it was the young republic's destiny to spread from ocean to ocean across the North American continent.[21]

Remarkably, before President John Tyler even reached Boston, it was as if the word had spread from city to city and hamlet to hamlet that he was a man under siege, vilified by his enemies, abandoned by his former Whig allies, and in dire need of some cheering up. To assuage the president's political woes and relieve his humiliation, each community did its utmost to honor him with a happy and boisterous celebration and the most joyous salutations. As many of his fellow citizens suspected, John Tyler loved a good time. And who could begrudge a scorned and disparaged president without a political party for happily basking in such unaccustomed public adulation? Even his daughter-in-law Priscilla Cooper Tyler confessed, "I am beginning to feel quite conceited and *grand* with all the fuss that is being made about us."[22]

As pleasant and gratifying as his newly gained celebrity status must have been, John Tyler saw this northern excursion as more than just a prolonged ego trip. It was a serious political foray to win converts to his reelection bid and lure large numbers of voters into the Tyler fold. At every opportunity along the way, the determined Virginia aristocrat behaved as any consummate politician would by eagerly pressing the flesh, giving countless speeches defending his presidential actions, urging Texas annexation, and seeking support for election to the presidency in his own right.

As the presidential entourage departed New York City and headed north through New England, another round of welcoming receptions and speeches unfolded with more processions of lovely girls bearing garlands of flowers, and scenes of John Tyler the gallant southern gentleman kissing as many of the young ladies as possible. But it was apparent that Boston, the principal destination of the eastern leg of the tour, might prove to be different. Unlike New York, whose merchants and businesses were deeply involved in the cotton trade and where many of its citizens took a lenient view of slavery, Boston was a hotbed of abolitionism. It threatened to be a potential lion's den for a slaveowner president, no matter how gallant and charming he might be.

It was a chilly, rainy, and altogether unpropitious Friday morning, June 16, 1843, when President Tyler arrived in Boston. He and his party had taken the early train from nearby Providence, Rhode Island. Although the streets leading from the rail station were jammed with gawking onlookers and the president received a proper military salute from the Roxbury Military & Musket corps, there was, according to one fascinated spectator, "*nothing like hearty cheers.*" The official reception for the slaveholder Tyler, whose attendance at the Bunker Hill ceremonies was decried by some prominent Bostonians as a desecration of this hallowed shrine of liberty, included respectful and cordial welcoming remarks from city and state dignitaries followed by a banquet at the Tremont House.[23]

The next morning dawned beautifully clear and crisp. It turned out to be a perfect day to dedicate the Bunker Hill Monument and mark the sixty-eighth anniversary of the 1775 battle. The festivities began at the Boston Statehouse, where a three-mile procession assembled. Led by fifty or more militia companies in magnificent regalia marching eight abreast, the parade slowly snaked its way to Charlestown, arriving in the early afternoon for the official celebration.

The man the curious citizens of Massachusetts had come to see, John Tyler, the president of the United States, rode immediately behind the military ensemble in an open carriage drawn by six splendid horses. In regal and decidedly nonrepublican fashion, President Tyler was shaded from the glaring sun by a black slave manservant holding a long-handled umbrella. If Tyler's arrogant in-your-face display of his attachment to the South's peculiar institution took Bostonians by surprise and offended their republican sensibilities, it was not readily apparent. All along the parade route thousands of people lined the streets to warmly and enthusiastically greet their chief magistrate.

A Fisher and Ives lithograph commemorating the 1843 dedication of the Bunker Hill Monument (copies of which are sold at this National Park Service historic site even today) depicts Daniel Webster speaking on an elevated reviewing stand filled with a host of dignitaries, presumably including President Tyler and members of his cabinet. The monument is portrayed with American flags festively draped from the four portals near the top of the structure. One hundred thousand people had assembled in the area surrounding the monument to hear their favorite son and renowned orator, Daniel Webster, deliver the main address.

Despite Webster's opposition to the extension of slave territory and his disagreement with the president over the desirability of annexing Texas, the two men still shared a nationalist vision of the American Union. Without question, on that glorious June day at Bunker Hill Tyler readily endorsed Webster's affirmation that Virginia and Massachusetts having been bound together by the Revolution, "there is now for them, in present possession as well as in future hope, but 'One Country, One Constitution, and One Destiny.'"[24]

To round out the daylong Bunker Hill pageantry a grand dinner was held that evening at Faneuil Hall. Seated at the head table in the places of honor were President Tyler and the hero of the hour, Daniel Webster. As the proceedings unfolded a number of the distinguished guests, including cabinet members Abel P. Upshur and John C. Spencer, offered brief remarks and repeated toasts to the health of the republic and its leaders. One of the toasts made to the president of the United States led to sustained applause and nine hearty cheers, which surely must have capped an exhilarating and gratifying day in Boston for John Tyler.

But not all Bostonians were cheering and applauding President Tyler's presence in their fair city. Among the local leaders boycotting the dedication ceremony was the antislavery congressman and former president, John Quincy Adams. "What a name in the annals of mankind is Bunker Hill! What a day was the 17th of June 1775! and what a burlesque on them both," he bitterly recorded in his diary, "is an oration upon them by Daniel Webster, and a pilgrimage of John Tyler, and his Cabinet of slave-drivers, to desecrate the solemnity by their presence!" And then the galling hypocrisy of "a dinner at Faneuil Hall in honor of a President of the United States, hated and despised by those who invited him to it, themselves as cordially hated and despised by him." Adams did not publicly express his disgust and outrage, but the former president's private sentiments reflected the thinking of any number of his antislavery constituents.[25]

In fact, the overwhelming majority of Boston's abolitionist community viewed the entire commemoration as a sacrilege committed on hallowed ground and a mockery of the true meaning of the 1775 battle. Led by their highly respected and renowned leader, Wendell Phillips, the city's abolitionists made an effort through moral suasion to reveal to the slaveholder president the error of his ways. Phillips and his colleagues in the New England Anti-Slavery Society hoped to persuade President Tyler that slavery was an evil and abhorrent practice totally at odds with America's ideals of liberty and justice.

Commissioned to be the Society's representative, Phillips wrote Tyler requesting an interview to present resolutions urging him to renounce the South's peculiar institution and accept his moral obligation to free his slaves. President Tyler ignored Phillips's presumptuous request and did not grant the abolitionist leader an interview. Whether or not Tyler was angered by Phillips's audacity is unrecorded, but the president probably saw this attempt to claim the moral high ground as one more example of the insufferable self-righteousness of his abolitionist antagonists.[26]

A resilient and determined President Tyler did not let these pesky abolitionist annoyances interfere with the main objectives of his generally successful political foray into New England. He met with business leaders such as Abbott Lawrence in a move to gain electoral backing from Boston bankers and textile industry magnates. Then, almost immediately after the Bunker Hill festivities had concluded, Lawrence invited President Tyler to tour the mill town of Lowell, where the Virginia aristocrat took the opportunity to press the flesh and seek votes from the community's factory workers and laboring classes. Upon his return to Boston after the hectic and busy excursion to Lowell, an exhausted Tyler received tragic news. Hugh Legare, the attorney general and interim secretary of state who had just arrived in Boston days earlier to join the president's entourage for the Bunker Hill dedication, had died unexpectedly at age forty-six.

John Tyler was devastated by the loss of his close confidant and ideological soul mate. The two men saw eye to eye on America's future destiny in the Pacific Rim and they agreed on the necessity to annex Texas as quickly as possible. Years later when musing on the deceased members of his cabinet, the former president not only lamented the loss of Hugh Legare but also candidly assessed its impact on his own political fortunes. Legare was one of the republic's "purest and noblest sons," Tyler recalled, and his "well-stored mind, which had shed broad light over the country on so many occasions, was now extinguished; that calm and unimpassioned friend, on whose counsel I had leaned in so much confidence, and by whom I was never deceived, was stricken from my side."

Legare's death also abruptly toppled Tyler's political bandwagon. His political foray to the major cities of the Northeast, "an excursion commenced in buoyancy and gladness, which had been accompanied on its whole line by the greetings and huzzas of unnumbered thousands, was terminated in sorrow and mourning." The remainder of the trip, with projected stops in Albany, Buffalo, and points west, was canceled.[27]

★ ANNEXATION PLACED ON THE FAST TRACK
★
★ The logical choice to fill the post of secretary of state after Hugh Legare's sudden death was Abel P. Upshur. Nearly two years of highly visible and outstanding service as secretary of the navy in the Tyler cabinet made Upshur one of the president's most trusted advisers. As had been the case in Tyler's relationship with Legare, the president and Upshur shared a similar expansionist outlook, like-minded views on slavery and states' rights, and both men distrusted the British. As a cabinet member, Upshur had participated in the formulation of foreign policy and knew something of its day-to-day execution. He also strongly favored the annexation of Texas and agreed with his chief that bringing the Lone Star Republic into the Union as a slave state should be the administration's number one diplomatic priority.

Initially, however, Upshur balked at accepting the premier cabinet post. He feared he "was not qualified" to be secretary of state. President Tyler thought otherwise and pressured Upshur to accept the appointment. After some hesitation, Upshur took the position. He explained his decision to William and Mary law professor Beverley Tucker by playfully inquiring of his friend, "What think you of my taking the State Dept.?" He quickly confessed that he had resisted "as long as I could," but "yielded at last from a sense of duty." Abel P. Upshur proved to be a wise and politically popular choice to head the State Department. Unlike several of Tyler's previous cabinet nominations that were summarily rejected by the Senate, Upshur was quickly confirmed. The Senate's approval of his appointment without opposition was a tribute to the widespread respect Upshur had earned while directing the Navy Department.[28]

The quest to annex Texas became the main focus of Upshur's diplomacy during the seven months he served as secretary of state. Using the same metaphor Julia Gardiner Tyler later employed to describe her husband's fixation on Texas, Upshur confided to Beverley Tucker that annexation was "the great object of my ambition. I do not care to control any measure of policy except this; & I have reason to believe that no person but myself can control it." He spent the first several weeks in office planning his expansionist strategy and seeking advice from his proslavery cronies Duff Green and John C. Calhoun.[29]

The British challenge to American ambitions in Texas was deemed highly dangerous by Senator Calhoun and the ever-alarmist Green, then in England on his second mission as Tyler's secret envoy. For both men Great Britain was a fearsome bogeyman intent on ending slavery everywhere. In addition, Calhoun warned, Britain sought dominant power and commercial monopoly, and did so as ruthlessly as any nation in history. In a dispatch to Upshur, Green spoke of an Anglo-American antislavery conspiracy supported by none other than the British foreign secretary, Lord Aberdeen, to abolish slavery in Texas and irretrievably place the Lone Star Republic in Britain's economic and commercial orbit. Secretary Upshur uncritically accepted this analysis and used it to justify immediate annexation, lest Great Britain succeed in the first phase of its global antislavery campaign.

President Tyler also was alarmed by unofficial intelligence coming from London detailing British diplomatic initiatives involving Texas and Mexico. Upon reviewing the correspondence from Duff Green, he immediately wrote Waddy Thompson, the American minister to Mexico, expressing his "apprehension and fears" and asking him to verify the accuracy of the reports that Britain was meddling in Texas. The information received in Washington, Tyler told Thompson, *"most confidentially,"* came from "the Texan minister of London." "Lord Aberdeen," the president continued, "avowed to the latter the great interest which England took in the abolition of slavery in Texas, and distinctly makes that the basis of interference."[30]

After Upshur and President Tyler consulted about a desired diplomatic course of action to meet the perceived British threat, the secretary of state was authorized to open secret treaty negotiations with Texas's minister in Washington, Isaac Van Zandt. It would not be a simple task. There were major hurdles facing Tyler and Upshur in their campaign to annex Texas. The Texans posed an initial obstacle because of fears they might again be the bride left at the altar by the fickle American groom and for several months played hard to get.

Primarily, Sam Houston's government wanted American guarantees against a possible Mexican retaliatory military attack. Granting such guarantees caused Tyler and Upshur serious concern as they fretted about the constitutional implications of promising military protection to a foreign nation without direct congressional sanction. Apparently an unnerved President Tyler momentarily wavered in his enthusiasm for annexation, prompting a less rattled Upshur to announce privately, "I shall get Texas, if I can make the President *stick*."[31]

Reservations about the desirability and legality of annexing Texas existed among the American public at large and not solely within the abolitionist ranks. For instance, a sizable number of citizens in the free states were troubled by the argument that annexation of a sovereign republic was unconstitutional; they questioned a policy that would add new slave territory to the Union in this seemingly extralegal fashion. Hesitation about the merits of Texas annexation among influential segments of the American public in turn made Secretary Upshur's task of securing a two-thirds majority for a treaty in the Senate quite formidable.

The secretary of state dealt with the Texans first. After five months of hard bargaining, he convinced enough members of Sam Houston's government of the sincerity of the Tyler administration's overtures and cajoled them into accepting American guarantees of protection and quick action. To overcome resistance among northern senators, Upshur shrewdly linked a settlement of the Oregon boundary dispute with Texas annexation, a scheme later included in the platform of James K. Polk as part of his successful 1844 presidential race. Finally, to mold public opinion and gain popular support, Upshur placed a series of anonymous editorials in the *Madisonian* urging annexation and outlining the dire consequences for the Union if Texas slipped permanently under British influence.

Throughout his coordinated and adroitly managed campaign to add Texas to the Union, Secretary Upshur played the juggler constantly seeking to maintain a delicate and difficult political and diplomatic balance. On the political front, he privately confided to fellow southerner Beverley Tucker: "I am sanguine in the belief that I can make the question so clear that even the Yankees will go for annexation. They are you know, an 'uncommon moral & religious people' & greatly opposed to the sin of slavery since they ceased to carry on the slave trade; but there is one point you may be sure of them & that is, their *interest*. As I can show them that the annexation of

Texas will be for the good of their commerce & manufactures, I shall probably have their support." Publicly, Upshur exploited anti-British sentiment to fuel his countrymen's patriotic impulses in favor of Texas annexation. At the same time under diplomatic cover and out of public view, Upshur coolly began to pursue a negotiated settlement of the Oregon dispute with archrival Great Britain.[32]

One example of Upshur's effort to rally the American public in opposition to British machinations in Texas came a few months into his service as head of the State Department. With President Tyler's hearty approval he sent a dispatch to Edward Everett, the American minister in London, that outlined the administration's dissatisfaction with Britain's antislavery agenda. By taking the unusual course of making his private message to an American diplomat public and known to the entire nation and the world beyond, which was a breach of diplomatic protocol, Upshur unabashedly played to a home audience and pandered to his countrymen's visceral Anglophobia. The public nature of the message also had the effect of putting the British government on notice that meddling in Texas was of grave concern to the Tyler administration because it undermined the security of the southern states and was tantamount to direct interference "with the established institutions of the United States."

In confidential correspondence to Everett accompanying the public communiqué, Upshur did not soften the overall tone of the message. If anything, the secretary hardened the American position by charging that Britain was negotiating a loan agreement with Texas that included a provision calling for the abolition of slavery. Upshur reiterated his belief that it would be absurd to accept the explanation that England was motivated by "a mere feeling of philanthropy" in promoting "the abolition of African slavery throughout the Western World." Parroting the analysis recently offered him by Duff Green and John C. Calhoun, the secretary of state reminded his minister that all expressions by British leaders of a disinterested humanitarianism were pure subterfuge. Ignore the smoke and mirrors, Upshur advised, because for Britain empire was the name of the game. With that in mind, Upshur cautioned Minister Everett to be continually alert to the threat posed to the United States by British imperialism in its reach for global economic hegemony.[33]

After a series of interviews with Foreign Secretary Aberdeen in November 1843, Edward Everett reported back to Upshur that he had "in obedience to your instructions, alluded to the agency, which the British Government was supposed to be exercising, to procure the abolition of Slavery in Texas." In response to the American minister's queries, Lord Aberdeen denied Great Britain was scheming to end slavery in Texas and told Everett that "the suggestion, that England had made or intended to make the abolition of Slavery the condition of any treaty arrangement with her, was wholly without foundation." Minister Everett also informed the secretary of state that he had asked Aberdeen about his opinion of a newspaper article attributed to Duff Green in which was outlined the alleged British scheme for world domination. "Lord Aberdeen," Everett recorded, "treated it as a notion too absurd and unfounded to need serious contradiction."[34]

When Everett's correspondence reached Washington in early December, neither Secretary Upshur nor President Tyler was reassured by the American minister's report that Lord Aberdeen had unequivocally denied his nation was seeking to abolish slavery in Texas. As President Tyler later explained to John C. Calhoun, the British government's answer "to Mr. Everett's inquires as to the propositions made by certain persons to G. Britain for pecuniary aid to procure the emancipation of slaves in Texas, decided me on the question as it did our lamented friend Mr. Upshur." No matter what assurances Lord Aberdeen and his colleagues offered, the British were not to be trusted. Tyler and Upshur simply did not believe British claims of non-involvement were truthful. To their mind, the best way to safeguard American security was to keep the secret negotiations for a Texas annexation treaty on the fast track.[35]

To avoid an acrimonious public political wrangle over the merits of Texas annexation, secrecy was essential to the success of the diplomatic endeavor. But then as now, intelligence about Upshur's discreet undercover activities invariably leaked out. Waddy Thompson reported to Washington that rumors abounded in Mexico City that the United States was busily negotiating to annex Texas. The American minister further stated that if the rumors were true and an annexation deal was finalized, it would lead to war with Mexico.

Juan Almonte, the Mexican minister to the United States, also got wind of the American overtures to the Texans. In an official communiqué, Minister Almonte informed Secretary Upshur that his government had received credible information that at its upcoming session the U.S. Congress intended to consider a proposal to annex Texas. If Texas annexation were approved by Congress and sanctioned by President Tyler, Almonte bluntly warned, Mexico would sever diplomatic relations and immediately declare war.

But even the threat of war did not restrain either Upshur or Tyler, nor did it suppress their desire for Texas. Not only were the Americans unwavering in their quest for Texas, they were less than candid in their official response to Minister Almonte. The Tyler administration's first line of argument was that the United States regarded Texas as an independent and sovereign nation "competent to treat for itself." Second, Secretary Upshur in a "how dare you insinuate" tone deflected the Mexican accusation by announcing he was not obligated to answer for the actions of the U.S. Congress, "even if he can be presumed to know anything about the subject."

Minister Almonte had blundered by charging that Congress was the instigator of the alleged annexation schemes. Upshur took advantage of that mistake and technically was accurate in his response to Almonte. However, not getting caught in a lie is not the same as telling the truth. Secretary Upshur had initiated the treaty negotiations and was responsible for the secret dealings with the Texans and the actions of American diplomats on the scene in Texas and Mexico. To be sure, Upshur did not directly or explicitly deny the allegations, but his evasive and dismissive response to Almonte's queries betrayed an implicit disdain for the claims of the Mexican government.[36]

At the time Upshur was feigning any knowledge of U.S.-Texas negotiations to Minister Almonte, the secretary of state was writing his trusted confidant, Beverley Tucker, seeking advice about "what form" an annexation treaty should take. "Treaties are made between governments but the Texan government has no right to transfer the *country* without the consent *of the people*. How shall this be managed?" Not wishing to delay the process by waiting for Tucker's response, Upshur straightforwardly asked his friend to "draft the preamble of a treaty & the clauses transferring the territory." "It is not yet certain that I shall need it," Upshur confessed, "but the possibilities are that I shall & that too within the present month. This, however, is *entre nous*."[37]

Professor Tucker hardly was an impartial or disinterested counselor on the merits of annexation. In addition to agreeing with President Tyler and Secretary Upshur that annexation was indispensable to the future security of the South and the destiny of the whole country, Tucker had a direct personal pecuniary interest in Texas. He owned some fifty slaves in the vicinity of Galveston, where they worked on the land of his friend and fellow speculator Alfred T. Burnley. At an earlier time Tucker may have considered taking up residence in Texas, but being a Virginian to the core he was unable to make the move.

The decision to remain in Williamsburg created a problem for Tucker if he wished at some point to reclaim his bondsmen and bring them back to Virginia. As long as Texas remained foreign territory, federal statutes forbade the importation of his slaves into the United States. To guarantee ready and lawful access to his human chattel as well as to preserve the future of the South's peculiar institution, Tucker was quite anxious to aid his friends Upshur and Tyler in their campaign to bring Texas into the Union as a slaveholding state. At the very least, he was willing to write, as Upshur had requested, a preamble and a treaty and yes, if need be, to devise a way to make annexation by joint resolution appear legitimate and constitutional.

For his part in keeping the annexation scheme on course, President John Tyler did his utmost not to blow the lid off Upshur's promising secret negotiations. To date, he had not made a formal announcement or any public reference to his administration's vigorous diplomacy of annexation. An opportunity to take the American public into his confidence arose when he presented his annual message to Congress in December 1843. Instead of reporting on the progress of his Texas undertaking, President Tyler purposely continued his official silence and made no mention of the treaty negotiations. It was the prudent thing to do if he hoped to retain the trust of the Texans and keep them at the negotiating table.

The president, however, did take note of Minister Almonte's "extraordinary" correspondence with Secretary Upshur "relating to the annexation of Texas to the United States" and announcing the Mexican government's "determination to visit any such anticipated decision by a formal declaration of war against the United States." President Tyler thought Almonte's impertinent threat of war was based on the flimsiest hearsay evidence and dismissed it out of hand. If the intent of the Mexicans was to intimidate the United States it did not succeed. Congress and the chief executive would not be frightened by such scare tactics and fully intended to continue their "calm deliberation" of the annexation question.

It would be far better for the security and harmony of all concerned, President Tyler believed, for the Mexican government to stop its war with Texas. After eight years of sporadic fighting, predatory incursions, and a failure to mount major military campaigns by land or sea, the time had come for Mexico to let go of its wayward province and allow an independent Texas to join the international community. Continued hostilities simply invited unwanted foreign interference in North American affairs. After all, Tyler noted, had not even mighty Great Britain wisely succumbed to the inevitable by giving the United States its independence after seven years of bitter strife? Mexico should do the same with Texas and accept the reality of an independent Lone Star Republic.[38]

While instructing Mexico in his annual message to stop its war against Texas, President Tyler neither affirmed nor denied the United States was seeking a treaty of annexation. In the months since he had told Upshur to obtain a treaty, the president had made no public acknowledgment of his administration's secret negotiations with the Texans. Probably the only observers unconcerned about Tyler's lack of candor were the majority of his fellow Americans, although his abolitionist adversaries smelled a rat. The Mexicans definitely were not duped. They fully grasped the scope of Tyler's annexationist agenda. The British did as well. Lord Aberdeen resented Tyler's talk of foreign interference with its implication that Great Britain was bent on intruding in Texas. In a moment of pique the British foreign secretary instructed his minister in Washington to lodge a protest with the American government over Tyler's provocative language.

A highly agitated Aberdeen also alerted the British ambassador in Paris, Lord Cowley, that "it is sufficiently evident that the future annexation of Texas to the United States is contemplated by the President." Ironically, Tyler's fears of foreign intervention nearly proved a self-fulfilling prophecy. In response to the American president's insinuations about Britain's designs, Aberdeen had instructed Cowley to propose to the French a joint initiative to prevent the United States from annexing Texas. Fortunately for Tyler, Lord Aberdeen's proposal for a combined British-French diplomatic front to stifle the American ambitions in Texas came to naught.[39]

Kept in the dark by the administration, the American public did not fully comprehend that the normally judicious John Tyler was playing a game of high-stakes poker. In an incredible role reversal the man who claimed to be a strict constructionist had transformed into a gambler and risk taker who would play fast and loose with constitutional requirements. Tyler as adventurous leader was not the image most Americans had of their accidental president. But out of public view President John Tyler the commander-in-chief was simultaneously courting war with Mexico and toying with the idea of skirting the constitutional requirement to inform Congress of any executive military commitments to protect Texas from Mexican attack. Tyler apparently would go to any lengths to nab the proverbial brass ring.

Publicly President Tyler exuded confidence because by his reckoning the annexation project was going as planned. In early January 1844 the treaty negotiations remained on the fast track with Secretary Upshur close to finalizing an agreement with the Texans. Equally important, Upshur appeared to have accomplished the politically impossible by successfully lining up enough votes in the Senate for ratification. Quickly bringing Texas into the Union would situate Tyler as the frontrunner in the election campaign. His dream of being reelected to the presidency seemed tantalizingly within grasp.

★ A TREATY AND A TRAGEDY
★

★ Although Secretary of State Upshur initially may have favored Texas annexation as a narrow sectional measure to preserve the South's peculiar institution, he readily converted to President Tyler's more politically expedient argument stressing broader national interests. Tyler undoubtedly believed annexation would make the South more secure and less vulnerable to the threat posed by the antislavery movement. But the president also vigorously contended that acquiring Texas would be a milestone on the United States's path to national greatness. Without hesitation Upshur adopted the president's rationale. As a loyal Tyler partisan, Secretary Upshur launched a discreet and stealthy diplomatic campaign for annexation on the grounds that adding Texas to the constellation of states would be a political and commercial benefit to the entire Union, not just one part of it.

Secretary Upshur's message to his men in the field unequivocally emphasized this point. It was to be understood by all of America's diplomatic corps that the Tyler administration viewed Texas annexation as being national in all respects and "excludes every idea of mere sectional interest." Only months earlier while still secretary of the navy, Upshur privately had been confiding to friends that the South's salvation lay in the annexation of Texas. However, after being elevated to the helm of the State Department, the secretary of state preached a different sermon to the diplomatic corps: *"The salvation of our Union depends on its success."*

As a recently converted true believer in a nationalist agenda, Upshur also conveyed the same message about the benefits of Texas annexation to wary and suspicious members of the Senate. Promising them he would keep their commitment to vote for an annexation treaty strictly confidential, Upshur displayed the full range of his lobbying wizardry and unheralded powers of persuasion by bringing the required majority of senators on board for ratification. In late January 1844 a triumphant Upshur announced to his agent in Texas, William S. Murphy, that he had ascertained "the opinions and views of the Senators upon the subject, and *it is found that a clear constitutional majority of two thirds, are in favor of the measure.*"[40]

The Texans were not as easily persuaded. They doubted the sincerity of American promises that support for an annexation treaty was assured and thus continued to balk. The Texans' understandable caution stemmed from their memory of having been spurned before by Washington. Secretary Upshur was fully aware of their reluctance to seal an annexation deal. To remove their doubts about the trustworthiness of the United States's promises this time round, Upshur instructed Murphy to inform Texan officials that at least forty of fifty-two senators were solid for ratification, which was more than enough to guarantee Senate approval of an annexation treaty.

Texans also were hesitant to sign a treaty for fear it would precipitate a full-scale Mexican attack on their nation. The head of the Lone Star Republic's legation in Washington, Minister Isaac Van Zandt, in a note to Secretary Upshur asked directly if the United States would place military forces on the borders of Texas "as shall be sufficient to protect her against foreign aggression." Upshur at this stage was unwilling to put such a commitment in writing. But speaking by the authority of the president, Secretary Upshur verbally assured Van Zandt that "at the moment a treaty of annexation shall be signed" the United States would send army and navy forces to prevent a Mexican invasion of Texas.[41]

It would take another four or five weeks of tough negotiations before Upshur completed a draft annexation treaty with Texas. Word of the secretary of state's unforeseen success ultimately spilled out and reached opponents of the administration's annexation scheme. Among those was none other than John Tyler's number one nemesis, the Whig leader Henry Clay. Writing from New Orleans, an incredulous Clay sought confirmation of Upshur's astounding diplomatic and political achievement from fellow Kentuckian John J. Crittenden.

Henry Clay reported to Crittenden that he heard the unwelcome news from General Charles F. Mercer, who "has just arrived here from Texas, and brings intelligence which has greatly surprized me, but which in part I cannot believe to be true. It is in substance, that it has been ascertained by a vote in Secret Session, or in some other way, that 42 American Senators are in favor of the annexation of Texas, and have advised the President that they will confirm a treaty to that effect; that a negotiation has been opened accordingly in Texas, and that a treaty will be speedily concluded, & c." Clay then asked Crittenden: "Is this true? Especially that 42 Senators have concurred in the project." Henry Clay was a politician accustomed to being in the know and requested an immediate reply. He dejectedly confessed to his friend, "If it be true, I shall regret extremely that I have had no hint of it." Indeed it was true. And had John Tyler known of Henry Clay's chagrin, the president surely would have danced a jig and rubbed his hands in glee.[42]

While Secretary Upshur quietly lined up the required number of senators for ratification and secretly continued to nail down treaty specifics with
the Texans, Senator Robert J. Walker joined the fray by opening a public
campaign urging annexation. A slaveowning Democrat from Mississippi
and valued point man for the Tyler administration in Congress, Senator
Walker spent his young life in Pennsylvania and understood the political
mores and racial prejudices of both the North and South. As a speculator in Texas lands and bonds, the Mississippi senator also had a financial
as well as a political interest in bringing Texas into the Union. Walker's
monetary stake in Texas was not unusual among enthusiasts for annexation. Several members and friends of the Tyler administration, including
Thomas Gilmer and John Y. Mason, both of whom served in the cabinet as
secretary of the navy, the undercover diplomat Duff Green, and informal
presidential adviser Beverley Tucker, had significant investments in Texas
properties. Although President Tyler speculated in Kentucky lands, there is
no evidence that he owned land or slaves in Texas.

In early February 1844 Senator Walker published a lengthy pro-annexation letter in the *Washington Globe*, one of the nation's leading newspapers.
Walker's message to the American people outlined the manifold reasons
why the United States should annex Texas by reiterating the arguments
made publicly the year before by Thomas Gilmer and more recently by Secretary Upshur. The Walker letter was the last and the most successful of the
trial balloons sent up by Tyler's allies. It quickly was reprinted in pamphlet
form and millions of copies were circulated to rally public support for annexation, especially among uncommitted northern Democrats and skeptical fence sitters throughout the country.

Senator Walker's brief for annexation proved to be a multipurpose mas-
terwork of propaganda. He deftly pressed the right buttons in the debate
and offered something for everyone. For those who had constitutional or
legal qualms about annexation, his advice was simple—"not to worry." Taking Texas actually would be the reannexation of territory earlier claimed by
the United States and unwisely ceded to Spain in the Florida treaty of 1819.
"This is no question of the purchase of new territory," Walker reassured
his countrymen, "but of the re-annexation of that which once was all our
own. It is not a question of the extension of our limits, but of the restora-
tion of former boundaries." Also, the senator believed the reannexation of
Texas could be accomplished in three possible ways—by treaty, by an act
of Congress without a treaty, or by the authority the states had to "annex
additional territory with the sanction of Congress." Senator Walker was con-

fident that all three of his suggested methods of annexation met the requirements of the Constitution.

For Americans who worried that bringing Texas into the Union would be too great an extension of territory and thus a threat to the viability of the republic, Walker reminded them of their young nation's successful historical record of territorial expansion. Similar concerns had been raised about the Louisiana Purchase, concerns Walker believed had been laid to rest by President James Monroe in his 1823 annual message: "It is manifest, that by enlarging the basis of our system, and increasing the number of States, the system itself has been greatly strengthened in both its branches. Consolidation and disunion have thereby been rendered equally impracticable."

By citing President Monroe's reiteration of the Madisonian formula, Senator Walker expressed his fervent belief that the "extend the sphere" analysis of Federalist no. 10 was the correct prescription for the continued health and prosperity of the American republic. He was not alone in that belief. James Madison's expansionist concept was a powerful idea that continually reverberated in the thinking and policy of the post-Revolutionary generation of American leadership.

Assuming that he had disposed of several of the more troubling constitutional and legal objections to annexation, Senator Walker moved on to confront the highly charged issues of race and the role of blacks in American society. He initially cast his racial argument in the context of the expansion of the South's peculiar institution by declaring that on the question of annexation the "only remaining objection is the question of slavery." But Walker quickly broadened his analysis in an appeal to the racial fears of northern whites by pointing out "that the presence of blacks throughout the country, not their enslavement in the South, threatened the nation's well-being."

To rid the nation of what many white Americans perceived to be a looming black peril, Senator Walker called for the immediate annexation of Texas. Such a course of action would eventually drain most free blacks from the northern states and diffuse the slave population of the upper southern states to Texas and beyond. This diffusion of free and enslaved blacks would occur, Walker explained, because annexation "is the only safety-valve for the whole Union, and the only practicable outlet for the African population through Texas, into Mexico and Central and Southern America."[43]

Senator Robert Walker's draconian prescription of racial cleansing — that to solve the race problem you had to remove the black race — was not uncommon or out of the political mainstream in antebellum America. The overwhelming majority of Walker's white contemporaries shared his views and rejected any suggestion that they should live harmoniously side by side with African Americans. That racial outlook had deep roots in American culture and had been sanctioned by none other than founding father Thomas Jefferson in his *Notes on the State of Virginia*, published in 1785. The idea of removing blacks by shipping them to Africa or the Caribbean was a solution Jefferson, James Madison, and John Tyler had embraced, and later was pursued by Abraham Lincoln during the first year of the Civil War when he attempted to launch a Haitian colonization scheme.

In addition to playing the race card in his pro-annexation polemic, Walker raised, as did Thomas Gilmer and others before him, the specter of two other bogeymen that bedeviled many of his fellow Americans. One was the ever-threatening British who were intent on preventing the annexation of Texas as part of their overall plan to undercut America's national destiny. Walker coupled his Anglophobic warnings with a second threat, that of the abolitionist movement. The Mississippi slaveholder loathed abolitionists as much or more so than did President Tyler. Both men denounced abolitionists as traitors in the service of England. In his letter Walker did not mince words: "their hearts are filled with treason" and they were "Americans in name, but Englishmen in feelings and principles."

To counteract the combined threats of British imperialism and the international antislavery enterprise, Senator Walker once again proposed the all-purpose remedy of annexation. In a succinct restatement of President Tyler's oft-expressed national greatness theme, Walker proclaimed that the "reannexation of Texas would strengthen and fortify the whole Union, and antedate the period when our own country would be the first and greatest of all the powers of the earth."[44]

Senator Walker probably issued his racially charged letter with President Tyler's approval, although the aristocratic and genteel Virginian never publicly endorsed his friend's blatantly racist screed. That was not John Tyler's style. Rarely, if ever, did he make disparaging racist remarks about free or enslaved blacks in either his private correspondence or his public discourse. That is not to say that President Tyler disagreed with Walker's analysis. He was in full agreement with all of Walker's pro-annexation arguments, including his appeal to the racial anxieties of white Americans. Nonetheless, at this stage of the game President Tyler wisely remained aloof from Walker's blatantly racist safety valve analysis, although in truth it was remarkably similar to the diffusion theory he earlier had formulated at the time of the Missouri controversy.

President Tyler was content to let Senator Walker be the administration's attack dog on the Texas question. This tactic shielded Tyler from being identified publicly with the contention that the campaign for Texas annexation was nothing more than a proslavery plot and the design of the slave power. The president intended to keep his hands clean of the highly contentious issue of slavery's expansion and neutralize its impact on the national debate over annexation. Later, when he entered the public arena in support of annexation, Tyler followed the script he and Upshur had perfected by taking the political high ground. Acquiring Texas, the president emphasized, would serve broad national interests, not the narrow and potentially divisive interests of sectionalism.

In the weeks and months following the publication of Senator Walker's letter, the public debate over the merits of annexation was shaped and framed by his analysis. Progress in the quest for annexation at the public level was accompanied by a corresponding breakthrough at the diplomatic level. On February 27, 1844, Secretary of State Upshur successfully completed negotiations for a draft treaty with the emissaries of the Lone Star Republic. The terms of the draft treaty called for the annexation of Texas as a slave territory of the United States. The institution of slavery would remain intact. Citizens of the Lone Star Republic were to be granted all the rights and privileges of American citizens. Texas public lands were to be ceded to the United States and in return the American government would assume responsibility for Texas's public debt. Finally, the treaty stipulated that both parties would ratify the agreement within six months after the initial signing.

The day after he hammered out the agreement with the Texans an exhausted Secretary of State Upshur was ready for some needed and well-deserved relaxation. He accepted an invitation from Captain Robert Stockton, skipper of the uss *Princeton*, to join him, President Tyler, some fellow cabinet members, and 300 other guests for a happy and carefree cruise on the Potomac aboard America's most technologically advanced warship. The pride of the U.S. Navy, the *Princeton* was a screw-propelled steam frigate that ran silent and smokeless on a high-grade anthracite coal. She was designed to have her engines and propeller shaft housed below the waterline, an innovation that made the ship less vulnerable to enemy fire than existing paddlewheel steam vessels. Upshur took self-satisfaction in the *Princeton* as well, because as secretary of the navy he had encouraged Captain Stockton and the Swedish naval architect John Ericsson to develop what became the American navy's state-of-the-art nautical wonder.

As President Tyler, Secretary Upshur, Secretary of the Navy Gilmer, and a host of other dignitaries, including members of Congress, diplomats, and army and navy officers, boarded that morning they were treated to the sight of the *Princeton* splendidly festooned with the flags of all the nations formally represented in Washington. The feature event of the gala river excursion was to be the firing of the "Peacemaker," an awesome twelve-inch-diameter wrought iron cannon with a fifteen-foot barrel. In the early afternoon of a brisk and sunny winter day, the *Princeton* pushed away from her moorings to begin a fateful journey down the Potomac River through unusually abundant ice floes. For some two hours or more the guests were entertained by the repeated firing of the "Peacemaker" and the other guns of the warship's battery, after which they went below for a sumptuous feast of food and drink, highlighted by plenty of champagne, one of the president's favorite libations.

John Tyler was about to begin the afternoon's round of toasts when he noticed that someone dear to his heart, Julia Gardiner, was missing and had remained above deck. The president sent a messenger to fetch Julia and her father, David Gardiner, a prominent New Yorker and former state senator. It was an open secret and source of much tongue-wagging among the elite of Washington society that the widower Tyler was courting Miss Gardiner, a captivating beauty known as the "Belle of Long Island." Initially laughing off the summons, the dawdling and bemused Julia presently obeyed the presidential directive. Upon joining the party below she immediately was seated and given a glass of champagne. A satisfied and happy President Tyler then began the round of toasts in a wash of champagne—one to the Navy, a second to the "Peacemaker," and a third to the gallant Captain Stockton. Other toasts quickly followed, led off by one from the captain of the *Princeton* to the president of the United States.

Amid the merriment, hilarity, and spontaneous outbreak of song, one party reveler, noticing they were passing Mount Vernon, requested a last firing of the "Peacemaker" in honor of the first president, George Washington. At first Captain Stockton refused and said, "No more guns to-night." But he relented when Secretary of Navy Gilmer pulled rank and asked for another firing of the big gun. A number of the slightly inebriated crowd, including Stockton, Upshur, Gilmer, and David Gardiner, went topside to witness the final ceremonial salvo. Once again the loquacious Julia Gardiner tarried below as did the president, who hesitated at the bottom of the stairs to hear a song his son-in-law, William Waller, had just begun singing. That momentary diversion may have saved John Tyler's life.[45]

In an instant there was a loud boom on deck, which the guests below initially cheered, then shrieked in anguish when they realized a catastrophe had occurred. The "Peacemaker" had exploded, killing Abel Upshur, Thomas Gilmer, David Gardiner, Virgil Maxcy, a retired diplomat from Maryland, Commodore Beverly Kennon of the United States Navy, two regular seamen, and Henry, Tyler's black slave and body servant. Captain Stockton was dazed and wounded, as were several others, including Senator Thomas Hart Benton of Missouri.

When a horrified President Tyler came upon the scene of carnage, he immediately grasped the full extent of the tragedy that had befallen the nation—and his administration. As he sorrowfully observed in describing the calamity to one of his daughters a few days later, "A more heart-rending scene scarcely ever occurred. What a loss I have sustained in Upshur and Gilmer. They were truly my friends, and would have aided me for the next twelve months with effect."[46]

After absorbing the shock of the bloodbath he encountered on the deck of the *Princeton*, President Tyler turned his attention to the distraught and grief-stricken Julia Gardiner. She had fainted upon learning of her father's death. When Julia regained consciousness, the president carried her across a gangplank to a rescue vessel that had come alongside to take the wounded and many of the dazed passengers ashore. Over the following weeks Tyler consoled and comforted Miss Gardiner in her sorrow and grief. Four months later, on June 26, 1844, the fifty-four-year-old president married his twenty-four-year-old sweetheart in a private ceremony at the Church of the Ascension on Fifth Avenue in New York City. Across the nation the tittering gossips and salacious scandalmongers had a field day, but the happy May–December couple ignored the hubbub. John and Julia Gardiner Tyler lived happily together for almost two decades. They had seven children and shared a blissful union until John Tyler's death in 1862.

Tyler ultimately may have found personal happiness after a brief bout of pain and grief, but as he instinctively understood the *Princeton* tragedy devastated his Texas agenda. The deaths of Upshur and Gilmer deprived him of two of his best people and the most important architects of the administration's annexation policy. Tyler was not alone in that realization. Both friend and foe of the administration recognized that the political landscape had been rocked as if by an earthquake by the February blast on the Potomac.

For instance, a shocked Isaac Van Zandt, the Texas diplomat who alongside Secretary Upshur had forged the draft treaty, was a guest on board the *Princeton* that fateful day and absorbed the full meaning of the disaster. He wrote Anson Jones, the new president of the Lone Star Republic, that this "occurrence will have, I fear, an unfavorable influence on our affairs here. Texas has lost two of her best friends in this country: their places it will be difficult to fill."[47]

Abolitionist enemies of the Tyler administration saw the explosion of the *Princeton* as an act of Providence which, in the judgment of Joshua Leavitt, "will probably defeat the Texas scheme for the present." Lewis Tappan wrote a fellow abolitionist in England that an "awful lesson has been taught our pro-slavery men at Washington by the explosion aboard the *Princeton*. Upshur & Gilmer, thus cut down at a blow, were the chief actors in the nefarious scheme of introducing Texas into the Union. Mr. Tyler is no better." Tappan also believed this tragic event would derail the campaign for annexation temporarily, although he observed that "there is no knowing what the Satanic designs of wicked men may achieve." In any event, both Leavitt and Tappan hoped that the Tyler administration would not be able to annex Texas prior to the presidential election, opening the way for the victory of an anti-annexationist candidate who once and for all would scuttle the Texas project.[48]

The *Princeton* catastrophe was one of the more devastating disasters to befall a presidential administration in American history. Prior to the Civil War and the assassination of Abraham Lincoln, it unquestionably was the most severe and debilitating tragedy ever to confront a president of the United States. To have a secretary of state, a secretary of the navy, a high-ranking naval officer, and two other well-known public men perish in a single misadventure was unprecedented in the nation's history and remains the case to the present day.

Looking back on these tragic events more than a decade later, John Tyler coupled the loss of Upshur and Gilmer with the earlier sorrowful death of Hugh Legare. "Thus in the course of eight months," the former president lamented, "three members of the executive branch of the government had passed away, each a shining light, and at moments full of promise to themselves and the world." Of course, President Tyler immediately had recognized, as he tacitly admitted to his daughter Mary Jones just days after the tragedy, that the loss of Upshur and Gilmer sounded the death knell of his own political ambitions and snuffed out any hope for reelection.[49]

★ Once he had officially honored and mourned his lost comrades, John Tyler moved quickly to rebuild his cabinet. Less than a week after the *Princeton* horror, President Tyler tapped John C. Calhoun to head the State Department. The sixty-two-year-old Calhoun had received the dreadful news of the *Princeton* accident from his son Patrick, a second lieutenant in the U.S. Army who had been a guest on board the ship that day. As a former senator and leading public servant of the antebellum era with vast experience in government, John C. Calhoun appeared to be a solid choice for secretary of state. He had been secretary of war in James Monroe's administration and had held the vice presidency under John Quincy Adams and during Andrew Jackson's first term. He also was known as a staunch defender of slavery and a pillar of southern conservatism in the Senate.[50]

John C. Calhoun ranked with Daniel Webster and Henry Clay as America's leading political icons of the early republic. Each renowned member of this illustrious triumvirate was considered prime presidential timber, but to the dismay of many of their countrymen none of them ever made it to the White House. In the 1840s many observers of the American political landscape rightly assumed that each of these three men jealously harbored feelings that he was better qualified and more deserving of the position of chief magistrate than the incumbent John Tyler.

Apparently President Tyler momentarily balked at the idea of appointing Calhoun as secretary of state because the South Carolinian might adversely polarize public opinion on the Texas question. But feeling embarrassed and trapped by an unauthorized overture Henry Wise imprudently had made to the Calhoun camp, the president put aside any reservations he may have had and agreed to offer Calhoun the premier cabinet post. It was a decision he later came to regret.

President Tyler initially employed Senator George McDuffie of South Carolina, a close ally of Calhoun, to convey his proposal. "The President is very anxious that you should accept & come on immediately as the Texas negociation [*sic*] admits of no delay," McDuffie dutifully wrote his friend, "and requested me to say so to you." Senator McDuffie further informed Calhoun that if he agreed to become secretary of state "in ten days after your arrival the Treaty of annexation would be signed, and from poor Upshur's count 40 senators would vote for it." Bringing Texas into the Union would be the capstone of your long career in public service, McDuffie predicted in an appeal to Calhoun's vanity, and "a great occasion involving the peace of the country & the salvation of the South."[51]

Before receiving official word from Calhoun accepting the offer, President Tyler sent the nomination to the Senate. "I have been prompted to this course," Tyler explained to Calhoun, "by reference to your great talents and deservedly high standing with the Country at large." "The annexation of Texas to the Union, and the settlement of the Oregon question on a satisfactory basis, are the great ends to be accomplished: The first is in the act of completion and will admit of no delay. The last had but barely opened, when death snatched from me my lamented friend." Within hours the Senate unanimously confirmed the appointment of John C. Calhoun as President Tyler's third secretary of state.[52]

Under this friendly pressure from the president and a host of other leading politicians to aid the nation in its hour of need, and in appreciation of the flattering unanimous vote of confidence from his former colleagues in the Senate, Calhoun capitulated and reluctantly accepted the appointment. Upon reaching Washington and formally taking the oath of office, the newly minted secretary of state quickly went to work. Calhoun's first order of business was to meet with the representatives of the Texas republic to finalize the annexation agreement that virtually had been completed six weeks earlier by his predecessor. However, securing a mutually agreeable treaty of annexation was not the casual and easy mopping up exercise of crossing the t's and dotting the i's that the South Carolinian had expected. Even so, Secretary Calhoun almost met the ten-day deadline McDuffie arbitrarily had imposed for the signing of a treaty.

Since agreeing to a preliminary draft with the late Secretary Upshur, the Texans had hardened their stance on the question of American military protection in the event of a Mexican attack. They were not content with the verbal assurances given by Upshur and now wanted a written guarantee. Eager to overcome this last obstacle, Calhoun readily obliged. He wrote Texan ministers Isaac Van Zandt and J. Pinckney Henderson that "I am directed by the President to say that the Secretary of the Navy has been instructed to order a strong naval force to concentrate in the gulf of Mexico, to meet any emergency, and that similar orders have been issued by the Secretary of War to move the disposable military forces on our Southwestern frontier for the same purpose." Calhoun said he was further directed to assure them the American chief executive "would deem it his duty to use all the means placed within his power by the Constitution to protect Texas from all foreign invasion."[53]

Secretary Calhoun's prompt and unequivocal written promise of military protection sealed the deal. On April 12, 1844, a formal treaty of annexation was signed. Just over a week later President Tyler submitted the Texas treaty to the Senate for ratification. The terms of the treaty were nearly identical—the exception being the explicit pledge of a military shield against invasion—to those contained in Upshur's draft. Texas would enter as a U.S. territory and in return the federal government would assume all of Texas's debts. In addition, Ministers Van Zandt and Henderson explained in a dispatch to their superiors, "We have the right to claim the preservation of all of our property as secured in our domestic institutions as well as to claim admission into the Union as a State or States." Although they felt "obliged to avoid any allusion" to slavery in the treaty to assure quick ratification by the Senate, Van Zandt and Henderson were confident that the property provisions in the document "include our right to slaves, as the constitution of the United States recognizes that species of property."[54]

Van Zandt and Henderson also detailed how American forces would be deployed "for the protection of Texas." They had "strong assurances" that President Tyler would meet his promised obligations. It was agreed that the main body of the American army "shall be concentrated and stationed at Fort Jessup," in Louisiana near the Texas border. John Tyler was true to his word. Shortly after the treaty was signed he ordered the deployment of a large number of soldiers to Fort Jessup. This garrison aptly was named the Army of Observation and it remained in place at Fort Jessup throughout the remainder of Tyler's presidency. To guard against a possible Mexican marine assault on the Texas coast, President Tyler ordered the dispatch of a powerful naval force to the Gulf of Mexico. All the president's actions to defend Texas were taken under his authority as commander-in-chief and without the knowledge or approval of Congress.

It is clear that Tyler and Calhoun had lengthy discussions with the Texan ministers about how to make certain their annexation project succeeded. Every contingency appears to have been discussed, including the possibility that the Senate would reject the treaty. If that occurred, Van Zandt and Henderson noted that "the President of the United States assured us, before we agreed to sign and submit it, that he would, immediately upon its rejection by that body, should it be so disposed of, send to both Houses of Congress a message, recommending to them, in the strongest terms, the passage of a law annexing Texas as a State, under that provision of the constitution of this Government, which authorizes Congress to admit new States into the Union." Again, as events would demonstrate, John Tyler was true to his word.[55]

In the letter of transmittal accompanying the treaty, President Tyler presented what was the first official announcement of his administration's rationale for annexation. He pointedly emphasized the innumerable national as opposed to purely sectional benefits that would accrue from bringing Texas into the Union. To his mind the reasons justifying annexation were "so replete with all that can add to national greatness and wealth" as to be unassailable. After six months of confidential and arduous negotiations, a relieved and elated John Tyler finally had emerged from the weeds to reap the long-awaited reward of his carefully calculated secret diplomacy.[56]

Even so, Tyler understood, as he candidly had told the Texans, that Upshur's death meant quick ratification was no longer a certainty. To placate and win over senators who were having second thoughts and now questioned the necessity and wisdom of further territorial expansion, President Tyler once again trotted out the tried and true republican formula of founding father James Madison. The "proposed enlargement of our territory" made some Americans uneasy, Tyler conceded. "From this, I am free to confess, I see no danger. The federative system is susceptible of the greatest extension compatible with the ability of the representation of the most distant State or Territory to reach the seat of Government," and the president concluded, the "addition of new States has served to strengthen rather than to weaken the Union."[57]

Public speculation about the status of the Texas negotiations had been rife for several weeks before the treaty was signed. After it was formally submitted, the Tyler administration assumed that the Senate would consider the annexation treaty in executive session, which meant that the text of the treaty and the accompanying documents would not be made public until after the vote on ratification. That was not to be the case. Five days after the Senate received the Texas treaty, Benjamin Tappan of Ohio, older brother of abolitionist leaders Lewis and Arthur Tappan, released his confidential package of treaty documents to the press. Tappan was duly reprimanded by his colleagues for his "flagrant violation" of Senate rules, but the cover of official secrecy had been blown. The details of the annexation treaty were now in the public domain. Consequently, the Senate lifted the ban of secrecy and had twenty thousand copies of the documents printed for congressional and public use.[58]

Immediately newspaper columns throughout the country were filled with the text and fine print of the treaty material, creating a national uproar because the documents appeared to verify that the sole objective of Texas annexation was the preservation of slavery. For the American public to have a perception of the treaty as being narrowly sectional was exactly what John Tyler had sought to avoid. Secretary Upshur's exaggerated claims of a British abolitionist conspiracy in his dispatches to Minister Everett raised a number of eyebrows. But what caused the most sensation was the aggressive defense of the peculiar institution expressed in Secretary of State Calhoun's April 18, 1844, letter to the British minister in Washington, Richard Pakenham.

In language uncharacteristically blunt for diplomatic discourse, Secretary Calhoun told Pakenham that Britain's intention to abolish slavery throughout the world was a direct threat to the security of the United States. Calhoun also questioned the sincerity of British denials that they were aiding the abolitionist cause in Texas. The secretary of state justified his government's right to annex Texas as a defensive measure to protect slave states from the encroachments of abolitionism. For Calhoun slavery was beneficial and a positive good. Citing what proved to be inaccurate data from the U.S. census of 1840, Calhoun asserted that the mental and physical health of black slaves in the South was demonstrably better than their free black counterparts in the North. On the basis of that faulty analysis Calhoun concluded that "what is called Slavery, is, in reality, a political institution, essential to the peace, safety, and prosperity of those States of the Union in which it exists."[59]

Secretary Calhoun's confidential, soon to be made public, lecture to Minister Pakenham on the merits of the South's peculiar institution was symptomatic of the widespread discussion of the slavery controversy rippling through American society in the spring of 1844. The question of whether or not Texas should be annexed and slavery allowed to expand was being hotly debated in a number of the nation's cities and towns. For instance, in New York City the venerable Albert Gallatin, Jefferson's secretary of the treasury and a distinguished republican of the old school, presided over an Anti-Annexation meeting at the Tabernacle on Broadway. The meeting had been called by several of Gotham's leading citizens, including the poet and editor William Cullen Bryant and the merchant and entrepreneur William B. Astor.

The capacity crowd in the auditorium listened attentively as the eighty-three-year-old Gallatin spoke passionately against Texas annexation. He denounced Tyler's treaty as a transparent southern scheme to protect slavery and he feared annexing Texas would provoke war with Mexico. After several bursts of applause from a mostly appreciative audience, Gallatin was interrupted by a loud chorus of hisses from Mike Walsh and about twenty toughs from his Spartan band. Walsh and his accomplices momentarily drowned out the feeble and frail Gallatin with shouts of "Hurrah for Texas" and "Three cheers for Calhoun." But, as George Templeton Strong recorded in his diary after attending the gathering, "Their impertinent blackguardism only made the meeting applaud the louder and feel the more magnanimously hostile to Tyler Texas."[60]

It was ironic that an earlier ardent territorial expansionist who had done much to calm President Thomas Jefferson's constitutional qualms about the legality of purchasing Louisiana now questioned the wisdom of acquiring Texas. In 1803 as a member of Jefferson's cabinet, Albert Gallatin had advised the president that the purchase of Louisiana clearly was constitutional because "the United States as a nation have an inherent right to acquire territory." Gallatin added that "whenever that acquisition is by treaty, the same constitutional authority in whom the treaty-making power is vested have a constitutional right to sanction the acquisition."[61]

Gallatin's change of heart on the virtues of unbridled territorial expansion came several years after his service as Jefferson's secretary of the treasury. He became an abolitionist sometime after 1814 and for the remainder of his life opposed the extension of slavery. Gallatin had been one of Jefferson's chief advisers and trusted political confidants. By turning against slavery on moral grounds Gallatin did what his idol Jefferson privately agonized about but could not do publicly—he became antislavery in action as well as in word. And unlike John Tyler, Albert Gallatin saw the inherent contradiction of perpetuating a slaveholding republic. He was one Jeffersonian republican able to reject and discard the "extend the sphere" rationale as an inapplicable and antiquated doctrine.

Beyond the metropolis of New York City and the urban centers of the Northeast, other communities also were debating the Texas treaty. Out on the prairies of the West a meeting was called at the State House in Springfield, Illinois, to consider "the question of immediate Annexation." One of those in attendance was a young, ambitious politician named Abraham Lincoln, who as a loyal Whig had enthusiastically supported and vigorously campaigned for the 1840 ticket of Tippecanoe and Tyler too. The death of Harrison and the ascension of the "accidental" President Tyler had not totally eroded Lincoln's political support for the administration. But that evening, after briefly reviewing the arguments of various critics of the treaty, Mr. Lincoln concurred in the opinion "that Annexation at this time upon the terms agreed upon by John Tyler was altogether inexpedient."[62]

As opposition to the Texas treaty mounted, the two leading candidates for the Whig and Democratic presidential nominations came out against immediate annexation. The Whig frontrunner, Henry Clay, opposed Texas annexation on a number of counts, but primarily because it would provoke war with Mexico and might lead to a breakup of the Union. Democrat Martin Van Buren's main objection to annexation was that it likely would lead to an unwanted war with Mexico. A prominent Democrat in the Senate, Thomas Hart Benton, also spoke out against the treaty because he believed it threatened disunion. Within a few weeks after its submission to the Senate, Tyler's Texas treaty seemed doomed and his carefully planned and secretly organized Texas crusade was in shambles.

Even members of John Tyler's cabinet were split on the wisdom of his Texas machinations. Secretary of War William Wilkins, a Democrat from Pennsylvania, was solidly behind Tyler on Texas. In an address to the people of his home state, Secretary Wilkins stressed the economic benefits of annexation for Pennsylvania's industry and agriculture. He also warned that American rejection of an annexation treaty at this point would surely result in Texas becoming a commercial dependency of Great Britain. It was imperative to approve a treaty of annexation now, Wilkins advised, or else the nation's exporters of agricultural and manufactured products would face the prospect of being shut out of the markets of Texas by British monopolists.[63]

Taking exception to the president's Texas policy was Secretary of the Treasury John C. Spencer of New York, one of the last Whigs remaining in the cabinet. Secretary Spencer, who as a loyal cabinet member had carried out Tyler's patronage purge, feared taking Texas might incite sectional discord and undermine the Union. But more troubling to Secretary Spencer was President Tyler's willingness to skirt constitutional restraints in his rush to annex Texas. To fulfill his promise to protect the Texans from a Mexican naval assault, President Tyler ordered the secretary of the treasury to deposit $100,000 of secret service contingency funds with a secret agent in New York City to finance the dispatch of a naval force to the Gulf of Mexico.

Secretary Spencer thought Tyler's directive was illegal without congressional approval and a clear violation of the republican principle of the separation of "the sword and the purse." In Spencer's opinion, President Tyler was acting unconstitutionally by exerting the executive power of the sword as well as the legislative power of the purse. After twice refusing to execute the presidential order, Secretary Spencer resigned his cabinet post in protest on May 2, 1844. Tyler was unfazed by Spencer's charges of illegality and remained determined to carry out his Texas agenda. He simply appointed a more pliant individual to be secretary of the treasury, someone who would obey orders without question or hesitation.[64]

In a desperate attempt to salvage his presidential candidacy and to gain approval of his Texas annexation treaty, John Tyler sanctioned his diehard supporters to launch a third-party movement. A band of Tyler's followers, many of them postmasters and other recipients of his executive patronage, assembled in early April 1844 to endorse his reelection and to draw up resolutions hailing the domestic and diplomatic achievements of his three years in office. This wan crew of Tyler partisans also called for the reannexation of Texas. Nobody's fool, President Tyler knew this last-minute effort offered little if any prospect for victory in the fall election, but he hoped that this tactical maneuver might pressure the Democrats to adopt an expansionist platform favoring the annexation of Texas.

As expected, in their May convention the Whigs nominated Henry Clay as the party's presidential candidate by acclamation. The Whig platform ignored the Texas issue entirely. The Democrats met later that month in Baltimore. After bitter wrangling they denied Martin Van Buren the nomination and instead chose a dark horse candidate, James K. Polk of Tennessee. Polk was an outspoken expansionist and his campaign platform called for the reannexation of Texas and the reoccupation of Oregon. John Tyler's third-party forces also met in Baltimore on the same day the Democratic convention assembled. This shadow third-party convention duly nominated John Tyler as its presidential candidate and came out strongly in support of Texas annexation.

In his letter of acceptance candidate Tyler clarified his priorities—"the question with me is between Texas and the presidency." If forced to select between the two, Tyler said that "even if within my grasp" he would forego another four years in the White House to take Texas. By consummating the annexation of Texas, President Tyler "felt that, as an instrument of Providence, I would have been able in accomplishing for my country the greatest possible good." A few years later Tyler explained to Henry Wise that the third-party ploy worked because it made the Democrats realize that a "Texas man or defeat was the choice left,—and they took a Texas man." "Texas," he candidly acknowledged to Wise, "was the great scheme that occupied me."[65]

The Texas annexation treaty was defeated on June 8 by the lopsided vote of 35-16. The Senate's rejection of the treaty was an outcome President Tyler had anticipated. Untroubled by this initial failure, Tyler carefully had prepared for just such a contingency. He quickly sent a message to the House of Representatives noting the Senate's decision and recommending they consider another path to annexation. Readily admitting that he had long considered annexation by treaty the "most suitable form," the president now suggested that "should Congress deem it proper to resort to any other expedient compatible with the constitution," they would have his prompt cooperation. Although Congress adjourned without taking action on the president's suggestion, the stage was set to achieve the annexation of Texas by joint resolution when it reconvened in December.[66]

Having accomplished his objective with the third-party gambit, Tyler withdrew from the presidential race in August and threw his support to Democrat James K. Polk. In November Polk narrowly defeated Henry Clay in the popular vote by just over 38,000 out of 2.7 million votes cast (1,338,464 to 1,300,097). The tally in the Electoral College was Polk 170, Clay 105. Voter participation in the 1844 election was one of the highest recorded in the antebellum era — 78.9 percent of the eligible electorate cast ballots. Tyler's switch to Polk may have been a decisive factor in providing the Democrat his slim edge in the popular vote. Another explanation for Polk's victory was the antislavery Liberty Party's strong showing in New York, which denied Henry Clay the electoral votes of that crucial state and, ironically, placed another pro-Texas slaveowner in the White House.

There was glee in President John Tyler's household when news of Polk's triumph arrived. The new mistress of the presidential mansion, Julia Gardiner Tyler, happily wrote her sister: "Hurrah for Polk! What *will* become of Henry Clay and of the downfall of our Whig friends! — We shall have a very pleasant winter here I can now promise." The vivacious First Lady did indeed have a pleasant winter social season, her only one during a brief eight-month reign as White House hostess. She enthusiastically joined her husband's lobbying team in behalf of Texas annexation, entertaining lavishly and graciously at receptions and dinners for congressional leaders and other dignitaries.

Unexpectedly, the young Mrs. John Tyler became an instantaneous smash hit among Washington's political and social elite. To be sure, there remained a few sniping critics. But a precedent-setter in her own right — she reportedly began the tradition of having the Marine Band play "Hail to the Chief" when the president appeared at official functions — Julia Tyler had laid the groundwork for her ready social acceptance by secretly hiring a New York journalist to serve as her public relations agent. The favorably constructed press releases did the trick. "Mrs. Presidentess," as Julia Tyler came to be toasted, received widespread and approving coverage in the nation's newspapers, which did much to burnish and enhance her public image.[67]

John Tyler's strategy in the post-election Texas drama was to seize upon James K. Polk's narrow victory at the polls as a mandate for annexation. In his fourth and final annual message, the president announced that a "controlling majority of the people and a large majority of the States have declared in favor of immediate annexation." "It is the will of both the people and the States," Tyler proclaimed, "that Texas shall be annexed to the Union promptly and immediately." Since both the United States and the Republic of Texas had already agreed on the terms of annexation, President Tyler recommended "their adoption by Congress in the form of a joint resolution" which would authorize him to finalize the treaty with the Texans.[68]

When Congress reconvened it acted upon President Tyler's request but not before considerable debate on the issue of the legality and constitutionality of annexing Texas by joint resolution. On January 25, 1845, the House of Representatives voted 120-98 in favor of a joint resolution that called for annexation and admission of Texas as a state in the Union. The Senate balked at accepting the House resolution and proceeded to amend it to allow the president to decide whether or not to begin negotiations for a new Texas treaty or go forward with the House plan of immediate annexation. On February 28, 1845, exactly one year after Secretary Upshur died in the *Princeton* explosion, the House voted to accept the Senate's amended version of the joint resolution.[69]

Although a number of senators had voted for the compromise resolution with the expectation that President-elect Polk would be the one to choose between the options of immediate annexation or renewed negotiations, Tyler once again surprised his adversaries by coolly preempting them in the last days of his presidency. He signed the joint resolution on March 1 and two days later, after first touching base with Polk, sent a dispatch to the Texans offering annexation and admission on the House plan. In this glorious moment of ultimate victory when he achieved the great object of his ambition, an overjoyed and triumphant John Tyler presented the gold pen with which he signed the legislation to his wife. The "immortal golden pen," which Mrs. Tyler wore around her neck as a battle trophy, was a fitting token of appreciation in recognition of her helpful role in the lobbying campaign for Texas annexation.[70]

During their last two weeks in the White House, John and Julia Tyler hosted a series of memorable galas and dinners where the champagne and wine "flowed like water." Climaxing the controversial presidency of "His

Accidency" in grand style, the Tylers began the farewell festivities with a presidential ball attended by over three thousand guests and concluded with a glorious dinner honoring James and Sarah Polk and celebrating the annexation of Texas. After accepting congratulations from a guest on the huge success of one of these glittering White House receptions, John Tyler wryly observed: "Yes, they cannot say *now* that I am a President *without a party*."[71]

However, the fun and merriment of an extended round of parties could not mask a glaring inconsistency of principle evident in John Tyler's ultimate victory, one that involved the negation of his most cherished republican beliefs. In devising the joint resolution scheme, President Tyler and his fellow southern strict constructionists had played fast and loose with the Constitution. To many contemporary observers across the nation the questionable constitutionality of the Tyler administration's actions to secure Texas annexation was all too apparent. Upset that southerners planned and executed the entire scheme, Henry Clay asked Beverley Tucker what was to be made of men who vowed strict adherence to the Constitution and now conveniently argued for Texas annexation by joint resolution. Clay provided his own answer—these men "forfeit all consideration of respect to principle." Undoubtedly, Clay was bitter because these unprincipled Tyler men had helped deny him a last hope of winning the presidency, but what troubled him more was the thought that the South had sold its soul for Texas.[72]

A few days after the annexation process was completed, Robert J. Walker, the leader of the joint resolution forces in the Senate, spoke with former secretary of state Daniel Webster, a longstanding opponent of Texas annexation. In the course of their conversation, Webster realistically conceded that the constitutionality of the joint resolution procedure "can not now be questioned by any judicial power," but pointedly told Senator Walker as well "that Mr. Calhoun and myself may live to regret this dispensing with the conservative ⅔ vote of the Senate." Half-jokingly, Webster went on to warn Walker that at some future date he and Calhoun might "wake up some morning and find the Canadas and perhaps all British North America annexed by a joint resolution by a bare majority of the two Houses of Congress."[73]

Probably the most trenchant commentary on the illegality of annexing Texas by joint resolution came from Albert Gallatin, a surviving Jeffersonian with impeccable credentials. He remained convinced that territory could only be annexed by treaty and declared the resolution was "an undisguised usurpation of power and a violation of the Constitution." In a telling observation about the sanctity and protection of states' rights, Gallatin pointed out "that the provision which requires the consent of two-thirds of the Senate was intended as a guarantee of the States' rights, and to protect the weaker against the abuse of a treaty-making power, if vested in a bare majority." Tyler, Calhoun, Tucker, Walker, and other southerners intent on annexation at whatever cost cavalierly dismissed such critiques of the constitutionality of their actions as nothing but sour grapes. In any event, to get Texas they willingly suffered and rebutted the charges of inconsistency and hypocrisy.[74]

From the very beginning of his administration John Tyler recognized that his dream of annexing Texas would not be achieved easily or quickly. For over three years he displayed a single-minded persistence of purpose, overcoming not only political and constitutional objections, but personal grief and despair as well, first with the death of Hugh Legare and then with the horrible toll of the *Princeton* tragedy. Texas was brought into the Union through sheer presidential determination and not by clear electoral mandate. Arguably, Tyler was correct when he proudly recalled a few years after leaving the White House that "Texas was lost but for my prompt action."[75]

President John Tyler rarely if ever had self-doubts about his presidential policies. Barely seven months after leaving the White House, he wrote John C. Calhoun that he had no remorse and "never doubted the wisdom of the prompt decision in favour of the House-resolution." Tyler was supremely confident about his actions, even when they transparently transgressed his dearly held republican principles. Perhaps such self-assurance and absence of self-doubt are indispensable characteristics of a successful leader. But such unthinking determination and resoluteness can be risky and may lead to undesired consequences. By pushing Texas annexation through during his last days in office, John Tyler recklessly courted war with Mexico.[76]

The Mexican minister, Juan Almonte, immediately protested the annexation of Texas. And five days after President Tyler signed the joint resolution, Almonte requested his passports and returned home. In international diplomacy the protest and departure of a minister usually, but not always, lead to a break in diplomatic relations and war. John Tyler had been warned repeatedly by the Mexicans that annexation would mean war. In the face of those warnings Tyler persisted and consequently bears a measure of responsibility for the ensuing war with Mexico.

★ ★ ★ ★ ★ ★ ★ ★ ★ ★

Retirement
& Secession

7

A small body of men planted on this spot the
seed of a mighty empire.

★ *John Tyler, address at Jamestown on the 250th*
  Anniversary of English Settlement in America,
  May 13, 1857

But the disease—the root of the thing, is not in
cotton or slavery, nor in the election of Lincoln.
But it is deep down in the human heart. The real
question is a question of empire.

★ *Matthew Fontaine Maury, 1861*

t did not take long for ordinary Texans to thank John Tyler for annexing their country. Within a few short months after he left the White House to retire to the life of a tidewater Virginia planter the appreciative accolades began to appear. One of the first tributes came from the Ladies of Brazoria County, which is in eastern Texas, south of Houston. They presented the former president with a beautiful inscribed silver pitcher "as a small token of their gratitude for the benefits conferred upon their Country by procuring its Annexation to the United States." In a letter sent with the silver pitcher, the Brazoria ladies praised John Tyler for his wisdom, zeal, and political sagacity and thanked him for acquiring Texas "without the effusion of blood or loss of treasure." The ladies assured the former president that all of Texas "hails your name with reverence and contemplates your character with admiration."[1]

The unexpected gift and accompanying words of praise and adulation arrived at Sherwood Forest, Tyler's 1,200-acre plantation on the north bank of the James River in Charles City County, on January 1, 1846. The much-maligned former president was quite touched by this totally unanticipated gesture of approval for his Texas policy. It was a most welcome tribute that lifted the spirits of the entire Tyler family at the beginning of the New Year. Tyler immediately responded with a gracious letter to the ladies of Brazoria thanking them for their "kind expressions" and warm commendations. His letter and the heart-warming story of the gift pitcher received widespread national publicity after initially appearing in the columns of a Richmond newspaper. The favorable press coverage given the tale of the grateful Brazoria ladies delighted John and Julia Tyler, both of whom desperately sought an enduring acknowledgment by the American people that the annexation of Texas was a major accomplishment of his presidency.[2]

Another expression of appreciation to "Ex-President Tyler and his Cabinet" came from a convention of Texans assembled in Austin in July 1845 to vote on whether or not to accept the terms of annexation offered by the United States. After readily approving the annexation agreement, the convention resolved that "the early and resolute stand taken by John Tyler, whilst he was President of the United States, to restore Texas to the bosom of the Republican family has secured to him the gratitude and veneration of the people of Texas." The convention delegates also thanked John C. Calhoun and other cabinet members as well as the families of the deceased friends of Texas, Abel P. Upshur and Thomas W. Gilmer, for their "noble enthusiasm" in support of annexation.[3]

The prestigious awards Texans showered upon John Tyler in the immediate aftermath of annexation, including naming a city and county for him, were unique localized state honors that were not duplicated nationally or elsewhere among the other states of the Union. It readily became apparent that Tyler's exclusive claim to Texas laurels was precarious at best and destined to be challenged by other prominent players in the Texas drama. Sure enough, other prominent claimants or their surrogates quickly came forth to demand their share of credit for annexation. Such an unbridled scramble for glory was a scenario that John Tyler and his entire family dreaded because it threatened to further tarnish his already blemished reputation and consign his presidential legacy to history's ash heap.

★ RESCUING A REPUTATION
★
★ To avoid being forgotten and to assure he would be placed alongside his republican idols Jefferson and Madison in the pantheon of American heroes, Tyler made every effort to remind the American people that he and he alone was the architect of Texas annexation. In this battle to guarantee his historical reputation, the publicity-conscious sage of Sherwood Forest took virtually every opportunity to play the role of elder statesman and national oracle. Perhaps deep down Tyler also hoped that by displaying his wisdom and grasp of the issues of the day, the American people might turn to him in their hour of need and give him another crack at the White House.

John Tyler's orchestrated campaign for historical vindication suffered an initial setback in early 1847 when his former secretary of state, John C. Calhoun, now once again a senator from South Carolina, announced during debate on the Senate floor that he alone was "the author of that great event" of Texas annexation. The entire Tyler clan flew into a rage when they learned of Calhoun's arrogant and impertinent claim of authorship, a claim they felt totally ignored John Tyler's brilliant and sustained leadership of the annexation campaign.

Privately, the former president denounced his friend Calhoun for his unwarranted assumption of unilateral credit and bitterly complained, "He is the great 'I am,' and myself and cabinet have no voice in the matter." "Rely upon it," Tyler assured a family member, "no man can win laurels by pursuing such a course." History has proved John Tyler correct on this point. Most historians have relegated John C. Calhoun to the role of supporting member, not lead actor, in the Texas cast.[4]

John Tyler was "chafed" not only by Calhoun's "extreme selfishness" but also by the fact that his former secretary of state once again had carelessly inflamed sectional passions on the slavery issue. "It is too bad!" he groaned to his son Robert, that Calhoun allowed "the whole question to turn on the question of slavery." That "Calhoun should make it appear that the object & end of annexation was to extend slavery to Texas for the protection of other slave states" was deplorable. John Tyler consistently had maintained throughout the Texas venture, beginning with the secret diplomacy of Abel P. Upshur, that national interests, not narrow sectional concerns, were the uppermost consideration in his quest for annexation. As he explained to his brother-in-law Alexander Gardiner, "If ever there was an American question, the Texas was that very question."[5]

It was a measure of the man that although John Tyler was angry with Calhoun, his private outbursts to family members remained confidential. He rarely carried his personal emotions and grudges into the public arena. Ever the southern gentleman, Tyler maintained a level of civility and in this instance refrained from attacking his friend and former colleague publicly. In fact, in the midst of the contretemps over who should get credit for taking Texas, the former president wrote Calhoun telling him of "the entire falsity" of a newspaper article that "ascribes to me any unfriendly intentions towards you while you were a member of my Cabinet." Be assured, Tyler continued, "you possessed my entire confidence." Explaining that he normally ignored such politically motivated attacks, Tyler told Calhoun that in this case he felt obligated to break his "uniform silence" to affirm that the allegations were "wholly unfounded."[6]

In the wake of Calhoun's preemptive strike to seize credit for Texas, a leading Whig newspaper, the *National Intelligencer*, aired charges that President Tyler had been surrounded, counseled and impelled to push the annexation venture to completion by speculators in Texas lands and bonds. These charges were not new. In their nine-year struggle to block annexation, the abolitionists repeatedly had asserted that the lust for Texas was driven by personal greed and corruption. As one abolitionist editor pointed out, the floating Texas bonds "constitute a vast corruption fund to secure the support of a sufficient number of *Senators* and other public men" for annexation. Tyler and his allies had easily dismissed such predictable abolitionist allegations, but the fact that the accusations now appeared in one of "the most respectable journals of the day" seriously challenged the tenth president's campaign to salvage his reputation and historical legacy.[7]

In two letters that were published in the *Richmond Enquirer* and subsequently circulated in the northern press, Tyler directly refuted the charges that the Texas deal was a corrupt bargain. He denied that any speculator in Texas stocks or lands had influenced his decisions on the matter or impelled him to action. "Certain it is," he declared, "that I never owned a foot of Texas land or a dollar of Texas stock in my life." In promoting and securing Texas annexation, the former president reiterated "that I saw nothing but the country, and the whole country; not this or that section, this or that local interest, but the WHOLE — the good, the strength, the glory of the whole country in the measure."[8]

However, in his response claiming that national interests were his only motivation, Tyler failed to mention that several individuals who had served in his administration were heavily involved in Texas bonds and lands. Among Tyler's advisers and colleagues were Texas speculators and cabinet members Thomas J. Gilmer and John Y. Mason, and his informal roving "ambassador of slavery," Duff Green. In addition, the administration's main ally in the Senate, Robert J. Walker, and the president's longtime friend and informal counselor, William and Mary law professor Beverley Tucker, had investments in Texas lands and owned slaves in Texas. There is no direct evidence that John Tyler was swayed by the arguments of those around him who held slaves and had pecuniary interests in Texas, but for a number of his contemporary critics a strong odor of corruption and personal enrichment surrounded the Texas scheme.

Some politicians did profit from their votes in favor of Texas annexation. Ironically, one of them was Senator Benjamin Tappan of Ohio, the older brother of the famous abolitionists Arthur and Lewis Tappan. An early antislavery opponent of the Tyler administration's annexation treaty, Senator Tappan leaked the treaty documents to the press in his successful bid to have the Senate reject ratification of the original agreement. Senator Tappan's anti-Texas stance angered members of the Ohio legislature and they instructed him to vote for annexation if it came before the Senate at a future date. Since the Ohio legislature had selected him to be senator and could remove him as well, Tappan did as instructed. In February 1845 he voted in favor of the joint resolution approving Texas annexation, thus assuring its passage by the narrow margin of 27 to 25. Had Benjamin Tappan voted against the resolution, it would have been defeated by a tie vote.

In explaining his vote for Texas annexation, Senator Tappan was not entirely candid when he claimed he was simply obeying instructions and abiding by the will of the people of Ohio. After the joint resolution passed and received President Tyler's signature, the senator told his brother Lewis, a New York City merchant, "to cast all the money you have of mine in Texas stock" because "I say to you privately that the debt of Texas will be provided for by our government." Lewis Tappan objected to his brother's request, but the senator went ahead with his investment in Texas bonds and netted a cool $50,000 profit from the transaction.[9]

In his public disclaimer on the Texas speculation charges, John Tyler did not mention or attack John C. Calhoun. Instead, the former president made clear that he and Secretary of State Upshur had started the annexation bandwagon in secret negotiations long before Calhoun came on board to head the State Department after Upshur's tragic death in the *Princeton* disaster. Thus Tyler was at once able to deny the involvement of speculators in the decisions impelling his Texas initiative and to take exclusive credit for the success of the annexation endeavor without impugning the integrity of John C. Calhoun. John Tyler had silenced Calhoun. There was no further public response from the South Carolina senator on the question of authorship of the Texas project.

Another leading partisan player in the Texas sweepstakes, Sam Houston, did choose to enter the fray after reading Tyler's rendition of events leading to annexation. Houston, a founding father of the Lone Star Republic and now a senator from the state of Texas, had been president of the Texas republic during crucial phases of the treaty negotiations with the Tyler administration. His main objection to Tyler's historical interpretation of the annexation process was the damning claim that the Republic of Texas and its leaders were caught up in a web of intrigue with other powers, namely Great Britain, to gain better terms from the United States.

Houston charged that by raising the specter of the British bogeyman, Tyler was engaged in fear mongering, having "originated phantasies and conjured up notions of intrigues, which had existence only in imagination." And although he chose not to champion Calhoun's cause, Senator Houston did object to John Tyler's hogging all the credit for the initiative that brought Texas into the Union. In Houston's opinion, Andrew Jackson also merited some recognition for his role in bringing about the success of that measure.[10]

Fully caught up in the emerging battle for his historical reputation and annoyed by the Texan's denigrating broadside, Tyler could not resist answering Houston. The former president dispatched another letter to the *Richmond Enquirer* asserting once again that the Texas treaty was entirely his work. He also reiterated that his Texas initiative benefited the entire country. Trotting out another of his oft-repeated arguments, Tyler insisted that the acquisition of Texas gave the United States a "virtual monopoly of the cotton plant," a monopoly of "more potential in the affairs of the world than millions of armed men." The idea that control of the world's cotton production would make the United States economically and militarily invincible may have comforted the old man during his retirement years. But John Tyler's "monopoly of the cotton plant" scenario was pure fantasy. Nonetheless, it was in tune with the thinking that brought forth the ill-fated King Cotton thesis that guided the course of Confederate diplomacy after 1861.[11]

Tyler's dismissive treatment of Sam Houston's version of the annexation story backfired. In a rebuttal that appeared in newspapers nationwide, the Texan lashed back, angered that the former president had cast him as a devious "coquette," flirting with Great Britain in order to extract a better and swifter annexation deal from the United States. Houston opened with the defense that his diplomacy with Britain was designed to protect the national interests of the Lone Star Republic. The national interest rationale was the standard answer that leaders under fire typically use to justify their actions, and during his administration a beleaguered President Tyler had given the same defense when responding to his critics.

Then, warming to the task, Senator Houston accused Tyler of not only being the deceptive coquette in the Texas negotiations but a transgressor of the American Constitution as well. By posing a series of rhetorical questions, Houston laid bare Tyler's dilemma when attempting to justify his pledges to shield Texas from a Mexican attack. Houston asked, did the Constitution authorize the president to make war without the approval of Congress? What if Texas had been invaded? Was the president bound by his promises to repel the Mexican invader? If Tyler had done so, would he have been in violation of the Constitution? Had he not done so, would the American president have been guilty of deceiving Texas?

"The Ex-President," Senator Houston concluded, "with all his constitutional wisdom and strict regard for its privileges, may choose whichever horn of the dilemma he thinks proper, and acknowledge himself as a wilful [sic] and flagrant violator of the constitution, or remain a confirmed 'coquette.'" After being so exquisitely skewered by the wily frontiersman, John Tyler knew he had met his match. He wisely withdrew from the field of battle and hoped a future generation of scholars might restore his reputation as a statesman and true republican.[12]

Years later a seemingly remorseful Sam Houston extended the olive branch to John Tyler through an intermediary. Although ready to patch things up, Houston was still slightly resentful of the numerous accolades Tyler had received from Texans. Referring to the silver pitcher given the

Virginian by the Brazoria ladies, Houston told a mutual friend "that was intended as a hit at me." Houston added that for all his military victories and civil triumphs he was never given a present by Texans or even a mere vote of thanks. Despite being jealous of the recognition fellow Texans had heaped upon Tyler, Houston expressed his high esteem for the former president and invited him to visit Texas.

In response to Houston's peace offering, Tyler extended his thanks but doubted he would be able to accept General Houston's invitation any time soon, if ever. Perhaps taking Houston's expression of hurt feelings a bit more seriously than was intended, Tyler assured the Texan leader that the presentation of the silver pitcher did not originate "in any unkind feelings towards him." Besides, Tyler continued, what was such a trivial testimonial compared to the exalted political offices conferred upon Houston by the people of Texas?[13]

Tyler need not have fretted about his rival's historical legacy in Texas. Posterity has been much kinder to the hero of San Jacinto than to the tenth president of the United States. Sam Houston is an icon of Texan independence, and the city of Houston has become the fourth most populous city in the United States, the home of NASA's mission control, and a world center of oil and natural gas technology. Today, President John Tyler is scarcely mentioned in the official tours of the state capital in Austin and his significant historical role in bringing about Texas annexation goes totally unrecognized at the Alamo. At best, the citizens and high school students of the eastern Texas city named in his honor occasionally may remember and celebrate John Tyler's historical legacy.

★ AN ELDER STATESMAN
★
★ After the problematic skirmishes with John C. Calhoun and Sam Houston for favorable historical recognition of the achievements of his presidency, John Tyler wisely opted to settle into the role of an elder statesman of the republic. In the tradition of the distinguished oracles and venerated philosophers of the Roman republic, the sage of Sherwood Forest was content to periodically weigh in on the pressing issues of the day, especially those involving slavery and sectional threats to the Union of the fathers. In retirement, Tyler also remained active as a spokesman for America's future national glory and greatness, and on one occasion he quixotically fancied himself a statesman of international stature and fame by offering to negotiate a peaceful solution to the Crimean War.

In addition to his faith in America's national destiny and future international prominence, Tyler shared his successor James K. Polk's passion for territorial expansion across the continent to the Pacific Ocean. The two men had cooperated to secure Texas annexation by joint resolution in the four months between Polk's election and inauguration. In this awkward period of delayed transition, the lame-duck Tyler forged a bond with Polk that allowed them to pull off a neat bit of political trickery that thwarted opponents of the immediate annexation of Texas.

Senator Thomas Hart Benton of Missouri had fashioned the wording of the Senate annexation resolution to give the incoming president the option of beginning new negotiations with Texas on the terms of annexation. Senator Benton's approach presumably offered the incoming Polk administration the possibility of winning Mexico's assent to annexation and of leaving open for future discussion the status of slavery in Texas. To win their support, President-elect Polk apparently promised Benton and several other senators that if they voted for the joint resolution he would take the option to start fresh negotiations.

Of course, Benton's option was anathema to John Tyler. He ignored it and readily signed the annexation resolution. And just before leaving the White House President Tyler, apparently with the approval of his successor, dispatched his old friend Captain Robert Stockton to Texas with an offer of admission to the Union on the previously negotiated terms. After his inauguration, President Polk accepted Tyler's fait accompli and did not rescind his predecessor's offer of annexation. The Texans accepted admission as a state in July 1845, Congress formally approved the measure in December, and Texas officially entered the Union in early 1846. Senator Benton and his allies cried foul at Polk's betrayal, with one of their number suggesting that not one but two presidents had defrauded them. The protests were to no avail. To their chagrin and embarrassment, the Bentonites realized that the opportunistic duo of Tyler and Polk had outfoxed them.[14]

President Tyler was gratified by Polk's cooperation in the Texas annexation deal. Had Polk honored his pledge to the Benton crew by initiating a new round of negotiations with Texas, John Tyler would not have accomplished the great object of his ambition. If the new round of talks succeeded, Texas annexation would have been President Polk's solo achievement. Under those circumstances, John Tyler would have little credible claim to being the "father" of Texas annexation. President-elect Polk's willing collusion with the outgoing president was crucial to the success of Tyler's Texas project.

Of course, President Polk had his own agenda. It would be naive to assume he was motivated by a desire to secure John Tyler's place in history. Polk realized that beginning anew on the terms of annexation was a dangerous option that easily might fail. Taking Texas, no matter the author of the terms, was a feather in Polk's cap. Because the deal was consummated on Polk's watch, John Tyler's place in historical memory has been minimized and obscured, and many, if not all, presidential scholars award James K. Polk high marks for fulfilling his campaign pledge to reannex Texas.

Polk's actions in pursuit of Texas were not surprising. He was a territorial expansionist par excellence of the old Jeffersonian school. More so than most of his contemporaries, James K. Polk and his immediate forebears lived and died as true believers in and avid practitioners of the "extend the sphere" dogma. Polk's clan, slaveowners all, epitomized the cult of the American Dream—restless Americans on the move, men on the make, ever eager for life's main chance in the rough-and-tumble world of the western frontier. His grandfather and father before him had moved from North Carolina to Tennessee in search of virgin land and economic opportunity. Polk himself started out with a plantation in western Tennessee, then transferred his slaveholding enterprise to Mississippi, and at the time he became president was considering another move to Arkansas. Throughout his life Polk's course of action in both the private and public spheres was guided by the popular dictum of his era: "Westward the course of empire."[15]

In his inaugural address President Polk trumpeted his republican expansionist vision and echoed the "extend the sphere" reasoning of his predecessors Jefferson, Madison, Monroe, and Tyler. Confirming once again the remarkable consistency in outlook and analysis that existed among antebellum disciples of Madison and Jefferson, Polk reiterated the standard argument about expansion as the binding of union. "In the earlier stages of our national existence the opinion prevailed with some that our system of confederated States could not operate successfully over an extended territory, and serious objections have at different times been made to the enlargement of our boundaries." These objections, according to President Polk, were unfounded. He believed the reverse was true because as the nation's territory and population "expanded, the Union has been cemented and strengthened."[16]

Polk's justification for continued territorial growth must have been music to John Tyler's ears. The two men definitely were of the same expansionist mindset. In several of his state addresses and messages to Congress, former president Tyler had presented an identical brief for the necessity of expansion to the health of the republic. Although pleased and proud that Texas was now in the Union fold, Tyler was disappointed that he had been unable to extend America's boundaries to the Pacific Ocean. He eagerly had wanted to plant the Stars and Stripes in California and to gain undisputed title to the Oregon territory. It now appeared that his successor, James K. Polk, was intent upon picking up where Tyler had left off by getting on with the job and fulfilling the nation's continental destiny.

However, the aggressive methods President Polk employed to gain more territory troubled Tyler. In correspondence with family and friends, he criticized his successor for having unnecessarily provoked war with Mexico. To some degree, this was a case of the pot calling the kettle black given Tyler's similar provocative action the year before when he sent troops to Fort Jessup, Louisiana, to protect Texas from Mexican invasion. Perhaps as a matter of friendship and in gratitude for Polk's help in annexing Texas, Tyler was discreet and did not express his concerns publicly nor did he leak them to the press.

The two men remained on cordial terms after the outbreak of hostilities with Mexico, even while Tyler privately was second-guessing Polk's policies. In late May 1846, just two weeks after the United States's formal declaration of war, John Tyler was in Washington to testify before a congressional committee investigating former secretary of state Daniel Webster's alleged improper use of secret service funds. Tyler's vigorous defense of his colleague's actions while serving in the cabinet led to Webster's quick exoneration. While in the nation's capital, Tyler took the opportunity to have an audience with President Polk at the White House. They had an "agreeable conversation" in which the president commiserated with his predecessor about the investigation, decrying it as an "unjust annoyance," and then generously "invited him to dine on Saturday next."

President Polk had a long meeting with his cabinet the following Saturday at which a plan for the military campaign against Mexico was discussed. At the cabinet session, the president also outlined his war aims. He told his colleagues that the United States should be in "military possession of California at the time peace was made, and I declared my purpose to be to acquire for the U.S. California, New Mexico, and perhaps some others of the Northern Provinces of Mexico whenever a peace was made." Without equivocation, Polk had detailed his ambitious agenda for imperial aggrandizement and made clear that he intended to be the builder of an American empire on the Pacific.[17]

John Tyler and a number of other dignitaries dined at the executive mansion that evening. Among the dinner guests was John Slidell, who had served as President Polk's special emissary to Mexico before the war. Slidell's instructions for his failed mission had been to purchase California and other territories from Mexico. Having earlier in the day informed his cabinet that he would take California and large chunks of other Mexican territory by conquest, President Polk may have hinted at the secrecy of his war plans that evening in conversations with Tyler, Slidell, and a few of the other guests. If so, the news would have underscored John Tyler's ambivalence about his successor's unjust war of aggression—while he welcomed the spoils of conquest, he deplored the method of acquisition.[18]

Polk's war with Mexico also troubled many northerners who feared its sole purpose was to expand slave territory. To foreclose the possibility of slavery's unimpeded march into conquered Mexican lands, Congressman David Wilmot of Pennsylvania offered a simple solution. In an attachment to a war appropriations bill, he proposed legislation that would prohibit slavery in any territory acquired by the United States as the result of its victory in the war with Mexico. The Wilmot Proviso, as the proposal was labeled, outraged the slave South and further enflamed the passions of sectionalism. The Proviso never was enacted. Southern senators led by John C. Calhoun blocked its passage in the Senate. Nonetheless, the Proviso did put the volatile issue of the further expansion of the South's peculiar institution on the front burner of national politics.

The memory of the bruising encounters in the press with Sam Houston over the diplomacy of Texas annexation caused Tyler to stay out of the public limelight during the Wilmot Proviso controversy. Instead, the circumspect elder statesman expressed his opposition to this latest northern humiliation of the South in an anonymous letter to a local Virginia newspaper. What was it, Tyler queried, that excited such distrust of the South and the desire to "exclude the Southern States from equal participation in the full benefits of Union?" He failed to comprehend why fair-minded northerners did not see that the "Wilmot Proviso is at this moment nothing less than a gratuitous insult on the slave-States." Either the slaveholding states "stand on a footing of equality with the non-slave-holding," Tyler observed, "or they are inferior and degraded." Better by far the less hypocritical "language of the Abolitionists," for in their calls for a break-up of the Union there was by "fair inference" a recognition of "the equality of the States."[19]

In his denunciation of the Wilmot Proviso, Tyler also argued that it was unnecessary because "no man doubts but that California and New Mexico will be free-States" when the time arrived for their entry into the Union. Soon after his anonymous letter appeared in the press, Tyler elaborated on this observation about the natural limits to slavery's expansion in correspondence with his brother-in-law Alexander Gardiner. Expressing a view that had some currency in the nineteenth century, Tyler believed that geography and climate would determine the fate of the institution of slavery.

In this geographically deterministic formula, the globe's subtropical and tropical climes were seen as the ideal zones for slavery to succeed and flourish. However, in the world's more temperate regions, such as the northeastern United States, the institution of slavery had no long-term future and was slowly disappearing. "Climate," Tyler told his brother-in-law, "should be left to determine the question of slavery, as it will most assuredly. It has already abolished it as far as Delaware, and if left to work out its results, will, at no distant day, produce similar effects in Delaware, Maryland, and Virginia."

Tyler's belief in the climate-driven demise of slavery was an updated variation of his earlier diffusion theory, which had been outlined nearly three decades earlier during the Missouri crisis. At that time he argued that slavery gradually would disappear by an amoebic diffusion process that would carry it southward to Mexico and Central America. Senator Robert Walker had employed the same analysis in his famous letter urging Texas annexation. One of Tyler's recent converts to the theory was Alexander Gardiner, who succinctly summed up its comforting main premise in answering northern objections to taking conquered Mexican territory: "The peculiar institution is doomed to disappear faster than it can be extended."[20]

The 1848 treaty of peace that ended the Mexican War resulted in a nearly 50 percent expansion of American territory—more than 500,000 square miles in all had been added to the national domain. A defeated Mexico, in return for a monetary indemnity of $15 million and the assumption of just over $3 million in claims by American citizens against the Mexican government, gave up more than half its territory, by relinquishing its title to California, New Mexico, and the Southwest territory, and accepting the Rio Grande as the boundary with Texas. Given the United States's clear military victory in the war, some Americans were disappointed that the Polk administration did not take all of Mexico. In reply to his carping critics, a proud President Polk told Congress after the ratification of the treaty that the territories of California and New Mexico "constitute of themselves a country large enough for a great empire, and their acquisition is second only in importance to that of Louisiana in 1803."[21]

John Tyler originally welcomed Polk's peace treaty and the acquisition of the Southwest and California with its magnificent harbors. After more careful consideration, however, Tyler began to grouse privately that he could have done better. Perhaps reflecting his lingering disappointment that his administration had failed to obtain the coveted "windows on the Pacific," the former president sought a measure of credit for Polk's success in bringing California into the American fold. He explained his reasoning to another of his wife's older brothers, David L. Gardiner, by asserting that if "the Senate had ratified the Texas Treaty that ratification would have been followed by immediate negociations [*sic*] and I do not doubt that California would have been peaceably acquired." Tyler's exaggerated claim that "Texas drew after it California" was nothing more than a harmless example of the power of self-delusion.[22]

When news of the discovery of gold at Sutter's Mill Creek reached the East in late 1848 several members of the extended Tyler-Gardiner family immediately lit out for California in search of adventure and riches. Chief among them were David Gardiner and John Beeckman, husband of Julia's younger sister Margaret. Comfortable and content at his Sherwood Forest plantation, gentleman farmer John Tyler initially disparaged the gold rush frenzy. Almost sixty years old, he told his family he had no desire to begin life anew panning for gold on the rugged frontier. "The President," Julia Tyler explained to her mother in New York, was not much taken with "this California fever. . . . He thinks a good farm on James River with plenty of slaves is gold mine enough."[23]

But a few months later John Tyler became a full-fledged California booster. The ex-president apparently became infected with a severe case of gold rush fever that resulted in his becoming a vicarious "forty-niner." For instance, when asked by members of the New York branch of the clan for advice and counsel about prospects in California, the family patriarch heartily encouraged his brothers-in-law to seek their fortunes in the new El Dorado on the Pacific. Tyler told them that the "future destiny of California is too plainly written to be mistaken."

Actually, John Beeckman and David Gardiner had needed little coaxing to join the gold rush. They were among the thousands of eager speculators and freebooters known as "forty-niners" who, in a time before transcontinental railroad existed, made the hazardous journey around Cape Horn or overland through Panama in hopes of lining their pockets with gold nuggets. Despite all their boyish enthusiasm and high hopes neither man made his fortune in the California gold fields. Beeckman died out West of an accidental gunshot wound and Gardiner returned to New York a wiser man with little to show for months of hard labor and deprivation panning for gold on the rugged frontier.

Prior to the tragic and disappointing experiences of his kin in the Promised Land, John Tyler himself toyed with the idea of going to California. The supposedly contented plantation owner "with plenty of slaves" dreamed about the main chance that lay beckoning "on some choice spot of the Sacramento" River and oftentimes in his imaginings about California "fancied that country an Eden." "There is nothing like the elbow room of a new country," Tyler wistfully had confessed to one of the relatives who had chosen not to go to California. Tyler's frontier logic was the inspiration of the man on the make. His phrase, "the elbow room of a new country," was the perfect nineteenth-century metaphor for the restless American hustler seeking one more chance to start over again and hit the jackpot of fame and fortune.[24]

John Tyler became so mesmerized by California's commercial and economic potential that he was willing to welcome the former Mexican province into the Union as a free state. In this case Tyler's position was entirely consistent with his bedrock states' rights philosophy. He explained why when answering a query from David Gardiner about a clause in the proposed California constitution prohibiting slavery. Tyler doubted any opposition would arise because of that restriction. Speaking for all southerners, he said they respected the right of the people to regulate their own internal affairs and "hence your power to *admit* domestic slavery is the same with the corresponding power to *prohibit* it." Although some southern spokesmen balked at accepting Tyler's argument for local/state control, it became the basis for a sectional compromise that included California's admission as a free state.[25]

Before a political settlement on the question of California's admission to the Union as a free state was hammered out, sectional tensions rose to a fever pitch. Former president Tyler was not alone in worriedly expressing grave doubts about the future of the American union. In the midst of the crisis he correctly observed that "we are destined to great trouble upon this slavery question and that the end is not yet." Tyler did, however, retain "much confidence in the good sense of the American people" and was in the forefront of a cadre of southern leaders who opted for compromise.[26]

The man who helped broker the Compromise of 1850 — with the invaluable assistance of Illinois senator Stephen A. Douglas — was Tyler's old nemesis, Henry Clay of Kentucky. Already renowned as antebellum America's

"Great Compromiser" for his earlier role in settling the Missouri and nullification crises, Clay once again managed to allay sectional differences, avoid
secession and civil war, and preserve the Union. The terms of the last of the
three great reconciliation measures called for the admission of California
as a free state and the organization of the territories of New Mexico and
Utah on the basis of local sovereignty without a restriction on slavery. In
addition, the compromise ended the slave trade in the District of Columbia
and created a new stringent Fugitive Slave Act for the capture and return
of runaway slaves.

As part of a campaign to build strong public support for the compromise
measure in the South as well as throughout the nation, Senator Henry S.
Foote of Mississippi asked John Tyler to give his views on the subject. Tyler
responded to his friend's request in a lengthy public letter that detailed his
approval of the compromise proposal. He remained consistent in his position that the people of California had the constitutional right to prohibit
slavery and petition to enter the Union as a free state. The other features of
the compromise measure also received Tyler's blessing. He was particularly
gratified by the abolition of the slave trade in the nation's capital and pointed
out that as a member of the Senate in the early 1830s he had authored an
unsuccessful proposal to end the sale of slaves in the District.[27]

Senator Foote circulated Tyler's letter among his moderate southern colleagues in Congress to telling effect. Former president Tyler's endorsement,
which subsequently was published in newspapers nationwide, ironically
helped gain widespread public support for his erstwhile archenemy's compromise package. To the relief of Tyler and other Americans who wished to
avoid civil conflict, Congress approved the compromise of 1850. President
Millard Fillmore, who followed John Tyler's succession precedent by assuming the presidency when Zachary Taylor died, signed the measure into law.

The notoriety and widespread circulation of Tyler's letter urging sectional compromise put him back in the national limelight. Apparently now
politically rehabilitated and even admired by many people, the reviled former president was as surprised as the next person by this improbable turn
of good fortune. But to some degree Tyler's recently acquired fame was
illusory because he was not universally popular and his infamy as a traitor
to the Whig Party remained uppermost in the minds of some of his countrymen. Predictably, abolitionists denounced his support for the Fugitive Slave
Act and on one occasion he was loudly hissed while giving an address on the
topic to a gathering of law students in New York City.

Actually, not all of John Tyler's new-found popularity and renewed good standing with southern Democrats like Senator Foote stemmed from his speaking out for sectional harmony, national unity, and Henry Clay's compromise. The tide of public opinion began shifting in Tyler's favor earlier as the result of his heartfelt support for the Hungarian revolutionary struggle to break free of Austrian rule. An admirer of the Hungarian people and their gallant leader, Louis Kossuth, Tyler saluted their bravery and thought them entitled to "the first place among nations ripe for liberty." The former president also was appalled at the barbarity of the Austrians in their suppression of the uprising and urged his nation to protest such uncivilized behavior. If such protest was unavailing, the United States should suspend diplomatic relations with Austria.[28]

Henry Foote was impressed by John Tyler's brave and forthright stand on behalf of Hungarian independence. Addressing his fellow senators, the Mississippian not only recommended suspension of diplomatic relations with Austria but also praised Tyler's courageous defense of universal liberty. Foote thought Tyler's "beautiful and soul-stirring" appeal should inspire all Americans to "be properly mindful of the importance of our example as the model republic of the world." Although the United States did not break diplomatic relations with Austria over the Hungarian issue, Senator Foote's laudatory tribute to Tyler did succeed in further resuscitating the former president's discredited and moribund reputation.[29]

The repeated assertions by numerous political leaders that the United States was an exemplary republican model for the world made some citizens uneasy. They wondered about the troubling implications of an American mission to spread liberty and the principles of self-government to the rest of humankind. Did support for a Hungarian independence movement obligate the American government to intervene to prevent Austria from putting down the revolt? The possibility that America might take on a global mission to preserve liberty everywhere prompted the membership of the Jefferson Literary Society of Philadelphia to seek John Tyler's opinion on the matter. They asked him, in his capacity as an outspoken defender of the Hungarian cause, whether he thought sympathy for foreign revolutions might lead the United States to intervene "to prevent intervention by other governments in the internal affairs of nations."

Private citizen Tyler, himself a proud honorary member of the Jefferson Literary Society, did retain an unswerving faith in the United States as "a mighty empire" and the world's model republic. But the former president also emphatically believed that America should lead by example and not by force of arms. In response to the Jefferson Society's query, Tyler unequivocally endorsed the principle of non-intervention in the affairs of other nations. He believed Americans should foreswear both military escapades and blustery self-satisfying "paper bulletins" in their attempts to spread republican principles abroad.

Otherwise, he cautioned, we candidly "should announce to all nations our determination to advance with the sword the doctrines of republicanism" and "proclaim ourselves the knights errant of liberty and organize at once a crusade against all despotic governments." If the nation changed its traditional policy of non-intervention for one of interventionism in behalf of liberty, Tyler thought Americans might as well shout to the world that *"there is but one form of gov't upon earth which we will tolerate and that is a republic."*[30]

In his discussion of whether or not it was in America's interest to intervene in the affairs of other societies, John Tyler had exposed a dilemma that bedeviled his generation as well the earlier Revolutionary War generation before him. Should the United States lead by example or intervene in behalf of every revolutionary movement that espoused the cause of liberty and freedom? It is a question that repeatedly has vexed and haunted makers of American foreign policy to the present day. Each new generation of Americans appears to be hopelessly trapped by the same dilemma, and predictably the nation as a whole endlessly debates whether or not to embark on another "crusade" for freedom and democracy.

John Tyler was not the only antebellum American statesman to warn of the perils of interventionism. A number of prominent nineteenth-century Americans had preceded him in recommending a non-interventionist course. John Quincy Adams enunciated the most famous expression of non-interventionism on July 4, 1821. In this patriotic address Adams immortalized the dictum that Americans should not go abroad in search of monsters to destroy. Adams's "monsters" metaphor has an eerie contemporary ring and it remains a favorite example for historians, journalists, opinion makers, and pundits to reference when cautioning Americans about the dangers inherent in a policy of overseas intervention.

No such enduring fame in American historical memory has been accorded John Tyler. His objections to an interventionist foreign policy are totally forgotten, even though Tyler's non-interventionist prescription was virtually identical to the advice offered decades earlier by John Quincy Adams. Although they had been poles apart on a number of political issues, especially on the question of Texas annexation, both men were convinced it would be folly for the United States to assume the task of being the world's policeman. Undoubtedly, Adams's prose was loftier and more eloquent than Tyler's in expressing this shared sentiment. But the Virginian's message to his countrymen drove home the same point. He echoed Adams in warning that if the United States issued a declaration to intervene in order to prevent other interventions, "we take upon ourselves innumerable wars all over the Earth, not for liberty to the human race only, but for all conceivable causes."[31]

In the early years of his retirement John Tyler had been preoccupied with securing his historical reputation and guaranteeing that posterity would acknowledge him as the architect of Texas annexation. But after settling into the blissful, bucolic routine at Sherwood Forest, Tyler's busy life as a gentleman farmer and adored patriarch of a large and growing family left him little time to worry about his historical legacy. Still a vigorous and active man in his mid-sixties, the former president was at peace with himself and satisfied that he had finally achieved the status and attendant honor of being a respected elder statesman of the republic.

In the 1850s the increasingly popular sage of Sherwood Forest frequently was called upon to address his fellow citizens and lecture before literary, civic, and agricultural societies. On those occasions Tyler, who now proudly identified himself as the last of the Virginia dynasty of presidents, never tired of reminding his audiences to keep faith in America's national destiny and future glory. Even as he glimpsed the storm clouds of disunion and civil strife on the horizon, Tyler remained hopeful that if his countrymen retained a communal commitment to national greatness the Union might be preserved. For Tyler it was an article of faith that the "future of the civilized world is in our hands if we be but true to ourselves."[32]

Faith in America's national destiny was a commonly held belief in the Tyler household at Sherwood Forest. Julia Gardiner Tyler was as fascinated as her husband with dreams of the United States's future glory and greatness. On one famous occasion Mrs. Tyler even went public with her convictions. The young mother and plantation mistress responded to an open letter addressed to the women of the South by several titled and aristocratic ladies of England who were horrified by the cruelties of American slavery depicted in Harriet Beecher Stowe's *Uncle Tom's Cabin*. In their transatlantic appeal, the Duchess of Sutherland, the Countess of Carlisle, Vicountess Palmerston, the Countess of Derby, and Lady John Russell implored southern women of conscience to use their moral influence to end the evils of slavery.

In a letter that originally appeared in a Richmond newspaper and subsequently was reprinted throughout the nation, Julia Gardiner Tyler defended the South's morality and its peculiar institution from the attacks of her British cousins. Mrs. Tyler thought the English ladies ill-mannered meddlers and chided them for their impertinent interference in the South's domestic affairs. Although she did not contend that slavery was a flawless institution, Julia Tyler did assert that slaves in the South lived in better conditions than many English laborers. At the very least, she pointed out, black bondsmen enjoyed regular meals, warm clothing, and a roof over their heads, necessities of life routinely denied to vast numbers of the English working class. In her youth during Gardiner family trips to the British Isles, Julia Tyler had observed firsthand the appalling poverty of England's laboring classes and was aware that the people of Ireland were "recently starving for food." If the noble ladies wished to satisfy their philanthropic needs, Mrs. Tyler suggested they should begin at home nourishing and comforting the poor of their own kingdom.[33]

Julia Tyler's defense of the South's peculiar institution was a fairly commonplace response to critics of the American slaveholding republic. She believed, as did other defenders of slavery, that the South's labor system was more benign and much less harsh than that of industrial capitalism. But perhaps the more striking theme of Mrs. Tyler's rejoinder to the British noblewomen was her detailed rendition of the glories of America's "new destiny" and its "future, unrivalled in point of power, by any thing the world has heretofore seen." America's former first lady shared her husband's Anglophobia and distrust of Great Britain and she warned her English audience that the United States was a nation not to be trifled with in the international arena. Her country soon would rival Great Britain as a major world player and, sounding a theme dear to her husband's heart, Julia Tyler predicted America would achieve global preeminence not by "power of the sword" but by "the power of example."[34]

The ideas and opinions expressed by Julia Gardiner Tyler in her reply exactly mirrored those of her husband. Although an exceptionally outspoken and independently minded planter's wife, Julia Tyler nonetheless remained strongly influenced by the much more experienced ex-president's political views. Her world outlook was virtually identical to that of her husband. Much like her husband, she too was outraged that male British aristocrats had instigated this hypocritical moral message and then had used their wives as political cover to invite sectional discord and disunion in the United States. But despite her reliance on her husband's ideas, the authorship of the letter was not in doubt. Julia Tyler wrote it. She struggled for a week to get her thoughts on paper and was rewarded for her labors by unanticipated national acclaim as well as transatlantic celebrity. For a fleeting moment, both Julia and John Tyler basked in the glory of being one of America's most famous and prominent couples.

One might wonder why John Tyler, a man who believed woman's place was to tend home and hearth and who earlier had harshly denounced politically active northern abolitionist women as agents of the devil, not only approved but took pride in his wife's foray into the public arena. The key to understanding the Virginia gentleman's acceptance of his wife's unconventional behavior was the fact that Mrs. Tyler had effectively defended the South's peculiar institution and had forecast the impending glories of America's national destiny. To her husband's immense satisfaction, Julia Tyler had properly chastised the meddling British ladies.

Equally important, Julia Tyler's letter was nonthreatening to her husband's nineteenth-century gender norms because she had reinforced, not challenged, the female's traditional role in the family as wife, mother, and homemaker. Rest assured, Mrs. Tyler told her readers, women in the United States were content to confine themselves to the sphere that God had designed for them. The American woman's circle was that of her family. Mrs. Tyler emphatically stressed that neither she nor the majority of her right-thinking American sisters ever intended to scandalize their husbands by embarking upon a career of political activism.

The mid-nineteenth century was an exhilarating as well as an unnerving time for believers in America's national destiny and future greatness. John Tyler's frequent patriotic orations and his wife's solo venture rebuking the Duchess of Sutherland placed the master and mistress of Sherwood Forest among those who took great pride in their young nation's economic growth and technological progress. At the same time, however, it was the patriarch himself who observed with dread the sectional discord over the issue of slavery's expansion that was ravaging the country. Perhaps more so than even his wife, John Tyler feared for the future of the Union and thought civil war was increasingly likely.

Tyler's uneasiness about how the United States might avoid the fate of earlier republics that fell prey to internal disintegration was never more evident than when he hit the lecture circuit. His foreboding about disunion became a recurring theme in his presentations to societies such as the Maryland Institute for the Promotion of the Mechanic Arts in Baltimore. On that occasion in March 1855 sectional tensions were uppermost on Tyler's mind as he reviewed the brief but crisis-laden history of the early American republic. In his telling, the most serious of these previous controversies over slavery's expansion came during the Missouri crisis of 1820–21. Tyler reminded his audience that none other than Thomas Jefferson had been frightened to the point that he admitted "this momentous question, like a firebell in the night awakened and filled me with terror. I considered it the knell of the Union."[35]

The Missouri crisis had proven not to be the death knell of the Union. A compromise had been reached that brought Missouri into the Union as a slave state and stipulated that in the future slavery would be forbidden in territory above the line of 36°30'. As a young slaveowning congressman from Virginia John Tyler had voted against the compromise. Now, quite remarkably, an older and wiser Tyler conceded he had been wrong. The ex-president told the members of the Maryland Institute that he wished the line of 36°30' had "been made universal in its application to all the territory then possessed or at any future day to be acquired by the United States." Had that been done, Tyler suggested the terribly divisive turmoil of the current Kansas-Nebraska crisis might have been avoided.

At the conclusion of his talk, Tyler did what he frequently did at such gatherings. Cloaking his anxiety about the dangers ahead in the rhetoric of national destiny and greatness, he reassured his listeners that all was not yet lost. Perhaps inadvertently, perhaps not, Tyler the well-read elder statesman appeared to mimic the haunting macabre refrain of one of Baltimore's most illustrious and tragic literary sons, Edgar Allan Poe. "I listen to no raven-like croakings foretelling 'disastrous twilight' to this confederacy," Tyler boldly announced, and "I will give no audience to those dark prophets who profess to foretell a dissolution of this Union." The day shall come "when this great Republic shall have reached the fullness of its glory" and will become "the paragon of government, the exemplar of the world."[36]

Staying with his literary allusions and assuming his audience also knew their Shakespeare, Tyler cited *Othello* to illustrate his final point about the necessity of preserving the precious Union of the United States. Speaking from the heart to his fellow Americans, Tyler told them: "I will not adopt the belief that a people so favored by heaven, will most wickedly and foolishly 'throw away a pearl richer than all the tribe.'" Tyler's ironic reference was to the lament of the tragic black Moor Othello, whose exact words were: "Like the base Indian, threw a pearl away Richer than all his tribe."

A few years later, after the election of Abraham Lincoln, John Tyler would ignore his own admonition by "wickedly and foolishly" throwing away the prized "pearl" of Union. Perhaps Tyler's later disunionist stance can be understood as the consequence of his definition of the union. He believed the United States should remain a slaveholding republic, as it had been from its inception in 1789. As an unrepentant slaveholder, Tyler was unwilling to contemplate universal emancipation and the possibility that the union of the fathers might evolve into a nonslaveholding republic. Ironically, such a transformation probably would have been welcomed by his idol Thomas Jefferson.[37]

Although Tyler continued to encourage Americans to stay true to their belief in America's national destiny, his doubts and concerns about the future of the union of the fathers began to surface more frequently in his private correspondence. This pessimistic shift in Tyler's thinking was barely perceptible in his public addresses. He remained upbeat during a demanding round of speaking engagements in the mid-1850s that ranged from an appearance at an agricultural fair in Rochester, New York, to presiding over a commercial convention in tidewater Virginia that explored the possibility of establishing direct trade between Norfolk and Liverpool, England. The ex-president continued to reign as the nation's wise and elderly counselor, and the man once derided as "His Accidency" had won a commanding place in the hearts of many of his countrymen.

Tyler gloried in this public adulation, as ephemeral as it would prove to be. His flourishing speaking career peaked in the spring of 1857 when he was offered and readily accepted an invitation to be the principal speaker at the celebration of the 250th anniversary of the founding of Jamestown, Virginia. The Jamestown 250th bash was a gala affair with an estimated crowd of 8,000–10,000 enjoying the festivities. An array of reception and entertainment tents dotted Jamestown Island as military bands and companies of soldiers paraded on the main field before the speaker's stand. A host of dignitaries were present, including most notably Henry A. Wise, Tyler's old political ally and close friend and now the governor of Virginia.

Amid the gaiety, merrymaking, and raucous hoopla, Tyler lent a serious note to the proceeding. In a speech that lasted over three hours he meticulously reviewed Virginia's history from the settlement at Jamestown to the events of the American Revolution. Predictably, Tyler laced his talk with the usual paeans of praise to American empire. He pointed with pride to the fact that "a small body of men planted on this spot the seed of a mighty empire." And near the conclusion of his lengthy peroration he paid homage to the pioneering settlers who struggled and perished, "but out of their ashes has arisen an empire of almost boundless extent." Although this was vintage John Tyler rhetoric about America's unprecedented potential great-ness, there was a noticeably different and defensive tone to this address.[38]

Tyler was exasperated and angered by the activities of his old antislav-ery antagonists, in this instance a coterie of New England abolitionists who mocked and disparaged the significance of Virginia's role in the nation's history. Among them was Theodore Parker, a Unitarian minister in Boston, who delivered a sermon to his congregation questioning Virginia's contribu-tion to victory in the American Revolution. In Parker's reading of history, Virginia's participation in the fight for freedom had been exaggerated, and he argued it was the North and not the South that had made the greater sacrifice in men and blood to the cause of independence. Reverend Parker's provocative and goading assault on the heroic past of the Old Dominion infuriated many a proud Virginian, including elder statesman Tyler.

In his Jamestown address at the birthplace of English settlement in Amer-ica, the ex-president took the opportunity to defend Virginia from the scur-rilous attacks of Parker and other Massachusetts abolitionists. He believed Virginians "have a right to demand of all such as revile and abuse Virginia" to ask when did the Old Dominion "give stintingly of her blood or treasure to the public good?" "Political demagogues may revile and abuse," Tyler told the patriotic Americans gathered that day at Virginia's most sacred historic shrine, "but they cannot detract from the high and lofty fame which belongs to this time-honored commonwealth." On this occasion Tyler was unable to concentrate on his preferred theme of national destiny and instead found himself defensively extolling the virtues of Virginia's eminent sons who had done their part to guarantee the nation's liberty and freedom.[39]

In the late 1850s other members of Virginia's slaveholding elite also had grown weary of what they considered unwarranted and gratuitous northern abuse. Some even had taken their state patriotism and southern loyalty to the point of favoring secession from the Union. Edmund Ruffin undoubt-edly was one of the more fanatical of these secessionist fire-eaters, as their more moderate contemporaries labeled these radical disunionists. A native Virginian, Ruffin had attended William and Mary, served in the state leg-islature, and gained prominence as a leading agricultural reformer in the South.

After having spent some years studying the political and economic rela-tionship of the North and South, Ruffin concluded it was in his region's best interest to leave the Union. When the South seceded and created the Con-federacy, Edmund Ruffin was overjoyed and eagerly rushed to the colors. But the Union victory in the Civil War proved mortifyingly unbearable for the man who had dedicated himself to the cause of southern independence. On June 15, 1865, the seventy-year-old Ruffin wrapped himself in the Confederate flag and committed suicide by shooting himself.

Even though their political paths had crossed frequently over the years, John Tyler's relationship with Edmund Ruffin had been properly cordial and respectful at best. Ruffin had not been an admirer of Tyler prior to his presidency. He changed his mind when President Tyler displayed his mettle in his struggle with Henry Clay and the Whigs. After Tyler left the White House the two men gradually became closer friends as they occasionally corresponded on the practice of farming and the political events of the day. In November 1857 the recently retired Ruffin had abundant free time on his hands and decided to travel to Sherwood Forest for an extended visit with John and Julia Tyler and their six children.

In the years of his retirement Ruffin was in the habit of keeping a detailed diary, and during his stay at Sherwood Forest he copiously recorded each day's happenings. He was greeted warmly by the Tylers and much appreciated their hospitality. The two Virginian farmers and slaveowners had much in common and over a three-day period "talked incessantly" as they sat before the fireplace or walked or rode horseback over the plantation grounds. Ruffin found the former president in good health and was surprised to see a man who once "wielded the power of a constitutional King—as truly does a President of the United States" now satisfied with his station in life as an "unassuming country gentleman & farmer."

Equally surprising for Ruffin was the realization that he had come to admire Tyler and that the newfound admiration was mutual. Above the fireplace in the family's sitting room at Sherwood Forest hung two engraved portraits, one of Daniel Webster and the other of Edmund Ruffin. Tyler explained to his friend that one was "the first among American statesmen, & the other the first of American agriculturists." Ruffin was flattered by this high compliment and pleased to see as well that other portraits that graced the walls of Tyler's home placed him in company with Patrick Henry, John C. Calhoun, Abel Upshur, and Henry Wise. But perhaps most gratifying for the confirmed secessionist Ruffin was the discovery that John Tyler apparently agreed with him and appeared to favor disunion as well. After only one day of conversation in which he exchanged ideas with Tyler, Ruffin felt confident enough to record in his diary that "I do not think we differ much as to the expediency of a separation of the Union."[40]

Ruffin was mistaken in his assessment since Tyler had not fully embraced a policy of secession at this stage of the sectional crisis. Tyler's polite comments to Ruffin must be understood as those of a southern gentleman being cordial and agreeable to his houseguest. Ruffin heard what he wanted to hear from the ex-president. In late 1857 John Tyler still retained a faith in the Union and a pride in the triumphs of his presidency that he was loath to throw away. Just a few months before Ruffin paid his visit to Sherwood Forest, Tyler had made clear his unionist preferences in a public rebuke to "fire-eaters" for "reviving the agitations of the slave question."[41]

A movement among southern proslavery extremists to turn the clock back by once again reopening the African slave trade had alarmed the former president. The opening wedge of this reactionary effort was a call from delegates meeting at a southern convention in Nashville for the repeal of the eighth article of the 1842 Webster-Ashburton Treaty. Article eight, which President Tyler helped fashion, had created a joint Anglo-American squadron to suppress the African slave trade. Fire-eaters at the Nashville convention such as Alabama planter William L. Yancey condemned the African squadron as an insult to the South and ruinous to the institution of slavery. Shortly after the Nashville convention adjourned, resolutions were introduced in the legislatures of South Carolina and Georgia demanding that the United States abrogate article eight of the Webster-Ashburton Treaty.

The logic developed by proponents of the effort to restore the African slave trade was based on a desire for and presumption of moral consistency. If federal laws prohibited the slave trade as an immoral act of piracy, they argued, then all slaveholders were pirates and plunderers and "slavery itself must be wrong." That was precisely the position taken by abolitionists, who argued that both slavery and the slave trade were wrong and morally reprehensible. But advocates of a revival of the slave trade believed the reverse should hold true. They wished to legitimize the slave trade in order to make the point that both slavery and the African slave trade were morally acceptable practices.

Even a longtime defender of slavery such as John Tyler was baffled by what he believed to be a peculiar logic in defense of the South's peculiar institution. In a letter to the *Richmond Enquirer* that was reprinted in newspapers throughout the country, he pointed out that southern states "had voted for an act of Congress declaring that all citizens of the United States who should engage in the slave-trade should be regarded, and if convicted, punished as pirates." Tyler now wondered how the provision of a treaty to enforce that law "for which the South had voted, can be rightly regarded as an insult to the South, I must say passes my comprehension."[42]

Tyler's widely published response to the fire-eaters expressed the views of southern moderates like himself who saw no moral inconsistency in believing the slave trade to be wrong and slavery itself to be right. In all sections of the nation a majority of Americans and their representatives in Congress seemed to agree with Tyler's blurred moral distinctions, and consequently the effort to revive the African slave trade failed. As one prominent historian of the era has observed, the "nuances of the slavery debate" in antebellum America "suggest a lost intellectual world irrevocably altered by the Civil War and nearly beyond contemporary comprehension."[43]

Over a long career of public involvement that spanned the entire antebellum era, Tyler had grown accustomed to living with the moral ambiguities of the South's peculiar institution. As a young man he had been hopeful that slavery would gradually disappear through the process of diffusion, but now in old age and retirement Tyler's optimism about its eventual demise faded. He became less concerned with the question of slavery as a moral institution and simply assumed it would remain a viable labor system for the foreseeable future. The alternative of abolition and emancipation was inconceivable to him unless freed blacks were diffused and scattered to locations beyond the borders of the United States. A slaveholding republic had been what his generation had inherited from the founding fathers. As a slaveholder Tyler remained committed to that legacy. But in the end it would be the anachronism of slavery and not the Union of the fathers that mattered most to him.

Tyler was content and happy as patriarch of Sherwood Forest. He had a beautiful and adoring wife and was the father of a brood of young children living on a James River plantation "with plenty of slaves." During the years of his retirement Tyler owned anywhere between sixty and ninety slaves who lived in some twenty cabins on Sherwood Forest. Some ten to thirteen of the slaves were house servants, including three who lived in the mansion—Louisa, Sarry, and Fanny Johnston. Old Marse John was reputed to be a kind and benign master who treated his slaves humanely. As far as is known, there were no whips or lashes and none of Tyler's slaves were held in chains, handcuffs, or irons. On occasion, when he did sell slaves, some of them undoubtedly would have been shipped to the Deep South coffled in chains and shackles.

One northern visitor to Sherwood Forest in the 1850s, Eben Horsford, a renowned chemist and Harvard professor, confessed to finding "the system of slavery" in many respects "much different from what I expected." In a letter to his mother, Horsford recounted the highlights of his visit to the Tylers and gave a detailed description of life on a James River plantation, including "a very tolerable sketch" of Sherwood Forest and its surrounding grounds. Slavery "in its best form," Horsford observed, "may be expressed in a simple phrase — 'a minority that never terminates.' The slaves are treated like children — punished when they deserve it, rewarded when they should be." No longer a skeptical Yankee, Horsford thought Tyler's paternalistic management style accounted for the fact that the slaves at Sherwood Forest were "uniformly cheerful and happy."[44]

If part of Tyler's self-identity hinged on his success as a slavemaster and his ability to control slaves, Horsford's testimony confirmed that the ex-president was secure and confident in his accomplishments as a plantation administrator. And although his wife had been raised in the North, Julia Gardiner Tyler readily took on the duties of directing a slave household and energetically assumed her new role as the young mistress of Sherwood Forest. In the early years of her wedded life, Mrs. Tyler especially enjoyed the challenge of furnishing and decorating the mansion and looking after the domestic needs of the plantation.

Julia Tyler took great pride in one of her initial purchases — a splendid new carriage for the family. The carriage's black coachmen and footmen were outfitted in "handsome light grey dress coats (livery cut) with black covered buttons (made in uniform style) white pantaloons and black hats." Another important mode of transportation for the Tylers was their river-boat, the *Pocahontas*, which had been given to them by friends as a farewell gift when they left Washington. Mrs. Tyler decked out the *Pocahontas* in a bright blue paint with matching blue damask cushions. The four black oarsmen who manned the "Royal Barge" on the James River were dressed in "bright blue and white check calico shirts, white linen pants, black patent leather belts, straw hats painted blue." As a finishing touch one corner of the oarsman's shirt collar bore a braided bow and arrow to signify Sherwood Forest. On the occasions when the Tylers went about visiting other James River plantations, either by land or water, they must have made a magnifi-cent impression on their friends and neighbors.[45]

Still residing in New York, Juliana Gardiner, Julia Tyler's mother, found these extravagances a bit unsettling. She thought her daughter was putting on airs and questioned whether such ostentatious costumes and uniforms were consistent with the simple virtues held dear in a republic. Livery brought to mind for the elderly Mrs. Gardiner the practices of aristocracy and royalty where retainers to a feudal lord wore distinctive insignia, cos-tumes, or uniforms. By dressing her slave coachmen and oarsmen in such elaborate garb Julia Tyler was guilty of flaunting her aristocratic status in a

Drawing of Sherwood Forest plantation sketched by Eben N. Horsford. Eben N. Horsford to M. C. Horsford, February 14, 1852. *Horsford Family Papers. Institute Archives and Special Collections, Rensselaer Polytechnic Institute, Troy, N.Y.*

republic. Taking her daughter to task, Juliana Gardiner told her that "liveries in our country are bad taste. I have always thought so." Unfazed by her mother's criticism, Julia Tyler came to relish traveling in style to neighboring estates in her resplendent carriage and shiny blue boat.[46]

Another quite different and highly critical appraisal of John Tyler the slavemaster appeared in a published record of the Underground Railroad by the contemporaneous chronicler William Still. Working out of Philadelphia, Still was a freeborn black who in the 1840s and 1850s spent fourteen years in service to the Underground Railroad as a member of the Vigilance Committee. During that time William Still interviewed several hundred fugitives and compiled a series of brief vignettes describing their backgrounds and experiences on the road of escape from the "barbarism" of slavery.

One of the runaways William Still encountered at the Philadelphia station of the Underground Railroad was James Hambleton Christian, who claimed to have been a slave of ex-president John Tyler. James Christian was a mulatto of about "fifty per cent of Anglo-Saxon blood" which "was visible in his features and his hair." The fugitive Mr. Christian told William Still he was the son of Major Christian, father of Letitia Christian, John Tyler's first wife, and that he had served in the White House during Tyler's presidency. Quite incredibly, if James Christian's story was true, he would have been the mulatto half-brother of Mrs. Letitia Tyler and John Tyler's enslaved half-brother-in-law.

The runaway slave from Virginia also told members of the Philadelphia Vigilance Committee that he "had been to William and Mary's College in his younger days, to wait on his young master," and "where, through the kindness of some students he had picked up a trifling amount of book learning." Presumably, James H. Christian's young master who took him to Williamsburg was his half-brother, John B., later Judge Christian. When asked by one of the Vigilance Committee interviewers how he had liked John Tyler, James Christian answered that he did not much care for him. Asked why, Christian replied that on the plantation "Tyler was a very cross man and treated the servants very cruelly." Christian added that Tyler's "house servants were treated much better, owing to their having belonged to his wife, who protected them from persecution, as they had been favorite servants in her father's family."[47]

Another reason for Christian's unfavorable characterization of the ex-president stemmed from the slave's resentment that John Tyler was "a poor man" who had married up. Perhaps Christian was reflecting the snobbery of his masters when he explained to William Still and the Vigilance Committee that "I didn't like his marrying into our family, who were considered very far Tyler's superiors." When Letitia Tyler died, "James and his old mother were handed over to her nephew, William H. Christian, Esq., a merchant of Richmond." Eventually James Christian decided to escape from his bondage in Richmond and made "tracks for Canada."[48]

It is difficult for the historian and biographer to know what to make of this tale. William Still is a well-known and well-respected chronicler of the lives of runaway slaves, and his account of James Hambleton Christian's life and escape is not inherently implausible. Nonetheless, the reliability of the story in all its details is open to serious question because of factual errors and a garbled chronology. To cite just one example of factual error, the Christian family estate was named Cedar Grove, not Glen Plantation, and it was in New Kent County, not Charles City County. Clearly, historians have the obligation to judge the worth of oral anecdotal reminiscences of this sort cautiously and skeptically. And while parts of Christian's rendition may ring true and his depiction of John Tyler as slavemaster may be believable, the overall veracity of the story remains problematic.

Certainly, Tyler's image of himself was that of a kind and considerate master. He took pride in his slaves at Sherwood Forest and believed his treatment of them was compassionate and just. As far as one may tell from his private correspondence and public utterances, his conscience was clear. Tyler was not guilt-ridden and felt no obligation to manumit some or all his slaves upon his death, as his Virginia predecessors Washington and Jefferson had done. Even his successor, James K. Polk, the hard-driving slavemaster and opportunistic proprietor of extensive cotton plantations, provided in his will for the emancipation of his slaves upon his death.

Tyler's total acceptance of the South's peculiar institution and its future continuation was apparent in the fall of 1859 when, approaching the age of seventy, he began to put his affairs in order. For posterity's sake Tyler agreed to sit for a portrait by the famed painter George P. A. Healy. Two distinguished likenesses of the former president were painted at these sittings, one a famous half-portrait that has been continually reproduced in copy form over the years. A larger three-quarter-length rendition of Tyler was sent to the White House, as stipulated by the terms of Healy's commission, where it hangs to the present day. The larger portrait of Tyler also has been freely duplicated and holds a place in American history as the most recognizable depiction of the tenth president of the United States.

That autumn Tyler also drew up his last will and testament. Not surprisingly, his entire estate, including some seventy slaves, was left to his wife with the request that she "will take good care of my faithful servants, William Short and Fanny Hall," in their old age. No provision was included to free even one slave upon the patriarch's death. Quite the reverse was the case as John Tyler made provisions for his young male children to inherit slaves at a future date. "I hope," he stipulated, "that my wife will upon each of our children (the boys) attaining the age of twenty-one years, select for each a Negro boy as his own separate property."[49]

At the time Tyler composed and signed his will on October 10, 1859, he and his wife had five sons, all under the age of twenty-one. The youngest male heir, three-year-old Robert Fitzwalter (1856–1927), would have reached his maturity and inherited his "Negro boy" in 1877. The terms of John Tyler's last will and testament revealed that the ex-president anticipated the South's peculiar institution would survive for at least another generation and that conceivably the United States would remain a slaveholding republic well into the twentieth century. Tragically, Tyler seemed totally oblivious to the fact that most of the rest of the western world thought slavery an anachronism and decidedly did not see it as the wave of the future for humankind.

Less than a week after Tyler completed his will and was satisfied that he had put most of his affairs in order, the tranquility and peace of his beloved South was shattered by John Brown's raid at Harpers Ferry, Virginia. Leading a small band of men he called the "Provisional Army of the United States," the abolitionist Brown captured the federal arsenal at Harpers Ferry and announced that he had come to free all the Negro slaves in Virginia. No slave insurrection ensued and within two days Brown's band was subdued by federal troops and taken into custody. "Commander-in-Chief" Brown was quickly tried and convicted for treason against the commonwealth of Virginia. He was hanged in Charles Town on December 2, 1859. Shortly before his execution, Brown handed one of his jailers a hand-scrawled and hauntingly prophetic (and strangely punctuated) note: "I John Brown am now quite *certain* that the crimes of this *guilty, land: will* never be purged *away*; but with Blood."[50]

Terror and panic struck the South's slaveholding aristocracy as Jefferson's proverbial "firebell in the night" once again had sounded. At Sherwood Forest the Tyler family was aghast at the boldness and audacity of John Brown's raid and his call for a violent slave uprising. John Tyler's immediate fear was that local slave revolts would spring up after John Brown's hanging, a truly horrifying prospect for a slaveowner who lived in Charles City County, where whites were outnumbered by blacks by more than two to one. To prevent a possible black insurrection, the able men of the county volunteered for armed and mounted security patrols to keep the peace and, as Julia Tyler informed her mother, to "keep the black people where they ought to be at night." Too frail to join the roaming "Charles City Cavalry," John Tyler signed up to captain the "Silver Greys," a mounted security force of older men "who cannot leave home to do active service."[51]

Tidewater Virginia remained peaceful and calm in the aftermath of Brown's execution. But for John Tyler the attack on Harpers Ferry marked a turning point, one that in short order led him down a path of despair for the future of the Union. He wrote his old friend James Lyons that abolitionists and other individuals in the North who were identified with the Brown movement should forthwith be arrested by a federal marshal under the direct orders of President James Buchanan. If such arrests were not made rather quickly, he feared "the Union would exist only in name, and would afford neither protection or security." Buchanan took no action against John Brown's alleged collaborators, which further heightened Tyler's apprehensions about a coming breakup of the American nation.[52]

Another sign of the extent to which Tyler had been unnerved by the Harpers Ferry raid came in March 1860 when he added a codicil to his last will and testament, though it was less than six months old. In his own handwriting the fearful patriarch added a provision that gave his wife Julia explicit legal power to deal with obstinate and intractable slaves. The codicil stated: "I invest her also with authority to sell and dispose of any slave or slaves who may prove refranctory [sic], either reinvesting in other [slaves] or after such manner as she may deem most conclusive to the interest of my estate." By giving his widow direct authority to punish unruly slaves by selling them off and shipping them away, John Tyler also implicitly verified the contention that even on the most benign and paternalistic plantations harsh measures were employed to control a restless slave workforce yearning to be free.[53]

For a brief period prior to the 1860 Democratic convention in Charleston, South Carolina, Tyler entertained the delusion that he might be the party's nominee. He had been buoyed by the enormously warm and enthusiastic reception accorded two of his recent speeches, one at William and Mary College in Williamsburg, the other in Richmond at the commemoration of the unveiling of a Henry Clay statue. Anticipating that his immense popularity in his home state would make him an attractive compromise candidate at a sure-to-be-deadlocked convention, Tyler believed that if his name were placed in nomination, "the whole South would rally with a shout." But Tyler's hopes of being the savior of the Democratic Party and the South were unrealistic, as the convention never for a moment contemplated his candidacy.[54]

Instead of nominating a potential unifier of national reputation to their ticket, the Democrats at Charleston split into two factions when the delegates from a number, but not all, of the slave states defiantly withdrew from the convention on the question of protection for slavery in the territories. Acting separately, these bolting Democrats nominated John Breckinridge of Kentucky as their presidential candidate. The platform of the Breckinridge Democrats called for the extension of slavery into the territories and included a plank favoring the acquisition of Cuba to allow for the future expansion of slavery. The other faction of regular Democrats selected Stephen Douglas of Illinois as their presidential nominee. Their platform advocated popular sovereignty, called for the Supreme Court to settle issues pertaining to slavery in the territories, and also urged the acquisition of Cuba.

Meeting in Chicago and sensing victory over their hopelessly divided opponents, a confident Republican Party nominated Abraham Lincoln and adopted a platform that included a plank prohibiting any further extension of slavery in the territories. A fourth middle-of-the-road candidate, John Bell of Tennessee, entered the crowded field as the nominee of a new party, the Constitutional Unionists. Conspicuously avoiding the issue of the extension of slavery into the territories, they resolved to enforce existing laws, defend the Constitution, and preserve the Union.

Of the four presidential candidates, Abraham Lincoln posed the biggest threat to the South and its peculiar institution. The "rail splitter" from Illinois not only thought slavery an evil, he also had rejected the argument made by Tyler and others that the preservation of the Union depended upon unhindered territorial expansion. In an 1848 speech to a delegation of Whigs at Worcester, Massachusetts, Congressman Lincoln had opposed the extension of slavery into the new territories conquered from Mexico. As was his patented style, Lincoln used a folksy rendition to make his point. He spoke for "all those who wished to keep up the character of the Union, who did not believe in enlarging our field, but in keeping our fences where they are and cultivating our present possession, making it a garden, improving the morals and education of the people." Merely cultivating the nation's existing possessions was anathema to all those who adhered to the Madisonian formula of extending the sphere and who believed continued territorial expansion served as the adhesive of the Union.[55]

★ When announcing his support for Breckinridge during the 1860 campaign, John Tyler emotionally pledged on the graves of his Virginia ancestors to protect the South against the onslaught of Republican abolitionists at all cost—"live or die, survive or perish." He was confronted with his worst nightmare when Lincoln was elected with just under 40 percent of the popular vote and a clear electoral majority (180 of 303 votes). Gloomy and despondent after the Republican victory, Tyler feared that Lincoln would destroy the South's peculiar institution and bring a future race war between whites and blacks. To live and survive and not perish and die, the ex-president contemplated "casting away the pearl" and going for secession and disunion. It was a course of action that previously had been unthinkable for John Tyler.

A week or so after the election results were known, Tyler lamented to an old friend that "we have fallen on evil times" and "the day of doom for the great model Republic is at hand." In the course of his lamentation Virginia's elder statesman also candidly explained how slavery and expansion were inextricably linked to his anxieties about the racial question. Virginia, Tyler declared, "will never consent to have her blacks cribbed and confined within proscribed and specified limits—and thus be involved in the consequences of a war of the races in some 20 or 30 years. She must have expansion, and if she cannot obtain for herself and sisters that expansion in the Union, she may sooner or later look to Mexico, the West India Islands, and Central America as the ultimate reservations of the African race."[56]

John Tyler's anguish about a future in which slavery would be "cribbed and confined" revealed a man who above all else was terrified that white supremacy was jeopardized. For the former president and a decided majority of his fellow southerners, discarding the pearl of Union became preferable to the horrible prospect of living in a sea of freed black bondsmen.

South Carolina's secessionists led the way in breaking up the Union of the fathers. They had threatened to secede if Abraham Lincoln was elected president and the fire-eaters were true to their word. Almost immediately after Lincoln's victory, Robert Barnwell Rhett and other rabid secessionists spearheaded a drive for a special convention that met in Charleston and unanimously voted to secede on December 20, 1860. Just over a month later all the other six cotton states of the Deep South—Mississippi, Florida, Alabama, Georgia, Louisiana, and Texas—followed South Carolina's lead and seceded from the United States.

As those Deep South states debated secession over the winter of 1860–61, moderate politicians in other regions of the country sought a compromise to adjust sectional differences and save the Union. In Congress Senator John J. Crittenden of Kentucky proposed an expansionist solution that would extend the Missouri Compromise line of 36°30′ to the Pacific Ocean. Crittenden's proposal stipulated that in "all the territory south of said line of latitude, now held or hereafter to be acquired, slavery of the African race is hereby recognized as existing, and shall not be interfered with by Congress, but shall be protected as property."[57]

Elder statesman Tyler desperately hoped the expansionist panacea would work one more time to preserve the Union. He supported the compromise presented by Senator Crittenden, his boyhood chum from their days at William and Mary. The Crittenden compromise was a serious last-ditch effort by a member of Tyler's generation to invoke the previously reliable Madisonian formula to maintain the slaveholding republic created in 1789. For Tyler, who was torn between his loyalty to the Union and his gut feeling that secession was inevitable, the key provision in the compromise was the "hereafter to be acquired" clause. The "hereafter" guarantee would allow Virginia and her sister states to create a slave empire in the Caribbean basin by expanding their peculiar institution to Mexico, Central America, and the West India Islands.

That open-ended expansionist provision was the rub for President-elect Lincoln. When asked by a fellow Republican for his opinion on the compromise, Lincoln responded that he and the party had won the election fair and square, and now "we are told in advance, the government shall be broken up, unless we surrender to those we have beaten, before we take the offices." That game of "stick 'em up" would never cease, Lincoln believed, and they "will repeat the experiment upon us *ad libitum*. A year will not pass, till we shall have to take Cuba as a condition upon which they will stay in the Union." "There is," Lincoln concluded, "in my judgment, but one compromise which would really settle the slavery question, and that would be a prohibition against acquiring any more territory."[58]

Most of Lincoln's Republican compatriots were satisfied that he unequivocally rejected an extension of the 36°30′ compromise line and stood "firm as an oak." His adamant stand against the Crittenden proposal and other compromise schemes stiffened the spine of wavering Republicans in Congress. For example, one freshman Republican congressman, Roscoe Conkling of upstate New York, heartily endorsed Lincoln's denunciation of the "hereafter" clause, remarking that "it would amount to a perpetual covenant of war against every people, tribe, and state owning a foot of land between here and Tierra del Fuego. It would make the Government the armed missionary of slavery." Apparently, Republican reluctance to accept Crittenden's compromise line was justified if southern moderates including John Tyler saw the "hereafter" provision as the scenario for slavery's future expansion in the Caribbean and beyond.[59]

Certainly, there was no question or doubt about the imperial designs of the fire-eating secessionists in the cotton states. On the day that South Carolina seceded, Robert Barnwell Rhett grandiosely predicted that the historian of the twenty-first century would heap praise and glory on the Southern Confederacy for its imperial and cultural achievements. Rhett believed the new confederation of slaveholding states soon would extend its "empire across the continent to the Pacific, and down through Mexico, to the other side of the Gulf, and over the isles of the sea." This new empire would create "a civilization that has never been equaled or surpassed—a civilization teeming with orators, poets, philosophers, statesmen, and historians equal to those of Greece and Rome." Arch-secessionist Rhett proved a poor prophet. His Southern Confederacy crumbled within five years, and the empire Americans were to create in the Caribbean and the Pacific Rim came under the red, white, and blue banner of the Stars and Stripes and not the Stars and Bars.[60]

In the last years of his retirement from public office, John Tyler fancied himself something of an international statesman who might be called upon to mediate an end to brutal conflicts such as the Crimean War. Although he was not summoned to negotiate the peace that ended the mid-1850s struggle for dominance in the eastern Mediterranean between czarist Russia and its imperial adversaries Britain and France, Tyler had the opportunity to test his peacemaking skills at home during the secession crisis of 1860–61. To halt a blind rush to civil war, the former president proposed a peace conference of twelve border states, six free and six slave, to devise a way to avoid bloodshed and preserve the Union.

Tyler's suggestion led Virginia to issue an expanded call to all the states to send delegates to a peace convention to be held in Washington, D.C. In addition to being named a representative to the Washington peace conference, Tyler was tapped for two other assignments by his native state. The aspiring peacemaker was appointed as a commissioner to President James Buchanan to urge him to maintain the status quo and not provoke hostilities with South Carolina or the other seceded states. Tyler also was selected as a delegate to a state convention that was to meet in Richmond to debate whether Virginia should secede or remain in the Union.

The septuagenarian John Tyler became the man of the hour. His mission to President Buchanan accomplished its goal and was crowned with success when the chief executive pledged not to take military action against the seceded states. While in Washington to see Buchanan, Tyler also met with his old friend Matthew Fontaine Maury, the renowned maritime scientist and superintendent of the U.S. Naval Observatory and Hydrographical Office. Tyler originally had appointed Maury to the Naval Observatory post and the two like-minded southern expansionists now shared a despairing and wan hope that the disintegrating Union might be saved.

After Maury's interview with his former patron, he reported to a colleague that "I had a long talk with Mr. Tyler—found him full of Va. abstractions" on "the right of Secession in the Constitution." "I think I satisfied him," Maury emphasized, "that no parchment provision would stand." At this perilous juncture of the sectional crisis, both Tyler and Maury with heavy hearts sensed that the old republic of the founders was doomed. Within two months after their meeting in Washington these two staunch lifetime unionists came to the conclusion that the best course for Virginia was to secede and join the new slaveholding Confederacy.[61]

Maury's decision in favor of secession hinged on the question of empire. As a geopolitical thinker and acclaimed "pathfinder of the seas," Maury correctly surmised that the sectional conflict between the free and slave states was a contest over empire. He explained his thinking on the centrality of empire in an exchange of correspondence with his pro-Union first cousin, New York merchant Ruston Maury. Unsparingly candid in his analysis, Matthew Maury dispensed with pleasantries and bluntly wrote: "But the disease—the root of the thing, is not in cotton or slavery, nor in the election of Lincoln. But it is deep down in the human heart. The real question is a question of empire." "The instincts of the South," Maury continued, "also warn her that she is being belted in by the North with a cordon of free States, which in the end will lead to her own destruction." For self-preservation, the "South looks abroad and sees a vast domain. She thinks of seed, room and empire" and seeks "the promised land." To make sure he was perfectly understood, Matthew Maury emphatically reiterated to his Yankee cousin that "the real cause of the difficulty is a question of *empire.*"[62]

Maury's fascinating analysis of the sectional crisis was the ultimate expression of the "extend the sphere" argument made by James Madison at the inception the American nation. As a believer in the Madisonian formula, Maury understood that the South confronted what amounted to the last stand of the "extend the sphere" argument. If the Union under Abraham Lincoln no longer would follow the Madisonian path, then the South's new Confederacy would honor Federalist no. 10 on its own in pursuit of the "promised land." Maury's arguments about southerners wanting the promised land for their children was the South's retooled version of the American Dream, a new dream and new destiny that apparently also beguiled John Tyler into casting away the pearl of union.

★ SECESSION
★
★ The precise moment at which elder statesman Tyler became a secessionist is difficult to determine. Arguably, he was leaning in that direction but still undecided before the Washington Peace Conference convened on February 4, 1861. When the delegates, most of whom were old men, elected him president of the conference an ambivalent Tyler was at center stage in the final act of an unparalleled American tragedy. Julia Gardiner Tyler had accompanied her husband to Washington and perceived that perhaps "I am here during the last days of the Republic." But with some pride she wrote her mother in Staten Island, New York, that everybody at the Peace Conference still looked to John Tyler to save the Union. "They all say," Mrs. Tyler told her mother, "if through him it cannot be accomplished, it could not be through any one else." Tyler was flattered at all the attention he received; his wife said it was "honor enough to satisfy the most ambitious." As one veteran politician told Mrs. Tyler, "President Tyler has had the great happiness accorded him of living to see himself fully appreciated."[63]

All the adulation showered on him by the panicky delegates prompted John Tyler to play it straight in the opening phase of the Washington conference. During the first week of sessions he apparently was sincere in his efforts to resolve the sectional crisis and was not simply going through the motions to disguise his true loyalties. Certainly the tone and content of his opening address to the Peace Conference conveyed a commitment to finding a solution that would restore the Union. "Our god-like fathers created—we have to preserve," he declared to the conference members. But quite uncharacteristically, Tyler also criticized the founding fathers, something he had rarely done before in his lifetime. He said the framers had "probably committed a blunder" by making it so difficult to amend the Constitution. Even so, "your patriotism," Tyler assured his fellow delegates, "will surmount the difficulties" and rescue the "country from danger."[64]

Not all Americans observing the proceedings of the Washington Peace Conference thought John Tyler was really interested in preserving the Union. Many Republicans in the free states were deeply suspicious of the Virginia slaveholder and questioned his loyalty to the United States. Northern newspapers mocked the old southern gentleman as a cadaverous political retrograde and labeled him a "tottering ashen ruin." The pro-Republican *New York Times* openly called him a traitor. A cartoon in *Vanity Fair* repeated that charge, depicting ex-president Tyler as an old biddy dressed in apron and maid's cap admitting "I am identified with the traitors as openly working for the disruption of the Union." And then to northern eyes there was the infuriating spectacle of his nineteen-year-old granddaughter, Letitia Tyler, who had been born in the White House during his presidency, raising the new Confederate flag, the Stars and Bars, at dedication ceremonies in the capital of the Confederacy, Montgomery, Alabama.[65]

John Tyler did not publicly reveal his secessionist beliefs until the last days of the Washington Conference when he stepped down as presiding officer and voted against the compromise proposal. Two troublesome developments removed Tyler's ambivalence and hardened his thinking. The first was the convention's decision to revise the wording of the Crittenden compromise proposal by dropping the "hereafter to be acquired" clause from their recommended amendment to the Constitution. That change was intolerable for Tyler and he opposed it.

Second, Tyler irrevocably moved to the secessionist camp after he and the other peace conference delegates had an audience with Abraham Lincoln when he arrived in Washington for his inauguration. In the tense and confrontational meeting, one delegate asked Lincoln if he would "yield to the just demands of the South" and "not go to war on account of slavery." The president-elect said he was not sure he understood the questioner's meaning, but what he wished to make clear was that after taking office he would "preserve, protect, and defend the Constitution of the United States" as it is, not as one might like it to be. Lincoln also emphasized to his guests that the "Constitution will not be preserved and defended until it is enforced and obeyed in every part of every one of the United States." It was readily apparent to John Tyler that the president-elect meant what he said and there would be no backing away from the pledge to halt the further expansion of slavery.[66]

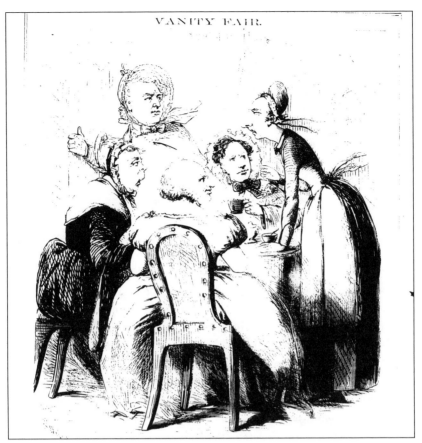

An imaginary meeting of President James Buchanan with four former presidents. Buchanan is seated at left, Van Buren sits in front, with Pierce sitting opposite; Fillmore has his hand on the door to depart. Tyler stands at the right. *Vanity Fair*, May 11, 1861. The original caption that appeared with the cartoon, under the rubric "Proposed Meeting of Ex-Presidents," featured the following dialogue:

VAN BUREN — "I think I should preside at this meeting, for I laid the foundation of this treason by splitting the Democratic Party on the Buffalo platform."

PIERCE — "I think I deserve especial consideration, for I put Jeff Davis in my Cabinet as Secretary of War, after he had been rejected by the people of Mississippi for his disunion sentiments."

BUCHANAN — "I should have precedence, for with Floyd and the rest of my Cabinet I brought about the present rebellion."

TYLER — "I deserve the first place, for I am identified with the traitors as openly working for the disruption of the Union."

FILLMORE — As positive councils are now only available, and as I am not in that line, I'll leave."

The day after the old gentlemen's convention adjourned in obvious failure, John Tyler delivered an impassioned speech on the steps of a Richmond hotel denouncing the Peace Conference's handiwork and urging his fellow Virginians to secede at once. The ex-president then proceeded to take his seat at the Virginia State Convention to support the cause of secession. Several weeks later with Abraham Lincoln in the White House, an embittered Tyler addressed the state convention and explained his reasons for wanting to leave the Union. The necessity of future territorial expansion for the South and its peculiar institution was high on his list. Tyler believed the revision of the Crittenden compromise offered at the peace convention was fatally flawed because "you cannot acquire a foot of land under this provision of the Peace Conference, for it effectually closes the door to further expansion on the part of the South." To illustrate what this meant, Tyler warned, "You will never get Cuba under this Administration."[67]

Tied to the need for territorial expansion was John Tyler's concern for the maintenance of white supremacy. This became evident when the usually circumspect Virginia patriarch overtly expressed his racism in behalf of his case for secession. Staying in the Union, Tyler warned, ultimately would necessitate accepting members of the African race as citizens with equality at the polls. Such was the case in Massachusetts, where conceivably a runaway slave like Frederick Douglass might be elected to a seat in Congress. Taunting a convention delegate who opposed secession, Tyler sarcastically predicted that some day that Unionist might find himself "down by the side of Fred. Douglass, in the Senate of the United States, cheek by jowl, and in fellowship with him as his fellow citizen."[68]

The delegates at the Virginia convention were not automatically swayed by the arguments of Tyler and his secessionist allies. Not even his assurances that the economic clout of King Cotton in world markets would pave the way for the Confederacy to achieve its independence changed many minds. Virginians were not yet ready to abandon the Union. On April 4 the convention defeated a motion for secession by a vote of 90 to 45. Only after President Lincoln, in response to the Confederate bombardment of Fort Sumter in Charleston Harbor, called for 75,000 volunteers to put down the southern rebellion did the tide shift in the convention. In secret session on April 17, 1861, the delegates of the Virginia State Convention voted 88 to 55 for an ordinance of secession.

An exhausted and emotionally drained John Tyler was jubilant that Virginia finally had taken the fateful step to leave the Union. After the vote for secession he and his compatriot Henry Wise went to Richmond's Metropolitan Hall to attend the Spontaneous Southern Rights Assembly, which was an extralegal secessionist enclave meeting in the city. Just as they arrived news that Virginia had seceded was greeted with thunderous applause by the assembly. "President Tyler and Gov. Wise," according to one witness, "were conducted arm-in-arm, and bare-headed, down the center aisle amid a din of cheers, while every member rose to his feet." Both men were escorted to the platform to give brief speeches. John Tyler invoked the forefathers of 1776 and hoped a benign Providence "would again crown our efforts with similar success." Henry Wise ignited the already delirious crowd with the chant of "Independence or Death." Although hundreds of thousands of Americans would die in the ensuing Civil War, Wise's juxtaposition did not accurately reflect his personal history. The Confederacy failed and he lived to write his memoirs.[69]

That evening John Tyler wrote his wife at Sherwood Forest of the day's momentous events. "Well, my dearest one," he began, "Virginia has severed her connection with the Northern hive of abolitionists, and takes her stand as a sovereign and independent State." Virginia, he continued, decided "to resume the powers she had granted to the Federal government and to stand before the world clothed in the full vestments of sovereignty." The Old Dominion's fortunes were now in the hands "of the God of Battle." Conveying a sense of dread and anxiety, John Tyler admitted to his wife that the "contest into which we enter is one full of peril." The loving and caring husband closed his message to his wife that night on a cautious and sobering note: "Do dearest, live as frugally as possible in the household—trying times are before us." Indeed, little did Tyler realize just how trying and tragic the times that lay ahead would be.[70]

★ ★ ★ ★ ★ ★ ★ ★ ★ ★ ★

Conclusion
Precedents &
Legacies

We have one country, one Constitution, and one future
that binds us. And when we come together and work
together, there is no limit to the greatness of America.

★ *President George W. Bush, November 3, 2004*

O n January 18, 1862, nine months after voting for secession and warning his wife of the trying times ahead, John Tyler died in a hotel room in Richmond, Virginia. The seventy-one-year-old former president of the United States was in the capital of the Confederacy to take his seat as the representative from Charles City County in the upcoming session of the Confederate Congress. In the brief period between secession and his death, Tyler had served his home state and the new Southern Confederacy well. As the head of a commission that successfully negotiated terms for Virginia's admission into the Confederate States of America, Tyler and his colleagues sealed the deal that moved the capital of the Confederacy from Montgomery, Alabama, to Richmond.

To the end a loyal and revered son of Virginia and only rather briefly a faithful servant of the Confederate States of America, John Tyler was fondly remembered and deeply mourned by his fellow citizens of the South. In Richmond, he was eulogized and given an elaborate funeral that included a 150-carriage cortege. In Washington, the capital of the United States, Tyler's death was ignored. President Abraham Lincoln did not issue an official proclamation marking the former president's death, nor were flags lowered to half-staff on federal buildings. The passing of the disgraced and reviled "traitor" ex-president was greeted with official silence as well in the capitals of the states that had remained faithful to the Union of the fathers.

Prior to his death, in the opening months of what would become a horrific and devastating civil war, John Tyler took considerable satisfaction in several notable Confederate military victories in the struggle for southern independence. An early Confederate triumph in June 1861 on the Virginia peninsula against Union forces stationed at Fortress Monroe, a federal stronghold on the Chesapeake Bay, was greeted with great excitement by the Tyler clan at Sherwood Forest. Mrs. Julia Tyler exclaimed that the "fight on the Southern side was more wonderful than the taking of Sumter." "How can it be otherwise than that?" she innocently wondered, because surely the "hand of Providence should assist this holy Southern cause."[1]

Her husband was equally ecstatic. Still serving at the time in the Virginia state convention that adopted the secession ordinance, John Tyler sponsored unanimously adopted resolutions that declared "that this convention has heard with high satisfaction of the brilliant victory recently obtained by the combined forces of North Carolina and Virginia at Bethel, in the county of York, the first regular conflict between those who, under usurped authority, have invaded our soil and the brave defenders of that soil." Tyler and his colleagues also commended the troops and officers for their gallantry, courage under fire, and military skill.[2]

Weeks later southern arms again repelled the Yankee invaders and achieved a glorious victory at Manassas (Bull Run) in northern Virginia. On that occasion the Tylers thrilled to the news accounts and editorial comment they read in the Richmond newspapers describing the total rout of Union forces. The *Richmond Whig* brashly and prematurely claimed that the splendid triumph at Manassas confirmed that the "break-down of the Yankees, their utter unfitness for empire, forces dominion upon us of the South." Giddy over what this stunning success of Confederate arms foretold, the *Whig* editors challenged their fellow white brethren of the South: "We must adapt ourselves to our destinies. We must elevate our race, every man of it,—breed them up to arms, to command—to empire."

A few months later in September 1861, the equally euphoric *Richmond Daily Examiner* proclaimed that Confederate successes on the battlefield "demonstrated, at once and forever, the superiority of the Southern soldier." The Yankee enemies "know, now, that when they go forth to the field they will encounter a master race. The consciousness of this fact will cause their knees to tremble beneath them in the day of battle."[3]

Weaned and nurtured on visions of national destiny, John Tyler and other southern rebels such as his old expansionist compatriot, Matthew Fontaine Maury, may have been exhilarated by the dizzying prospects for the Confederacy's glorious destiny and future empire outlined in their infant nation's leading newspapers. But for present-day Americans, such outlandish and ephemeral rhetoric hailing an empire of the master race is as incomprehensible as it is chilling. Justifiably or not, it brings to mind Adolf Hitler's boasts of a thousand-year Reich. In the end, Confederate hubris and prideful boasting led to crushing defeat. The rule of a southern master race was as short-lived as it was disastrous.[4]

John Tyler was not entirely spared the pain and sorrow of America's fratricidal conflict. To a limited but frightening measure, he tasted the anguish and loss wrought by a civil war he had hoped to avert and tragically had helped bring on. After secession and the firing on Fort Sumter, a torrent of bitterness and recrimination against Confederate sympathizers erupted in many northern communities. In Philadelphia and towns nearby, Robert Tyler, the former president's eldest son and a defender of slavery and states' rights, faced arrest for treason. At one gathering the mention of Robert Tyler's name and his pro-southern proclivities aroused some in the crowd to cry: "He ought to be lynched!" More terrifying was the rage and anger of

Robert Tyler's former neighbors. They built a bonfire in front of his home and hanged him in effigy from a nearby tree. Panic-stricken, Robert Tyler and his family fled for their lives to the safety of Virginia. But even after reaching Sherwood Forest, the refugees as well as other members of the Tyler clan felt the war's ominous presence as Union gunboats patrolled the James River and the boom of cannons could be heard in the distance.[5]

In the early summer of 1861 Julia Tyler confessed in a letter to her mother in New York that "more and more we have the *realization* of war." In addition to the sounds of battle and the arrival of Robert Tyler's fleeing family, the routine of plantation life at Sherwood Forest also had been noticeably disrupted when half of Tyler's slaves were requisitioned for digging duty in the Peninsula campaign "to throw up intrenchments at Williamsburg." Six weeks later as harvest time approached, an annoyed John Tyler complained to the Confederate secretary of war about the length and legality of the requisition. "The much longer detention of the slaves, which has delayed the thrashing of the wheat crop," he wrote, "has engendered some little feeling of discontent among some of our people, who begin to question the legal authority of the proceedings."

The patriarch of Sherwood Forest also was agitated because some of the requisitioned slaves had run away. As a corrective, John Tyler suggested to the war secretary that "the officer having charge of the laborers should give a certificate for the negroes of each proprietor, so as to protect the master against possible contingencies of loss." Although unsettling, slave requisitions were the least of the disruptions that ultimately would destroy the harmony and tranquility of plantation life at Sherwood Forest.[6]

The "realization of war" also struck home when Union soldiers, sent from Massachusetts to garrison Fortress Monroe and launch the Peninsula campaign, quickly commandeered Villa Margaret, the Tyler summer home near Hampton, for barracks use. These Yankee troops evidently hated and loathed Tyler for his apostasy and treason, and took their revenge at the villa, according to one rebel war clerk, "in a barbarous manner. They cut his carpets, defaced the pictures, broke the statues, and made kindling wood of the piano, sofas, etc." Emotions at Sherwood Forest ran high at this outrage, and an infuriated Julia Tyler repeated a family friend's rant that the men and boys of the Massachusetts company were "the scum of the earth."[7]

The Civil War not only ripped apart a nation; it also tore families asunder as brother fought brother and cousin fought cousin. The closely knit Tyler-Gardiner family was no exception to this human tragedy as its members split into a pro-Confederacy Tyler faction centered in Virginia, and a pro-

Union Gardiner contingent based in New York. Juliana Gardiner, Tyler's mother-in-law, was the lone exception. Her sympathies were with the Virginia Tylers and the Confederacy. David Gardiner, the California gold rush survivor and Juliana's eldest son, was a loyal and outspoken Unionist. Julia Tyler was at a loss to explain and understand her brother's position and was sure he had "been bitten by the rabid tone of those around him." But David Gardiner was true to his convictions. He and his immediate family broke with John and Julia Tyler; it was an acrimonious split that outlasted the war and poisoned brother-sister relations for years thereafter.

John Tyler also lived to see the early stages of the separation of his beloved Virginia into two states. After the Virginia ordinance of secession was approved by a public referendum in May 1861, the northwestern counties extending to the Ohio River chose in a convention to stay with the Union. To Tyler's dismay, the Old Dominion was disintegrating before his very eyes. In 1863, just over a year after his death, the separation was finalized when the state of West Virginia officially entered the Union. In the final year of his life, the aged ex-president suffered the pain and heartache of three tragic divisions and losses—the break-up of the Union and of the commonwealth of Virginia, and the dissolution of his family into feuding camps.

Mercifully, John Tyler did not live to witness and endure the agony and humiliation of the defeat and unconditional surrender of the Confederacy. The numbers detailing the loss of human life and the destruction of property in the South are staggering. At war's end in April 1865, after four years of brutal fighting, one quarter of the military-age white men in the Confederate states had been killed. The Confederate economy lay in ruins with two-thirds of the wealth of the southern states destroyed, including the property value of some four million enslaved African Americans who had been emancipated. The devastated southern landscape was marked by trackless railroad lines, smashed bridges and factories, and burned plantations and flaming cities plagued by lawlessness and looting, including the once proud capital of Richmond, set ablaze by its own retreating defenders. The old economic and social order of the South had been demolished.

Along the shores of the James River and foremost in Tyler's home base, Charles City County, the world of the slavemaster and plantation owner had crumbled as well. Union forces occupied Virginia's mid-peninsula from Hampton west to the Confederate barricades defending Richmond. These invading Yankee troops confiscated farms and plantations, freed slaves, and scavenged the countryside for food and supplies. Gone forever was John Tyler's vision of the idyllic life on "a good farm on James River with plenty of slaves." After his death, Tyler's large family scattered. His older sons did service for the Confederacy. His widow, who had inherited Sherwood Forest and its seventy slaves, ran north with the younger children to the safety of her mother's home on Staten Island. Now a woman in her mid-forties with seven children, Mrs. Ex-President Tyler, as she came to be called, faced financial uncertainty and the hardships of rebuilding a war-torn estate, with many of its fields growing up in weeds and its slave labor force liberated.

The plundering and pillaging had begun in earnest in the spring of 1864 as the fighting engulfed Charles City and the surrounding locales. Union soldiers confiscated the *Pocahontas*, Julia Tyler's prized blue boat, which in former times had been the "Royal Barge" of the James. Tyler's Sherwood Forest estate, its mansion reputed to have been the longest antebellum house in Virginia—three hundred feet from end to end, including a sixty-eight-foot ballroom—was devastated by the United States Colored Troops with help from some of Tyler's former slaves. General Edward H. Wild, the commander of the black troops, liberated *"two canes* and a *secession flag"* as war booty from the former president's home. General Wild, a passionate abolitionist who two years earlier had lost an arm on the field of battle, sent Tyler's trophy walking sticks and the rebel flag to General Benjamin Butler with the request that they be forwarded to the Sanitary Commission Fair in Philadelphia, "where they would doubtless realize a very large sum of money, for the benefit of our soldiers."[8]

One of the ex-president's nieces later confirmed to a Union officer investigating the incident that "the negro troops under Genl Wild had Sacked the Mansion of Sherwood." Out of duty and curiosity, the same officer "rode over to see the place" and recorded "such a scene as the inside presented I never saw." Everything had been broken up and smashed to pieces—mirrors, furniture, china, and beds. John Tyler's valuable and extensive library was vandalized, with the "books & papers mutilated—simply for mischief" and to the woe and dismay of future biographers and historians. In addition, some of his remaining private papers that had been stored in a bank vault for safekeeping were destroyed in the burning of Richmond. The loss of his private papers, including an unfinished autobiographical manuscript, deprived future historians of a vast documentary treasure and to a degree helped obscure the tenth president's historical legacy.[9]

Several weeks after General Wild's soldiers trashed Sherwood Forest, another Yankee caller named Stephen Farnum Peckham visited the Tyler residence. A hospital steward in the 7th Regiment, Rhode Island Volunteers, Peckham claimed almost fifty years after the war to have come upon "a package of yellow manifold paper that appeared to have been pressed hard together from having been carried in a pocket." What he found inside were telegrams "that had been sent President Tyler from all over the South, while he was the presiding officer of the 'Peace Convention,' giving him all sorts of information concerning the preparations that were being made to put the South in a condition to fight."

Upon reflection, Peckham believed that the information in the packet of telegrams, which he left at Sherwood Forest and was unable to retrieve later, established "beyond any possibility of doubt the fact that John Tyler, a man who had filled the exalted position of President of the United States, had run the 'Peace Convention' simply to kill time, while the South got ready to fight." Unfortunately, the packet of telegrams was never found and this crucial documentary evidence was lost to history. Thus, Peckham's indignant post–Civil War claim that former president Tyler betrayed the Union while serving as head of the peace convention cannot be fully verified.[10]

But Peckham's charge that Tyler had been disloyal was not new and had been raised earlier. At the time of the Peace Conference in February 1861, some northern newspapers had accused the ex-president of being in league with "the Montgomery conspirators," including Jefferson Davis, the leader of the Confederacy. Such press reports led Tyler's former countrymen in the North to suspect that his actions during the peace convention were treasonous. The suspicions of Tyler's disloyalty were confirmed and etched in historical memory after the former president became a full-fledged secessionist and an open enemy of the nation he had served for almost five decades.

At the time of his death the obituaries that did appear in a scattering of northern papers, most especially the one in the *New York Times*, were unforgiving, emphasizing Tyler's betrayal of the Union as the tragic last act for which he would be most remembered. That contemporary verdict was endorsed more than a century later by one of his leading biographers, Robert Seager, who succinctly concluded that "John Tyler had died a rebel and a 'traitor.'"[11]

Death may have spared John Tyler the anguish of seeing the Confederacy go down in flames, but he was unable to escape the tragedy and historical disgrace of being labeled a rebel, an apostate American, and the United States's sole "traitor" president. In fact, in his lifetime Tyler had the distinction of twice being labeled a traitor. The first occasion came in 1841 after he had succeeded to the presidency upon the death of William Henry Harrison. "His Accidency," as his critics derided him, chose to steer an independent course and vetoed bills to create a national bank and other Whig

Let It Be Ever Thus With Traitors. Columbia, with her sword of Liberty and Union, is astride the figure of Secession. Vanity Fair, *April 27, 1861.*

legislation. Immediately, the Whigs bitterly denounced Tyler as a double-crosser for betraying their legislative program. Tyler the reviled traitor then was drummed out of the party, hanged in effigy, and threatened with impeachment.

Such strong feelings against John Tyler among the Whig faithful did not dissipate even after he left the White House. Edmund Ruffin recorded upon Tyler's retirement and return to Charles City County that the former president faced hostility and rejection because nearly "every neighbor, & most of his countymen were whigs & followers of Clay, & who had learned to hate Tyler as a traitor, a renegade, & everything that was esteemed bad in their party creed." Nor was he forgiven at his alma mater, William and Mary, where the Swem Library copy of Alexander Gordon Abell's 1844 campaign biography, *Life of John Tyler*, is inscribed in pencil on the frontispiece: "A traitor to the Whig Party. Sic Semper Tyrannis," the motto of Virginia, Latin for "Thus [death] always to tyrants."[12]

Ex-president Tyler's treason to the Union he had served and upheld for most of his adult life was a far more serious error than his political break with the Whigs. In supporting secession, Tyler adopted the course he believed every loyal Virginian should follow. But not every son of Virginia of his generation went for secession and the Confederacy. At least two of his William and Mary classmates who were native-born Virginians and prominent national leaders, General Winfield Scott and Senator John J. Crittenden of Kentucky, remained loyal to the Union and condemned the treason of turncoats such as Tyler. For these two men, following their native state on its secessionist path was dishonorable and unthinkable. Perhaps the major difference between them and secessionist John Tyler was that they did not value the institution of slavery, and the need for its continued expansion, above that of saving the Union. Scott and Crittenden treasured the preservation of the Union above all else.

A military hero of the Mexican War, Scott was born near Petersburg, Virginia, and enrolled at William and Mary in 1805 to study with the famed legal scholar St. George Tucker. Known as "Old Fuss and Feathers" for his pedantry and pomposity—he was fond of gold braid and yellow plumes—Scott was commanding general of the U.S. Army when the secession crisis erupted. In April 1861 the rumor spread that the seventy-five-year-old General Scott would defect to the Confederacy. Tyler, who as president had appointed his fellow Virginian to the post as the nation's top general, was overjoyed at the news. He wrote to his wife, "General Scott has resigned. It is as always I thought it would be. He comes to offer his sword to Virginia."

Bookplate in Abell, *Life of John Tyler.* *Special Collections, Swem Library, College of William and Mary.*

Claiborne Memorial Library

COLLEGII GULIELMI ET MARIÆ IN VIRGINIA · SIC ·

A traitor to the Whig Party
Sic semper tyrannis

The rumor proved false. Tyler, who had come to doubt the story, and other secessionists were disappointed and angered to learn that Winfield Scott had declined the offer to command Virginia's armed forces. It was a "mortal insult," the old warrior told the delegation of Virginians who asked him to betray the United States. "I have served my country under the flag of the Union, for more than fifty years, and so long as God permits me to live, I will defend that flag with my sword, even if my own native state assails it." Although the General-in-Chief of the Army was frail and much past his prime, Winfield Scott's decision to remain loyal to the United States was a reassuring boost to beleaguered Unionists everywhere.[13]

At the onset of the secession crisis, Senator Crittenden, who was born in Kentucky when it was still a part of Virginia, had tried, along with Tyler, to broker a compromise to preserve the Union and avoid a civil war. When those efforts failed, Crittenden chose to stay in the republic of the founders. He believed secession was unconstitutional and an act of rebellion. But it was a "rebellion without cause" or justification. President Lincoln, Crittenden believed, had done nothing to warrant secession and rebellion. The secessionists were to blame for provoking an unjust war that placed "the destiny of mankind" and human liberty in jeopardy. Had they not seceded, representatives of the southern slave states in Congress had the votes to block any Republican efforts to eliminate slavery where it existed. For Senator Crittenden, the unjustified rebellion was treason and his old William and Mary school chum John Tyler was a traitor.[14]

The memory of Tyler within the rank and file of the triumphant Republican Party of Abraham Lincoln also was that of a rebel and traitor. His transgressions in support of the Confederacy were not easily forgiven. One victor's history of the early republic, entitled *The Rise and Fall of the Slave Power in America*, detailed slavemaster Tyler's apostasy. Henry Wilson, a leading abolitionist from Massachusetts and vice president during Ulysses S. Grant's second term, formally pinned the rebel label on the tenth president in his book, declaring that John Tyler would be "remembered as the only traitor president."[15]

Tyler's historical reputation suffered further damage when his legacy as a proponent of the pursuit of national destiny was almost totally erased from American memory. In fact, his oft-repeated refrain linking destiny and national unity was co-opted by the leader who had saved the Union. In a political gesture both aimed at healing the wounds of civil war and laden with irony, President Lincoln's second inaugural coat, tailored by Brooks Brothers, was embroidered on the inside panels with the inscription, "One Country, One Destiny."

Another Republican president, Ulysses S. Grant, also appropriated John Tyler's national destiny rhetoric and mirrored his views on the future greatness of the American republic. In 1832 Senator Tyler had imagined America bringing "tidings of great joy to distant nations" and "overturning the strong places of despotism, and restoring to man his long-lost rights." Some forty years later in his second inaugural address, Grant repeated Tyler's lofty sentiments, pronouncing that "our own great Republic is destined to be the guiding star to all others." Remarkably, the Civil War hero proved as well to be a believer in the Jeffersonian rationale, held dear by Tyler, that expansion strengthened republics. Now that slavery had been abolished, Grant could readily adopt the view that there was no "danger of governments becoming weakened and destroyed by reason of their extension of territory." Obviously, the belief in an American exceptionalism and the expansive potential of republics had survived the trauma and disruption of civil war. It did not matter that the Civil War had in fact put the lie to any claim of an American exceptionalism.[16]

To the present day, Republicans and Democrats honor and glorify the national destiny and national greatness shibboleths that guided and shaped America's nineteenth-century expansion and empire. Woodrow Wilson hoped America would make the world safe for democracy. Franklin D. Roosevelt believed all the peoples of the world, not just Americans, should enjoy Four Freedoms—freedom of speech and worship, and freedom from want and fear. Ronald Reagan repeatedly invoked America's destiny as a beacon of liberty and proudly proclaimed that the United States was an empire of ideals.

On the morning following his victorious election to a second term, George W. Bush echoed the words of at least two of his predecessors, the Great Emancipator and the virtually forgotten traitor president from Virginia. "We have one country, one Constitution, and one future that binds us," Bush declared. "And when we come together and work together, there is no limit to the greatness of America." President Bush also has expressed, as did John Tyler before him, a mystical faith in America's national destiny and the belief that "the United States is the beacon for freedom in the world."[17]

Although his accomplishments are little remembered and his presidency usually is dismissed by scholars as a dismal failure, John Tyler's initiatives and actions did influence the course of American history and in a few cases had a lasting impact. Anyone familiar with the history of the American presidency knows the significance of the Tyler precedent, which established by usage the precedent for the vice president to become president on the death of the incumbent. Tyler's bold precedent has been reaffirmed seven times, first within a decade by Millard Fillmore, and later by Andrew Johnson, Chester A. Arthur, Theodore Roosevelt, Calvin Coolidge, Harry Truman, and Lyndon Johnson.

Ultimately, the Tyler precedent was codified in the American Constitution by the adoption of the Twenty-fifth Amendment in 1967. Section 1 of the amendment stipulates, "In the case of the removal of the President from office or of his death or resignation, the Vice-President shall become President." The amendment was applied for the first time in 1974 when Vice President Gerald Ford became president on the resignation of Richard Nixon. Through his decisive action in 1841, John Tyler had placed all future vice presidents a heartbeat from the presidency. He also had stabilized and strengthened the institution of the presidency by making it independent of death.

Tyler also set path-breaking precedents for nineteenth-century American foreign policy in the Pacific Rim. In 1842 he announced the Tyler Doctrine, which recognized the sovereignty of the Hawaiian Kingdom and extended the Monroe Doctrine to the crossroads of the Pacific. Two of his successors, Zachary Taylor and Millard Fillmore, publicly upheld the Tyler Doctrine during their administrations. In outlining their goals for American diplomacy in the Pacific, both Taylor and Fillmore declared that the United States would act to guarantee Hawaiian independence and expected other leading maritime nations to do the same. These endorsements of the Tyler Doctrine paved the way for a dominant American missionary and economic presence in the Hawaiian Islands for the remainder of the century.

John Tyler also opened the door to the China market and its 400 million inhabitants. In 1844 his emissary Caleb Cushing negotiated the United States's first treaty with the Celestial Kingdom. Cushing's treaty granted American merchants and entrepreneurs favorable trading privileges, equal access to five Chinese ports, and extraterritorial rights for all Americans residing or doing business in China. In addition, the Tyler administration was the first in the history of the American republic to extend the official protection of the United States government to missionaries serving in foreign lands, including China. President Tyler's diplomatic initiatives in China helped lay the groundwork for the creation of the Open Door Policy, which was established by Secretary of State John Hay at the end of the nineteenth century.

Another of President Tyler's far-reaching precedents was his use of a congressional joint resolution to annex Texas. Unable to secure ratification of an annexation treaty by a two-thirds majority in the Senate as required by the Constitution, Tyler evaded that requirement. He gained House and Senate passage of a joint resolution, which required only a majority vote in each chamber, to approve the annexation of Texas.

Tyler's extralegal joint resolution ploy, which belied his pretensions to being a strict constructionist when it came to interpreting the Constitution, appealed to late-nineteenth-century imperialists who sought ways to circumvent Senate opposition to a Hawaiian annexation treaty. In early 1893 Republican president Benjamin Harrison, the grandson of Tyler's 1840 running mate William Henry Harrison, submitted a Hawaiian annexation treaty to the Senate. Harrison was a lame duck who had but a few weeks left in his term. It was doubtful that the Senate would ratify the annexation treaty before he left office. To expedite the process, the expansionist *Chicago Tribune* called upon President Harrison to employ the Tyler joint resolution precedent as the means to gain approval of the treaty before his term expired. Harrison chose not to do so and the Senate failed to ratify the treaty. His successor, Democrat Grover Cleveland, withdrew the treaty and Hawaiian annexation was delayed until Republican William McKinley became president in 1897.[18]

Within months of his inauguration, McKinley answered the prayers of the imperialists who favored American territorial expansion in the Pacific by submitting a Hawaiian annexation treaty to the Senate. Once again the two-thirds required for Senate ratification of a treaty presented a huge obstacle to overcome. But as the *New York Times* earlier had reported, the joint resolution gambit was alive and well—"It is understood that a joint resolution is being prepared with much care for introduction in Congress which will provide for the annexation of the Hawaiian Islands to the United States," and the "case of Texas is referred to as furnishing a precedent for Hawaii." Indeed, separate committee reports were issued in the spring of 1898 in both the Senate and the House that recommended Tyler's Texas precedent as justification for annexation by joint resolution. Not long afterward, in July 1898 during the last weeks of the Spanish-American War, the McKinley administration and its allies in Congress successfully pushed through a joint resolution approving the annexation of Hawaii.[19]

In addition to the joint resolution stratagem to bypass constitutional restraints on the chief executive, John Tyler established another empowering precedent during his embattled effort to annex Texas. Without legislative sanction, Tyler extended the war powers of the president when he pledged the United States would defend the Texans from foreign invasion while ratification of the annexation treaty was pending in the Senate. In 1869–70 President Grant sought to annex the Dominican Republic and cited the Tyler war powers precedent as justification for sending warships to protect Dominican territory from invasion while the Senate considered approval of an annexation treaty. In this instance, Grant's actions aroused serious constitutional objections in Congress and the Dominican annexation treaty failed ratification by the Senate. Although the Dominican annexation scheme was thwarted, Tyler's war powers precedent was upheld when the Senate defeated resolutions denouncing Grant's actions as an unconstitutional extension of executive authority.[20]

So powerful was the pull of empire "deep down in the human heart" that the victorious Republicans who initially had demonized John Tyler as a traitor president now were more than willing to employ his precedents in the chase for imperial glory in the Caribbean and the Pacific. Presidents Grant and McKinley, both of whom were Union officers who had led the Union to victory in the Civil War, unabashedly relied on Tyler's extralegal extensions of presidential power in pursuit of their imperialist agenda. America's imperial purpose proved resilient in the face of adversity and failure. Neither partisan politics nor deadly internecine conflict long stifled

America's global mission and its quest for national greatness. As unlikely as it may seem, the dishonored and little remembered tenth president cast a long shadow over the United States's late-nineteenth-century imperial expansion. His precedents fostered the building of an antebellum continental empire and guided the creation of a post–Civil War overseas empire in the vast reaches of the Pacific Rim.

Contrary to the frequent historical characterization of John Tyler as the archetypal states' righter and defender of limited government, as president of the United States he considerably extended and enhanced executive power. He helped establish the tradition of a strong and forceful executive, independent of Congress and independent of death. Through his autonomous course of action, confident foreign policy initiatives, and fearless use of the presidential veto, Tyler administered a severe body blow to Henry Clay's Whig concept of legislative dominance and a restricted and tethered chief executive. President Tyler freely used the secret service fund, which was not directly monitored by Congress, and utilized secret executive agents to achieve his diplomatic goals. In addition to extending presidential war powers in defense of the nation's inchoate interests, Tyler asserted the executive's right to withhold information from Congress in order to maintain the separation of powers.

A number of President Tyler's contemporaries thought his doctrine of executive power undermined the republican principles he formerly held so dear. For example, the editors of the prestigious and influential *National Intelligencer*, Joseph Gales and William W. Seaton, charged that Tyler's executive actions violated the Constitution because he assumed powers never intended to be employed by the chief executive. They claimed that the prerogative power Tyler exercised had no legal standing or constitutional sanction. The editors were correct. John Tyler had come to embrace and champion the broad executive prerogatives he found so objectionable when wielded by his predecessors.

Arthur Schlesinger, a historian who has traced the development of what he has labeled "the imperial presidency," credited John Tyler, along with James K. Polk, for the rescue and deliverance of the Jacksonian doctrine of executive power and independence. Schlesinger's assessment is valid. By acting on his belief that the Constitution had not designed the chief executive to be "a mere cipher," President Tyler set precedents that marked the birth of an imperial presidency.[21]

No occupant of the White House since John Tyler has followed his last calamitous precedent. His tragic act of treason was unique. He remains the sole former president to have turned against the republic he once led and the only traitor president in American history. Groomed from an early age to assume the reins of national power as the scion of one of Virginia's first families, Tyler never imagined his fate would be that of a turncoat like the disreputable revolutionary traitor Benedict Arnold. But Arnold's treachery has far overshadowed Tyler's apostasy. In American memory Benedict Arnold lives on as the country's most infamous traitor; his name is synonymous with treason. If remembered at all as a player in the national experience, John Tyler no longer is stigmatized by the taint of treason but merely is ignored for being an inept and hapless president.

Most tragic figures in history have suffered from a fatal or debilitating flaw in their physical makeup, personal character, mental stability, or capacity for self-delusion. Tyler's delusional defect was self-inflicted because it originated in his republican political philosophy. The crucial flaw in his thinking was an unswerving belief in the "extend the sphere" formula devised by his idols, James Madison and Thomas Jefferson. Those two founding fathers, along with their protégé James Monroe, had stressed the vital connection between territorial expansion and the viability of republican government. Tyler throughout his public life kept faith in the merits of an extended republic. He fervently believed in the Madisonian formula and struggled to preserve a slaveholding Union by emphasizing the necessity of territorial expansion and the promise of America's national destiny. Like the enticing siren's song leading seamen to disaster, John Tyler's tune beckoned Americans to stay true to themselves on the path to a glorious destiny of national greatness.

That expansionist blueprint and the accompanying lofty vision of national greatness failed in the end to rescue the anachronism of a slaveholding republic from the ash heap of history. Tyler was stunned and saddened when the Madisonian formula failed to preserve the Union of the fathers. Throughout his public career until the eve of the secession crisis, John Tyler had promoted a nationalism that combined the "extend the sphere" panacea with the dream of national destiny to sublimate sectionalism and prevent discord over slavery's future. It consistently had worked in the past as witnessed by the easy success in the antebellum era of republican territorial and commercial expansionism across the continent and over the seas.

But in the late 1850s that traditional nationalism based on territorial aggrandizement and the expansion of slavery had been challenged by a competing antislavery nationalism dedicated to free soil, free men, and an end to slavery's expansion. Former president Tyler rejected that vision of the future and abandoned both the Union and his lifelong pursuit of America's national destiny. John Tyler's historical reputation has yet to fully recover from that tragic decision to betray his loyalty and commitment to what he had once defined as "the first great American interest"—the preservation of the Union.

NOTES

Chapter 1

1. Seager, *and Tyler too*, 148; Wise, *Recollections*, 13.

2. Shelley, "The Vice President Receives Bad News," 337–39; James Lyons to John Tyler, April 3, 1841, John Tyler Papers, Library of Congress (microfilm edition).

3. Corwin, *The President*, 54; Morgan, *Whig Embattled*, 8–9.

4. Nathaniel Beverley Tucker to Thomas Ritchie, July 12, 1845, Tyler Scrapbook, Tyler Family Papers, Swem Library, William and Mary; Carpenter, "A Talk," 416–18.

5. Richardson, *Messages and Papers*, 4:31–32, 36–39.

6. Ibid., 37; Morgan, *Whig Embattled*, 78.

7. John Tyler to William C. Rives, April 9, 1841, in Tyler, *Letters and Times*, 2:20.

8. Silva, *Presidential Succession*, 22–23; "The Accession of John Tyler," 447–58; Stathis, "John Tyler's Presidential Succession," 223–36.

9. Tyler, *Letters and Times*, 1:622–23; Kesilman, "John Tyler and the Presidency," 48–49.

10. John Tyler to Littleton W. Tazewell, November 2, 1841; John Tyler to the Norfolk Democratic Association, September 2, 1844, in Tyler, *Letters and Times*, 2:131, 95.

11. Richardson, *Messages and Papers*, 5:51–60.

12. Tyler, *Letters and Times*, 2:171, 96.

13. Ibid., 2:33–34.

14. Cleaves, *Old Tippecanoe*, 326.

15. Holt, *Rise and Fall of the American Whig Party*, 104; Philip Hone diary entry of August 17, 1841, in Nevins, *Diary of Philip Hone*, 553.

16. Gunderson, *Log-Cabin Campaign*, 129.

17. Remini, *Henry Clay*, 581; Carl Schurz, *Henry Clay*, 1:215.

18. Henry Clay to the Whig Caucus, September 13, 1841, in Hopkins, *Papers of Henry Clay*, 9:608–9.

19. Nathaniel Beverley Tucker to Thomas Ritchie, July 12, 1845, Tyler Scrapbook, Tyler Family Papers, Swem Library, William and Mary.

20. James Madison to Thomas Jefferson, October 24, 1787, in Boyd, *Papers of Thomas Jefferson*, 12:271, 276; LaFeber, "Foreign Policies of a New Nation," 37; Alexander Hamilton concurred with Madison's view of the Constitution in the opening paragraph of *The Federalist*, 31: "The subject speaks of its own importance; comprehending in its consequences nothing less than the existence of the UNION, the safety and welfare of the parts of which it is composed, the fate of an empire in many respects the most interesting in the world."

21. Thomas Jefferson to Nathaniel Niles, March 22, 1801, Thomas Jefferson to James Madison, April 27, 1809, in Lipscomb and Bergh, *Writings of Thomas Jefferson*, 10:232–33; 12:277.

22. Richardson, *Messages and Papers*, 2:219.

23. Ibid., 4:40–51.

24. John Tyler to Daniel Webster, October 11, 1841, in Tyler, *Letters and Times*, 2:126.

25. Richardson, *Messages and Papers*, 4:41.

26. Tyler to Webster, October 11, 1841, in Tyler, *Letters and Times*, 2:126.

27. "Letter of President Tyler to a gathering of his political friends in Philadelphia, met to celebrate the birthday of Washington, Feb. 19, 1842," in *Philadelphia Ledger*, February 25, 1842, copy in John Tyler Collection, Alderman Library, University of Virginia; John Tyler to Robert Tyler, March 12, 1848, in Tyler, *Letters and Times*, 2:107.

Chapter 2

1. See advertisement for the sale of Greenway, *Richmond Enquirer*, September 10, 1805, in Tyler, *Letters and Times*, 2:188–90.

2. Ibid., 2:200–201.

3. Johnson, "James Madison," 1:168.

4. Madison, *Manifestations*; Holmes, *A Nation Mourns*, 31–32. See also Crowe, "Bishop James Madison and Republic of Virtue," 58–70.

5. Sprague, *Annals of Pulpit*, 5:321–23.

6. *Annals of Congress*, 8th Cong., 1st sess., 60.

7. John Tyler Sr. to Thomas Jefferson, June 10, 1804, in Tyler, *Letters and Times*, 1:206; Jefferson quoted in Malone, *Jefferson and His Time*, 4:316; Horsman, "Dimensions," 13.

8. John Tyler Sr. to James Madison, January 15, 1810, in Stagg, *Papers of James Madison*, 2:179.

9. Shepard, "John Tyler," 76–85; Tyler, *Letters and Times*, 1:281.

10. Wheeless, *Landmarks*, 109.

11. John Tyler to Thomas Jefferson, June 10, 1804, in Tyler, *Letters and Times*, 1:206.

12. Ibid., 1:321; Tyler, *Lecture Delivered before the Maryland Institute*, 14.

13. Tyler, *Letters and Times*, 1:317.

14. *Annals of Congress*, 16th Cong., 1st sess., 1956–60; Hunt, *Ideology*, 30–31.

15. Tyler, *Letters and Times*, 1:337, 348.

16. James Monroe to Governor John Tyler, August 13, 1826, James Monroe Papers, James Monroe Museum.

17. Wriston, *Executive Agents*, 206–7.

18. Belohlavek, *"Let the Eagle Soar!,"* 162–77, 253; Schroeder, *Shaping a Maritime Empire*, 32–33, 72–73.

19. Abell, *Life of John Tyler*, 129.

20. Speech of John Tyler, February 6, 1833, *Register of Debates*, 22nd Cong., 2nd sess., 362; John Tyler to John Coalter, May 29, 1834, Tyler Family Papers, Swem Library, William and Mary.

21. Robert, *Road from Monticello*, 92, 99; Freehling, *Drift Toward Dissolution*, xiii, 144–46; Richards, *Slave Power*, 104–6.

22. Child, *Appeal*, 30; Breen, "Female Antislavery Petition Campaign," 377–98.

23. The "Fathers and Rulers" petition is in Barnes and Dumond, *Letters of Weld*, 2:175–76.

24. Dillon, *Abolitionists*, 88–90; Simms, *Emotion at High Tide*, 84.

25. Dillon, *Abolitionists*, 90–91.

26. Richards, *"Gentlemen of Property,"* 64–71.

27. "Address at Gloucester Court House," August 22, 1835, in Tyler, *Letters and Times*, 1:574–79.

28. Ibid.

29. Ibid.

30. Newman, "Prelude to Gag Rule," 571–99.

31. Simms, *Emotion at High Tide*, 107.

32. Tyler, *Letters and Times*, 1:581; McKitrick, "Liberator," 55.

33. A. P. Upshur to N. B. Tucker, March 8, 1836, Tucker-Coleman Collection, Swem Library, William and Mary; Tucker, *Partisan Leader*; Upshur, "Domestic Slavery," 687; Wilentz, *Rise*, 198.

34. Tyler, "An Oration at York Town," 752.

35. "Address to the Virginia Colonization Society on January 10, 1838," in Tyler, *Letters and Times*, 1:567–70.

36. Legare, *Writings of Legare*, 1:322–28.

37. Cooper, *Liberty and Slavery*, 179.

38. McInerney, *Fortunate Heirs*, 149–50.

39. Crapol, "Foreign Policy of Antislavery," 92–93; James G. Birney to Myron Holley, Joshua Leavitt, and Elizur Wright Jr., May 11, 1840, in Dumond, *Letters of Birney*, 573.

Chapter 3

1. Fehrenbacher, *Slaveholding Republic*, xii.

2. Tyler, *Letters and Times*, 1:154.

3. Remarks of John Tyler, February 16, 1835, *Register of Debates*, 23rd Cong., 2nd sess., 456; Tyler, *Letters and Times*, 1:570–71; Seager, *and Tyler too*, 53.

4. Child, *Appeal*, 31.

5. Quoted in Chitwood, *John Tyler*, 142.

6. John Tyler, *Lecture Delivered before the Maryland Institute*, 14.

7. John Tyler to Henry Curtis, September 4, October 26, November 10, 1827, John Tyler Papers, Library of Congress.

8. Johnson, *Soul by Soul*, 78–79.

9. Diary entry of April 4, 1841, in *Memoirs of John Quincy Adams*, 10:456–57; Theodore D. Weld to Angelina G. Weld, January 2, 1842, January 1, 1843, in Barnes and Dumond, *Letters of Weld*, 2:885, 954.

10. Morgan, *Autobiography of Wilkes*, 521–22; Stevens, *Life of Peter Parker*, 220–23.

11. *Emancipator*, December 10, 1841.

12. *Madisonian*, December 28, 30, 1841; *Emancipator*, January 13, 1842.

13. Neiman, "Coincidence or Causal Connection," 198–210; *Richmond Times-Dispatch*, August 4, 1999.

14. *Liberator*, December 17, 1841; Richards, *Slave Power*, 1–2.

15. Richards, *Slave Power*, 93.

16. S. Jones, of Kings Creek, to John Tyler, April 14, 1841, in Tyler Family Papers, Swem Library, William and Mary.

17. For a full discussion of the Corn Law scheme, see Crapol, "Foreign Policy of Antislavery," 85–103.

18. Joseph Sturge to John G. Whittier, February 9, 1841, in Albree, *Whittier Correspondence*, 69–71; Sturge, *Visit*, 110.

19. Green, *Facts and Suggestions*, 119; Klunder, *Cass*, 106–10.

20. *Niles National Register*, November 4, 1843.

21. John Tyler to Samuel Gardiner, November 26, 1850, Tyler Family Papers, Swem Library, William and Mary; Abel P. Upshur to John C. Calhoun, August 14, 1843, reprinted in *William and Mary Quarterly* 16 (October 1936): 555.

22. Hall, *Upshur*, 120–22.

23. *Report of the Secretary of the Navy*, December 4, 1841, 27th Cong., 2nd sess., Senate Document #1, 379–81, 369.

24. Ibid., 380; Abel P. Upshur to Nathaniel B. Tucker, January 12, 1842, Tucker-Coleman Collection, Swem Library, William and Mary.

25. *Emancipator*, February 17, 1842.

26. Williams, *Maury*, 156.

27. *Southern Literary Messenger* 6 (April 1840): 233–40; (May 1840): 305–20; (December 1840): 785–800; 7 (January 1841): 2–25; (May 1841): 345–79.

28. Williams, *Maury*, 155–56; Hearn, *Tracks*, 103–8; Tyler, "Opening Address," 437–38.

29. MacLean, "Othello Scorned," 158.

30. Wise quoted in Simpson, *Good Southerner*, 36.

31. Quoted in Cleven, "First Panama Mission," 238.

32. *Emancipator*, February 17, 1842; Simpson, *Good Southerner*, 42–43; *National Intelligencer*, January 27, 1842.

33. Wriston, *Executive Agents*, 444–45.

34. Entry for January 22, 1858, in Scarborough, *Diary of Edmund Ruffin*, 1:149.

35. John Tyler to John C. Calhoun, October 7, 1845, in Jameson, *Calhoun Correspondence*, 2:1058; John Hogan to James Buchanan, received October 4, 1845, Senate Executive Document No. 17, 41st Cong., 3rd sess., Serial 1440, 41.

36. Fehrenbacher, *Slaveholding Republic*, 116.

Chapter 4

1. Sir Robert Peel to Queen Victoria, October 28, 1841, in Benson, *Letters of Queen Victoria*, 445–46.

2. John Tyler to Daniel Webster, March 12, 1846, in Van Tyne, *Letters of Daniel Webster*, 310–11.

3. Bourne, *Britain and the Balance of Power*, 94; Stevens, *Border Diplomacy*, 160–63; Watt, "Case of Alexander McLeod," 156–57.

4. Remarks of Francis W. Pickens, February 13, 1841, *Congressional Globe*, 26th Cong., 2nd sess., 170–75; Edmunds, *Pickens*, 22, 60–62.

5. Lord Sydenham to Lord John Russell, April 12, 1841, in Knaplund, *Letters from Lord Sydenham*, 133–34.

6. "Honors to the Brave," *Southern Literary Messenger* 7 (April 1841): 316–20; *Richmond Enquirer*, February 23, 1841; Heite, "Virginia Twists the Lion's Tail," 41–47.

7. Lewis Cass to Daniel Webster, March 5, 1841, in Shewmaker, *Papers of Daniel Webster*, 37–38.

8. Corey, *Crisis of 1830–1842*, 152–53; Woodward, "Age of Reinterpretation," 1–19.

9. Brescia, "'Defenses Strong Enough,'" 26.

10. Albert Fitz to Daniel Webster, July 21, 1842, in Shewmaker, *Papers of Daniel Webster*, 192.

11. Peel to Aberdeen, December 30, 1841, quoted in Remini, *Webster*, 537.

12. Jones, "Peculiar Institution," 28–50; Fehrenbacher, *Slaveholding Republic*, 108; Aptheker, *Documentary History*, 232.

13. Daniel Webster to Edward Everett, December 28, 1841, in Shewmaker, *Papers of Daniel Webster*, 170; Earl of Aberdeen to Queen Victoria, December 24, 1841, in Benson, *Letters of Queen Victoria*, 462.

14. Edward Everett to Daniel Webster, December 31, 1841, in Shewmaker, *Papers of Daniel Webster*, 173.

15. Edward Everett to Daniel Webster, January 3, 1842, ibid., 488; Carroll, *Good and Wise Measure*, 246, 388n7.

16. Daniel Webster to Edward Everett, January 29, 1842, in Shewmaker, *Papers of Daniel Webster*, 497; Edward Everett to Daniel Webster, January 31, 1842, 495.

17. Jones, "Peculiar Institution," 33–34; Richardson, *Messages and Papers*, 4:91.

18. *Madisonian*, January 21, 1842; Shewmaker, *Papers of Daniel Webster*, 521.

19. Joshua Leavitt to Joseph Sturge, January 28, 1842, quoted in Abel and Klingberg, *Side-Light*, 90–92; Hammond diary entry of March 21, 1842, in Bleser, *Secret and Sacred*, 88–89. A public charge of imbecility came in the August 17, 1842, issue of the *Daily Richmond Whig* when it denounced Tyler's rejection of a tariff bill: "Again has the imbecile, into whose hands accident has placed the power, vetoed a bill passed by a majority of those legally authorized to pass it." See Chitwood, *John Tyler*, 302.

20. Ashburton to Aberdeen, April 26, May 29, 1842, quoted in Jones, *To the Webster-Ashburton Treaty*, 118; Ashburton to Aberdeen, June 29, July 28, 1842, quoted in Jones, "Influence of Slavery," 49.

21. Remini, *Webster*, 548; diary entry of June 12, 1842, in Adams, *Memoirs*, 11:174–75.

22. John Tyler to Robert McCandlish, July 10, 1842, in Tyler, *Letters and Times*, 2:172–73.

23. Ibid.; remarks of John Minor Botts, January 10, 1843, *Congressional Globe*, 27th Cong., 3rd sess., 144–46.

24. Chitwood, *John Tyler*, 303–4; Peterson, *Presidencies*, 101–8; Seager, *and Tyler too*, 167–68.

25. *Richmond Enquirer*, November 16, 20, 23, 1838.

26. Richardson, *Messages and Papers*, 4:101.

27. Francis O. J. Smith to Daniel Webster, June 7, 1841, in Merk, *Fruits of Propaganda*, 143.

28. Francis O. J. Smith to Daniel Webster, August 12, 1842; Daniel Webster to Jared Sparks, May 14, 16, 1842; Jared Sparks to Daniel Webster, May 19, 1842, in Shewmaker, *Papers of Daniel Webster*, 681–82, 556, 562, 564–65.

29. Ashburton to Aberdeen, August 9, 1842, quoted in Jones and Rakestraw, *Prologue*, 130; Tyler quoted in Merk, *Fruits of Propaganda*, 65.

30. Daniel Webster to Jared Sparks, March 11, 1843, in Shewmaker, *Papers of Daniel Webster*, 786.

31. Tyler, *Letters and Times*, 2:216–18.

32. Daniel Webster to Lord Ashburton, August 8, 1842, in Shewmaker, *Papers of Daniel Webster*, 673–79.

33. Ashburton to Aberdeen, July 28, August 13, 1842, quoted in Jones, "Influence of Slavery," 49.

34. Daniel Webster to Henry Fox, April 24, 1841, in Shewmaker, *Papers of Daniel Webster*, 67; Tyler, *Letters and Times*, 2:207.

35. *New York Times*, September 27, 2002; Schlesinger, "Eyeless," 24–27.

36. John Tyler to Robert Tyler, August 29, 1858, in Tyler, *Letters and Times*, 2:240.

37. Jones, *To the Webster-Ashburton Treaty*, 150–52.

38. *National Intelligencer*, August 2, 1842; Philip Hone diary entry of August 2, 1842, in Nevins, *Diary of Philip Hone*, 613–14; Remini, *Webster*, 562–63.

39. John C. Calhoun to Thomas G. Clemson, August 22, 1842, in Jameson, *Calhoun Correspondence*, 2:515.

40. Jones, *To the Webster-Ashburton Treaty*, 165–67; *Emancipator*, October 20, 27, 1842; *National Anti-Slavery Standard*, September 22, 1842; *The Philanthropist*, September 10, 1842; Hone diary entry of September 2, 1842, in Nevins, *Diary of Philip Hone*, 618–19.

41. *Philanthropist*, October 1, 1842; Lewis Tappan to John Scoble, March 1, 1843, quoted in Abel and Klingberg, *Side-Light*, 113.

42. Zorn, "Criminal Extradition," 285, 288–89; Ashburton to John Scoble, November 4, 1842; quoted in Abel and Klingberg, *Side-Light*, 113.

43. Richardson, *Messages and Papers*, 4:196, 231; Peel's remarks of February 2, 1843, in *Hansard's Parliamentary Debates*, 3rd ser., 66 (1843): 88–91; Ashburton to Aberdeen, January 6, 1843, quoted in Jones, *American Problem*, 30; Aberdeen to Mr. Croker, February 25, 1843, in Jennings, *Croker Papers*, 2:397.

44. Richardson, *Messages and Papers*, 196; Aberdeen to Croker, February 25, 1843.

45. John Tyler to Edward Everett, April 27, 1843, Edward Everett Papers, Massachusetts Historical Society; Edward Everett to Charles Francis Adams, September 30, 1862, quoted in Frothingham, *Edward Everett*, 448.

46. *Letter from the Secretary of the Navy*, House Report 161, 28th Cong., 2nd sess., 1844–1845, 1–3; *Report from the Committee on Naval Affairs*, Senate Report 319, 31st Cong., 2nd sess., 1850–1851, 1–2.

47. John Tyler to John C. Calhoun, October 7, 1845, in Jameson, *Calhoun Correspondence*, 1058–60; Remarks of Andrew Kennedy, January 10, 1846, *Congressional Globe*, 29th Cong., 1st sess., 180.

48. Lord Ashburton to Mr. Croker, November 25, 1842, in Jennings, *Croker Papers*, 2:395.

49. "Official Misconduct of the Late Secretary of State," June 9, 1846, House Report No. 684, 29th Cong., 1st sess.; Merk, *Fruits of Propaganda*, 131–220.

50. Richardson, *Messages and Papers*, 4:431–36.

51. Remarks of Charles J. Ingersoll, April 27, 1846, *Congressional Globe*, 29th Cong., 1st sess., 730.

52. Daniel Webster to John Tyler, August 12, 1842, quoted in Remini, *Webster*, 565; Daniel Webster to Edward Everett, May 12, 1843, in Moser, *Papers of Daniel Webster*, 5:303–4.

Chapter 5

1. Tocqueville, *Democracy in America*, 1:421–22; *Report of the Secretary of the Navy*, December 7, 1842, House Document No. 2, 27th Cong., 3rd sess., 535.

2. Stevens and Martwick, *Life, Letters*, 326.

3. Ibid., 183, 327.

4. Peter Parker to Daniel Webster, January 30, 1841, ibid., 184–88.

5. Ibid., 327.

6. Ibid., 221; diary entry of June 2, 1842, in Adams, *Memoirs*, 11:166–67.

7. Journal entry of September 16, 1841, in the Peter Parker Papers, Historical Library, Cushing/Whitney Medical Library, Yale University; John Tyler to Daniel

Webster, March 12, 1846, in Van Tyne, *Letters of Daniel Webster*, 310–11; Roberts, *Embassy to the Eastern Courts*, 63–74.

8. Stevens and Martwick, *Life, Letters*, 223–24; Hammond diary entry of July 7, 1842, in Bleser, *Secret and Sacred*, 97–98.

9. Bradley, *American Frontier*, 311–15.

10. Hiram Bingham to Daniel Webster, July 10, 1841, Hiram Bingham to Rufus Anderson, July 23, 1841, ibid., 315.

11. Ibid., 403–5.

12. Hopkins, *Hawaii*, 275.

13. Peter Allan Brinsmade to Daniel Webster, April 8, 1842, in Shewmaker, *Papers of Daniel Webster*, 1:858–66.

14. Sullivan, *History of Brewer & Company*, 71; Peirce, *Biography*, 13.

15. Wilkes, *Narrative*, 4:8–9.

16. Hopkins, *Hawaii*, 254.

17. Sir George Simpson to Sir John H. Pelly, March 10, 1842, in Schafer, "Letters," 70–94.

18. See the informative essays in Viola and Margolis, *Magnificient Voyagers*.

19. Diary entry of June 15, 1842, Adams, *Memoirs*, 9:177; Henderson, *Hidden Coasts*, 207; Smith, "Wilkes," 148–51; Goetzmann, *New Lands*, 272, 275–76.

20. Julia Gardiner to Alexander Gardiner, December 13, 1842, Gardiner-Tyler Papers, Sterling Library, Yale University.

21. Journal of William Richards, December 13, 14, 1842, Hawaii State Archives, Honolulu.

22. Entry of December 7, 1842, ibid.; Richards, "Testimony," 97.

23. Journal of William Richards, December 8, 1842; diary entry of December 8, 1842, Adams, *Memoirs*, 11:274–75.

24. Adams, *Memoirs*.

25. Timoteo Haalilio and William Richards to Daniel Webster, December 14, 1842, in Shewmaker, *Papers of Daniel Webster*, 1:868–69.

26. Journal of William Richards, December 23, 24, 1842.

27. Ibid., December 27, 1842.

28. Daniel Webster to Timoteo Haalilio and William Richards, December 19, 1842, in Shewmaker, *Papers of Daniel Webster*, 1:870–71.

29. Journal of William Richards, December 30, 1842.

30. Daniel Webster to Edward Everett, December 29, 1842, March 23, 1843, in Shewmaker, *Papers of Daniel Webster*, 1:871, 876.

31. Richardson, *Messages and Papers*, 4:212.

32. Ibid., 4:214.

33. Caleb Cushing to John Tyler, December 27, 1842, Cushing Papers, Library of Congress.

34. Ibid.

35. See Daniel Webster to Isaac Rand Jackson, April 12, 1842, and Daniel Webster to David Porter, February 2, 1842, in Shewmaker, *Papers of Daniel Webster*, 1:264–65, 280–81.

36. *Emancipator*, January 12, 1843; diary entry of December 31, 1842, Adams, *Memoirs*, 11:284.

37. Timoteo Haalilio and William Richards to Daniel Webster, March 3, 1843, Daniel Webster to Edward Everett, March 23, 1843, in Shewmaker, *Papers of Daniel Webster*, 1:873, 876.

38. Richard Armstrong to Rueben A. Chapman, March 3, 1843, Richard Armstrong Papers, Library of Congress.

39. Edward Everett to Daniel Webster, November 30, 1842, quoted in Varg, *Edward Everett*, 95.

40. John Tyler to Hugh S. Legare, May 18, 1843, in Tyler, *Letters and Times*, 3:111.

41. Hugh S. Legare to Edward Everett, June 13, 1843, quoted in O'Brien, *Character*, 275–76.

42. John Tyler to Daniel Webster, July 8, 1843, in Tyler, *Letters and Times*, 2:272.

43. Timoteo Haalilio and William Richards to John C. Calhoun, July 1, 1844; John C. Calhoun to Timoteo Haalilio and William Richards, July 6, 1844, Hawaii State Archives, Honolulu.

44. Richardson, *Messages and Papers*, 4:194, 214.

45. Circular, Department of State, Washington, March 20, 1843, in Shewmaker, *Papers of Daniel Webster*, 1:901–2.

46. List of Articles for the Legation to China, April 11, 1843, ibid., 1:907–10.

47. Diary entry of August 2, 1842, Adams, *Memoirs*, 11:226.

48. Daniel Webster to Caleb Cushing, May 8, 1843, in Shewmaker, *Papers of Daniel Webster*, 1:922–23.

49. Ibid.

50. John Tyler to the Emperor of China, July 12, 1843, Senate Document #138, 28th Cong., 2nd sess., 8.

51. Cushing's speech quoted in Fuess, *Life of Cushing*, 1:414–15.

52. John Tyler to Daniel Webster, [January–February 1843], in Shewmaker, *Papers of Daniel Webster*, 1:894.

53. Cushing's Despatch #77, September 29, 1844, quoted in Downs, *Golden Ghetto*, 446.

54. Ch'i-ying quoted in Belohlavek, "Race, Progress," 35.

55. Quoted in Fuess, *Life of Cushing*, 1:437.

56. John Tyler to John C. Calhoun, August 3, 1844, in Wilson, *Papers of Calhoun*, 19:511; John Tyler to John S. Cunningham, November 4, 1855, in Tyler, *Letters and Times*, 2:200–201.

57. Julia Gardiner Tyler to Mrs. David Gardiner, December 6, 1844, in Tyler, *Letters and Times*, 2:358.

58. John Tyler to Caleb Cushing, October 14, 1845, ibid., 2:445.

59. Fuess, *Life of Cushing*, 2:19; Seager, *and Tyler too*, 304.

60. Pletcher, *Diplomacy of Involvement*, 99.

61. Richardson, *Messages and Papers*, 5:17, 120.

Chapter 6

1. Thomas Jefferson to James Monroe, May 14, 1820, in Lipscomb and Bergh, *Writings of Jefferson*, 15:251.

2. "Reminiscences of Mrs. Julia G. Tyler," in Tyler, *Letters and Times*, 3:200.

3. John Tyler to Daniel Webster, October 11, 1841, ibid., 2:126.

4. Henry A. Wise, "Speech in the House of Representatives," April 13, 1842, reprinted in Merk, *Slavery and Annexation of Texas*, 192–200.

5. Ibid., 192n8; *Congressional Globe*, 27 Cong., 2nd sess., 418. For a full account of Adams's reaction to Wise's speech see Lewis, *John Quincy Adams*, 132–33.

6. Thomas Walker Gilmer, letter to the *Baltimore Republican and Argus*, January 10, 1843, published January 19, 1843, reprinted in Merk, *Slavery and Annexation of Texas*, 200–204.

7. Ibid., 202.

8. Ibid., 203.

9. Ibid., 201.

10. Daniel Webster to Edward Everett, May 12, 1843, in Moser, *Papers of Webster*, 5:303–4; *National Intelligencer*, May 12, 1843.

11. Francis P. Blair to Andrew Jackson, April 4, 1841, in Bassett, *Correspondence of Jackson*, 6:98.

12. John Tyler to John C. Spencer, May 12, 1843, John Tyler Papers, Library of Congress. For data on Tyler's removals, see Fish, *Civil Service*, 151–54, 252.

13. Foos, *Short, Offhand*, 72–73; Burrows and Wallace, *Gotham*, 635.

14. Abell, *Life*; Alexander Abell to Ephraim Spooner, November 29, 1843, John Tyler Jr. to Ephraim Spooner, November 29, 1843, Abell to Spooner, December 20, 1843, Plymouth Antiquan Society, Plymouth, Massachusetts. I am grateful to my former student and longtime friend Robert W. Smith for bringing these letters to my attention.

15. Chitwood, *Tyler*, 319.

16. Coleman, *Priscilla Cooper Tyler*, 103–4.

17. Ibid., 104.

18. Entry of June 12, 1843, Nevins and Thomas, *Diary of Strong*, 1:205.

19. The *New York Morning Express* is quoted in Chitwood, *Tyler*, 320–21.

20. *New York Herald*, June 13, 1843.

21. Ibid.

22. Coleman, *Priscilla Cooper Tyler*, 104.

23. George Allen to Joseph Greenleaf, Postmaster, Brockport, Monroe County, New York, June 16, 1843, Tyler Family Papers, Swem Library, William and Mary.

24. "An Address delivered on Bunker Hill, on the 17th of June, 1843," in Webster, *Writings and Speeches*, 1:271.

25. Diary entry of June 17, 1843, in Adams, *Memoirs*, 11:383.

26. Bartlett, *Phillips*, 127.

27. "The Dead of the Cabinet," an address delivered at Petersburg on April 24, 1856, in Tyler, *Letters and Times*, 2:387.

28. Abel P. Upshur to Nathaniel B. Tucker, June 24, July 15, 1843, Tucker-Coleman Collection, Swem Library, William and Mary.

29. Abel P. Upshur to Nathaniel B. Tucker, October 26, 1843, ibid.

30. John Tyler to Waddy Thompson, August 28, 1843, *William and Mary Quarterly* 12 (January 1904): 140–41.

31. Abel P. Upshur to Nathaniel B. Tucker, November 2, 1843, Tucker-Coleman Collection, Swem Library, William and Mary.

32. Abel P. Upshur to Nathaniel B. Tucker, October 10, 1843, ibid.

33. Abel P. Upshur to Edward Everett, September 28, 1843, in Manning, *Diplomatic Correspondence*, 7:6–17.

34. Edward Everett to Abel P. Upshur, November 3, 16, 1843, 7:246–51, ibid.

35. John Tyler to John C. Calhoun, June 5, 1848, in Jameson, *Calhoun Correspondence*, 2:1173.

36. Abel P. Upshur to Juan Almonte, November 8, December 1, 1843, in Manning, *Diplomatic Correspondence*, 8:141, 147.

37. Abel P. Upshur to Nathaniel B. Tucker, December 4, 1843, Tucker-Coleman Collection, Swem Library, William and Mary.

38. Richardson, *Messages and Papers*, 4:260–62.

39. Aberdeen to Cowley, January 12, 1844, cited in Adams, *British Interests*, 158.

40. Abel P. Upshur to William S. Murphy, November 21, 1843, January 16, 23, 1844, in Manning, *Diplomatic Correspondence*, 12:58–69.

41. Isaac Van Zandt to Abel P. Upshur, January 17, 1844, H.R. Document 271, 28th Cong., 1st sess., 89; Van Zandt to Jones, January 20, 1844, cited in Rives, *United States and Mexico*, 582.

42. Henry Clay to John J. Crittenden, February 15, 1844, in Hopkins, *Papers of Henry Clay*, 10:6–7.

43. "Letter of Mr. Walker," reprinted in Merk, *Fruits of Propaganda*, 221–52. Citations from the letter are on pp. 1, 2, 8, 10, 11, and 14 of the facsimile of the original.

44. Ibid., 15.

45. Miles, "Princeton," 2225–45; Stockton, *Sketch*, 87–93; Hall, *Upshur*, 209–13.

46. John Tyler to Mary Jones, March 4, 1844, in Tyler, *Letters and Times*, 2:289.

47. Isaac Van Zandt to Anson Jones, February 27 [29th?], 1844, in Jones, *Memoranda*, 323.

48. Joshua Leavitt to John Scoble, March 1, 1844; Lewis Tappan to John Scoble, March 28, 1844, quoted in Abel and Klingberg, *Side-Light*, 177–78, 180.

49. "The Dead of the Cabinet," in Tyler, *Letters and Times*, 2:391.

50. Patrick Calhoun to John C. Calhoun, February 28, 1844, in Wilson, *Papers of Calhoun*, 17:806–7.

51. George McDuffie to John C. Calhoun, March 5, 1844, ibid., 17:815.

52. John Tyler to John C. Calhoun, March 6, 1844, ibid., 17:828.

53. John C. Calhoun to Isaac Van Zandt and J. Pinckney Henderson, April 11, 1844, ibid., 18:208–9.

54. Isaac Van Zandt and J. Pinckney Henderson to Anson Jones, April 12, 1844, ibid., 18:220–21.

55. Ibid.

56. Richardson, *Messages and Papers*, 4:312.

57. Ibid., 4:312–13.

58. Feller, "Brother in Arms," 66–67; "Proceedings of the Senate and Documents Relative to Texas, from which the Injunction of Secrecy Has Been Removed," May 16, 1844, Senate Document No. 341, 28th Cong., 1st sess.

59. John C. Calhoun to Richard Pakenham, April 18, 1844, in Wilson, *Papers of Calhoun*, 18:273–78; Stanton, *Leopard's Spots*, 61–65.

60. Walters, *Gallatin*, 376–77; entry of April 24, 1844, in Nevins and Thomas, *Diary of Strong*, 1:229.

61. LaFeber, "Expansionist's Dilemma," 7.

62. Speech on Annexation of Texas, May 22, 1844, in Basler, *Collected Works*, 1:337.

63. Address by Secretary of War William Wilkins to the People of Pennsylvania, April 13, 1844, in Williams, *Shaping*, 1:176–77.

64. Kesilman, "John Tyler and the Presidency," 189.

65. John Tyler to Thomas T. Cropper et al., May 30, 1844; John Tyler to Henry Wise, April 20, 1852, in Tyler, *Letters and Times*, 2:321, 317.

66. John Tyler to the House of Representatives, June 10, 1844, Richardson, *Messages and Papers*, 4:327.

67. Julia Gardiner Tyler to Margaret Gardiner Beekman, November 13, 1844, Gardiner-Tyler Papers, Sterling Library, Yale University; Kirk, *Music at White House*, 56; Seager, "Julia Gardiner Tyler," 3:494–96.

68. Richardson, *Messages and Papers*, 4:344–45.

69. Peterson, *Presidencies*, 255–59.

70. Julia Gardiner Tyler to Juliana Gardiner, March 6, 1845, in Tyler, *Letters and Times*, 2:368–70.

71. "Reminiscences," ibid., 3:200.

72. Henry Clay to Nathaniel Beverley Tucker, January 11, 1845, Tucker-Coleman Collection; Henry Clay to John J. Crittenden, January 9, 1845, in Hopkins, *Papers of Henry Clay*, 10:187.

73. "Walker Memoranda," in Tyler, *Letters and Times*, 3:152–53.

74. Albert Gallatin to D. Dudley Field, December 17, 1844, February 10, 1845, in Adams, *Writings of Gallatin*, 2:605–10.

75. John Tyler to Alexander Gardiner, August 7, 1848, Gardiner-Tyler Papers, Sterling Library, Yale University.

76. John Tyler to John C. Calhoun, October 7, 1845, in Jameson, *Calhoun Correspondence*, 2:1059.

Chapter 7

1. Tyler, "John Tyler and the Ladies," 1–4.

2. Ibid., 3–4.

3. "Convention of Texas, 1845, Resolution, Expression of the Gratitude of this Convention to Ex-President Tyler and his Cabinet," *William and Mary Quarterly*, 1st ser., 14 (July 1906): 41–42; Smith, *Annexation of Texas*, 459.

4. John C. Calhoun, "Speech in Reply to Thomas Hart Benton on the Mexican War," February 24, 1847, in Wilson, *Papers of Calhoun*, 24:196; John Tyler to Alexander Gardiner, March 11, 1847, in Tyler, *Letters and Times*, 2:420.

5. John Tyler to Alexander Gardiner, June 17, 1847, in Tyler, *Letters and Times*, 2:426; Julia Gardiner Tyler to Alexander Gardiner, March 4, 1847, Gardiner-Tyler Papers, Sterling Library, Yale University.

6. John Tyler to John C. Calhoun, March 27, 1847, in Wilson, *Papers of Calhoun*, 24:281.

7. Child, *American Anti-Slavery Almanac*, 39.

8. John Tyler to the *Richmond Enquirer*, June 5, 1847, in Tyler, *Letters and Times*, 2:425.

9. Wyatt-Brown, *Lewis Tappan*, 277–78.

10. Sam Houston to F. L. Hatch, editor of the *Texas Banner*, July 18, 1847, in Williams and Barker, *Writings*, 5:14–18.

11. John Tyler to the editor of the *Richmond Enquirer*, September 1, 1847, in Tyler, *Letters and Times*, 2:428–31.

12. Sam Houston to F. L. Hatch, October 20, 1847, in Williams and Barker, *Writings*, 5:26; Tyler, *Letters and Times*, 2:433.

13. John S. Cunningham to John Tyler, January 27, 1851, John Tyler to John S. Cunningham, February 5, 1851, in Tyler, *Letters and Times*, 2:411–13.

14. Sellers, *Polk*, 2:218–19.

15. Dusinberre, *Slavemaster President*, 132–33.

16. Richardson, *Messages and Papers*, 4:380.

17. Diary entries of May 27, 30, 1846, in Quaife, *Diary of Polk*, 1:431, 437–38.

18. Ibid., 1:440.

19. [John Tyler] to the editor of the *Portsmouth Pilot*, n.d. [February 1847] in Tyler, *Letters and Times*, 2:477–78.

20. John Tyler to Alexander Gardiner, March 2, 1847, ibid., 2:479.

21. Richardson, *Messages and Papers*, 4:588.

22. John Tyler to David L. Gardiner, March 7, 1849, Tyler Family Papers, Swem Library, William and Mary; John Tyler to Gen. Thomas Green, February 29, 1856, Huntington Library, Tyler Collection.

23. Julia Gardiner Tyler to Juliana Gardiner, December 15, 1848, Tyler Family Papers, Swem Library, William and Mary.

24. John Tyler to Alexander Gardiner, February 21, March 9, 1849, Gardiner-Tyler Papers, Sterling Library, Yale University.

25. John Tyler to David Gardiner, December 7, 1849, Tyler Family Papers, Swem Library, William and Mary.

26. Ibid.

27. John Tyler to Henry S. Foote, May 21, 1850, in Tyler, *Letters and Times*, 2:485–89.

28. John Tyler to Robert Tyler, July 16, 1849, ibid., 2:491; Sanka Knox, "Dealer Here Gets 1849 Tyler Letter," *New York Times*, December 7, 1958, 136.

29. "Diplomatic Relations with Austria," Speech of Mr. Foote of Mississippi, in the Senate, January 8, 1850, 31st Cong., 1st sess., Appendix, 43–47.

30. John Tyler to ———, February 3, 1852, Tyler Family Papers, Swem Library, William and Mary.

31. Ibid.; John Q. Adams, *Address on Fourth of July, 1821.*

32. Tyler, *Lecture at Petersburg*, 6.

33. Tyler, "To the Duchess of Sutherland," 120–26.

34. Ibid., 121–22; Pugh, "Women and Slavery," 186–202.

35. Thomas Jefferson to John Holmes, April 22, 1820, quoted in Bernstein, *Jefferson*, 185.

36. Tyler, *Lecture Delivered before the Maryland Institute*, 14–16, 23.

37. Ibid., 23.

38. "Address of John Tyler at Jamestown, May 13, 1857, on the Two Hundred and Fiftieth Anniversary of the First English Settlement in America," in Tyler, *Letters and Times*, 1:2, 33; Rives, "Jamestown Celebration," 259–71.

39. Tyler, *Letters and Times*, 1:33–34; Kiracofe, "Jamestown Jubilees," 53–55.

40. Tyler, "Ruffin's Visit," 193–211.

41. John Tyler to Robert Tyler, September 5, 1857, in Tyler, *Letters and Times*, 2:236–37.

42. Ibid., 2:237–38; Takaki, *Pro-Slavery Crusade*, 71–72.

43. Shade, *Democratizing the Old Dominion*, 191.

44. Eben N. Horsford to M. C. Horsford, February 14, 1852, Horsford Family Papers, Institute Archives and Special Collections, Rensselaer Polytechnic Institute.

45. Julia Gardiner Tyler to Margaret Gardiner, June 10, 1845; Julia Gardiner Tyler to Brother, [April 1845], Tyler Family Papers, Swem Library, William and Mary.

46. Juliana Gardiner to Julia Gardiner Tyler, November 18, 1845, in Seager, *and Tyler too*, 602.

47. "Ex-President Tyler's Household Loses an Aristocratic 'Article,'" in Still, *Underground Rail Road*, 69–70.

48. Ibid.

49. Collins and Weaver, *Wills*, 87–88.

50. Reynolds, *John Brown*, 395.

51. Julia Gardiner Tyler to Juliana Gardiner, November 14, December 1, 1859, Tyler Family Papers, Swem Library, William and Mary.

52. John Tyler to James Lyons, October 28, 1859, Brock Collection, Huntington Library.

53. Collins and Weaver, *Wills*, 88.

54. Tyler quoted in Chitwood, *Tyler*, 432.

55. Speech at Worcester, Massachusetts, September 12, 1848, in Basler, *Collected Works*, 2:4.

56. John Tyler to Silas Reed, November 16, 1860, John Tyler Papers, Library of Congress.

57. Reese, *Proceedings*, 1:650.

58. Abraham Lincoln to James T. Hale, January 11, 1861, in Basler, *Collected Works*, 4:172.

59. Remarks of Roscoe Conkling, January 30, 1861, *Congressional Globe*, 36th Cong., 2nd sess., 651.

60. Rhett quoted in Hesseltine and Smiley, *South*, 606.

61. Matthew Fontaine Maury to B. Franklin Minor, January 28, 1861, Matthew Fontaine Maury Papers, Library of Congress.

62. Matthew Fontaine Maury to Rutson Maury, January 24, 1861, ibid.

63. Julia Gardiner Tyler to Juliana Gardiner, February 3, 4, 1861, in Tyler, *Letters and Times*, 2:596–97.

64. "Address to the Peace Conference, February 5, 1861," ibid., 2:598–600.

65. Gunderson, *Old Gentlemen's Convention*, 10; Shaw, *Lincoln*, 159.

66. Sandburg, *Lincoln*, 1:89–90.

67. John Tyler's remarks of March 13, 1861, in Reese, *Proceedings*, 1:653.

68. Tyler's remarks of March 14, 1861, ibid., 1:669.

69. Jones, *Rebel War Clerk's Diary*, 6.

70. John Tyler to Julia Gardiner Tyler, April 17 [18?], 1861, in Tyler, *Letters and Times*, 2:641–42.

Conclusion

1. Julia Gardiner Tyler to Juliana Gardiner, June 16, 1861, in Tyler, *Letters and Times*, 2:651.

2. John Tyler's Resolutions, ibid., 2:660–61.

3. *Richmond Whig*, July 23, 1861; *Richmond Daily Examiner*, September 27, 1861.

4. McPherson, "Fruits of Preventive War," 5–6.

5. Coleman, *Priscilla Cooper Tyler*, 136–42.

6. John Tyler and Hill Carter to the Secretary of War, August 26, 1861, in *Official Records of the Union and Confederate Armies*, Series 1, 4:636.

7. Jones, *Rebel War Clerk's Diary*, 40; Julia Gardiner Tyler to Juliana Gardiner, April 25, 1861, in Tyler, *Letters and Times*, 2:648.

8. General Edward A. Wild to General Benjamin F. Butler, May 13, 1864, in Butler, *Correspondence*, 4:203.

9. "Introduction," *Index to the John Tyler Papers*, vi.

10. Peckham, "Echo," 613–14.

11. *New York Times*, January 22, 1862; Seager, *and Tyler too*, 472.

12. Entry for November 12, 1857, in Scarborough, *Diary of Ruffin*, 1:126; the

inscribed bookplate is in Abell, *Life of John Tyler*, Rare Book Collection, Swem Library, William and Mary.

13. John Tyler to Julia Tyler, April 16, 1861, in Tyler, *Letters and Times*, 2:640; Peskin, *Winfield Scott*, 244.

14. Kirwan, *Crittenden*, 469–70.

15. Wilson, *History of the Rise and Fall*, 1:564.

16. Tyler, *Letters and Times*, 1:436; Richardson, *Messages and Papers*, 7:221–22.

17. *Washington Post*, November 4, 2004; Woodward, *Plan*, 88.

18. *Chicago Tribune*, January 31, 1893.

19. *New York Times*, November 16, 1895; *Annexation of Hawaii*, March 16, 1898, Senate Report No. 681, 55th Cong., 2nd sess.; *Annexation of the Hawaiian Islands*, May 17, 1898, House Report No. 1355, 55th Cong., 2nd sess.

20. Tansill, "War Powers," 41–47; Nelson, *Almost a Territory*, 85.

21. Ames, *History of the National Intelligencer*, 269; Schlesinger, *Imperial Presidency*, 39–41, 46–47.

BIBLIOGRAPHY

Manuscript and Archival Collections
Boston, Massachusetts
    Massachusetts Historical Society
        Adams Family Papers (microfilm)
        Edward Everett Papers
Charlottesville, Virginia
    Alderman Library, University of Virginia
        John Tyler Collection
Durham, North Carolina
    Duke University
        John Tyler Collection
Fredricksburg, Virginia
    James Monroe Museum
        James Monroe Papers
Honolulu, Hawaii
    Hawaii State Archives
        Foreign Office & Executive Office Papers
        Journal of William Richards
    Mission Houses Museum
        Hawaiian Mission Children's Society Collections
Morgantown, West Virginia
    West Virginia and Regional History Collection, West Virginia University
        Oliver Perry Chitwood Papers
        John Tyler Collection
New Haven, Connecticut
    Historical Library, Cushing/Whitney Medical Library, Yale University
        Peter Parker Papers
    Sterling Library, Yale University
        Gardiner-Tyler Papers
Plymouth, Massachusetts
    Plymouth Antiquan Society
        Ephraim Spooner Papers

Richmond, Virginia
    Virginia Historical Society
        Tyler Family Papers
San Marino, California
    The Huntington Library
        Brock Collection, Tyler Papers
Troy, New York
    Institute Archives and Special Collections, Folsom Library, Rensselaer
            Polytechnic Institute
        Horsford Family Papers
Washington, D.C.
    Library of Congress
        Richard Armstrong Papers
        Caleb Cushing Papers
        Matthew Fontaine Maury Papers
        John Tyler Papers
Williamsburg, Virginia
    Special Collections, Swem Library, College of William and Mary
        Dew Family Papers
        Tucker-Coleman Collection
        Tyler Family Papers

Government Publications

United States

CONGRESSIONAL
Annals of Congress
Register of Debates
Congressional Globe
House of Representatives. *Annexation of the Hawaiian Islands*. House Report No.
    1355, 55th Cong., 2nd sess., 1898. Washington, D.C.: 1898.
———. *Letter from the Secretary of the Navy*. House Report No. 161, 28th Cong.,
    2nd sess., 1844–1845. Washington, D.C.: 1845.
———. *Official Misconduct of the Late Secretary of State*. House Report No. 684,
    29th Cong., 1st sess., 1846. Washington, D.C.: 1846.
———. *Report of the Secretary of the Navy*. House Document No. 2, 27th Cong.,
    3rd sess., 1842. Washington, D.C.: 1842.
Senate. *Annexation of Hawaii*. Senate Report No. 681, 55th Cong., 2nd sess., 1898.
    Washington, D.C.: 1898.
———. *John Tyler to the Emperor of China, July 12, 1843*. Senate Document No.
    138, 28th Cong., 2nd sess., 1843. Washington, D.C.: 1843.
———. *Proceedings of the Senate and Documents Relative to Texas, from which
    the Injunction of Secrecy Has Been Removed*. Senate Document No. 341, 28th
    Cong., 1st sess., 1844. Washington, D.C.: 1844.

————. *Report from the Committee on Naval Affairs*. Senate Report No. 319, 31st Cong., 2nd sess., 1850–1851. Washington, D.C.: 1851.

OTHER

War Department. *The War of the Rebellion: A Compilation of the Official Records of the Union and Confederate Armies*. 128 vols. Washington, D.C.: 1880–1901.

Library of Congress. Manuscript Division. Reference Department. *Index to the John Tyler Papers*. Washington, D.C.: 1961.

Great Britain
Hansard's Parliamentary Debates.

Newspapers and Magazines
Chicago Tribune
Debow's Review
Emancipator
Harper's Weekly
Madisonian
National Anti-Slavery Standard
National Intelligencer
New York Herald
New York Times
Niles National Register
North American Review
Philanthropist
Richmond Daily Examiner
Richmond Dispatch
Richmond Enquirer
Richmond Times-Dispatch
Richmond Whig
Southern Literary Messenger
Vanity Fair
Washington Post

Published Sources
Abel, Anne Heloise, and Frank J. Klingberg, eds. *A Side-Light on Anglo-American Relations, 1839–1858: Furnished by the Correspondence of Lewis Tappan and Others with the British and Foreign Anti-Slavery Society*. Lancaster, Pa.: Association for the Study of Negro Life and History, 1927.

Abell, Alexander Gordon. *Life of John Tyler*. New York: Harper and Brothers, 1844.

Adams, Charles Francis, ed. *Memoirs of John Quincy Adams*. Vols. 9–11. Reprint. Freeport, N.Y.: Books for Libraries Press, 1969.

Adams, Ephraim D. *British Interests and Activities in Texas, 1838–1846*. Reprint. Gloucester: Peter Smith, 1963.

Adams, Henry, ed. *The Writings of Albert Gallatin*. 3 vols. Philadelphia: J. B. Lippincott & Company, 1879.

Adams, John Quincy. *An Address Delivered at the Request of a Commission of the Citizens of Washington; on the Occasion of Reading the Declaration of Independence, on the Fourth of July, 1821*. Washington, D.C.: Davis and Force, 1821.

Albree, John, ed. *Whittier Correspondence from the Oak Knoll Collections, 1830–1892*. Salem: Essex Book and Print Club, 1911.

Allgor, Catherine. *Parlor Politics: in which the Ladies of Washington Help Build a City and a Government*. Charlottesville: University Press of Virginia, 2000.

Ames, William E. *A History of the National Intelligencer*. Chapel Hill: University of North Carolina Press, 1972.

Aptheker, Herbert, ed. *A Documentary History of the Negro People in the United States*. New York: Citadel Press, 1951.

Auchampaugh, Philip Gerald. *Robert Tyler, Southern Rights Champion, 1847–1866; A Documentary Study Chiefly of Antebellum Politics*. Duluth: Himan Stein, 1934.

Barnes, Gilbert H., and Dwight L. Dumond, eds. *Letters of Theodore Dwight Weld, Angelina Grimke Weld, and Sarah Grimke, 1822–1844*. 2 vols. Gloucester: Peter Smith Reprint, 1965.

Bartlett, Irving H. *Wendell Phillips, Brahmin Radical*. Boston: Beacon Press, 1961.

Basler, Roy P., ed. *The Collected Works of Abraham Lincoln*. 9 vols. New Brunswick, N.J.: Rutgers University Press, 1953.

Bassett, John Spencer, ed. *Correspondence of Andrew Jackson*. 7 vols. New York: Kraus, 1969.

Belohlavek, John M. *Broken Glass: Caleb Cushing and the Shattering of the Union*. Kent, Ohio: Kent State University Press, 2005.

———. *"Let the Eagle Soar!": The Foreign Policy of Andrew Jackson*. Lincoln: University of Nebraska Press, 1985.

———. "Race, Progress, and Destiny: Caleb Cushing and the Quest for American Empire." In *Manifest Destiny and Empire: American Antebellum Expansionism*, ed. Sam W. Haynes and Christopher Morris, 21–47. College Station: Texas A&M University Press, 1997.

Bemis, Samuel Flagg. *John Quincy Adams and the Foundations of American Foreign Policy*. New York: Alfred A. Knopf, 1949.

———. *John Quincy Adams and the Union*. New York: Alfred A. Knopf, 1956.

Benetz, Margaret Diamond, ed. *The Cushing Reports: Ambassador Caleb Cushing's Confidential Diplomatic Reports to the United States Secretary of State, 1843–1844: Mexico, Egypt, the Barbary States, India, Ceylon*. Salisbury, N.C.: Documentary Publications, 1976.

Benson, Arthur C., ed. *The Letters of Queen Victoria: A Selection from Her Majesty's Correspondence between the Years 1837 and 1861*. London: John Murray, 1907.

Benton, Thomas Hart. *Thirty Years' View, or a History of the Working of the*

American Government for Thirty Years from 1820 to 1850. 2 vols. New York: D. Appleton, 1854–56.

Bernstein, R. B. *Thomas Jefferson.* New York: Oxford University Press, 2003.

Bingham, Hiram. *A Residence of Twenty-One Years in the Sandwich Islands.* 2nd ed. Hartford: Hezehrah Huntington, 1848.

Bleser, Carol, ed. *Secret and Sacred: The Diaries of James Henry Hammond, a Southern Slaveholder.* New York: Oxford University Press, 1988.

Blight, David W. "Perceptions of Southern Intransigence and the Rise of Radical Antislavery Thought, 1816–1830." *Journal of the Early Republic* 3 (Summer 1983): 139–63.

Bourne, Kenneth. *Britain and the Balance of Power in North America, 1815–1908.* London: Longmans, 1967.

Bowers, Claude G. *John Tyler, An Address by Hon. Claude G. Bowers of New York at the Unveiling of the Bust of President Tyler in the State Capitol, Richmond, Virginia, June 16, 1931.* Richmond: Richmond Press, 1932.

Boyd, Julian, ed. *The Papers of Thomas Jefferson.* Vol. 12. Princeton, N.J.: Princeton University Press, 1955.

Bradley, Harold Whitman. *The American Frontier in Hawaii: The Pioneers 1789–1843.* Stanford, Calif.: Stanford University Press, 1942.

Brauer, Kinley J. "Economics and the Diplomacy of American Expansionism, 1821–1861." In *Economics and World Power: An Assessment of American Diplomacy since 1789,* ed. William H. Becker and Samuel F. Wells, Jr., 55–116. New York: Columbia University Press, 1984.

———. "The United States and British Imperial Expansion, 1815–60." *Diplomatic History* 12 (Winter 1988): 19–37.

Breen, Patrick H. "The Female Antislavery Petition Campaign of 1831–32." *Virginia Magazine of History and Biography* 110, no. 3 (2002): 377–398.

Brescia, Anthony M. "'Defenses Strong Enough to Defy the World': The Visit of a U.S. State Department Special Agent to Bermuda in 1841." *Bulletin of the Institute of Maritime History and Archaeology* 10 (December 1987): 11–12, 14, 16, 25–26.

Brugger, Robert J. *Beverley Tucker: Heart over Head in the Old South.* Baltimore: Johns Hopkins University Press, 1978.

Burrows, Edwin G., and Mike Wallace. *Gotham: A History of New York City to 1898.* New York: Oxford University Press, 1999.

Butler, Benjamin F. *Private and Official Correspondence of Gen. Benjamin F. Butler.* Vol. 4. Norwood: Plimpton Press, 1917.

Cain, Marvin R. "Return of Republicanism: A Reappraisal of Hugh Swinton Legare and The Tyler Presidency." *South Carolina Historical Magazine* 79 (October 1978): 264–80.

Carpenter, Fred G. "A Talk with a President's Son." *Lippincott's* 41 (March 1888): 416–18.

Carroll, Francis M. *A Good and Wise Measure: The Search for the Canadian-American Boundary, 1783–1842.* Toronto: University of Toronto Press, 2001.

Child, Lydia Maria. *The American Anti-Slavery Almanac for 1843*. New York: American Anti-Slavery Society, 1843.

———. *An Appeal in Favor of That Class of Americans Called Africans*. New York: John S. Taylor, 1836.

Chitwood, Oliver P. *John Tyler, Champion of the Old South*. New York: D. Appleton-Century Company, 1939.

Christian, George L. *John Tyler, Address Delivered before the Colonial Dames of America in the State of Virginia at Greenway, Charles City County, Va., on Monday, October 27, 1913, at the Unveiling of a Memorial to Mark the Birthplace of President Tyler*. Richmond: Whittet & Shepperson, 1913.

Cleaves, Freeman. *Old Tippecanoe: William Henry Harrison and His Time*. New York: Charles Scribner's Sons, 1939.

Cleven, Andrew N. "The First Panama Mission and the Congress of the United States." *Journal of Negro History* 13 (July 1928): 225–54.

Coffman, Tom. *Nation Within: The Story of America's Annexation of the Nation of Hawai'i*. Honolulu: Tom Coffman/Epicenter, 1998.

Cole, Donald B. *Martin Van Buren and the American Political System*. Princeton, N.J.: Princeton University Press, 1984.

Coleman, Elizabeth Tyler. *Priscilla Cooper Tyler and the American Scene, 1816–1889*. Nashville: Weatherford Printing Company, 1955.

Collins, Herbert R., and David B. Weaver. *Wills of the U.S. Presidents*. New York: Communication Channels, 1976.

Cooper, William J., Jr. *Liberty and Slavery: Southern Politics to 1860*. New York: Alfred A. Knopf, 1983.

Corey, Albert B. *The Crisis of 1830–1842 in Canadian-American Relations*. New Haven, Conn.: Yale University Press, 1941.

Corwin, Edward C. *The President, Office and Powers, 1787–1957*. 4th rev. ed. New York: New York University Press, 1962.

Crapol, Edward P. "The Foreign Policy of Antislavery, 1833–1846." In *Redefining the Past: Essays in Diplomatic History in Honor of William Appleman Williams*, ed. Lloyd C. Gardner, 85–103. Corvallis: Oregon State University Press, 1986.

———. "John Tyler and the Pursuit of National Destiny." *Journal of the Early Republic* 17 (Fall 1997): 467–91.

———. "Lydia Maria Child: Abolitionist Critic of American Foreign Policy." In *Women and American Foreign Policy: Lobbyists, Critics, and Insiders*, 2nd ed., ed. Edward P. Crapol, 1–18. Wilmington, Del.: Scholarly Resources, 1992.

Craven, Avery, and Frank E. Vandiver. *The American Tragedy: The Civil War in Retrospect*. Hampden-Sydney, Va.: Hampden-Sydney College, 1959.

Crofts, Daniel W. *Reluctant Confederates: Upper South Unionists in the Secession Crisis*. Chapel Hill: University of North Carolina Press, 1989.

Crowe, Charles. "Bishop James Madison and the Republic of Virtue." *Journal of Southern History* 30 (February 1964): 58–70.

Dalzell, Robert F., Jr. *Daniel Webster and the Trial of American Nationalism, 1845–1852*. Boston: Houghton Mifflin Company, 1973.

————. *Enterprising Elite: The Boston Associates and the World They Made.* Cambridge: Harvard University Press, 1987.

Davis, William C., ed. *A Fire-Eater Remembers: The Confederate Memoirs of Robert Barnwell Rhett.* Columbia: University of South Carolina Press, 2000.

DeLaney, Theodore C. "Surviving Defeat: The Trials of 'Mrs. Ex-President Tyler.'" In *Virginia's Civil War*, ed. Peter Wallenstein and Bertram Wyatt-Brown, 230–42. Charlottesville: University of Virginia Press, 2005.

DeLeon, Thomas C. *Four Years in Rebel Capitals.* Mobile: Gossip Printing Company, 1892.

Dew, Charles B. *Apostles of Disunion: Southern Secession Commissioners and the Causes of the Civil War.* Charlottesville: University Press of Virginia, 2001.

Dillon, Merton. *The Abolitionists: The Growth of a Dissenting Minority.* DeKalb: Northern Illinois University Press, 1974.

Dinnerstein, Leonard. "The Accession of John Tyler to the Presidency." *Virginia Magazine of History and Biography* 70 (October 1962): 447–58.

Dodge, Ernest S. *Islands and Empires: Western Impact on the Pacific and East Asia.* Minneapolis: University of Minnesota Press, 1976.

Downs, Jacques M. *The Golden Ghetto: The American Commercial Community at Canton and the Shaping of American China Policy, 1784–1844.* Bethlehem: Lehigh University Press, 1997.

Dudden, Arthur Power. *The American Pacific: From the Old China Trade to the Present.* New York: Oxford University Press, 1992.

Dumond, Dwight L., ed. *The Letters of James G. Birney.* Gloucester: Peter Smith, 1966.

Dusinberre, William. *Slavemaster President: The Double Career of James K. Polk.* New York: Oxford University Press, 2003.

Edmunds, John B., Jr. *Francis W. Pickens and the Politics of Destruction.* Chapel Hill: University of North Carolina Press, 1986.

Ellis, Joseph J. *Founding Brothers: The Revolutionary Generation.* New York: Alfred A. Knopf, 2001.

Faust, Drew Gilpin, ed. *The Ideology of Slavery: Proslavery Thought in the Antebellum South, 1830–1860.* Baton Rouge: Louisiana State University Press, 1981.

————. *A Sacred Circle: The Dilemma of the Intellectual in the Old South.* Baltimore: Johns Hopkins University Press, 1977.

Fehrenbacher, Don E., completed and edited by Ward M. McAfee. *The Slaveholding Republic, An Account of the United States Government's Relations to Slavery.* New York: Oxford University Press, 2001.

Feller, Daniel. "A Brother in Arms: Benjamin Tappan and the Antislavery Democracy." *Journal of American History* 88 (June 2001): 48–74.

Fish, Carl Russell. *The Civil Service and the Patronage.* Cambridge: Harvard University Press, 1920.

Fisher, Louis. *Presidential War Power.* Lawrence: University Press of Kansas, 1995.

Fladeland, Betty. *Men and Brothers: Anglo-American Antislavery Cooperation*. Urbana: University of Illinois Press, 1972.

Foner, Eric. *Free Soil, Free Labor, Free Men: The Ideology of the Republican Party before the Civil War*. New York: Oxford University Press, 1970.

Foos, Paul. *A Short, Offhand, Killing Affair: Soldiers and Social Conflict during the Mexican-American War*. Chapel Hill: University of North Carolina Press, 2002.

Foster, John W. *American Diplomacy in the Orient*. Boston: Houghton, Mifflin, 1903.

Fraser, Hugh Russell. *Democracy in the Making*. New York: Bobbs Merrill Company, 1938.

Freehling, Alison Goodyear. *Drift toward Dissolution: The Virginia Slavery Debate of 1831–1832*. Baton Rouge: Louisiana State University Press, 1982.

Freehling, William W. *The Road to Disunion: Secessionists at Bay 1776–1854*. New York: Oxford University Press, 1990.

Frothingham, Paul Revere. *Edward Everett: Orator and Statesman*. Boston: Houghton Mifflin Company, 1925.

Fry, Joseph A. *Dixie Looks Abroad: The South and U.S. Foreign Relations, 1789–1973*. Baton Rouge: Louisiana State University Press, 2002.

Fuess, Claude M. *The Life of Caleb Cushing*. 2 vols. New York: Harcourt, Brace & Company, 1923.

Goetzmann, William H. *New Lands, New Men: America and The Second Great Age of Discovery*. New York: Viking Penguin, 1986.

Goldsmith, William M. *The Growth of Presidential Power, A Documented History*. Vol. 2. New York: Chelsea House Publishers, 1974.

Gordon, Armistead C. *John Tyler, Tenth President of the United States; An Address by Armistead C. Gordon, at the Dedication, October 12, 1915, of the Monument Erected by Congress in Hollywood Cemetery, Richmond, Va., in Memory of President Tyler*. N.p., 1915.

Gotlieb, Howard B. "President Tyler and the Gardiners: A New Portrait." *Yale University Library Gazette* 34 (July 1959): 1–4.

Graebner, Norman A. *Empire on the Pacific: A Study in American Continental Expansion*. New York: Roland Press Company, 1955.

Green, Duff. *Facts and Suggestions, Biographical, Historical, Financial and Political, Addressed to the People of the United States*. New York: Richardson & Company, 1866.

Greenberg, Kenneth S. *Masters and Statesmen: The Political Culture of American Slavery*. Baltimore: Johns Hopkins University Press, 1985.

Gulick, Edward V. *Peter Parker and the Opening of China*. Cambridge: Harvard University Press, 1973.

Gunderson, Robert Gray. *The Log-Cabin Campaign*. Lexington: University of Kentucky Press, 1957.

———. *Old Gentleman's Convention: The Washington Peace Conference of 1861*. Madison: University of Wisconsin Press, 1961.

Hagan, Kenneth J. *This People's Navy: The Making of American Sea Power*. New York: Free Press, 1991.

Hall, Claude H. *Abel Parker Upshur: Conservative Virginian 1790–1844*. Madison: State Historical Society of Wisconsin, 1964.

Hamilton, Alexander, James Madison, and John Jay. *The Federalist*. Introduction by Clinton Rossiter. Reprint ed. New York: New American Library, 1961.

Harrison, Lowell Hayes. *John Breckinridge: Jeffersonian Republican*. Louisville: Filson Club, 1969.

Hartnett, Stephen. "Senator Robert Walker's 1844 Letter on Texas Annexation: The Rhetorical 'Logic' of Imperialism." *American Studies* 38 (Spring 1997): 27–54.

Haynes, Sam W. "Anglophobia and the Annexation of Texas: The Quest for National Security." In *Manifest Destiny and Empire: American Antebellum Expansionism*, ed. Sam W. Haynes and Christopher Morris, 115–45. College Station: Texas A&M University Press, 1997.

———. *James K. Polk and the Expansionist Impulse*. New York: Longman, 1997.

Hearn, Chester G. *Tracks in the Sea: Matthew Fontaine Maury and the Mapping of the Oceans*. Camden, Maine: International Marine/McGraw-Hill, 2002.

Heite, Edward F. "Virginia Twists the Lion's Tail." *Virginia Cavalcade* 17 (Spring 1968): 41–47.

Henderson, Daniel. *The Hidden Coasts: A Biography of Admiral Charles Wilkes*. Westport, Conn.: Greenwood Press, 1971.

Hesseltine, William B., and David L. Smiley. *The South in American History*. 2nd ed. Englewood Cliffs, N.J.: Prentice-Hall, 1960.

Hietala, Thomas R. *Manifest Design: American Exceptionalism & Empire*. Rev. ed. Ithaca, N.Y.: Cornell University Press, 2003.

Holmes, David, L., ed. *A Nation Mourns: Bishop James Madison's Memorial Eulogy on the Death of George Washington*. Mount Vernon: Mount Vernon Ladies' Association, 1999.

Holt, Michael F. *The Rise and Fall of the American Whig Party: Jacksonian Politics and the Onset of the Civil War*. New York: Oxford University Press, 1999.

Hopkins, James F., et al., eds. *The Papers of Henry Clay*. 11 vols. Lexington: University Press of Kentucky, 1992.

Hopkins, Manley. *Hawaii: The Past, Present and Future of the Island Kingdom*. London: Longman, Green, Long, and Roberts, 1862.

Horsman, Reginald. "The Dimensions of an 'Empire of Liberty': Expansion and Republicanism, 1775–1825." *Journal of the Early Republic* 9 (Spring 1989): 1–20.

Hunt, Michael H. *Ideology and U.S. Foreign Policy*. New Haven, Conn.: Yale University Press, 1987.

Jameson, J. Franklin, ed. *Calhoun Correspondence. Annual Report of the American Historical Association for the Year 1899*. Vol. 2. Washington, D.C.: Government Printing Office, 1900.

Jennings, Louis J., ed. *The Croker Papers: The Correspondence and Diaries of the Right Honourable John Wilson Croker*. 3 vols. London: John Murray, 1885.

Johnson, Ludwell H. III. "James Madison and the 'Long and Lingering Decline,' 1782–1812." In *The College of William and Mary: A History*, 2 vols., ed. Susan H. Godson et al., 165–98. Williamsburg: King and Queen Press, 1993.

Johnson, Timothy D. *Winfield Scott: The Quest for Military Glory*. Lawrence: University Press of Kansas, 1998.

Johnson, Walter. *Soul by Soul: Life Inside the Antebellum Slave Market*. Cambridge: Harvard University Press, 1999.

Jones, Anson. *Memoranda and Official Correspondence Relating to the Republic of Texas*. New York: D. Appleton and Company, 1859.

Jones, Howard. *Mutiny on the Amistad: The Saga of a Slave Revolt and Its Impact on American Abolition, Law, and Diplomacy*. New York: Oxford University Press, 1987.

————. "The Peculiar Institution and National Honor: The Case of the *Creole* Slave Revolt." *Civil War History* 21 (March 1975): 28–50.

————. *To the Webster-Ashburton Treaty: A Study in Anglo-American Relations, 1783–1843*. Chapel Hill: University of North Carolina Press, 1977.

Jones, Howard, and Donald A. Rakestraw. *Prologue to Manifest Destiny: Anglo-American Relations in the 1840s*. Wilmington, Del.: Scholarly Resources, 1997.

Jones, John B. *A Rebel War Clerk's Diary*. Condensed ed., ed. Earl Schenk Miers. New York: Sagamore Press, 1958.

Jones, Wilbur Devereux. *The American Problem in British Diplomacy, 1841–1861*. Athens: University of Georgia Press, 1974.

————. "The Influence of Slavery on the Webster-Ashburton Negotiations." *Journal of Southern History* 22 (February 1956): 48–58.

Kesilman, Sylvan H. "John Tyler as President: An Old School Republican in Search of Vindication." In *The Moment of Decision: Biographical Essays on American Character and Regional Identity*, ed. Randall M. Miller and John R. McKivigan, 74–98. Westport, Conn.: Greenwood Press, 1994.

Kiracofe, David James. "The Jamestown Jubilees: State Patriotism and Virginia Identity in the Early Nineteenth Century." *Virginia Magazine of History and Biography* 110, no. 1 (2002): 35–68.

Kirk, Elise K. *Music at the White House: A History of the American Spirit*. Urbana: University of Illinois Press, 1986.

Kirwan, Albert D. *John J. Crittenden: The Struggle for the Union*. Lexington: University of Kentucky Press, 1962.

Klein, Maury. *Days of Defiance: Sumter, Secession, and the Coming of the Civil War*. New York: Alfred A. Knopf, 1997.

Klunder, Willard Carl. *Lewis Cass and the Politics of Moderation*. Kent, Ohio: Kent State University Press, 1996.

Knaplund, Paul, ed. *Letters from Lord Sydenham to Lord John Russell*. London: George Allen & Unwin, 1931.

Kuykendall, Ralph S. *The Hawaiian Kingdom, 1778–1854, Foundation and Transformation*. Vol. 1. Honolulu: University of Hawaii Press, 1968.

LaFeber, Walter. "An Expansionist's Dilemma." *Constitution* 5 (Fall 1993): 4–13.
———. "Foreign Policies of a New Nation: Franklin, Madison, and the 'Dream of a New Land to Fulfill with People in Self-Control,' 1750–1804." In *From Colony to Empire: Essays in the History of American Foreign Relations*, ed. William Appleman Williams, 9–37. New York: John Wiley & Sons, 1972.

Larson, Gary, and Guy Seidman. *The Constitution of Empire: Territorial Expansion and American Legal History*. New Haven, Conn.: Yale University Press, 2004.

[Legare, Mary S., ed.] *Writings of Hugh Swinton Legare*. 2 vols. Charleston, S.C.: Burges & James, 1846.

Lewis, Charles Lee. *Matthew Fontaine Maury, The Pathfinder of the Seas*. Annapolis: United States Naval Institute, 1927.

Lewis, James E., Jr. *John Quincy Adams: Policymaker for the Union*. Wilmington, Del.: Scholarly Resources, 2001.

Link, William A. *Roots of Secession: Slavery and Politics in Antebellum Virginia*. Chapel Hill: University of North Carolina Press, 2003.

Lipscomb, Andrew A., and Albert E. Bergh, eds. *The Writings of Thomas Jefferson*. 20 vols. Washington, D.C.: Thomas Jefferson Memorial Association, 1907.

MacLean, William Jerry. "Othello Scorned: The Racial Thought of John Quincy Adams." *Journal of the Early Republic* 4 (Summer 1984): 143–60.

Madison, James. *Manifestations of the Beneficence of Divine Providence towards America*. Richmond: Printed by Thomas Nicolson, 1795.

Malone, Dumas. *Jefferson and His Time*. Vol. 4, *Jefferson the President, First Term, 1801–1805*. Boston: Little, Brown and Company, 1970.

Manning, William R., ed. *Diplomatic Correspondence of the United States: Inter-American Affairs, 1831–1860*. 12 vols. Washington, D.C.: Carnegie Endowment for International Peace, 1937.

Martin, Asa E. *After the White House*. State College, Penn.: Penn Valley Publishers, 1951.

May, Robert E. *The Southern Dream of Caribbean Empire, 1854–1861*. Baton Rouge: Louisiana State University Press, 1973.

McCoy, Drew R. *The Last of the Fathers: James Madison and the Republican Legacy*. New York: Cambridge University Press, 1989.

McInerney, Daniel J. *The Fortunate Heirs of Freedom: Abolition and Republican Thought*. Lincoln: University of Nebraska Press, 1994.

McKitrick, Eric. "The Liberator." *New York Review of Books*, October 21, 1999.

McPherson, James M. "The Fruits of Preventive War." *Perspectives, Newsmagazine of The American Historical Association* (May 2003): 5–6.

Merk, Frederick, with the Collaboration of Lois Banner Merk. *Fruits of Propaganda in the Tyler Administration*. Cambridge: Harvard University Press, 1971.

———. *Slavery and the Annexation of Texas*. New York: Alfred A. Knopf, 1972.

Merry, Sally Engle. *Colonizing Hawai'i: The Cultural Power of Law*. Princeton, N.J.: Princeton University Press, 2000.

Miles, Alfred H. "The Princeton Explosion." *United States Naval Institute Proceedings* 52 (November 1926): 2225-45.

Miller, Nathan. *Star-Spangled Men: America's Ten Worst Presidents*. New York: Scribner, 1998.

Monroe, Dan. *The Republican Vision of John Tyler*. College Station: Texas A&M University Press, 2003.

Morgan, Robert J. *A Whig Embattled: The Presidency under John Tyler*. Lincoln: University of Nebraska Press, 1954.

Morgan, William James, David B. Tyler, Joye L. Leonhart, and Mary F. Loughlin, eds. *Autobiography of Rear Admiral Charles Wilkes, U.S. Navy, 1798-1877*. Washington, D.C.: Naval History Division, Department of the Navy, 1978.

Morrison, Michael A. *Slavery and the American West: The Eclipse of Manifest Destiny and the Coming of the Civil War*. Chapel Hill: University of North Carolina Press, 1997.

Moser, Harold D., comp. *John Tyler, A Bibliography*. Westport, Conn.: Greenwood Press, 2001.

———, ed. *The Papers of Daniel Webster*. Vol. 5, *Correspondence, 1840-1843*. Hanover, N.H.: University Press of New England, 1982.

Neiman, Fraser D. "Coincidence or Causal Connection? The Relationship between Thomas Jefferson's Visits to Monticello and Sally Hemings's Conceptions." *William and Mary Quarterly* 57 (January 2000): 198-210.

Nelson, William Javier. *Almost a Territory: America's Attempt to Annex the Dominican Republic*. Newark: University of Delaware Press, 1990.

Nevins, Allan, ed. *The Diary of Philip Hone, 1828-1851*. New York: Dodd, Mead and Company, 1927.

Nevins, Allan, and Milton Halset Thomas, eds. *The Diary of George Templeton Strong*. Vol. 1, *Young Man in New York, 1845-1849*. New York: Macmillan Company, 1952.

Newman, Richard S. "Prelude to the Gag Rule: Southern Reaction to Antislavery Petitions in the First Federal Congress." *Journal of the Early Republic* 16 (Winter 1996): 571-99.

Oakes, James. *The Ruling Race: A History of American Slaveholders*. New York: Alfred A. Knopf, 1982.

O'Brien, Michael. *A Character of Hugh Legare*. Knoxville: University of Tennessee Press, 1985.

Osborne, Thomas J. *"Empire Can Wait": American Opposition to Hawaiian Annexation, 1893-1898*. Kent, Ohio: Kent State University Press, 1981.

Paul, James C. N. *Rift in the Democracy*. Philadelphia: University of Pennsylvania Press, 1951.

Peckham, Stephen Farnum. "An Echo from the Civil War." *Journal of American History* 5 (October 1911): 613-14.

Peirce, Augustus. *Biography of Henry Augustus Peirce*. San Francisco: A. L. Bancroft & Company, 1880.

Peskin, Allan. *Winfield Scott and the Profession of Arms*. Kent, Ohio: Kent State University Press, 2003.

Pessen, Edward. *The Log Cabin Myth: The Social Backgrounds of the Presidents*. New Haven, Conn.: Yale University Press, 1984.

Peterson, Norma Lois. *Littleton Waller Tazewell*. Charlottesville: University Press of Virginia, 1983.

———. *The Presidencies of William Henry Harrison & John Tyler*. Lawrence: University Press of Kansas, 1989.

Phillips, Clifton Jackson. *Protestant America and the Pagan World: The First Half Century of the American Board of Commissioners for Foreign Missions, 1810–1860*. Cambridge: Harvard University Press, 1969.

Pierson, Michael D. "'Slavery Cannot Be Covered Up with Broadcloth or a Bandanna': The Evolution of White Abolitionist Attacks on the 'Patriarchal Institution.'" *Journal of the Early Republic* 25 (Fall 2005): 383–415.

Pious, Richard M. "John Tyler, 10th President 1841–1845." In *"To the Best of My Ability": The American Presidents*, ed. James M. McPherson, 78–83. New York: Dorling Kindersley Publishing, 2000.

Pletcher, David M. *The Diplomacy of Annexation: Texas, Oregon, and the Mexican War*. Columbia: University of Missouri Press, 1973.

———. *The Diplomacy of Involvement: American Economic Expansion across the Pacific, 1784–1900*. Columbia: University of Missouri Press, 2001.

Porter, Kirk H., and Donald B. Johnson, comps. *National Party Platforms, 1840–1968*. Urbana: University of Illinois Press, 1970.

Pugh, Evelyn L. "Women and Slavery: Julia Gardiner Tyler and the Duchess of Sutherland." *Virginia Magazine of History and Biography* 88 (April 1980): 186–202.

Quaife, Milo Milton. *The Diary of James K. Polk during His Presidency, 1845–1849*. 4 vols. Chicago: A. C. McClurg, 1910.

Reese, George H. *Proceedings of the Virginia State Convention of 1861*. 4 vols. Richmond: Virginia State Library, 1965.

Reeves, Jesse S. *American Diplomacy under Tyler and Polk*. Baltimore: Johns Hopkins University Press, 1907.

Remini, Robert V. *Daniel Webster: The Man and His Time*. New York: W. W. Norton & Company, 1997.

———. *Henry Clay: Statesman for the Union*. New York: W. W. Norton & Company, 1991.

Reynolds, David S. *John Brown, Abolitionist: The Man Who Killed Slavery, Sparked the Civil War, and Seeded Civil Rights*. New York: Alfred A. Knopf, 2005.

Rhea, Linda. *Hugh Swinton Legaré: A Charleston Intellectual*. Chapel Hill: University of North Carolina Press, 1934.

Richards, Leonard L. *"Gentlemen of Property and Standing": Anti-Abolition Mobs in Jacksonian America*. New York: Oxford University Press, 1970.

———. *The Life and Times of Congressman John Quincy Adams*. New York: Oxford University Press, 1986.

———. *The Slave Power: The Free North and Southern Domination, 1780–1860*. Baton Rouge: Louisiana State University Press, 2000.

Richards, William. "Testimony of William Richards, September 1, 1846." In *Report of the Proceedings and Evidence in the Arbitration between the King and Government of the Hawaiian Islands and Messrs. Ladd & Co.* Honolulu: Charles E. Hitchcock, Printer, Government Press, 1846.

Richardson, James D. *A Compilation of the Messages and Papers of the Presidents, 1789–1902.* 10 vols. Washington, D.C.: Bureau of National Literature and Art, 1903.

Rigby, Barry. "American Expansion in Hawaii: The Contribution of Henry A. Peirce." *Diplomatic History* 4 (Fall 1980): 353–69.

Rives, George L. *The United States and Mexico, 1821–1848.* 2 vols. New York: Charles Scribner's Sons, 1913.

Rives, Ralph Hardee. "The Jamestown Celebration of 1857." *Virginia Magazine of History and Biography* 66 (July 1958): 258–71.

Robert, Joseph C. *The Road from Monticello: A Study of the Virginia Slavery Debate of 1832.* Durham, N.C.: Duke University Press, 1941.

Roberts, Edmund. *Embassy to the Eastern Courts of Cochin-China, Siam, and Muscat; in the U.S. Sloop-of-War Peacock, David Geisinger, Commander, During the Years 1832-3-4.* New York: Harper & Brothers, 1837.

Robinson, Armstead L. *Bitter Fruits of Bondage: The Demise of Slavery and the Collapse of the Confederacy, 1861–1865.* Charlottesville: University Press of Virginia, 2005.

Roeckell, Lelia M. "Bonds Over Bondage: British Opposition to the Annexation of Texas." *Journal of the Early Republic* 19 (Summer 1999): 257–78.

Sandburg, Carl. *Abraham Lincoln: The War Years.* 4 vols. New York: Harcourt, Brace & World, 1939.

Saul, Norman E. *Distant Friends: The United States and Russia, 1763–1867.* Lawrence: University Press of Kansas, 1991.

Scarborough, William K., ed. *The Diary of Edmund Ruffin.* Vol. 1, *Toward Independence, October 1856–April 1861.* Baton Rouge: Louisiana State University Press, 1972.

Schafer, Joseph. "Letters of Sir George Simpson, 1841–1843." *American Historical Review* 14 (October 1908): 70–94.

Schlesinger, Arthur M., Jr. "Eyeless in Iraq." *New York Review of Books*, October 23, 2003, 24–27.

———. *The Imperial Presidency.* Boston: Houghton Mifflin Company, 1973.

Schroeder, John H. *Shaping a Maritime Empire: The Commercial and Diplomatic Role of the Navy, 1829–1861.* Westport, Conn.: Greenwood Press, 1985.

Schurz, Carl. *Henry Clay.* 2 vols. New York: Frederick Ungar Publishing Company, 1915.

Scully, Eileen P. *Bargaining with the State from Afar: American Citizenship in Treaty Port China, 1844–1942*. New York: Columbia University Press, 2001.

Seager, Robert II. *and Tyler too: A Biography of John and Julia Gardiner Tyler*. New York: McGraw-Hill Book Company, 1963.

———. "John Tyler: The Planter of Sherwood Forest." *Virginia Cavalcade* 13 (Summer 1963): 4–11.

———. "Julia Gardiner Tyler." In *Notable American Women, 1607–1950, A Biographical Dictionary*, Vol. 3., ed. Edward T. Jones, 494–96. Cambridge: Harvard University Press, 1971.

Sellers, Charles G. *James K. Polk, Continentalist, 1843–1846*. Vol. 2. Princeton, N.J.: Princeton University Press, 1966.

———. *The Marketplace Revolution: Jacksonian America, 1815–1846*. New York: Oxford University Press, 1991.

Shade, William G. *Democratizing the Old Dominion: Virginia and the Second Party System, 1824–1861*. Charlottesville: University Press of Virginia, 1996.

Shanks, Henry Thomas. *The Secession Movement in Virginia, 1847–1861*. Richmond: Garrett and Massie, 1934.

Shaw, Albert. *Abraham Lincoln: The Year of His Election*. New York: Review of Reviews Corporation, 1930.

Shelley, Fred, ed. "The Vice President Receives Bad News in Williamsburg, A Letter of James Lyons to John Tyler." *Virginia Magazine of History and Biography* 76 (July 1968): 337–39.

Shenton, James B. *Robert John Walker: A Politician from Jackson to Lincoln*. New York: Columbia University Press, 1961.

Shepard, E. Lee. "John Tyler: Virginia Counsel." In *America's Lawyer-Presidents, From Law Office to Oval Office*, ed. Norman Gross, 76–85. Evanston, Ill.: Northwestern University Press, 2004.

Shewmaker, Kenneth E. "Daniel Webster and the Oregon Question." *Pacific Historical Review* 51 (May 1982): 195–201.

———. "Forging the 'Great Chain': Daniel Webster and the Origins of American Foreign Policy toward East Asia and the Pacific, 1841–1852." *Proceedings of the American Philosophical Society* 129 (1985): 225–59.

———, ed. *The Papers of Daniel Webster, Diplomatic Papers, 1841–1843*. Vol. 1. Hanover, N.H.: University Press of New England, 1983.

Silva, Ruth C. *Presidential Succession*. Ann Arbor: University of Michigan Press, 1951.

Simms, Henry H. *Emotion at High Tide: Abolition as a Controversial Factor, 1830–1845*. Richmond: William Byrd Press, 1960.

Simpson, Craig M. *A Good Southerner: The Life of Henry A. Wise of Virginia*. Chapel Hill: University of North Carolina Press, 1985.

Sioussat, St. George L. "Duff Green's 'England and the United States': With an Introductory Study of American Opposition to the Quintuple Treaty of 1841." *American Antiquarian Society* (October 1930): 175–276.

Skaggs, Jimmy M. *The Great Guano Rush: Entrepreneurs and American Overseas Expansion*. New York: St. Martin's Press, 1994.

Smith, Elbert B. *The Presidencies of Zachary Taylor and Millard Fillmore*. Lawrence: University Press of Kansas, 1988.

Smith, Gene A. *Thomas Ap Catesby Jones: Commodore of Manifest Destiny*. Annapolis: Naval Institute Press, 2000.

Smith, Geoffrey S. "Charles Wilkes and the Growth of American Naval Diplomacy." In *Makers of American Diplomacy: From Benjamin Franklin to Henry Kissinger*, ed. Frank J. Merli and Theodore A. Wilson, 135–63. New York: Charles Scribner's Sons, 1974.

Smith, Justin H. *The Annexation of Texas*. New York: Baker and Taylor Company, 1911.

Sprague, William B., ed. *Annals of the American Pulpit*. 9 vols. New York: Robert Carter & Brothers, 1859.

Stagg, J. C. A., et al., eds. *Papers of James Madison*. Vol. 2. Charlottesville: University Press of Virginia, 1992.

Stanton, William. *The Great United States Exploring Expedition of 1838–1842*. Berkeley: University of California Press, 1975.

———. *The Leopard's Spots: Scientific Attitudes toward Race in America, 1815–59*. Chicago: University of Chicago Press, 1960.

Stathis, Stephen W. "John Tyler's Presidential Succession: A Reappraisal." *Prologue* 8 (Winter 1976): 223–36.

Stephanson, Anders. *Manifest Destiny: American Exceptionalism and the Empire of Right*. New York: Hill and Wang, 1995.

Stevens, George B., and W. Fisher Martwick. *The Life, Letters, and Journals of the Rev. and Hon. Peter Parker, M.D., Missionary, Physician, and Diplomatist, the Father of Medical Missions and Founder of the Ophthalmic Hospital in Canton*. 1896. Reprint, Wilmington, Del.: Scholarly Resources, 1972.

Stevens, Kenneth R. *Border Diplomacy: The Caroline and McLeod Affairs in Anglo-American-Canadian Relations, 1837–1842*. Tuscaloosa: University of Alabama Press, 1989.

Still, William. *The Underground Rail Road: A Record*. Philadelphia: Porter & Coates, 1872.

Stockton, Robert F. *A Sketch in the Life of Com. Robert F. Stockton*. New York: Derby & Jackson, 1856.

Sturge, Joseph. *A Visit to the United States in 1841*. London: Hamilton, Adams, & Company, 1842.

Sullivan, Josephine. *A History of C. Brewer & Company, Limited: One Hundred Years in the Hawaiian Islands, 1826–1926*. Boston: Walton Advertising & Printing Company, 1926.

Takaki, Ronald T. *A Pro-Slavery Crusade: The Agitation to Reopen the African Slave Trade*. New York: Free Press, 1971.

Tansill, Charles C. "War Powers of the President." *Political Science Quarterly* 45 (March 1930): 40–55.

Tate, Merze. *The United States and the Hawaiian Kingdom: A Political History.* New Haven, Conn.: Yale University Press, 1965.

Tocqueville, Alexis de. *Democracy in America.* Introduction by Alan Ryan. 2 vols. New York: Alfred A. Knopf, Everyman's Library, 1994.

Tucker, Nathaniel Beverley. *The Partisan Leader, A Tale of the Future.* Washington, D.C.: Printed for Duff Green, 1836.

Tyler, John. "Early Times in Virginia—William and Mary College." *DeBow's Review* 27 (August 1859): 136–49.

———. *Lecture Delivered before the Maryland Institute for the Promotion of the Mechanic Arts, on Tuesday Evening, March 20 1855, by Hon. John Tyler, Subject: The Prominent Characters and Incidents of Our History from 1812 to 1836.* Baltimore: John Murray & Company, 1855.

———. *A Lecture Prepared at the Request of the Library Association of Petersburg, Delivered on the 4th of May 1854.* Petersburg, Va.: Banks & Lewellen, 1854.

———. "Opening Address of John Tyler, President of the United States and Patron of the National Institute, April 1, 1844." *Proceedings of the National Institute,* Bulletin No. 3. Washington, D.C.: National Institute for the Promotion of Science, 1844.

———. "An Oration Delivered by John Tyler, at York Town, October 19, 1837." *Southern Literary Messenger* 3 (December 1837): 747–52.

Tyler, Julia Gardiner. "To the Duchess of Sutherland and Ladies of England." *Southern Literary Messenger* 19 (February 1853): 120–26.

Tyler, Lyon G. "Edmund Ruffin's Visit to John Tyler." *William and Mary Quarterly,* 1st ser., 14 (January 1906): 193–211.

———. "John Tyler and His Presidency." *Eclectic Magazine* 148 (May 1907): 387–403.

———. "John Tyler and the Ladies of Brazoria." *Tyler's Quarterly Historical and Genealogical Magazine* 11 (July 1929): 1–4.

———. *The Letters and Times of the Tylers.* 3 vols. Richmond: Whittet & Shepperson, 1884, 1885, 1896.

Upshur, Abel P. "Domestic Slavery, as It Exists in our Southern States, with Reference to Its Influence on Free Government." *Southern Literary Messenger* 5 (October 1839): 677–87.

Van Tyne, Claude H., ed. *The Letters of Daniel Webster.* New York: Haskell House Publishers, 1969.

Varg, Paul A. *Edward Everett: The Intellectual in the Turmoil of Politics.* Selinsgrove, Pa.: Susquehanna University Press, 1992.

Varon, Elizabeth R. *We Mean to Be Counted: White Women & Politics in Antebellum Virginia.* Chapel Hill: University of North Carolina Press, 1998.

Viola, Herman J., and Carolyn Margolis, eds. *Magnificent Voyagers: The U.S. Exploring Expedition, 1838–1842.* Washington, D.C.: Smithsonian Institution Press, 1985.

Walters, Raymond, Jr. *Albert Gallatin: Jeffersonian Financier and Diplomat.* New York: Macmillan Company, 1957.

Watt, Alastair. "The Case of Alexander McLeod." *Canadian Historical Review* 12 (June 1931): 145–67.

Webster, Daniel. *The Writings and Speeches of Daniel Webster.* 18 vols. Boston: Little, Brown and Company, 1903.

Weeks, William Earl. *Building the Continental Empire: American Expansion from the Revolution to the Civil War.* Chicago: Ivan R. Dee, 1996.

———. "New Directions in the Study of Early American Foreign Relations." In *Paths to Power: The Historiography of American Foreign Relations to 1941,* ed. Michael J. Hogan, 8–43. New York: Cambridge University Press, 2000.

Wheeless, Carl. *Landmarks of American Presidents, A Traveler's Guide.* New York: Gale Research, 1995.

Whittenburg, James P., ed. *Charles City County, Virginia: An Official History.* [s.l.: s.n.], 1989.

Wilentz, Sean. *The Rise of American Democracy, Jefferson to Lincoln.* New York: W. W. Norton & Company, 2005.

Wilkes, Charles. *Narrative of the United States Exploring Expedition during the Years 1838, 1839, 1840, 1841, 1842.* 8 vols. Philadelphia: Lee and Blanchard, 1845.

Williams, Amelia W., and Eugene C. Barker, eds. *The Writings of Sam Houston.* 5 vols. Austin: University of Texas Press, 1941.

Williams, Elgin. *The Animating Pursuits of Speculation: Land Traffic in the Annexation of Texas.* New York: Columbia University Press, 1949.

Williams, Frances Leigh. *Matthew Fontaine Maury, Scientist of the Sea.* New Brunswick, N.J.: Rutgers University Press, 1963.

Williams, John Hoyt. *Sam Houston: A Biography of the Father of Texas.* New York: Simon & Schuster, 1993.

Williams, William Appleman, ed. *The Shaping of American Diplomacy.* 2 vols. 2nd ed. Chicago: Rand McNally & Company, 1970.

Williston, Samuel. *William Richards.* Cambridge, Mass.: Privately printed, 1938.

Wilson, Clyde N., ed. *The Papers of John C. Calhoun.* Vols. 16–21. Columbia: University of South Carolina Press, 1984–1993.

Wilson, Douglas L. *Honor's Voice: The Transformation of Abraham Lincoln.* New York: Alfred A. Knopf, 1998.

Wilson, Henry. *History of the Rise and Fall of the Slave Power in America.* 3 vols. Boston: Houghton, Mifflin and Company, 1872.

Wiltse, Charles M., and Michael J. Birkner, eds. *The Papers of Daniel Webster, Correspondence.* Vol. 7, *1850–1852.* Hanover, N.H.: University Press of New England, 1986.

Wise, Henry A. *Seven Decades of the Union.* Philadelphia: J. B. Lippincott & Company, 1881.

Wise, John S. *Recollections of Thirteen Presidents.* New York: Doubleday, Page & Company, 1906.

Woodward, Bob. *Plan of Attack.* New York: Simon & Schuster, 2004.

Woodward, C. Vann. "The Age of Reinterpretation." *American Historical Review* 66 (1960): 1–19.

Wriston, Henry M. *Executive Agents in American Foreign Relations*. Baltimore: Johns Hopkins University Press, 1929.

Wyatt-Brown, Bertram. *Lewis Tappan and the Evangelical War Against Slavery*. Cleveland: Press of Case Western University, 1969.

———. *Southern Honor: Ethics and Behavior in the Old South*. New York: Oxford University Press, 1982.

Zorn, Roman J. "Criminal Extradition Menaces the Canadian Haven for Fugitive Slaves, 1841–1861." *Canadian Historical Review* 38 (December 1957): 284–94.

Dissertations and Theses

DeLaney, Theodore C. "Julia Gardiner Tyler: A Nineteenth Century Southern Woman." Ph.D. dissertation, College of William and Mary, 1995.

Gray, Elizabeth Kelly. "American Attitudes toward British Imperialism, 1815–1860." Ph.D. dissertation, College of William and Mary, 2002.

Kesilman, Sylvan H. "John Tyler and the Presidency: Old School Republicanism, Partisan Realignment, and Support for His Administration." Ph.D. dissertation, The Ohio State University, 1973.

Smith, Kenneth L. "Duff Green and the *United States Telegraph*, 1826–1837." Ph.D. dissertation, College of William and Mary, 1981.

Sprague, Roberta A. "The Wilkes Expedition, Framework for American Expansionism; The U.S. Exploring Expedition, 1838–1842." M.A. thesis, University of Hawaii, 1988.

Wickman, John E. "Political Aspects of Charles Wilkes's Work and Testimony, 1842–1849." Ph.D. dissertation, Indiana University, 1964.

ACKNOWLEDGMENTS

I began working on this study of America's largely forgotten tenth president more than twenty years ago. Originally, I intended to focus primarily on analyzing John Tyler's foreign policy initiatives and achievements during the years of his presidency, 1841–45. Gradually the project expanded to become a full-scale biography. It highlights Tyler's mystical faith in America's national destiny and closely examines his life-long commitment to territorial expansion as the means to preserve the Union as a slaveholding republic. It is my belief that the book's broad emphasis on John Tyler's hopes and dreams for the future glory and greatness of the United States, and the centrality of slavery's expansion to that vision, offers a clearer understanding of the man and his place in American history.

The extended nature of this project has been beneficial in other respects as well. Over the last two decades I have enjoyed the generous support and friendship of President John Tyler's grandson, Harrison R. Tyler, and his wife, Payne Tyler. Their help and encouragement have been invaluable and I am most grateful to them both. I also am grateful to Robert Seager, an earlier biographer of John Tyler, for his advice at the initial stages of this endeavor and for kindly sharing his research notes from the Gardiner Family Papers at Yale University's Sterling Library.

My greatest intellectual and scholarly debt is to Andy Fry, a treasured friend who has encouraged and inspired me with his good humor, generosity, and enthusiasm for this project. He thoughtfully and helpfully commented on the manuscript from its inception to its completion. I also wish to thank a number of my William and Mary colleagues. Chan Brown read the entire manuscript and provided valuable suggestions for revision. Craig Canning's insightful critique of chapter 5 was most helpful. I also benefited from the guidance of Scott Nelson, who directed me to several important documents, and the assistance of Mel Ely, LuAnn Homza, and Tom Payne for interpreting some key primary sources. Thanks as well to Chuck Hobson and Dan Preston for research assistance. Once again Ed Pease has my gratitude for his intellectual support and mapmaking skills. Special thanks are due to Judy Ewell, Jim McCord, and Thad Tate for their friendship and encouragement along the way. Betty Flanigan and Roz Stearns generously and repeatedly offered me help and assistance, for which I am most grateful.

I am indebted to Tom Coffman and Bill Siener for their aid in locating several illustrations. For their research assistance and critical commentary at various stages of the project, I wish to thank Paul Burlin, Sam Haynes, Ken Stevens, John Coski, Ted DeLaney, Bob Smith, Kelly Gray, and Ken Smith.

It is my pleasure to thank the staff at William and Mary's Swem Library for their guidance and assistance, especially Margaret Cook, Susan Riggs, John Haskell, Allan Zoellner, Don Welsh, Hope Yelich, Mary Molineux, and Stacy Gould. At the University of North Carolina Press I wish to thank Chuck Grench, Katy O'Brien, Ron Maner, and Eric Schramm for their advice and guidance.

I wish to thank my daughters and sons-in-law for their moral support over the years, and I am grateful to my sons, Paul and Andrew, for their editorial and research assistance. Thanks as always to my wife and best friend, Jeanne Zeidler. Finally, I have dedicated this book to my five grandchildren—Jonathan, Layla, Bryce, Christopher, and Blake—and to any others that may come along in the future. I wish them well on life's journey and hope they succeed in making the twenty-first-century world a better place.

INDEX

Beeckman, John, 236
Bell, John, 256
Belohlavek, John, 41
Bennett, James Gordon, 189
Benson, Alfred, 120
Benton, Thomas Hart, 101, 122, 151,
    163, 209, 231; opposes recognition
    of Haiti, 82; opposes Webster-
    Ashburton Treaty, 115
Berkeley plantation, 30
Berlin, Germany, 105
Bermuda, 96
Berry, Henry, 44
Bethel, battle of, 268
Bill of Rights, 50
Bingham, Ann Louisa. *See* Ashburton,
    Lady
Bingham, Hiram, 139, 157, 172; meets
    with Tyler and Webster, 137–38
Bingham, William, 100
Birney, James G., 55, 56, 60, 69, 70, 71
Blair, Francis Preston, 183
Bolívar, Símon, 82
Booz, E. C., Distillery, 18
Boston, Mass., 46, 47, 130, 186, 190–93
Boston Museum of Fine Arts, 169
Botts, John Minor, 110; seeks Tyler's
    impeachment, 106–7
Brandywine (frigate), 167
Brazil, 72
Breckinridge, John, 34, 256, 257
Bridgman, E. C., 168
Brinkerhoff, Jacob, 124
Brinsmade, Peter, 149, 172; seeks
    recognition for Hawaii, 139–41
British and Foreign Anti-Slavery
    Society, 69, 70, 102, 117
British North America, 90
Brown, John, 254–55
Bruton Parish Church (Williamsburg,
    Va.), 33
Bryant, William Cullen, 215
Buchanan, James, 84, 255, 259–60
Buckingham Palace, 90

Bunker Hill Monument, 186, 191–92
Burnley, Alfred T., 199
Bush, George W., 112, 278
Butler, Benjamin, 272

Calhoun, John C., 43, 44, 50–51,
    68, 71, 74, 81, 83, 84, 101, 121,
    122, 135, 151, 162, 173, 195, 197,
    198, 221, 222, 224, 225–26, 228,
    230, 234, 247; favors Webster-
    Ashburton Treaty, 115; appointed
    secretary of state, 211–12; sends
    letter to Pakenham, 215
Calhoun, Patrick, 211
California, 25, 30, 119, 120; acquired
    by Polk, 233–35; and gold rush,
    236–37; admitted as free state, 238
Callender, James, 64, 66
Canada, 22, 36, 65, 85, 93, 96; and
    fugitive slaves, 116–17
Canton, China, 156, 169
Cape Horn, 78, 236
Caroline (American ship), 91, 93, 112
Carysfort (British warship), 159
Cass, Lewis, 72–73, 94–95, 96
Charles City Cavalry, 255
Charles City County, Va., 30, 35, 171,
    224, 253, 268, 271, 275; reaction to
    John Brown's raid, 254–55
Charleston, S.C., 46, 54, 101, 255–56,
    257
Chase, Salmon, 68
Chicago Tribune, 279
Child, David Lee, 115–16
Child, Lydia Maria, 44–45, 60, 67, 115
China, 42, 64, 78, 92, 130, 131, 132,
    133, 134, 135, 136, 142, 154, 155,
    156, 158, 160, 173, 279
Christian, James H., 252–53
Christian, John B., 252
Christian, Letitia. *See* Tyler, Letitia
    Christian
Christian, William H., 253
Christian Mirror (Portland, Maine), 108

Ford, Gerald, 278
Forsyth, John, 131
Fort Jessup, La., 213, 233
Fortress Monroe, 268, 270
Fort Sumter, 264, 268, 269
Fow-chow-fow (Fuzhou), China, 165
Fox, Henry S. (British minister to
    United States), 90–91, 92, 95, 97,
    112–13, 117, 118, 134, 161
France, 34, 72, 85, 133, 136, 137, 140,
    144, 145, 149, 162, 177, 259
Franklin, Benjamin, 109
"Free diplomacy," 55
Fugitive Slave Act, 238

"Gag rule," 50–51, 53
Gales, Joseph, 281
Gallatin, Albert, 215–16, 221–22
Gardiner, Alexander (Julia's brother),
    226, 235
Gardiner, David (Julia's father), 147;
    death of, 208–9
Gardiner, David L. (Julia's brother),
    236–37; as Unionist, 271
Gardiner, Julia. See Julia Gardiner Tyler
Gardiner, Juliana (Julia's mother):
    chides daughter, 250, 252; supports
    Confederacy, 271
Garfield, James A., 15
Garland, Samuel, 44
Garnett, Henry Highland, 98
Garrison, William Lloyd, 46, 47, 48,
    49, 67, 68
Georgia, 38, 46, 248; secedes, 257
Giddings, Joshua, 63
Gilmer, Thomas W., 71, 180–82, 204,
    206, 224, 227; death of, 208–9
Gloucester Court House, Va., 47–49
Grant, Ulysses S., 277, 280
Great Britain, 25, 35, 38, 39, 42, 47,
    58, 65, 69–76, 80, 85, 91–96, 100,
    101, 104, 118, 119, 120, 124, 133,
    134, 136, 140, 144, 145, 149, 157,
    161–62, 168, 173, 177, 181, 195,

197, 200–201, 217, 229, 242, 259;
    and boundary dispute with United
    States, 107–11
Greeley, Horace, 67
Green, Duff, 68, 86, 96, 119–20, 195,
    197, 122, 204, 227; as "ambassador
    of slavery," 71–74
Greenhow, Robert, 32
Greenway plantation, 30, 31
Gulf of Mexico, 213, 217

Haalilio, Timoteo, 142, 156, 157, 159;
    visits United States, 144, 147–54;
    death of, 162
"Hail to the Chief," 219
Haiti, 86, 151, 153, 206; recognition
    issue, 53–56, 80–85
Hamilton, Alexander, 33, 286 (n. 20)
Hammond, James H., 50, 102–3, 135
Harding, Warren G., 15
Harpers Ferry, 254–55
Harrison, Benjamin (father of William
    Harrison), 30
Harrison, Benjamin (U.S. president), 279
Harrison, William Henry (U.S.
    president), 2, 3, 10, 12–14, 27, 30–
    31, 63, 94, 130, 176, 182, 189, 273,
    279; death of, 8–9; 1840 campaign
    of, 17–18
Hawaii, 42, 76, 78, 130, 131, 135–
    37, 139–44, 147, 172–73, 185;
    recognition of sovereignty, 151–59;
    1843 takeover by British of, 160–62;
    U.S. annexation of, 279–80
Hay, John, 279
Healy, George P. A., 253
Hemings, Sally, 66–67
Henderson, J. Pinckney, 212–13
Henry, Patrick, 31, 247
Hewell, John, 97
Hogan, John B., 84, 96
Hone, Philip, 18, 116
Hong Kong, 156
Hopkins, Manley, 139–40, 143

Horsford, Eben, 249–50
Houston, Sam, 196, 228–30, 234
Hubbard's (Richmond slave market), 62–63
Hudson's Bay Company, 143, 158
Hunt, Michael H., 39
Hunter, Robert M. T., 84

Ingersoll, Charles J., makes charges against Webster, 123–26
Ireland, 242
Irving, Washington, 105

Jackson, Andrew, 11, 14, 41–42, 46, 50, 86, 110, 176, 177, 183, 189, 211, 224, 228
James River, 9, 30, 271
Jamestown, Va., 250th celebration, 245–46
Japan, 41–42, 131, 156, 169–70
Jefferson, Thomas, 3, 4, 6, 12, 19, 20–23, 26, 28, 30–31, 34, 36–37, 45, 52, 55, 56, 59, 61, 64, 80, 87, 107, 145, 176, 216, 225, 232, 244, 245, 253, 282; death of, 39–40; and Sally Hemings, 66–67; *Notes on the State of Virginia*, 206
Jefferson Literary Society, 239
Johnson, Andrew, 15, 278
Johnson, Lyndon B., 15, 91, 278
Johnson, Walter, 63
Jones, Anson, 210
Jones, John B., 69
Jones, Mary (President Tyler's daughter), 210

Kamehameha III (king of Hawaii), 78, 137, 144, 149; seeks recognition, 138–40, 142; relents to 1843 British occupation, 159
Kansas-Nebraska crisis, 244
Kendall, Amos, 46
Kennedy, Andrew, 121
Kennedy, John F., 15

Kennon, Beverly, 209
King Cotton, 69, 229, 264
King Wheat, 69
Kipling, Rudyard, 155
Kossuth, Louis, 239

Ladd & Company, 139
Ladies of Brazoria County (Tex.), 224, 230
Lafayette, Marquis de, 94, 189
LaFeber, Walter, 21
Laplace, Cyrille, 137, 138
Lawrence, Abbott, 193
Lazarus, Emma, 26
Leavitt, Joshua, 55, 63, 68, 69, 70, 77, 102–3, 113, 115, 158, 210; alleges Tyler had slave children, 64–66
Legare, Hugh S., 54, 68, 186, 210, 222; as interim secretary of state, 160–61; death of, 193–94
Leigh, Benjamin Watkins, 32
Liberator, 46, 67
Liberia, 53
Liberty Party, 55–56, 60, 67, 69, 71, 219
Lincoln, Abraham, 4, 15, 58, 68, 86, 206, 216, 244, 258, 260, 261, 264, 268, 276, 277; wins 1860 presidential election, 256–57; meets with peace conference delegates, 262
London *Times*, 99
Lone Star Republic, 25, 53, 56, 176, 177, 178, 181, 194, 195, 208. *See also* Texas
Louisiana, 102, 182; secedes, 257
Louisiana Purchase, 22, 34, 38, 176, 205, 216, 235
Louis Philippe (king of France), 73
Lyons, James, 8, 13, 255

Macao, 167, 169
Madison, Dolley, 105
Madison, James (bishop), 3, 32; eulogy for Washington, 33, 34, 36, 56, 59, 92

Russell, Lord John, 93
Russia, 72, 259

Sabine River, 176
Sacramento River, 237
St. Lawrence River, 111
St. Louis (sloop), 167
St. Petersburg, Russia, 105
Sandwich Islands. *See* Hawaii
San Francisco, Calif., 119
Sanitary Commission Fair, 272
Schlesinger, Arthur M., Jr., 281
Scott, Winfield, 32, 275–76
Seager, Robert, 273
Seaton, William W., 281
Seward, William H., 92, 120
Shakespeare, William, 4, 31, 244
Shanghai, China, 165
Shawnee Indians, 17
Sherwood Forest, 4, 114, 171, 172, 224,
    225, 230, 241, 243, 249–50, 253,
    265, 268, 270; sacked by United
    States Colored Troops, 272–73
"Silver Greys," 255
Simpson, Sir George, 143–44, 158, 173
Slave Power thesis, 67–68, 122
Slavery, 37–38, 58–59
Slidell, John, 233–34
Smith, Francis O. J., 96, 108–10, 125
Smithsonian Institution, 5, 146
South Carolina, 38, 43, 46, 50, 68, 93,
    248; secedes, 257
Southern Literary Messenger, 79, 94
Sparks, Jared, 109–11
Spencer, John C., 184, 192, 217
Spontaneous Southern Rights
    Assembly (Richmond, Va.), 265
Spooner, Ephraim, 185
Stanton, Elizabeth Cady, 46
Stanton, Henry B., 46, 69, 71
Staten Island, 261, 272
Still, William, 252–53
Stockton, Robert F., 187, 207–10, 231
Stowe, Harriet Beecher, 241

Strong, George Templeton, 188, 216
Stuart, Charles, 47
Sturge, Joseph, 70, 102
Sumner, Charles, 67
Sutherland, Duchess of, 241, 243
Sutter's Mill Creek, 236
Sydenham, Lord, 93
Syria, 157

Tahiti, 78
Tappan, Arthur, 46, 48, 214
Tappan, Benjamin, 214, 227–28
Tappan, Lewis, 45, 116, 210, 214,
    227–28
Taylor, Zachary, 15, 172, 238, 278–79
Tazewell, Littleton Waller, 8, 14–15,
    32, 41
Tennessee, 232
Texas, 26, 30, 35, 70, 72, 120, 123, 126,
    141; annexation opposed, 53–54,
    55; annexed, 220; secedes, 257; as
    annexation precedent, 279–80
Thailand, 41, 134
Thomas, Richard, 162
Thompson, George, 47, 48, 55, 70
Thompson, Waddy, 179, 195, 198
Tierra del Fuego, 259
Tippecanoe, battle of, 17
"Tippecanoe and Tyler too," 2, 17–18,
    130, 216
Tocqueville, Alexis de, 130
Todd, Charles S., 32
Treaty of 1819. *See* Adams-Onis Treaty
Treaty of Wangxia, 169, 170, 171
Truman, Harry, 15, 278
Tucker, Nathaniel Beverley, 9, 20, 51,
    75, 77, 194–95, 196, 199–200, 204,
    222, 227
Tucker, St. George, 275
Twenty-fifth Amendment, 15, 53, 278
Tyler, Harrison, 67
Tyler, John
—childhood and youth: disciple of
    Jefferson and Madison during, 3, 12,